SpringerWienNewYork

CISM COURSES AND LECTURES

The series presents lecture notes, monographs, edited works and proceedings in the field of Mechanics, Engineering, Computer Science and Applied Mathematics.
Purpose of the series is to make known in the international scientific and technical community results obtained in some of the activities organized by CISM, the International Centre for Mechanical Sciences.

INTERNATIONAL CENTRE FOR MECHANICAL SCIENCES

COURSES AND LECTURES - No. 476

NONLINEAR DYNAMICAL SYSTEMS IN ECONOMICS

EDITED BY

MARJI LINES
UNIVERSITY OF UDINE, ITALY

SpringerWien NewYork

This volume contains 90 illustrations

SPIN 11494331

In order to make this volume available as economically and as rapidly as possible the authors' typescripts have been reproduced in their original forms. This method unfortunately has its typographical limitations but it is hoped that they in no way distract the reader.

ISBN-10 3-211-26177-X SpringerWienNewYork
ISBN-13 978-3-211-26177-4 SpringerWienNewYork

PREFACE

Many problems in theoretical economics are mathematically formalized as dynamical systems of difference and differential equations. In recent years a truly open approach to studying the dynamical behavior of these models has begun to make its way into the mainstream. That is, economists formulate their hypotheses and study the dynamics of the resulting models rather than formulating the dynamics and studying hypotheses that could lead to models with such dynamics. This is a great progress over using linear models, or using nonlinear models with a linear approach, or even squeezing economic models into well-studied nonlinear systems from other fields.

There are today a number of economic journals open to publishing this type of work and some of these have become important. There are several societies which have annual meetings on the subject and participation at these has been growing at a good rate. And of course there are methods and techniques available to a more general audience, as well as a greater availability of software for numerical and graphical analysis that makes this type of research even more exciting. The lecturers for the Advanced School on Nonlinear Dynamical Systems in Economics, who represent a wide selection of the research areas to which the theory has been applied, agree on the importance of simulations and computer-based analysis. The School emphasized computer applications of models and methods, and all contributors ran computer lab sessions. The exigencies of space left us no room to include the related exercises and software, but you can get a taste of those (and access to a wealth of other useful material) by referring to contributors home pages.

The volume is structured as follows. The first three chapters are introductory (though not necessarily elementary). The first provides a quick introduction to nonlinear analysis: a short review of what is useful from linear systems theory in the analysis of nonlinear systems through first-order approximations; the essential theorems useful for local analysis; definitions and terminology for stability analysis; a discussion of limit sets and local bifurcation theory. The second chapter is a discussion of chaos and complexity at an intermediate level of difficulty. Typical examples of systems with chaotic trajectories are provided in order to discuss deeper issues including chaotic attractors as a form of global stability, random versus deterministic chaotic series, predictability of chaotic systems, statistical predictability of chaotic systems and financial and economic implications of deterministic chaos. The section on complexity focuses on the cellular automata approach, considering complexity classes, predictability and agent-based modeling in economics. The third chapter is an introduction to a relatively new line of research in economics, the ergodic approach, which investigates the probabilistic properties of dynamical systems. The basic concepts of elementary measure theory are used to understand the dynamics of nonlinear models. Concepts such as invariant, ergodic, absolutely continuous and natural measures are explained with simple examples. The issue of deterministic chaos and randomness is discussed from the point of view of predictability, by means of the notion of metric entropy. These three chapters, coming from quite different approaches, give a broad introduction to definitions, concepts and methods that are useful for the more applied chapters that follow.

The final four chapters are applications of local and global bifurcation theory to models coming from different approaches and fields in economics. In Chapter 4 the local approximation is used to understand the dynamics in two versions of one of the models currently dominating macroeconomics, the Overlapping Generations (OLG) model. From the basic 1-dimensional Diamond model, with standard choices of functions, hypotheses are altered to develop two other models, each illustrating problems that arise once the basic hypotheses are abandoned. A second type of OLG model is studied, in 2 and 3 dimensions, for which the Neimark-Sacker bifurcation is typical and invariant curves are common limit sets. Chapter 5 focuses on some very interesting work in modeling the dynamics of financial markets with heterogeneous agents, an approach receiving much attention in the field. The first part employs the cobweb model with rational versus naive agents to demonstrate a rational route to randomness as well as the existence of a homoclinic orbit. The second part develops an asset pricing model in which agents switch between different forecasting or trading strategies, using an evolutionary fitness measure. Prices and beliefs co-evolve over time, leading to instability and complicated price fluctuations. Chapter 6 is dedicated to complex dynamics in models from oligopoly theory, which is one of the fields that pioneered in the application of nonlinear dynamics. A model of duopolists with nonlinear reaction curves gives rise to a period-doubling scenario to chaos and the coexistence of cycles and complicated basins of attraction. The model is extended to include adaptive expectations, and stability is lost through the Neimark-Sacker bifurcation giving rise to a very complicated structure of periodic Arnol'd tongues observable in the two-parameter bifurcation diagram. The critical line approach is used to define the absorbing areas. In Chapter 7 an excellent review of definitions and properties concerning noninvertible maps is followed by a description of the method of critical lines and curves in determining the trapping region, with examples of global bifurcations causing nonconnected basins of attraction. These methods are applied to a Cournot duopoly game with best reply, naive expectations and adaptive behavior, and to a duopoly game with gradient dynamics. Finally the related phenomena of chaos synchronization and riddled basins are studied in a dynamic brand competition model with market shares and marketing effort.

The organization of a learning experience such as the Advanced School is amazingly complex in itself and I wish to thank Prof. Manuel Velarde, current Rector of CISM, for his support at all stages, the CISM staff for their patience and competence, my fellow lecturers for their efforts in preparing presentations, lab sessions, and the chapters that follow, and of course, the students, who gave themselves up for an entire week to the joys of nonlinearity.

Marji Lines

CONTENTS

Introductory Notes on the Dynamics of Linear and Linearized Systems

Marji Lines and Alfredo Medio

Department of Statistics, University of Udine, Udine, Italy

Abstract In the following we provide terminology and concepts which are central to understanding the dynamical behavior of nonlinear systems. The first four sections are a necessarily very brief introduction to the dynamics of linear systems, in which we concentrate on those aspects most useful for acquiring a sense of the basic behaviours characterising systems of differential and difference equations. The last four sections introduce basic notions of stability, the linear approximation and the Hartman-Grobman Theorem, the use of the Centre Manifold Theorem, local bifurcation theory.*

1 Linear systems in continuous time

In this section we discuss the form of the solutions to the general system of linear differential equations

$$\dot{x} = Ax \qquad x \in \mathbb{R}^m \tag{1.1}$$

where A is a $m \times m$ matrix of constants, also called the coefficient matrix.

An obvious solution to equation (1.1) is $x(t) = 0$, called the equilibrium solution because if $x = 0$, $\dot{x} = 0$ as well. That is, a system starting at equilibrium stays there forever. Notice that if A is nonsingular, $x = 0$ is the only equilibrium for linear systems like (1.1). Nontrivial solutions will be of the form

$$x(t) = e^{\lambda t}u \tag{1.2}$$

where u is a vector of real or complex constants and λ real or complex constants. Differentiating (1.2) with respect to time, and substituting into (1.1), we obtain $\lambda e^{\lambda t}u = Ae^{\lambda t}u$ which, for $e^{\lambda t} \neq 0$, implies

$$(A - \lambda I)u = 0 \tag{1.3}$$

where 0 is an m-dimensional null vector. A nonzero vector u satisfying (1.3) is called an eigenvector of matrix A associated with the eigenvalue λ. Equation (1.3) has a nontrivial solution $u \neq 0$ if and only if

$$det(A - \lambda I) = 0 \tag{1.4}$$

*For suggestions on further reading and an extended bibliography please see Medio and Lines, *Nonlinear Dynamics: A Primer*, Cambridge: Cambridge University Press, 2001.

Equation (1.4) is called the characteristic equation of system (1.1) and can be expressed in terms of a polynomial in λ, thus

$$det(A - \lambda I) = \mathcal{P}(\lambda) = \lambda^m + k_1\lambda^{m-1} + \ldots + k_{m-1}\lambda + k_m = 0 \tag{1.5}$$

and $\mathcal{P}(\lambda)$ is called the characteristic polynomial. Then (1.5) is a solution of (1.1) if λ is an eigenvalue and u is the associated eigenvector of A. The set of solution curves of a dynamical system, sketched in the state space, is known as the *phase diagram* or *phase portrait* of the system.

It should be appreciated that the problem of solving a functional equation (1.1) has been reduced to the algebraic problem of finding the roots of the polynomial (1.5) and solving the system of equations (1.4) which, for given λ, is linear. Notice that for each λ, if u is an eigenvector, so is cu for $c \neq 0$.

Equation (1.5) has m roots which may be real or complex and some of them may be repeated. Consider the general case that there exist n $(0 \leq n \leq m)$ real, distinct eigenvalues λ_i of the matrix A with corresponding n real, linearly independent eigenvectors u_i, and $p = (m-n)/2$ pairs of distinct complex conjugate eigenvalues $(\lambda_j, \bar{\lambda}_j)$ with corresponding eigenvectors $(u_j, \bar{u}_j)$ where $(0 \leq p \leq m/2)$. Then, in the real case, there are n linearly independent solutions of (1.1) with the form

$$x_i(t) = e^{\lambda_i t}u_i \qquad (i = 1, 2, \ldots, n). \tag{1.6}$$

In the complex case, each pair of eigenvalues and associated pair of eigenvectors can be written, respectively, as

$$\begin{aligned}(\lambda_j, \lambda_{j+1}) &= (\lambda_j, \bar{\lambda}_j) = (\alpha_j + i\beta_j, \alpha_j - i\beta_j)\\ (u_j, u_{j+1}) &= (u_j, \bar{u}_j) = (a_j + ib_j, a_j - ib_j)\end{aligned}$$

where α, β are real scalars, a_j and b_j are m-dimensional vectors, and $i^2 = -1$.

Making use of Euler's formula, polar coordinates and trigonometric identities the solutions of (1.1) can be written as m-dimensional vectors whose lth elements have the form

$$\begin{aligned}x_j^{(l)}(t) &= C_j^{(l)} e^{\alpha_j t}\cos(\beta_j t + \phi_j^{(l)})\\ x_{j+1}^{(l)}(t) &= C_j^{(l)} e^{\alpha_j t}\sin(\beta_j t + \phi_j^{(l)})\end{aligned} \tag{1.7}$$

Linear systems satisfy the *superposition principle*, defined as follows: if $\phi_1(t,x)$ and $\phi_2(t,x)$ are any two linearly independent solutions of system (1.1), then $S(t,x) = \alpha\phi_1(t,x)$ $+\beta\phi_2(t,x)$ is also a solution for any $\alpha, \beta \in \mathbb{R}$. Applying the superposition principle, we can write the general solution of (1.1) as a function of time and m arbitrary constants, namely:

$$x(t) = c_1x_1(t) + c_2x_2(t) + \ldots + c_mx_m(t) \tag{1.8}$$

where $x_i(t)$ $(i = 1, \ldots, m)$ are the individual solutions defined in (1.6) or (1.7) and the m constants c_i are determined by the initial conditions. It can be shown that formula (1.8) gives all of the possible solutions to (1.1).

Simple inspection of (1.6) and (1.7) suggests that if it any of the eigenvalues has a positive real part, solutions initiating from a generic point (one for which $c_i \neq 0 \ \forall_i$) diverge, i.e., variables tend to + or $-\infty$ as time tends to plus infinity. On the contrary, if *all* eigenvalues have negative real parts, solutions asymptotically tend to zero, that is, to the unique equilibrium point. In the latter case, the equilibrium is asymptotically stable, in the former case the equilibrium is unstable (see Section 6.) The situation is more complicated if there are no eigenvalues with positive real parts but some eigenvalues have zero real parts. If there is only one such eigenvalue, the system has an attenuated form of stability — it does not converge to equilibrium, but it does not diverge either. (If one of the eigenvalues is zero, the equilibrium need not be unique.)

Consider now, the case of a real eigenvalue λ_k and set the initial conditions so that $c_k \neq 0, c_i = 0 \ \forall_{i \neq k}$. From (1.6) and (1.8) we have

$$x(0) = c_k x_k(0) = c_k u_k. \tag{1.9}$$

Initial conditions have been chosen so as to position the system, at time zero, on the eigenvector associated with λ_k. Using (1.6), (1.8) and (1.9) the solution for $|t| > 0$ in this case is given by $x(t) = c_k x_k(t) = e^{\lambda_k t} c_k u_k = e^{\lambda_k t} x(0)$.

Then, if the initial conditions are on the eigenvector, the system either approaches or moves away from the equilibrium point (depending on the sign of the eigenvalue), *along that vector*. In other words, each real eigenvector u_k defines a direction of motion in the state space that is preserved by the matrix A. In this case, the eigenvectors are invariant sets. Broadly speaking, a certain region of the state space is said to be invariant with respect to the action of a continuous- or discrete-time dynamical system, if an orbit starting in the set remains there forever (unless disturbed by exogenous shocks). The speed of the motion along the eigenvector u_k is given by $\dot{x}(t) = \lambda_k e^{\lambda_k t} x(0) = \lambda_k x(t)$, that is, the speed is a constant proportion of the position of x.

The complex case is more difficult to analyze, but it is possible to show that the plane S spanned (or generated) by the two linearly independent real vectors associated with a pair of complex conjugate eigenvectors $(u_j, \bar{u}_j)$,

$$\begin{aligned} \frac{1}{2}(u_j + \bar{u}_j) &= a_j \\ -\frac{i}{2}(u_j + \bar{u}_j) &= b_j \end{aligned}$$

is invariant. (Vectors a_j and b_j are the real and imaginary parts of $(u_j, \bar{u}_j)$.) If we choose the initial conditions on S so that the coefficients c_i of the general solution are all zero except the two corresponding to the pair of complex eigenvalues $(\lambda_j, \bar{\lambda}_j)$, the orbits of the system remain on the plane S forever.

Again, assuming that the matrix A has m distinct eigenvalues, the eigenvectors (or, in the complex case, the vectors equal to the real and imaginary parts of them) are divided into three groups, according to whether the corresponding eigenvalues have negative, positive or zero real parts. Then the subsets of the state space spanned (or generated) by each group of vectors are known as the stable, unstable and center eigenspaces, respectively, and denoted by E_s, E_u and E_c. If m_s is the number of eigenvalues with negative real parts, m_u the number with positive real parts and m_c the number with zero real parts, the dimension of the stable, unstable and center eigenspaces are m_s, m_u and m_c, respectively, and $m = m_s + m_u + m_c$. The subspaces E_s, E_u and E_c are invariant.

2 Continuous systems in the plane

Systems in two dimensions are particularly easy to discuss in full detail and give rise to a number of interesting basic dynamic configurations.

The general form can be written as

$$\begin{pmatrix} \dot{x} \\ \dot{y} \end{pmatrix} = A \begin{pmatrix} x \\ y \end{pmatrix} = \begin{pmatrix} a_{11} & a_{12} \\ a_{21} & a_{22} \end{pmatrix} \begin{pmatrix} x \\ y \end{pmatrix} \tag{2.1}$$

with $x, y \in \mathbb{R}$, a_{ij} real constants. If $\det(A) \neq 0$, the unique equilibrium, for which $\dot{x} = \dot{y} = 0$, is $x = y = 0$. The characteristic equation is

$$0 = \begin{pmatrix} a_{11} - \lambda & a_{12} \\ a_{21} & a_{22} - \lambda \end{pmatrix}$$

and the eigenvalues are

$$\lambda_{1,2} = \frac{1}{2}\left(\text{tr } (A) \pm \sqrt{\Delta} \right) \tag{2.2}$$

where $\Delta \equiv \left([\text{tr}(A)]^2 - 4\det(A)\right)$ is called the *discriminant*. For system (2.1) we have $\Delta = (a_{11} - a_{22})^2 + 4a_{12}a_{21}$. The different types of dynamical behavior of (2.1) can be described in terms of the two eigenvalues of the matrix A, which in planar systems can be completely characterised by the trace and determinant of A. In the following we consider nondegenerate equilibria (for which λ_1 and λ_2 are both nonzero), unless otherwise stated. Dynamical behaviour is distinguished according to the sign of the discriminant.

CASE 1 $\Delta > 0$

Eigenvalues and eigenvectors are real. Solutions have the form

$$\begin{aligned} x(t) &= c_1 e^{\lambda_1 t} u_1^{(1)} + c_2 e^{\lambda_2 t} u_2^{(1)} \\ y(t) &= c_1 e^{\lambda_1 t} u_1^{(2)} + c_2 e^{\lambda_2 t} u_2^{(2)}. \end{aligned}$$

Off-equilibrium, the slope of the orbits in the (x, y) plane asymptotically tend to a common, definite limit equal to

$$\lim_{t \to \infty} \frac{dy(t)}{dx(t)} = \lim_{t \to \infty} \frac{c_1 \lambda_1 e^{\lambda_1 t} u_1^{(2)} + c_2 \lambda_2 e^{\lambda_2 t} u_2^{(2)}}{c_1 \lambda_1 e^{\lambda_1 t} u_1^{(1)} + c_2 \lambda_2 e^{\lambda_2 t} u_2^{(1)}} = \frac{u_1^{(2)}}{u_1^{(1)}}$$

if either c_1 or c_2 is nonzero. The last equality was derived by assuming $\lambda_1 > \lambda_2$, dividing throughout by $e^{\lambda_1 t}$, and taking the limit. It is the slope of the eigenvector associated with the dominant eigenvalue, that is, the largest eigenvalue, λ_1. It defines the direction with which orbits asymptotically converge to the fixed point for $t \to +\infty$ or $t \to -\infty$. There are three basic subcases corresponding to Figure 1(a), (b), (e), respectively (eigenvalues are plotted in the complex plane).

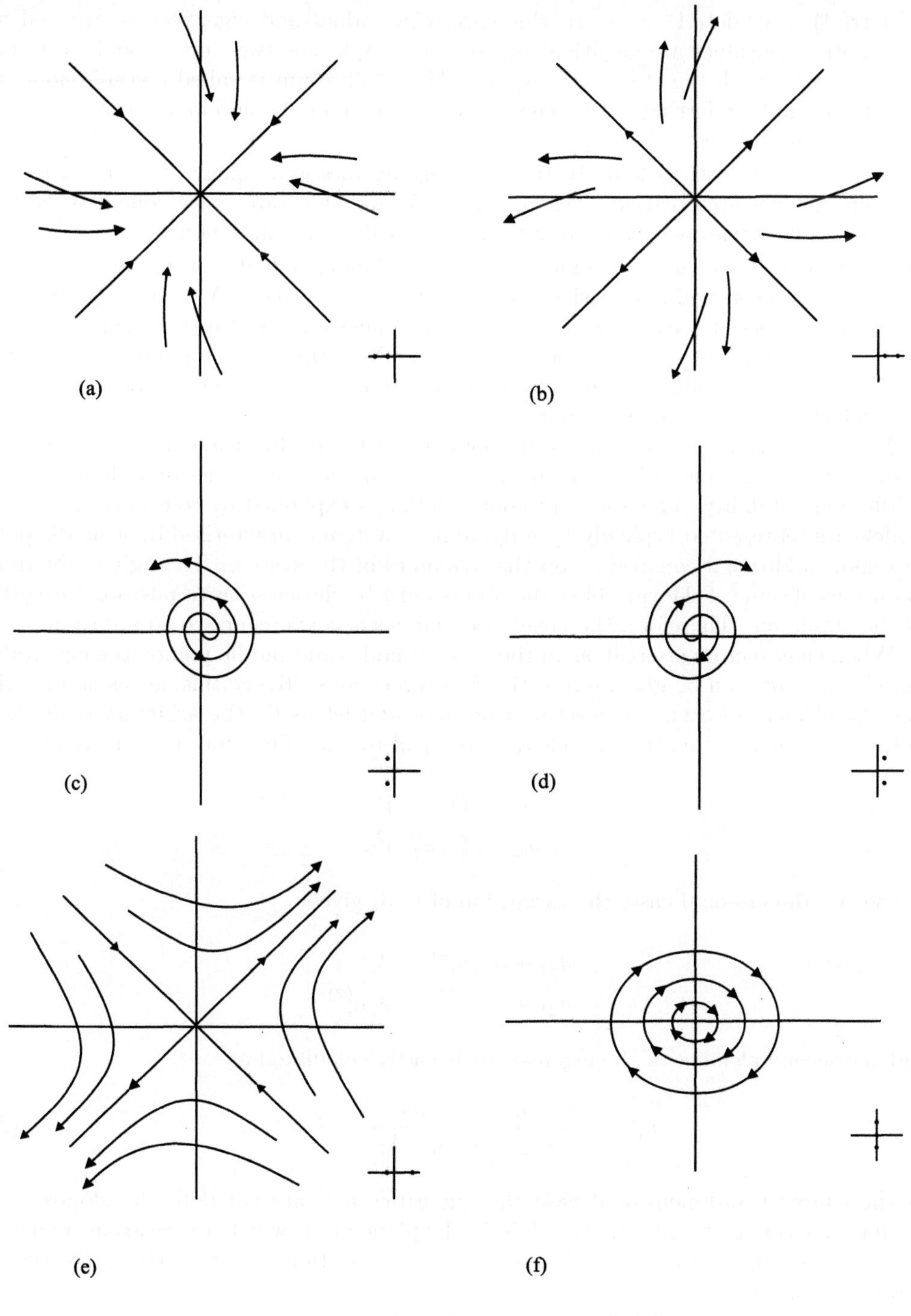

Figure 1. Equilibrium types in the plane, continuous systems

(i) $\text{tr}(A) < 0$, $\det(A) > 0$. In this case, eigenvalues and eigenvectors are real and both eigenvalues are negative (say, $0 > \lambda_1 > \lambda_2$). The two-dimensional state space coincides with the stable eigenspace. The equilibrium is called a stable node, the term 'node' referring to the characteristic shape of the ensemble of orbits around the equilibrium.

(ii) $\text{tr}\ (A) > 0$, $\det(A) > 0$. In this case, eigenvalues and eigenvectors are real, both eigenvalues are positive (say, $\lambda_1 > \lambda_2 > 0$) and the state space coincides with the unstable eigenspace. The equilibrium is called an unstable node.

(iii) $\det(A) < 0$. In this case, which implies $\Delta > 0$ independently of the sign of the trace of A, one eigenvalue is positive, the other is negative (say, $\lambda_1 > 0 > \lambda_2$). There is, then, a one-dimensional stable and a one-dimensional unstable eigenspace and the equilibrium is known as a saddle point. All orbits starting off-equilibrium eventually diverge from equilibrium except those originating in points on the stable eigenspace which converge to equilibrium.

Mathematically speaking, a saddle point is unstable. In economic literature, especially in rational expectations or optimal growth models, we often find the concept of saddle point stability. The apparent contradiction is explained by considering that such models are represented typically by a dynamical system characterised by a saddle point, *plus* some additional constraints on the dynamics of the system. Then given the initial conditions of some of the variables, the others must be chosen so as to position the system on the stable set. Therefore, the ensuing dynamics is convergence to equilibrium.

When eigenvectors are real, as in the cases of nodes and saddle points, the eigenvalues and eigenvectors can be given interesting interpretations. To see this, let us assume that the first element of each eigenvector is nonzero and let us fix the arbitrary scale factor so that, for each vector, the first element is equal to one. Therefore we can write

$$\begin{aligned} u_1 &= (1, u_1^{(2)})^T \\ u_2 &= (1, u_2^{(2)})^T. \end{aligned}$$

In the two-dimensional case, the expansion of (1.3) gives

$$\begin{aligned} a_{11} + a_{12}u_i^{(2)} &= \lambda_i \\ a_{21} + a_{22}u_i^{(2)} &= \lambda_i u_i^{(2)} \end{aligned}$$

and the second element of the eigenvector is easily calculated as

$$u_i^{(2)} = \frac{\lambda_i - a_{11}}{a_{12}} = \frac{a_{21}}{\lambda_i - a_{22}} \qquad i = 1, 2. \tag{2.3}$$

In the simple two-dimensional case the quantities $u_i^{(2)}$ are equal to the slopes of the straight lines emanating from the origin in the plane (x, y) which are invariant under the law of motion defined by (2.1). From (2.1) the proportional rates of change of the two variables x, y are

$$\frac{d \ln x}{dt} = \frac{\dot{x}}{x} = \frac{a_{11}x + a_{12}y}{x} = a_{11} + a_{12}\frac{y}{x}$$

$$\frac{d\ln y}{dt} = \frac{\dot{y}}{y} = \frac{a_{21}x + a_{22}y}{y} = a_{21}\frac{x}{y} + a_{22}. \tag{2.4}$$

Using (2.4) we can see that for initial conditions on one or the other of the lines defined by (2.3), we have

$$\frac{\dot{x}}{x} = \frac{\dot{y}}{y} = \lambda_i$$

that is, the proportional rates of change for both variables are constant and equal to the corresponding eigenvalue. The lines defined by (2.3) are sometimes denoted as *balanced growth paths*. On these paths the two variables evolve in time maintaining a constant ratio. These paths can be of special significance in applications. For example, in an economic context, if y denotes capital stock and x is output, along a balanced growth path there is a growing (or declining) output with a constant capital/output ratio. Alternatively, if $y = \dot{x}$, and x is income, along the balanced growth path there is a constant proportional rate of growth (or decline) of income.

Notice that on the balanced growth paths the value of the variables may increase or decrease according to the sign of the eigenvalues *and* the initial conditions. A positive proportional growth rate may result either from positive rate of change ($\dot{x} > 0$) and positive level ($x > 0$) *or* from negative rate of change ($\dot{x} < 0$) and negative level ($x < 0$). A negative proportional growth rate results from the rate of change and level being of opposite sign. Finally, from the discussion above, it follows that the balanced growth path corresponding to the largest eigenvalue (in algebraic terms) is attracting in the sense that almost all orbits (i.e., all orbits except those starting on the other eigenvector) asymptotically converge to it in time.

CASE 2 $\Delta < 0$

The eigenvalues and eigenvectors are complex conjugate pairs and we have

$$(\lambda_1, \lambda_2) = (\lambda, \bar{\lambda}) = \alpha \pm i\beta \text{ and } \alpha = \frac{\text{tr }(A)}{2}, \qquad \beta = \frac{\sqrt{-\Delta}}{2}.$$

The solutions have the form

$$\begin{aligned} x(t) &= Ce^{\alpha t}\cos(\beta t + \phi) \\ y(t) &= Ce^{\alpha t}\sin(\beta t + \phi) \end{aligned} \tag{2.5}$$

and the motion is oscillatory. If $\alpha \neq 0$ there is no strict periodicity in the sense that there exists no τ such that $x(t) = x(t+\tau)$. However, a conditional period can be defined as the length of time between two successive maxima of a variable, which is equal to $2\pi/\beta$. The frequency is simply the number of oscillations per time unit, that is, $\beta/2\pi$. The amplitude or size of the oscillations, depends on the initial conditions and $e^{\alpha t}$.

The complex conjugate eigenvectors can be calculated as follows. Once again use the degree of freedom and, assuming that the real (denoted Re) and imaginary (denoted Im) parts are nonzero, set $u_1^{(1)} = 1 + i$, $u_2^{(1)} = 1 - i$. Then, expanding (1.3) we obtain

$$\begin{aligned} u_1 &= \left(1 + i, \frac{\alpha - \beta - a_{11}}{a_{12}} + i\frac{\alpha + \beta - a_{11}}{a_{12}}\right)^T \\ u_2 &= \left(1 - i, \frac{\alpha - \beta - a_{11}}{a_{12}} - i\frac{\alpha + \beta - a_{11}}{a_{12}}\right)^T \end{aligned}$$

and two real and linearly independent vectors can be constructed

$$e_R = \frac{1}{2}(u_1 + u_2) = \left(1, \frac{\alpha - \beta - a_{11}}{a_{12}}\right)^T$$
$$e_I = \frac{i}{2}(u_1 - u_2) = \left(-1, \frac{-\alpha - \beta + a_{11}}{a_{12}}\right)^T$$

which span a plane that is invariant. Notice that in this particular case, the invariant plane coincides with the state space and with the stable or unstable eigenspace. This is no longer the case in higher-dimensional systems. There are three subcases depending on the sign of $\mathrm{tr}(A)$ and therefore of $\mathrm{Re}(\lambda) = \alpha$, see the corrresponding figures in Figure 1(c), (d), (f), respectively:

(i) $\mathrm{tr}(A) < 0$, $\mathrm{Re}\,\lambda = \alpha < 0$. The oscillations are dampened and the system converges to equilibrium. The equilibrium point is known as a *focus* or, sometimes, a *vortex*, due to the characteristic shape of the orbits around the equilibrium. In this case the focus or vortex is stable and the stable eigenspace coincides with the state space.

(ii) $\mathrm{tr}(A) > 0$, $\mathrm{Re}\,\lambda = \alpha > 0$. The amplitude of the oscillations gets larger with time and the system diverges from equilibrium. The unstable eigenspace coincides with the state space and the equilibrium point is called an unstable focus or vortex.

(iii) $\mathrm{tr}(A) = 0$, $\mathrm{Re}\,\lambda = \alpha = 0$, $\det(A) > 0$. In this special case we have a pair of purely imaginary eigenvalues. Orbits neither converge to, nor diverge from, the equilibrium point, but they oscillate regularly around it with a constant amplitude that depends only on initial conditions and a frequency equal to $\sqrt{\det(A)}/2\pi$. The centre eigenspace coincides with the state space and the equilibrium point is called a *centre*.

CASE 3 $\Delta = 0$

The eigenvalues are real and equal, $\lambda_1 = \lambda_2 = \lambda$. In this case, if $A \neq \lambda I$, only one eigenvector can be determined, call it $u = (u^{(1)}, u^{(2)})^T$, defining a single straight line through the origin. The second solution is associated with constant c_2 (the second and third terms on the RHS below) so that the general solution can be written as

$$x(t) = (c_1 u^{(1)} + c_2 v^{(1)})e^{\lambda t} + tc_2 u^{(1)} e^{\lambda t} y(t) = (c_1 u^{(2)} + c_2 v^{(2)})e^{\lambda t} + tc_2 u^{(2)} e^{\lambda t}$$

whence

$$x(0) = c_1 u^{(1)} + c_2 v^{(1)} y(0) = c_1 u^{(2)} + c_2 v^{(2)}.$$

The equilibrium type is again a node, sometimes called a Jordan node. Finally, if $A = \lambda I$ the equilibrium is still a node, sometimes called a bicritical node. However, all half-lines from the origin are solutions, giving a star shaped form.

3 Linear systems in discrete time

Let us consider now the linear, discrete-time system

$$x_{n+1} = Bx_n \qquad x \in \mathbb{R}^m. \tag{3.1}$$

Once again observe that $x = 0$ is an equilibrium solution and that for linear systems like (3.1) it is, generically, the only equilibrium. The general solution of (3.1) can be obtained in a manner analogous to that of (1.1). If κ_i is a real, distinct eigenvalue of the $(m \times m)$ matrix B and v_i is the corresponding real eigenvector so that $Bv_i = \kappa_i v_i$, it can be verified that

$$x_i(n) = \kappa_i^n v_i \tag{3.2}$$

is a solution of (3.1). It is important to note a basic difference between solutions of continuous-time systems and solutions of discrete-time systems regarding the status of the invariant lines defined by the eigenvectors. The real eigenvectors associated with real eigenvalues for systems of difference equations are still invariant sets, that is, sequences of points initiating on these sets remain on the sets. However the invariant, continuous, straight lines are *not solution orbits* as they were in the continuous case. Also recall the interesting peculiarity of discrete-time systems in the case of negative, real eigenvalues known as improper oscillations. In such a case, we may have the following interesting situation. Consider again system (3.1). Suppose that there is one real eigenvalue $\kappa_1 < 0$, $|\kappa_1| > 1$ and that the initial condition is $x(0) = v_1$ (the eigenvector corresponding to κ_1). The solution is $x(n) = \kappa_1^n v_1$, that is, the system stays forever on the straight line through the origin defined by v_1. At each iterate the system moves towards the equilibrium point $\bar{x} = 0$, but always overshoots it, so that the distance from equilibrium becomes ever larger in time, tending to ∞ as $n \to +\infty$. Therefore, when there are negative real eigenvalues in discrete-time systems, great care should be applied in the use and, in particular, the interpretation of arrows in the phase diagram.

Notice that if system (3.1) is characterised by improper oscillations then the system $x_{n+1} = B^2 x_n$, with $B^2 = BB$, will have the same stability properties, but no improper oscillations. In fact, if κ is an eigenvalue of B, then $\rho = \kappa^2$ is an eigenvalue of B^2 and $|\rho| = |\kappa|^2$. Then $|\rho| \geq 1$ if $|\kappa| \geq 1$. If the (nonsingular) matrix B has an odd number of negative eigenvalues (and therefore $\det(B) < 0$), system (3.1) is said to be orientation-reversing (whereas for $\det(B) > 0$ it will be said to be orientation-preserving). The justification for these phrases can be readily seen in the simplest case of a one-dimensional system $x_{n+1} = G(x_n) = -x_n$, $x_n \in \mathbb{R}$. The oriented interval $[a, b]$ is mapped by G to an interval $[G(a), G(b)]$ with reversed orientation. However, $G^2[a, b]$ preserves orientation.

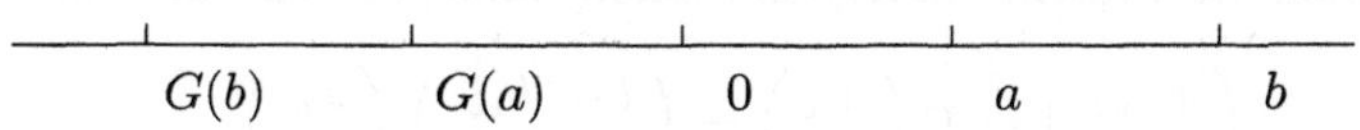

As usual, dealing with complex conjugate eigenvalues is more complicated. Suppose that there is a pair of eigenvalues and corresponding pair of eigenvectors of B

$$\begin{aligned}(\kappa_j, \kappa_{j+1}) &= (\kappa_j, \bar{\kappa}_j) = \sigma_j \pm i\theta_j \\ (v_j, v_{j+1}) &= (v_j, \bar{v}_j) = p_j \pm iq_j\end{aligned}$$

where p_j and q_j are m-dimensional vectors. Making use of polar coordinate transformations, a theorem due to de Moivre, trigonometric identities and r, the modulus of the complex eigenvalues, the solutions can be re-written as m-dimensional vectors whose lth elements have the form

$$\begin{aligned} x_j^{(l)}(n) &= C_j^{(l)} r_j^n \cos(\omega_j n + \phi_j^{(l)}) \\ x_{j+1}^{(l)}(n) &= C_j^{(l)} r_j^n \sin(\omega_j n + \phi_j^{(l)}). \end{aligned} \tag{3.3}$$

Notice the similarities and differences with solutions to continuous-time systems with complex eigenvalues in (1.7).

Stable, unstable and centre eigenspaces are defined in a manner similar to that used for continuous-time systems, with the obvious difference that the discriminating factor for discrete-time systems is whether the *moduli* of the relevant eigenvalues are, respectively, smaller, greater or equal to *one.*

Once again, assuming that there are m linearly independent solutions defined by (3.2) and (3.3), by the superposition principle the general solution of (3.1) can be written as a linear combination of the individual solutions

$$x(n) = c_1 x_1(n) + c_2 x_2(n) + \ldots + c_m x_m(n) \tag{3.4}$$

where c_i are constants depending on the initial conditions.

Inspection of (3.2) and (3.3) indicates that if the modulus of *any* of the eigenvalues is greater than one, solutions tend to + or $-\infty$ as time tends to plus infinity. On the contrary, if *all* eigenvalues have modulus smaller than one, solutions converge asymptotically to the equilibrium point. In the latter case, we say that the equilibrium is asymptotically stable, in the former case we say it is unstable. For distinct eigenvalues, the solution in the long run is determined by the term (or terms in the complex case) corresponding to the eigenvalue (or the pair of eigenvalues) with the largest modulus. When the dominant real eigenvalue or complex eigenvalue pair has modulus exactly equal to one, we have a weaker form of stability discussed below. If that eigenvalue or eigenvalue pair is repeated, the equilibrium is unstable. As for continuous-time systems, there are criteria that can be applied to the coefficient matrix B to ensure stability. In this case, stability conditions guarantee that all eigenvalues have moduli inside the unit circle of the complex plane.

4 Discrete-time systems in the plane

The discrete autonomous system analogous to continuous system (2.1) is:

$$\begin{pmatrix} x_{n+1} \\ y_{n+1} \end{pmatrix} = B \begin{pmatrix} x_n \\ y_n \end{pmatrix} = \begin{pmatrix} b_{11} & b_{12} \\ b_{21} & b_{22} \end{pmatrix} \begin{pmatrix} x_n \\ y_n \end{pmatrix} \tag{4.1}$$

If the matrix $(I-B)$ is nonsingular, as assumed here, there exists a unique equilibrium point for (4.1), situated at the origin. The characteristic equation is analogous to the continuous case, that is,

$$\kappa^2 - \text{ tr } (B) \quad \kappa + \text{ det } (B) = 0$$

and the eigenvalues are

$$\kappa_{1,2} = \frac{1}{2}\left(\text{ tr } (B) \pm \sqrt{[\text{ tr } (B)]^2 - 4 \text{ det } (B)}\right)$$

The dynamics for the discrete system (4.1) are discussed case by case, again considering nondegenerate equilibria (κ_1, κ_2 nonzero):

CASE 1 $\Delta > 0$

The eigenvalues are real and solutions take the form

$$\begin{aligned} x(n) &= c_1\kappa_1^n v_1^{(1)} + c_2\kappa_2^n v_2^{(1)} \\ y(n) &= c_1\kappa_1^n v_1^{(2)} + c_2\kappa_2^n v_2^{(2)}. \end{aligned}$$

There are three basic subcases corresponding to the state space representations in Figure 2, where again, eigenvalues are plotted in the complex plane.

(i) If $|\kappa_1| < 1$ and $|\kappa_2| < 1$ the fixed point is a stable node. In discrete time this means that solutions are sequences of points approaching the equilibrium as $n \to +\infty$. If κ_1, $\kappa_2 > 0$ the approach is monotonic, otherwise, there are improper oscillations (see Figure 2(a) and (c), respectively). In this case, the stable eigenspace coincides with the state space.

(ii) If $|\kappa_1| > 1$ and $|\kappa_2| > 1$ the fixed point is an unstable node, that is, solutions are sequences of points approaching equilibrium as $n \to -\infty$. If κ_1, $\kappa_2 > 0$ the approach is monotonic, otherwise, there are improper oscillations (as in Figure 2(a) and (c), respectively, but arrows point in the opposite direction and the time order of points is reversed). In this case, the unstable eigenspace coincides with the state space.

(iii) If $|\kappa_1| > 1$ and $|\kappa_2| < 1$ the fixed point is a saddle point. No sequences of points approach the equilibrium for $n \to \pm\infty$ except those originating from points on the eigenvectors associated with κ_1 or κ_2. Again, if κ_1, $\kappa_2 > 0$ orbits move monotonically (see Figure 2(b)), otherwise they oscillate improperly (see Figure 2(d)). The stable and unstable eigenspaces are one-dimensional.

CASE 2 $\Delta < 0$ Then $\det(B) > 0$ and eigenvalues are a complex conjugate pair

$$(\kappa_1, \kappa_2) = (\kappa, \bar{\kappa}) = \sigma \pm i\theta$$

and solutions are sequences of points situated on spirals whose amplitude increases or decreases in time according to the factor r^n where $r = |\sigma \pm i\theta| = \sqrt{\sigma^2 + \theta^2} = \sqrt{\det(B)}$, the modulus of the complex eigenvalue pair. The invariant plane in the two-dimensional problem coincides with the state space as well as the (stable, unstable or centre) eigenspace. Solutions are of the form

$$\begin{aligned} x(n) &= Cr^n \cos(\omega n + \phi) \\ y(n) &= Cr^n \sin(\omega n + \phi). \end{aligned}$$

(i) If $r < 1$ solutions converge to equilibrium and the equilibrium point is a stable focus (see Figure 2(e)).

(ii) If $r > 1$ solutions diverge and the equilibrium point is an unstable focus (as in Figure 2(e), but arrows point in the opposite direction and the time order of points is reversed).

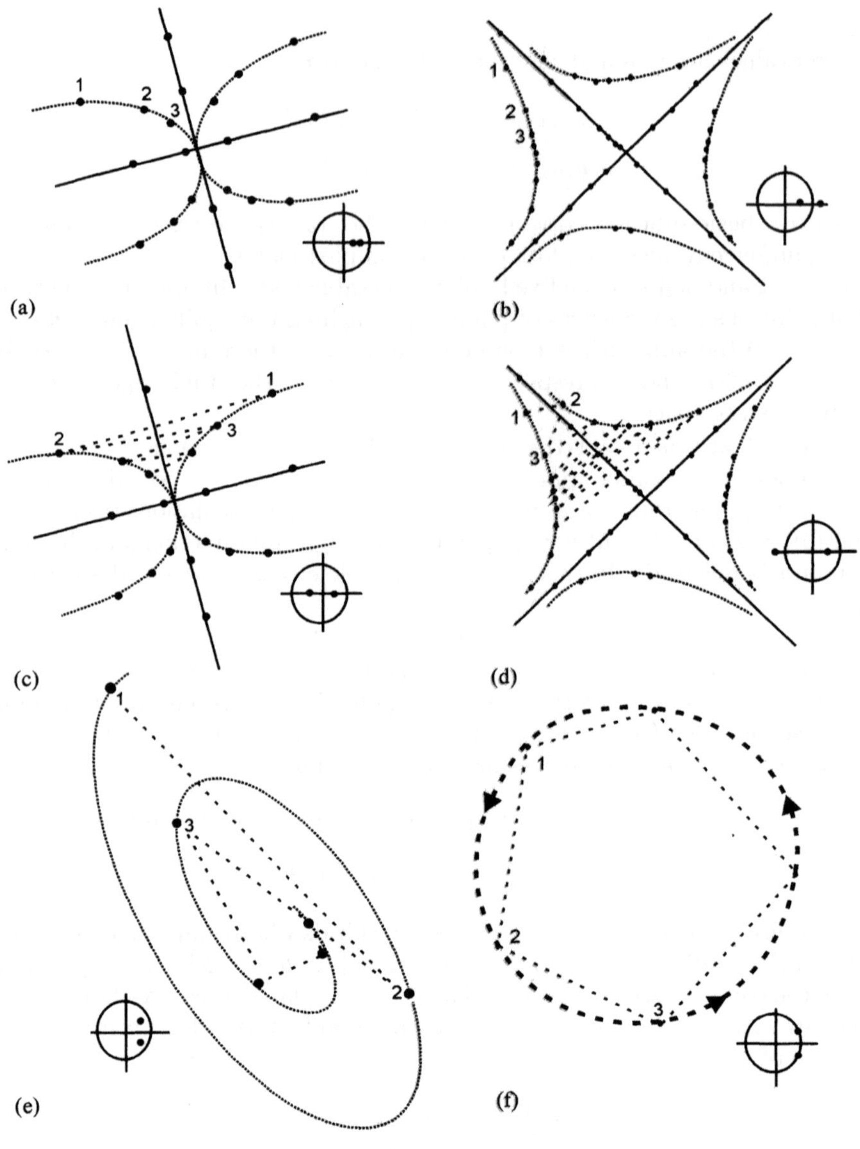

Figure 2. Equilibrium types in the plane, discrete systems

(iii) If $r = 1$ the eigenvalues lie exactly on the unit circle, an exceptional case. There are two subcases which depend on the frequency of the oscillation $\omega/2\pi$, $\omega = \arccos[\,\text{tr}\,(B)/2]$:

(a) $\omega/2\pi$ is rational and the orbit in the state space is a periodic sequence of points situated on a circle, the radius of which depends on initial conditions (see Figure 2(f));

(b) $\omega/2\pi$ is irrational, the sequence is nonperiodic or quasiperiodic. The sequence of quasiperiodic motion is as follows. Starting from any point on the circle, orbits stay on the circle but no sequence returns to the initial point in finite time. Therefore, solutions wander on the circle filling it up, without ever becoming periodic. Periodic and quasiperiodic solutions are not exceptional for nonlinear systems.

CASE 3 $\Delta = 0$

There is a repeated real eigenvalue $\kappa_1 = \text{tr}\,(B)/2$. Considerations analogous to those made for continuous systems could be developed to arrive at the general form of solutions to planar systems with a repeated eigenvalue κ, namely

$$\begin{aligned} x(n) &= (c_1 v^{(1)} + c_2 u^{(1)})\kappa^n + n c_2 v^{(1)} \kappa^n \\ y(n) &= (c_1 v^{(2)} + c_2 u^{(2)})\kappa^n + n c_2 v^{(2)} \kappa^n . \end{aligned}$$

If $|\kappa| < 1$, $\lim_{n\to\infty} n\kappa^n = 0$ and the multiplicative expansion due to n is dominated by the exponential contraction implied by κ^n. If the repeated eigenvalue is equal to one in absolute value, the equilibrium is unstable (with improper oscillations for $\kappa_1 = -1$). However, divergence is linear not exponential.

The equilibrium types illustrated in Figure 2 are presented in such a way as to emphasise the differences with equilibrium types for continuous planar systems. First, it should be observed that the points of the orbit sequences lie on the (dotted) curves but the curves themselves are not orbits. Moreover, points have been given a time reference so as to avoid any confusion about the direction of motion.

In the two-dimensional case the conditions for stability, that is for which $|\kappa| < 1$, can be given a simple representation in terms of the trace and determinant of the constant matrix B as follows

$$\begin{aligned} 1 + \text{tr}\,(B) + \det\,(B) &> 0 \quad (i) \\ 1 - \text{tr}\,(B) + \det\,(B) &> 0 \quad (ii) \\ 1 - \det\,(B) &> 0. \quad (iii) \end{aligned}$$

If we replace the greater-than sign with the equal sign in conditions (i)–(iii), we obtain three lines intersecting in the $(\text{tr}(B), \det(B))$ plane, defining a triangle. Points inside the triangle correspond to stable combinations of the trace and determinant of B. Typically, stability is lost, as a parameter is varied, by intersecting one of these lines (see Section 8).

5 Stability - some definitions

Consider the autonomous system of nonlinear differential equations

$$\dot{x} = f(x) \quad x \in \mathbb{R}^m \tag{5.1}$$

with an *isolated* fixed point, that is, it has a surrounding neighbourhood containing no other fixed point (refer to Figure 3 for graphical representations of the following definitions). Let $x(t)$ denote the state of the system at time t, $x(0) = x_0$ the initial point and $\|\cdot\|$ indicate the Euclidean distance in $\mathbb{R}^m$. With this notation we can now introduce the following definitions of stability.

Definition 5.1. *The fixed point $\bar{x}$ is said to be* Lyapunov stable *(or simply* stable*) if for any $\epsilon > 0$ there exists a number $\delta(\epsilon) > 0$ such that if $\|x_0 - \bar{x}\| < \delta$ then $\|x(t) - \bar{x}\| < \epsilon$ for all $t > 0$.*

Important aspects of stability in the sense of Lyapunov are: (i) the constraint on the initial condition is that $\delta(\epsilon)$ must exist for *any* $\epsilon > 0$; (ii) for the generality of nonautonomous systems of differential equations, the number δ depends also on the initial time t_0, whereas, for autonomous systems δ depends only on ϵ. In this case we say that stability is uniform. Uniformity also holds for nonautonomous systems which are periodic in the sense that we have $\dot{x} = f(t, x) = f(t + \omega, x)$ for some ω.

Definition 5.2. *The fixed point $\bar{x}$ is said to be* asymptotically stable *if*
(a) it is stable; and
(b) there exists an $\eta > 0$ such that whenever $\|x_0 - \bar{x}\| < \eta$

$$\lim_{t\to\infty} \|x(t) - \bar{x}\| = 0.$$

Because system (5.1) is autonomous, asymptotic stability is uniform and property *(b)* of definition of asymptotically stable can be replaced by the equivalent property

(b′) there exists a number $\eta > 0$ and, for each $\epsilon > 0$, a real positive number $T = T(\eta, \epsilon)$, such that if $\|x_0 - \bar{x}\| < \eta$ then $\|x(t) - \bar{x}\| < \epsilon$ for all $t > T$.

Notice that because of uniformity, T does not depend on initial time but only on η and ϵ.

Definition 5.3. *Let $\bar{x}$ be an asymptotically stable fixed point of (5.1), then the set $B(\bar{x}) = \{x \in \mathbb{R}^m \mid \lim_{t\to\infty} \|x(t) - \bar{x}\| = 0\}$ is the* domain *or* basin of attraction *of $\bar{x}$. If $B(\bar{x}) = \mathbb{R}^m$ (or, at any rate, if it coincides with the state space) then $\bar{x}$ is said to be* globally asymptotically stable. *If stability only holds in a neighbourhood of $\bar{x}$, it is said to be* locally stable.

Broadly speaking, when defined in terms of the union of properties *(a)* and *(b)*, asymptotic stability implies that if orbits start near equilibrium they stay near it and eventually converge to it. The equivalent formulation *(b′)* indicates that, starting sufficiently near equilibrium, any arbitrarily small neighbourhood of it is reached in finite time.

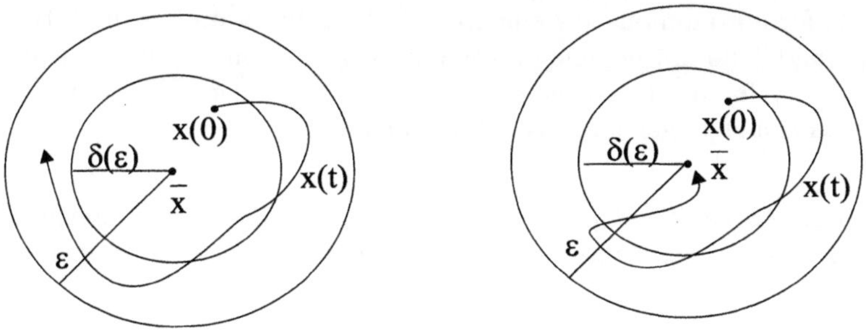

Figure 3. Left, Lyapunov stability; right, asymptotic stability

Note that property *(b)*, or *(b′)*, (convergence to equilibrium) does not imply property *(a)* (stability). That is, if *(b)*, or *(b′)*, holds but *(a)* does not, we could have solutions that, before converging to $\bar{x}$, wander arbitrarily far from it. (Alternatively, it might take an arbitrarily long time to reach a given neighbourhood of equilibrium.)

Systems for which property *(a)* holds, but property *(b)*, or *(b′)*, does not, are called *weakly stable.* Centres are examples of this type of stability. Examples of asymptotic stability were given by stable nodes or foci. Systems for which property *(b)*, or *(b′)*, holds, but property *(a)* does not, are sometimes called *quasi-asymptotically stable.* However, for *linear systems*, property *(b)*, or *(b′)*, does imply property *(a)*.

There exist analogous definitions of stability for autonomous dynamical systems in discrete time with the general form of

$$x_{n+1} = G(x_n) \qquad x \in \mathbb{R}^m. \tag{5.2}$$

Suppose $\bar{x}$ is an isolated equilibrium point of (5.2), such that $G(\bar{x}) = \bar{x}$.

Definition 5.4. *The equilibrium point $\bar{x}$ is* Lyapunov stable *(or, simply,* stable*) if for every $\epsilon > 0$, there exists $\delta(\epsilon)$ such that*

$$[\|x_0 - \bar{x}\| < \delta(\epsilon)] \Rightarrow [\|G^n(x_0) - \bar{x}\| < \epsilon \ \forall n > 0] .$$

Definition 5.5. *The equilibrium point $\bar{x}$ is* asymptotically stable *if*

(a) it is stable and

(b) there exists $\eta > 0$ such that

$$[\|x_0 - \bar{x}\| < \eta] \Rightarrow \left[\lim_{n\to\infty} \|G^n(x_0) - \bar{x}\| = 0 \ \forall n > 0\right] .$$

Property *(b)* can be replaced by the equivalent property

(b′) there exists $\eta > 0$ and for each $\epsilon > 0$, there exists an integer $T = T(\eta, \epsilon) > 0$ such that

$$[\|x_0 - \bar{x}\| < \eta] \Rightarrow [\|G^n(x_0) - \bar{x}\| < \epsilon \ \forall n \geq T] .$$

Notice that for autonomous systems like (5.2), stability and asymptotic stability are uniform and δ and T do not depend on the initial time. Convergence to equilibrium does not imply stability for discrete-time systems either. For certain systems, asymptotical stability may take a stronger form as defined below.

Definition 5.6. *An equilibrium $\bar{x}$ of system (5.1) is said to be* exponentially stable *if there exist two positive constants α and β such that, if $\|x_0 - \bar{x}\| < \eta$ for some $\eta > 0$, then*

$$\|x(t) - \bar{x}\| < \beta\|x_0 - \bar{x}\|e^{-\alpha t} \; \forall t > 0.$$

The constants α and β may depend on η.

An entirely analogous definition can be written for a discrete-time system.

Asymptotically stable *linear* systems (in both continuous and discrete time), such as those studied above, are all exponentially stable. It should be observed that the properties *stable* and *unstable* are not symmetric in the sense that stability is defined in terms of the behaviour of a family of orbits, whereas instability occurs whenever even a single orbit violates the conditions for stability.

Definition 5.7. *A fixed point of systems (5.1) or (5.2) is called* unstable *if it is not stable.*

This means that there exists a number $\epsilon > 0$ and an orbit starting from a point x_0 arbitrarily close to the fixed point such that $\|x(t) - \bar{x}\| \geq \epsilon$ for some $t > 0$. Unstable nodes, unstable foci, and saddle points discussed for linear systems are examples of unstable fixed points according to the definitions given above. Again, analogous definitions exist for discrete-time systems.

Linear systems generally have only one equilibrium point. If they are homogeneous, the point is the origin. For those systems, asymptotic stability is global and exponential always; weakly stable systems are exceptional (for example, the centre). Nonlinear systems, on the other hand, may have any finite, or a countably infinite number of fixed points; local asymptotic stability does not necessarily imply global stability, nor is it necessarily exponential; weak stability is not exceptional.

6 The linear approximation

Consider again the nonlinear system of differential equations $\dot{x} = f(x)$, $x \in \mathbb{R}^m$ with a fixed point $\bar{x}$. Assume that f is differentiable in each of the m variables of the vector x. A local linear approximation of the nonlinear system near the fixed point $\bar{x}$ is given by the expansion in a Taylor series of the coordinate functions f_i (the elements of the vector f) truncated after the first-order terms. Let $\xi = x - \bar{x}$, whence $\dot{\xi} = \dot{x}$. Then in first approximation

$$
\begin{aligned}
\dot{\xi}_1 &= f_1(\bar{x}) + \frac{\partial f_1(\bar{x})}{\partial x_1}\xi_1 + \frac{\partial f_1(\bar{x})}{\partial x_2}\xi_2 + \cdots + \frac{\partial f_1(\bar{x})}{\partial x_m}\xi_m \\
\dot{\xi}_2 &= f_2(\bar{x}) + \frac{\partial f_2(\bar{x})}{\partial x_1}\xi_1 + \frac{\partial f_2(\bar{x})}{\partial x_2}\xi_2 + \cdots + \frac{\partial f_3(\bar{x})}{\partial x_m}\xi_m \\
\vdots \quad & \quad \vdots \\
\dot{\xi}_m &= f_m(\bar{x}) + \frac{\partial f_m(\bar{x})}{\partial x_1}\xi_1 + \frac{\partial f_m(\bar{x})}{\partial x_2}\xi_2 + \cdots + \frac{\partial f_m(\bar{x})}{\partial x_m}\xi_m
\end{aligned}
$$

Considering that the first term on the RHS of each equation is equal to zero, the linearised system can be written compactly as

$$\dot{\xi} = Df(\bar{x})\xi \tag{6.1}$$

where, in general, $Df(x)$ denotes the matrix of first partial derivatives (often called the Jacobian matrix).

It is important to know how much of the dynamics characterising the original nonlinear system (5.1) is preserved by the approximation (6.1). There exists a general result in the theory of differential equations known as the Hartman-Grobman theorem, which guarantees that, under appropriate conditions, in a neighbourhood of the equilibrium point the qualitative properties of the nonlinear system are preserved by the linearisation. The conditions regard the hyperbolicity of the fixed point.

Definition 6.1. *A fixed point of a system of differential equations is* hyperbolic *if the Jacobian matrix calculated at that point has no zero or purely imaginary eigenvalues (no eigenvalue has real part equal to zero).*

Definition 6.2. *A continuous map g that is one-to-one (injective) and onto (surjective), and therefore invertible, with the property that both g and g^{-1} are k times differentiable, is called a C^k diffeomorphism. If $k = 0$ the map is called a homeomorphism.*

Now we can state the following known as the Hartman-Grobman theorem

Theorem 6.3. *If $\bar{x}$ is a hyperbolic fixed point of (5.1), then there is a homeomorphism h defined on some neighbourhood N of $\bar{x}$ in $\mathbb{R}^m$, locally taking orbits of the nonlinear system (5.1) to those of the linear system (6.1). The map h preserves the sense of orbits and can also be chosen so as to preserve parametrisation by time.*

If h is a homeomorphism, then from the Hartman-Grobman theorem we can deduct that asymptotic stability (or the lack of it) for the linear system (6.1) implies local asymptotic stability of the nonlinear system (5.1) (or the lack of it), see Figure 4. However, homeomorphic equivalence does not preserve all the interesting geometric features of a dynamical system. For example, a linear system characterised by an asymptotically stable node is topologically conjugate to another linear system characterised by an asymptotically stable focus.

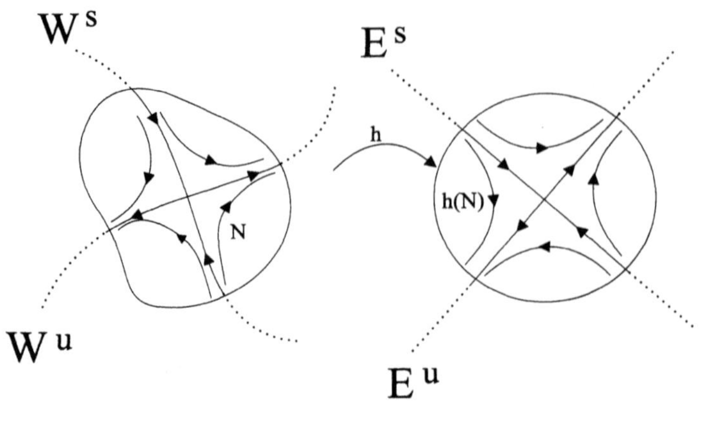

Figure 4. The Hartman-Grobman theorem

The equivalence between a nonlinear system such as (5.1) and its linearisation (6.1) would be stronger if h were a diffeomorphism. This has been proved to be the case for the nonlinear system (5.1) whenever the eigenvalues of the corresponding matrix $Df(\bar{x})$ satisfy a *nonresonance condition*, that for any choice of coefficients $c_i \geq 0$ with $\sum_{i=1}^{m} c_i \geq 2$, and for any eigenvalue λ_k of $DF(\bar{x})$, $\lambda_k \neq \sum_{i=1}^{m} c_i \lambda_i$.

If the equilibrium point is not hyperbolic, that is to say, if there exists at least one eigenvalue with real part exactly equal to 0, the Hartman-Grobman theorem cannot be applied. The reason is that the linearised system is not sufficiently informative. In particular, the stability properties of the system depend on the higher-degree terms of the expansion which have been ignored in the approximation (6.1).

In the discussion of linear systems the importance of certain invariant subspaces, the eigenspaces, defined by the eigenvectors of the controlling matrix were emphasised. If the nonlinear system (5.1) has an isolated, hyperbolic equilibrium $\bar{x}$, in the neighbourhood of $\bar{x}$ there exist certain invariant surfaces, called stable and unstable manifolds, which are the nonlinear counterparts of the stable and unstable eigenspaces. Locally, these manifolds are continuous deformations, respectively, of the stable and unstable eigenspaces of the linear system (6.1) (because $\bar{x}$ is hyperbolic, there is no centre eigenspace) and they are tangent to them at $\bar{x}$.

The method of linear approximation can be applied in a perfectly analogous manner to nonlinear systems of difference equations. Consider system (5.2), with a fixed point $\bar{x}$, and assume that G is differentiable in the m variables of the vector x. A local linear approximation of (5.2) near $\bar{x}$ is again given by truncated Taylor expansions of the functions G_i. Letting $\xi = x - \bar{x}$, the first approximation

$$\begin{aligned}
x_{n+1}^{(1)} &= \xi_{n+1}^{(1)} + \bar{x}^{(1)} = G_1(\bar{x}) + \frac{\partial G_1(\bar{x})}{\partial x_n^{(1)}}\xi_n^{(1)} + \cdots + \frac{\partial G_1(\bar{x})}{\partial x_n^{(m)}}\xi_n^{(m)} \\
x_{n+1}^{(2)} &= \xi_{n+1}^{(2)} + \bar{x}^{(2)} = G_2(\bar{x}) + \frac{\partial G_2(\bar{x})}{\partial x_n^{(1)}}\xi_n^{(1)} + \cdots + \frac{\partial G_2(\bar{x})}{\partial x_n^{(m)}}\xi_n^{(m)} \\
\vdots \quad & \quad \vdots \qquad\qquad \vdots \\
x_{n+1}^{(m)} &= \xi_{n+1}^{(m)} + \bar{x}^{(m)} = G_m(\bar{x}) + \frac{\partial G_m(\bar{x})}{\partial x_n^{(1)}}\xi_n^{(1)} + \cdots + \frac{\partial G_m(\bar{x})}{\partial x_n^{(m)}}\xi_n^{(m)}
\end{aligned}$$

where $x_n^{(i)}$, $\xi_n^{(i)}$, $\bar{x}^{(i)}$ denote, respectively, the ith element of the vectors x_n, ξ_n, $\bar{x}$ and G_i is the ith coordinate function of G.

In equilibrium, $\bar{x}^{(i)} = G_i(\bar{x})$ for all i and therefore the linearised system can be written compactly as

$$\xi_{n+1} = DG(\bar{x})\xi_n \tag{6.2}$$

where $DG(\bar{x})$ is the Jacobian matrix of partial derivatives of G, evaluated at $\bar{x}$.

The version of the Hartman-Grobman theorem for diffeomorphisms of the form $x_{n+1} = G(x_n)$ is perfectly analogous to that for flows, but the following important differences should be stressed. For discrete-time systems, fixed points are hyperbolic if none of the eigenvalues of the Jacobian matrix, evaluated at the equilibrium, is *equal to 1 in modulus.* The map h of the Hartman-Grobman theorem defining the local relation between the nonlinear system (5.2) and the linearised system (6.2) is a diffeomorphism if the eigenvalues of $DG(\bar{x})$ satisfy a nonresonance condition. In the case of maps this condition requires that for no eigenvalue κ_k of $DG(\bar{x})$ we have $\kappa_k = \prod_{i=1}^{m} \kappa_i^{c_i}$ for any choice of $c_i \geq 0$ with $\sum_i c_i \geq 2$.

7 The centre manifold theorem

Local bifurcations depending on one parameter essentially involve one real eigenvalue or a pair of complex conjugate eigenvalues. It is then possible to characterise them completely in a reduced one- or two-dimensional space, even when the phenomenon takes place in a multi-dimensional state space. The most general approach for performing this reduction is based on the notion of a *centre manifold.* Centre manifold theory involves many difficult technical details and for this introduction only general notions will be presented.

The stable and unstable manifolds of a nonlinear system in a neighbourhood of a hyperbolic fixed point are related to the corresponding eigenspaces of the linearised system. The following theorem states this relation in a more precise manner, and extends it to the centre manifold. The Theorem is presented for fixed points of differential systems.

Theorem 7.1. *Consider the system of differential equations*

$$\dot{w} = f(w) \qquad w \in \mathbb{R}^m \tag{7.1}$$

where $f \in C^r$ and $f(0) = 0$. Let E^s, E^u and E^c denote, respectively, the stable, unstable and centre eigenspaces of the matrix $A \equiv Df(0)$ (the Jacobian matrix evaluated at $w =$

0). Then there exist C^r stable and unstable invariant manifolds W^s and W^u tangent to E^s and E^u at $w = 0$, and a C^{r-1} centre invariant manifold to E^c at $w = 0$. W^s and W^u are unique, but W^c is not necessarily so. (If $f \in C^\infty$, then a C^r centre manifold exists for any finite r.)

From the centre manifold theorem it follows that, at a bifurcation point where the fixed point is not hyperbolic and W^c is not empty, in a neighbourhood of $w = 0$ system (7.1) is topologically equivalent to

$$\begin{aligned} \dot{x} &= H(x) \qquad && x \in W^c \\ \dot{y} &= -By && y \in W^s \\ \dot{z} &= Cz && z \in W^u \end{aligned}$$

where x, y and z are appropriately chosen local coordinates and B, C are positive definite matrices. Locally, the time evolution of the variables y and z is governed by two *linear* subsystems of differential equations with equilibria in $y = 0$ and $z = 0$, respectively. Recalling that the eigenvalues of a positive definite matrix are real and positive, then for initial points on W^s or W^u, the motion will converge asymptotically to equilibrium for $t \to +$ or $-\infty$, respectively. In order to complete the study of the dynamics near equilibrium, we need only investigate the reduced nonlinear subsystem

$$\dot{x} = H(x) \qquad x \in W^c \tag{7.2}$$

whose dimension is equal to the number of eigenvalues of the matrix $A \equiv Df(0)$ with zero real part. In most cases we cannot hope to calculate (7.2) exactly but, under certain regularity assumptions on W^c, its dynamics can be approximated arbitrarily closely by means of power series expansions around $\bar{x} = 0$. Also the description of the qualitative properties of each type of local bifurcation can be simplified by certain coordinate transformations that reduce the analytical expression of the vector field on the centre manifold to the simplest form (sometimes called normal form equation) exhibiting those properties.

Suppose now that the vector field f of the centre manifold theorem depends on a parameter vector $\mu \in \mathbb{R}^k$ and that a bifurcation occurs for $\mu = 0$. To investigate the behaviour of families of systems depending on μ near the bifurcation point we need to extend the basic vector field and its centre manifold so as to include a *variable* μ. This is done by adding the trivial equation $\dot{\mu} = 0$ with obvious solution $\mu =$ constant. The extended centre manifold $\tilde{W}^c$ has dimension equal to $\dim(E^c) + k$ and is tangent to $E^c(0)$ ($E^c(0) = \{(x, y, z) | y = 0, z = 0\}$) at $x = y = z = 0; \mu = 0$. The *extended* centre manifold and the dynamics on it can be approximated in a neighbourhood of $(x = y = z = 0; \mu = 0)$ by the same procedure as for the *nonextended* vector field. The resulting reduced system has the form

$$\begin{pmatrix} \dot{x} \\ \dot{\mu} \end{pmatrix} = F(x, \mu) = \begin{pmatrix} G(x, \mu) \\ 0 \end{pmatrix}$$

A bifurcation depending on parameters is called a *codimension-k bifurcation* where k is the smallest number for which that bifurcation occurs in a persistent way for a k-parameter family of systems.

Notice that the local stable and unstable manifolds of a fixed point $\bar{x}$ of a vector field $\dot{x} = f(x)$ can be characterised by the stability properties of orbits, as follows:

$$\begin{aligned} W^s(\bar{x}) &= \{x \in N \mid d[\phi(t,x), \bar{x}] \to 0 \text{ as } t \to +\infty \text{ and } \phi(t,x) \in N \ \forall t \geq 0\} \\ W^u(\bar{x}) &= \{x \in N \mid d[\phi(t,x), \bar{x}] \to 0 \text{ as } t \to -\infty \text{ and } \phi(t,x) \in N \ \forall t \leq 0\} \end{aligned}$$

where N denotes a neighbourhood of $\bar{x}$ and, as usual, $\phi(t,x)$ is the flow generated by the vector field, d is a distance function; $t \in \mathbb{R}$. On the contrary, convergence to the fixed point (or divergence from it) of the orbits on the centre manifold W^c cannot be specified without further investigation.

Similar considerations can be developed for discrete-time dynamical systems characterised by *diffeomorphisms* (smooth, invertible maps). In particular, there exists a centre manifold theorem for diffeomorphisms entirely analogous to the centre manifold theorem for differential systems except that the eigenvalues of the Jacobian matrix at equilibrium are split according to whether their moduli are greater, less than or equal to one. We can also define local stable and unstable manifolds of a fixed point $\bar{x} = G(\bar{x})$ of a diffeomorphism G, in terms of their stability properties, as follows:

$$W^s(\bar{x}) = \{x \in N \mid \lim_{n\to\infty} d[G^n(x), \bar{x}] = 0 \text{ and } G^n(x) \in N \ \forall n \geq 0\} \tag{7.3}$$

$$W^u(\bar{x}) = \{x \in N \mid \lim_{n\to-\infty} d[G^n(x), \bar{x}] = 0 \text{ and } G^n(x) \in N \ \forall n \leq 0\} \tag{7.4}$$

where, again, N is a neighbourhood of $\bar{x}$, $n \in \mathbb{Z}$.

The situation is more complicated, of course, if G is noninvertible. The local *stable* manifold of $\bar{x}$ can be defined exactly as in (7.3), but if G is not invertible, the function G^{-1} is not defined and the unstable manifold of $\bar{x}$ cannot be obtained trivially from (7.4) by simply replacing forward with backward iterates of G. We need the following, more complicated definition to replace (7.4)

$$\begin{aligned} W^u(\bar{x}) = \{x \in N \mid &\text{ there exists a sequence } \{x_i\}_0^\infty \text{ s.t. } x_0 = x, \\ &G(x_i) = x_{i-1} \ \forall i \geq 1 \quad \text{and} \quad \lim_{i\to\infty} d(x_i, \ \bar{x}) = 0\}. \end{aligned}$$

That is, if G is not invertible, each point x_0 in the state space has many 'past histories' and in order to define the unstable manifold of a fixed point, we need to choose those of them that, if 'read backward', converge asymptotically to $\bar{x}$.

8 Local bifurcations

In this section we introduce only some basic terminology and concepts regarding simple local bifurcations, without any pretense to a complete treatment of the subject.

Consider families of systems whose members are identical except for the value of one parameter, that is, equations such as

$$\begin{aligned} \dot{x} &= f(x;\mu) \quad \mu \in \mathbb{R} \quad \text{or} \\ x_{n+1} &= G(x_n;\mu) \quad \mu \in \mathbb{R}. \end{aligned}$$

Suppose now that a certain property (e.g., the number of equilibria or their stability) holds for μ in an open interval (a, b), but this property does not hold on any other larger interval. The endpoints a and b are called *bifurcation points.*

Bifurcations can be classified as local, global and local/global. We have a *local* bifurcation when the qualitative changes in the orbit structure can be analysed in a neighbourhood of a fixed or a periodic point of a map, or a fixed point of a flow. (Bifurcations of periodic points of flows can be similarly treated by means of Poincaré maps.) *Global* bifurcations are characterised instead by changes in the orbit structure of the system which are not accompanied by changes in the properties of its fixed or periodic points. *Local/global* bifurcations occur when a local bifurcation has also global repercussions that qualitatively change the orbit structure far from the fixed point. In what follows, we consider only local bifurcations of flows and maps.

Local bifurcations of fixed points are closely related to the (loss of) hyperbolicity of these points. When a system is subject to small perturbations in the parameter space (i.e., a parameter value is slightly changed), near each hyperbolic fixed point of the unperturbed system there will be a hyperbolic point of the perturbed system with the same properties. In particular, the Jacobian matrix of the perturbed system, evaluated at the 'new' fixed point will have the same eigenvalue structure as the Jacobian matrix of the 'old' fixed point. That is to say: for flows, it will have the same number of eigenvalues with positive and negative real parts; for maps, the same number of eigenvalues inside and outside the unit circle in the complex plane. Thus, when we look for local bifurcations of fixed points, we shall try to find those parameter values for which hyperbolicity is lost, i.e., for which the real part of an eigenvalues goes through zero (flows) or its modulus goes through one (maps).

8.1 Local bifurcations for flows

Consider the one-parameter family of functions $f(x; \mu)$ will be treated as a function of two variables, x and μ.

For a generic function $f(x; \mu)$, $x, \mu \in \mathbb{R}$, the necessary condition for the existence of any local bifurcation is that a fixed point $\bar{x}$ be nonhyperbolic at a critical value of $\mu = \mu_c$. For flows this condition is:

$$\frac{\partial f(\bar{x}; \mu_c)}{\partial x} = 0 \qquad (i)$$

Notice that $\partial f(\bar{x}; \mu_c)/\partial x$ can be thought of as the (1×1) Jacobian matrix from the linear approximation of the system $\dot{x} = f(x; \mu)$, calculated at $\bar{x}$, μ_c. Condition (i) means that the single eigenvalue of the Jacobian matrix calculated at equilibrium is zero at the bifurcation point $\mu = \mu_c$.

If besides the nonhyperbolicity condition the following two conditions are satisfied

$$\frac{\partial^2 f(\bar{x}; \mu_c)}{\partial x^2} \neq 0 \qquad (ii)$$

$$\frac{\partial f(\bar{x}; \mu_c)}{\partial \mu} \neq 0 \qquad (iii)$$

the local bifurcation is called a fold or saddle-node bifurcation (or a tangent bifurcation in one-dimensional systems). Fold bifurcations are generic in the sense that if, starting from a value of μ for which those bifurcations occur, we slightly perturb the systems, the family of the perturbed systems will also undergo a fold bifurcation. Typically these systems have two branches of fixed points which, as the parameter μ is varied, coalesce and disappear at μ_c. The name saddle-node derives from the fact that, in the general, multi-dimensional case, the stable branch is composed of nodes, and the unstable branch of saddles. The qualitative change in the dynamical properties of the system can be represented in the bifurcation diagram which plots limit sets against the parameter. On one side of the critical parameter value there are two equilibrium branches (one stable, one unstable), at the critical value there is a unique fixed point, on the other side there are no fixed points.

The fold bifurcation is particularly important in applications because, on the one hand, it helps define the parametric range for which equilibria exist. On the other hand, if it can be shown that a fold bifurcation occurs at the endpoint of an open interval of values of the controlling parameter, then at least one stable equilibrium exists over that interval.

Other non-generic bifurcations, which satisfy the nonhyperbolicity condition, but different sets of conditons (*ii*) and (*iii*) are known as the transcritical and pitchfork bifurcations.

The Hopf bifurcation is the second generic way in which equilibria of systems of differential equations can lose their stability when one control parameter is changed. In this case, local stability is lost when, changing the value of the controlling parameter, the real part of a pair of complex conjugate eigenvalues of the Jacobian matrix calculated at the equilibrium goes through zero and becomes positive. Near the bifurcation value of the parameter, periodic solutions occur. Of course, the simplest family of systems of differential equations characterised by a Hopf bifurcation must have at least two state variables. The name of the bifurcation derives from a celebrated theorem by Hopf, which generalises certain earlier results of Poincaré and Andronov (and is also known as the Poincaré-Andronov-Hopf theorem).

The nonhyperbolicity condition requires that the Jacobian matrix of f with respect to x, evaluated at $(\bar{x}(\mu); \mu)$, has a pair of simple complex conjugate eigenvalues $\lambda(\mu)$ and $\bar{\lambda}(\mu)$ such that, at a critical value μ_c of the parameter, we have

$$\text{Re } \lambda(\mu_c) = 0 \qquad \text{Im } \lambda(\mu_c) \neq 0 \qquad \frac{d}{d\mu} \text{ Re } \lambda(\mu_c) \neq 0,$$

while Re $\rho(\mu_c) < 0$ for any other eigenvalue ρ.

In the bifurcation diagram, on one side of the critical value solutions locally behave as a focus, at μ_c solutions become periodic but with zero amplitude, on the other side of the critical value the periodic solutions have positive amplitude.

Other sufficient conditions must be satisfied to prove the existence of the Hopf bifurcation and the determination of stability of the resulting limit cycle solutions requires calculating second and third order partial derivatives. This can be a problem in applications where typically only certain general properties of the relevant functions are known (e.g., that the relevant function is concave).

8.2 Local bifurcations for maps

To determine bifurcation points in maps we look for situations in which a fixed point of the map ceases to be hyperbolic for a certain critical value of the parameter. This happens typically in three cases, the Jacobian matrix calculated at the fixed point has all eigenvalues with modulus less than one except: (i) one real eigenvalue equals one; (ii) one real eigenvalue equals minus one; (iii) a pair of complex conjugate eigenvalues have modulus equal to one. We can once more use the centre manifold theorem to reduce the dimensionality of the problem. The analysis can be reduced to a one-dimensional map in cases (i) and (ii), to a two-dimensional map in case (iii). Once again the one-parameter family of maps $G(x;\mu)$ will be treated as a function of two variables.

The nonhyperbolicity condition for the existence of a bifurcation is that

$$\frac{\partial G(\bar{x};\mu_c)}{\partial x_n} = 1 \qquad (i)$$

If, in addition, the following conditions are met

$$\frac{\partial^2 G(\bar{x};\mu_c)}{\partial x_n^2} \neq 0 \qquad (ii)$$

$$\frac{\partial G(\bar{x};\mu_c)}{\partial \mu} \neq 0 \qquad (iii)$$

a fold bifurcation occurs at the critical vaule μ_c. As for the case of differential systems, the fold bifurcation occurs at the value of the parameter for which two branches of fixed points intersect (typically at the last value for which fixed points are real). Other sets of sufficient conditions are used to prove the existence of the nongeneric transcritical and pitchfork bifurcations.

For maps the stability of an equilibrium point of a map can also be lost when a real eigenvalue goes through *minus* one. This leads to a new phenomenon, known as a flip bifurcation. To understand this bifurcation better, consider the equation $\xi_{n+1} = -\xi_n$. Solution of equations of this type were mentioned in section 4, where we discussed improper oscillations. Starting from an initial value ξ_0, the temporal sequence of points would be $\{\xi_0, -\xi_0, \xi_0, -\xi_0, ...\}$, that is, the alternation of two values of the variable, or a cycle of period two. If the map ξ is the linear representation of a nonlinear map, because the eigenvalue is equal to one in modulus, we cannot invoke the Hartman-Grobman theorem and take solutions as a 'correct' representation of local behaviour of the nonlinear map. However, if a the occurrence of a flip bifurcation can be guaranteed, at the critical value of the parameter the dynamics characterising the map alter from a fixed point to a a period-2 cycle (or vice versa).

For a general one-dimensional family of maps $G(x_n;\mu)$, the necessary condition for a flip bifurcation to occur at $\bar{x}(\mu_c)$ is

$$\partial G(\bar{x};\mu_c)\partial x_n = -1 \qquad (i')$$

Sufficient conditions can be defined either on the map itself or on its second iterate

G^2:

$$\frac{\partial^2 G^2(\bar{x};\mu_c)}{\partial x_n^2} = 0 \quad \text{and} \quad \frac{\partial^3 G^2(\bar{x};\mu_c)}{\partial x_n^3} \neq 0 \qquad (ii'')$$

$$\frac{\partial G^2(\bar{x};\mu_c)}{\partial \mu} = 0 \quad \text{and} \quad \frac{\partial^2 G^2(\bar{x};\mu_c)}{\partial \mu \partial x_n} \neq 0 \qquad (iii'')$$

Finally, the case in which a pair of complex eigenvalues of the Jacobian matrix at a fixed point of a map has modulus one is analogous, but not quite the same as the corresponding case for flows. The nonhyperbolicity condition is that the Jacobian matrix has two complex, conjugate eigenvalues $\kappa(\mu_c)$ and $\bar{\kappa}(\mu_c)$ with $|\kappa(\mu_c)| = 1$.

The periodic solutions arising from the Neimark-Sacker bifurcation are different from the limit cycle solutions of the Hopf bifurcation for there are many orbits, sequences of points, on the resulting invariant set. Moreover the dynamics of the solution orbits can be either periodic or quasiperiodic.

For two-dimensional maps the search for nonhyperbolic fixed points and the determination of the way in which the stability frontier is crossed is simplified by the use of stability conditions on the coefficients of the characteristic equation. Recall from Section 6 that a fixed point $\bar{x}$ is (locally) asymptotically stable if the eigenvalues κ_1 and κ_2 of the Jacobian matrix, calculated at the fixed point, are less than one in modulus. The set of necessary and sufficient conditions guaranteeing that $|\kappa_1| < 1$ and $|\kappa_2| < 1$ are:

$$\begin{aligned} 1 + \text{ tr } DG(\bar{x}) + \text{ det } DG(\bar{x}) &> 0 \qquad (i) \\ 1 - \text{ tr } DG(\bar{x}) + \text{ det } DG(\bar{x}) &> 0 \qquad (ii) \\ 1 - \text{ det } DG(\bar{x}) &> 0. \qquad (iii) \end{aligned}$$

Each of the three generic bifurcations results from the loss of stability through the violation of one of these three conditions:

(a) There is a potential flip bifurcation if a single eigenvalue becomes equal to -1, that is, the first condition holds as an equality while (ii) and (iii) are simultaneously satisfied.

(b) There is a potential fold bifurcation if a single eigenvalue becomes equal to $+1$, that is, the second condition holds as an equality while conditions (i) and (iii) are simultaneously satisfied. For particular cases, the violation of (ii) might lead to a transcritical or pitchfork bifurcation.

(c) There is a potential Neimark-Sacker bifurcation if the modulus of a pair of complex, conjugate eigenvalues is equal to one, that is, the determinant is equal to one while conditions (i) and (ii) are simultaneously satisfied.

These are, of course, necessary conditions for the existence of the associated bifurcation. However, combined with numerical simulations suggesting that such bifurcations do occur, they constitute strong evidence. In applications where analytical proofs can be difficult to provide, this procedure is, at times, the only available.

Complex and Chaotic Dynamics in Economics

Duncan Foley

Graduate Faculty, New School University, New York

Abstract Like a limit cycle, a chaotic attractor is a locally unstable but globally stable form of dynamic behavior. Examples of chaotic attractors including the Lorenz attractor, the Rössler attractor, and the logistic system are studied. The deterministic unpredictability of chaotic systems is contrasted with their statistical predictability. Chaotic systems are a tempting model for economics, particularly financial economics.

Complex systems include the cell, the brain and nervous system, the capitalist social division of labor, and the universe. Complex systems theory attempts to understand the general properties of such systems. Systems with stable point attractors or limit cycles cannot sustain long-term evolving structures, which collapse into their limits; chaotic systems also cannot sustain evolving structures because they are dispersed in the divergence of nearby points on chaotic attractors. Type I and II cellular automata provide examples of stable dynamics, and Type III of chaotic dynamics. Type IV cellular automata, which lie on the boundary of stability, exhibit long-term evolving and interacting structures and serve as a paradigm of complex systems. Topology and global interaction have special roles in agent-based models of complex economic interactions. Simulation of agent-based models constitutes a research frontier that can complement and supplement analytical approaches to understanding economic interactions.

Programs implementing a model of spatially decentralized exchange are presented as an example and basis for exercises exploring the issues involved in agent-based models of economic interaction.

1 Chaos is a form of global stability

In studying bifurcations of nonlinear dynamical systems, you have encountered the important concept of systems that have locally unstable equilibria, but are globally stable. Limit cycles, such as those that arise from a supercritical Hopf bifurcation, are a good example. When the bifurcation parameter is in the unstable region, the system converges toward a limit cycle around an equilibrium point which is itself unstable. If we perturb the system from the limit cycle, it tends to return to it, so the limit cycle is an *attractor* for the system.

The combination of global stability and local instability is particularly intriguing as a representation of economic systems. There are many reasons to suspect that economic interactions give rise to locally unstable feedbacks. One example is the tendency of higher-than-average growth to induce higher-than-average expenditure (due to accelerator effects on investment), which tends to de-stabilize the macroeconomy. Another example is the effect of trend-following expectations among speculators, which tend to amplify deviations of prices in asset markets. On the other hand, we rarely see historical examples of global economic instability. There are few, if any, cases of economies that actually melt down or explode due to accelerator feedbacks, or of markets that implode due to speculative feedbacks. The possibility of regarding economic systems as locally unstable but globally stable is an appealing way to reconcile these facts. In other words, extreme unstable motions of prices or output in economic systems bring into play non-linear compensating forces (even those as drastic as institutional changes).

Chaotic motions generalize the properties of local instability and global stability beyond the realm of limit cycles. Chaotic systems undergo complicated oscillations, but remain in a neighborhood of an unstable equilibrium (or perhaps shift back and forth between neighborhoods of several unstable equilibria). As in the case of limit cycles, there is an attracting set for the chaotic orbits. The structure of this set, however, can in principle be very complicated. The attractors of chaotic systems have a self-similar, fractal structure in fine detail. From a mathematical point of view the crucial difference between a limit cycle (which itself may have a very complicated structure if it has arisen from multiple Hopf bifurcations) and a chaotic attractor is that chaotic orbits never return exactly to the same state (though they return indefinitely often to states arbitrarily close to any given attracting state). Thus mathematically chaotic orbits are aperiodic.

From an economic point of view, however, this distinction may not be of much real significance, because we only ever observe a finite sample of economic data. It may not, in fact, make much difference economically whether the system is truly chaotic in the mathematical sense, or is attracted to a very complicated periodic motion.

2 Some Examples of Chaotic Systems and their Attractors

2.1 The Lorenz Attractor

One of the first episodes to draw the attention of contemporary scientists and mathematicians to the phenomenon of chaos (which was known to Poincaré) was the attempt of the M.I.T. meteorologist Lorenz to use an early and not-very-powerful computer to simulate the basic dynamics of the Navier-Stokes equations describing flows in fluids (such as the atmosphere) (Gleick, 1988, 27–31). Lorenz reduced the complicated Navier-Stokes partial differential equations, which would have been hopeless to solve on his computer, to a simplified system of ordinary differential equations[1]:

```
In[1]:= LorenzSystem = {x' == -σx + σy, y' == -xz + rx - y, z' == xy - bz}

Out[1]= {x' == -xσ + yσ, y' == rx - y - xz, z' == xy - bz}
```

This system has three equilibria:

[1] These lectures were created as Mathematica 5.0 notebooks. I have retained the Mathematica expressions so that the examples can serve as a tutorial both on chaotic and complex dynamics and in Mathematica programming.

```
In[2]:= LorenzEquilibria = Solve[LorenzSystem/.{x' → 0, y' → 0, z' → 0},
           {x, y, z}]
```

$$\text{Out[2]}= \{\{y\to 0, z\to 0, x\to 0\}, \{y\to -\sqrt{-b+b\,r}, z\to -1+r, x\to -\sqrt{-b+b\,r}\}, \{y\to \sqrt{-b+b\,r}, z\to -1+r, x\to \sqrt{-b+b\,r}\}\}$$

Lorenz chose the parameters $\sigma = 10, r = 28, b = 8/3$ to represent the regime representing the earth's atmosphere.

```
In[3]:= LorenzParameters = {σ → 10, r → 28, b → 8/3}
```

$$\text{Out[3]}= \{\sigma\to 10, r\to 28, b\to \frac{8}{3}\}$$

```
In[4]:= LorenzEquilibria/.LorenzParameters//N
```

```
Out[4]= {{y → 0., z → 0., x → 0.}, {y → -8.48528, z → 27., x → -8.48528},
          {y → 8.48528, z → 27., x → 8.48528}}
```

He set his computer up to simulate this system recursively, went to lunch, and was surprised to find that the system had not converged to an equilibrium. In fact, the program continued to produce orbits that never seemed to converge to an equilibrium point nor to a limit cycle. We can see what is going on if we let *Mathematica* solve the Lorenz system:

```
In[5]:= LorenzAttractor[σ_, r_, b_, T_] :=
          {x[t], y[t], z[t]}/.
           Flatten[NDSolve[{x'[t] == -σ x[t] + σ y[t], x[0] == -10,
                 y'[t] == -x[t] z[t] + r x[t] - y[t], y[0] == -10,
                 z'[t] == x[t] y[t] - b z[t], z[0] == 25}, {x[t], y[t], z[t]},
               {t, 0, T }, Method → ExplicitRungeKutta, AccuracyGoal- > 32]];
```

```
In[6]:= ParametricPlot3D[Evaluate[LorenzAttractor[10, 28, 8/3, 50]],
          {t, 0, 50}, PlotPoints → 1000, PlotRange → All,
          AxesLabel → {"x", "y", "z"}];
```

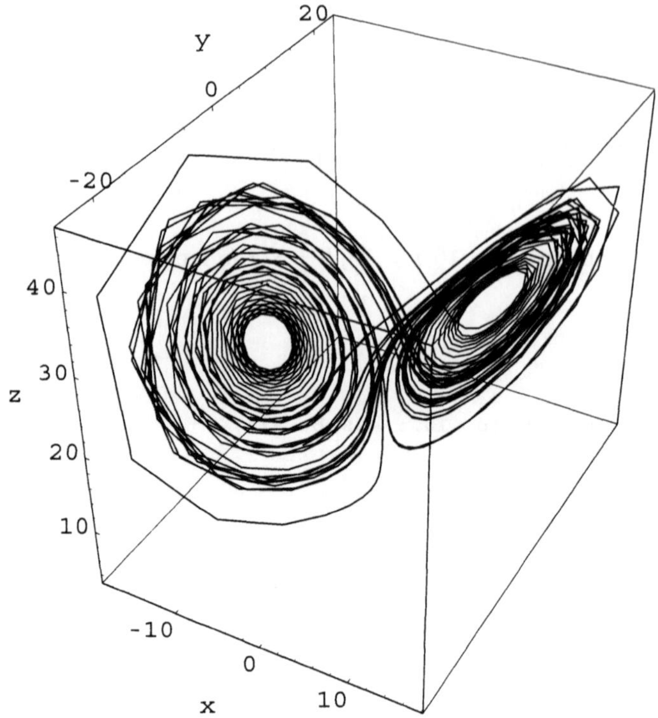

Notice that the stable eigenvalues at each equilibria tend to compress the motion of the system into a two-dimensional manifold near the equilibrium. (The attractor is sometimes called the "Lorenz Butterfly".)

A systematic examination of the Lorenz system's dynamics gives a good deal of insight into what is going on here.

The stability of the system can be analyzed by calculating the Jacobian at its equilibria:

```
In[7]:= LorenzJacobian = D[LorenzSystem[[All, 2]], #]&/@{x, y, z}
Out[7]= {{-σ, r - z, y}, {σ, -1, x}, {0, -x, -b}}
```

The Jacobians at the three equilibria are:

```
In[8]:= LorenzJacobian/.LorenzEquilibria/.LorenzParameters//
          N
Out[8]= {{{-10., 28., 0.}, {10., -1., 0.}, {0., 0., -2.66667}},
         {{-10., 1., -8.48528}, {10., -1., -8.48528}, {0., 8.48528, -2.66667}},
         {{-10., 1., 8.48528}, {10., -1., 8.48528}, {0., -8.48528, -2.66667}}}
```

The stability of these equilibria depends on the eigenvalues:

```
In[9]:= Eigenvalues[#]&/@
          (LorenzJacobian/.LorenzEquilibria/.LorenzParameters//N)
Out[9]= {{-22.8277, 11.8277, -2.66667},
          {-13.8546, 0.0939556 + 10.1945 i, 0.0939556 - 10.1945 i},
          {-13.8546, 0.0939556 + 10.1945 i, 0.0939556 - 10.1945 i}}
```

We can see that the second two equilibria have a pair of unstable complex roots. What happens is that when the system starts in the neighborhood of one of these equilibria, it begins a spiralling orbit away from the equilibrium, which after a longer or shorter period of time leads to the neighborhood of the second equilibrium, where a spiralling outward motion again takes place, which eventually shifts the orbit back toward the first equilibrium. The non-linear interactions, simple as they are in this system, are sufficient to prevent the orbits from escaping from this pattern. These orbits never return to exactly the same point in the space, so they are aperiodic. The motions of the individual components shift unpredictably between the two equilibria:

```
In[10]:= Table[Plot[Evaluate[LorenzAttractor[10, 28, 8/3, 50][[i]]],
            {t, 0, 50}, PlotRange → All, AxesLabel → {"t", {x, y, z}[[i]]}],
          {i, 3}];
```

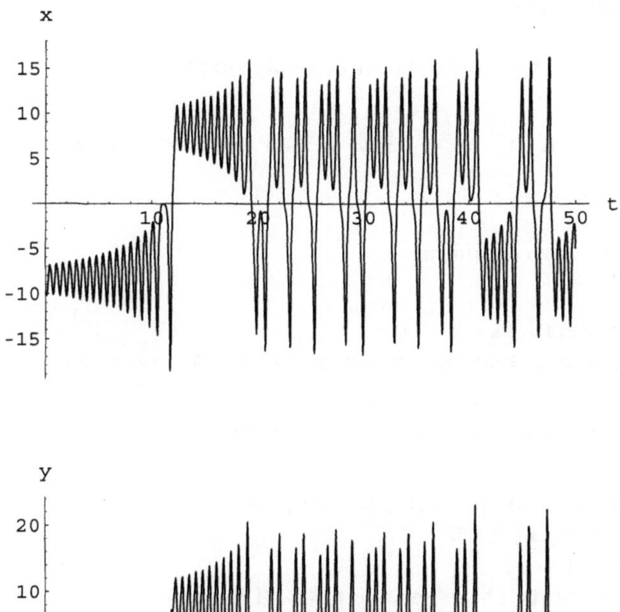

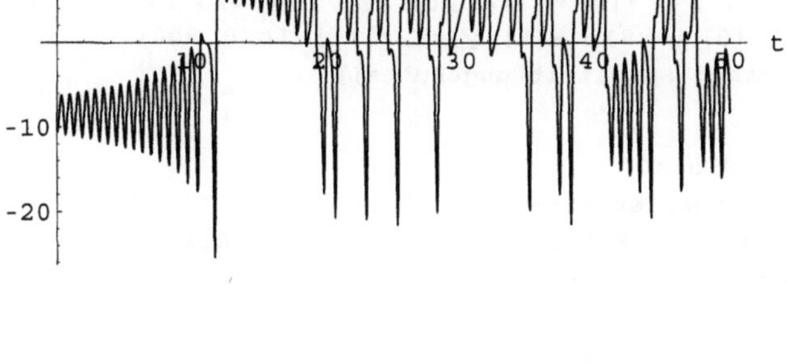

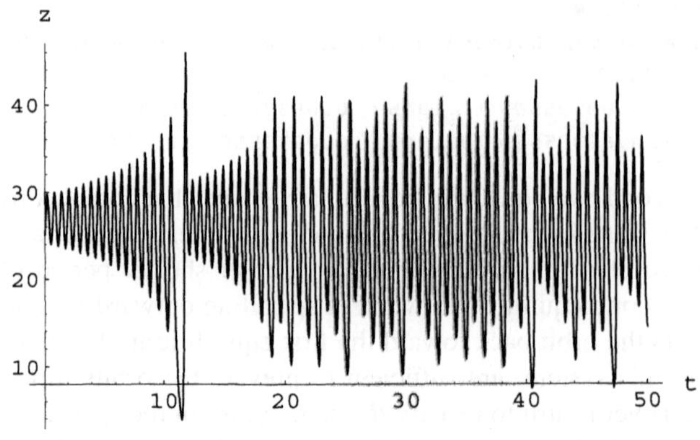

It is perhaps enlightening to ponder the characteristics of these time-series in the context of widely-used econometric models.

2.2 The Røssler Attractor

Røssler proposed a somewhat similar, but structurally simpler system:

```
In[11]:= RosslerSystem = {x′ == -y - z, y′ == x + 0.425 y, z′ == 2 - z (4 - x)}

Out[11]= {x′ == -y - z, y′ == x + 0.425 y, z′ == 2 - (4 - x) z}
```

The Røssler system has two equilibria:

```
In[12]:= RosslerEquilibria =
           Solve[RosslerSystem/.{x′ → 0, y′ → 0, z′ → 0}, {x, y, z}]

Out[12]= {{y → -8.88194, x → 3.77482, z → 8.88194},
           {y → -0.529826, x → 0.225176, z → 0.529826}}

In[13]:= RosslerAttractor[{x0_, y0_, z0_}, T_] :=
           {x[t], y[t], z[t]}/.
             Flatten[
               NDSolve[{x′[t] == -y[t] - z[t], x[0] == x0,
                   y′[t] == x[t] + 0.425 y[t], y[0] == y0, z′[t] == 2 - z[t] (4 - x[t]),
                   z[0] == z0}, {x[t], y[t], z[t]}, {t, 0, 900},
                 Method → ExplicitRungeKutta]];

In[14]:= ParametricPlot3D[
           Evaluate[RosslerAttractor[{-0.04, -0.3, 0.52}, 900]],
           {t, 0, 900}, PlotPoints → 5000, PlotRange → All,
           AxesLabel → {x, y, z}];
```

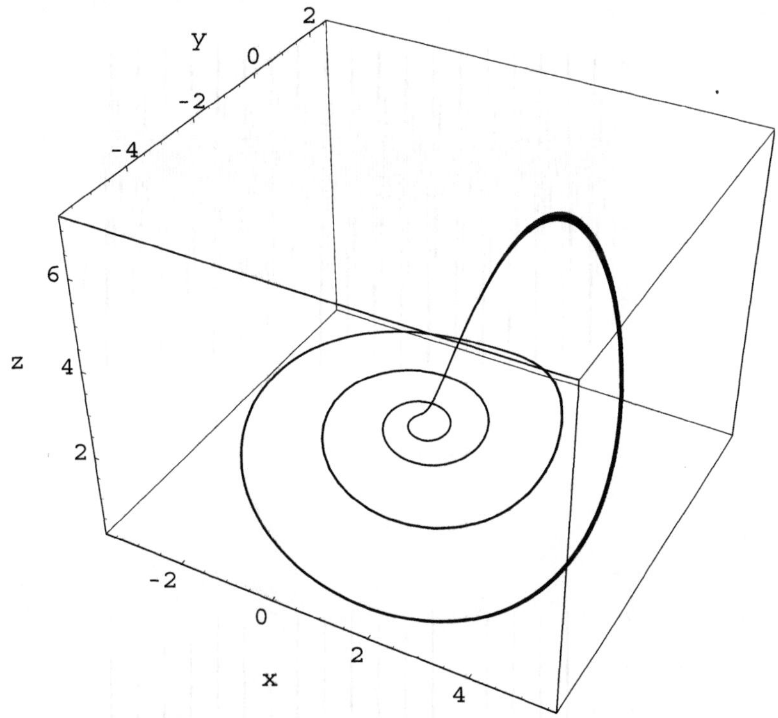


```
In[15]:= Table[
    Plot[Evaluate[RosslerAttractor[{-0.04, -0.3, 0.52}, 900][[i]]],
      {t, 0, 500}, PlotRange → All, AxesLabel → {"t", {x, y, z}[[i]]}],
   {i, 3}];
```

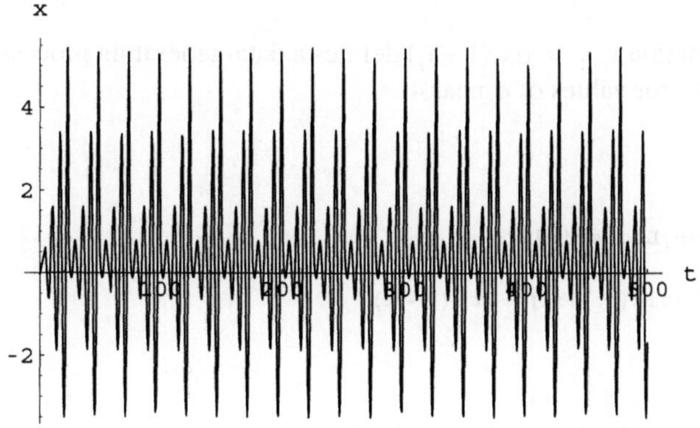

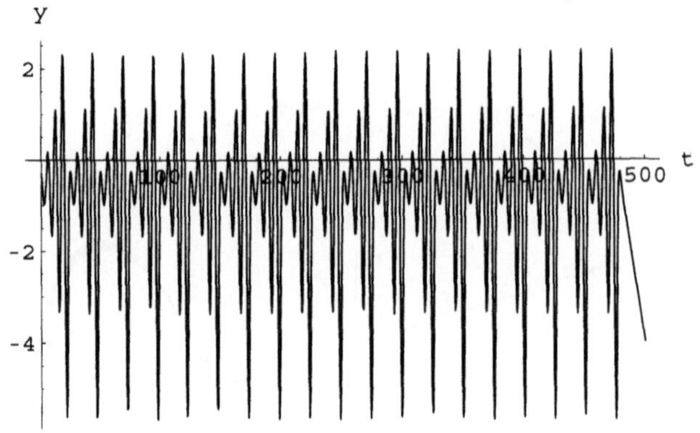

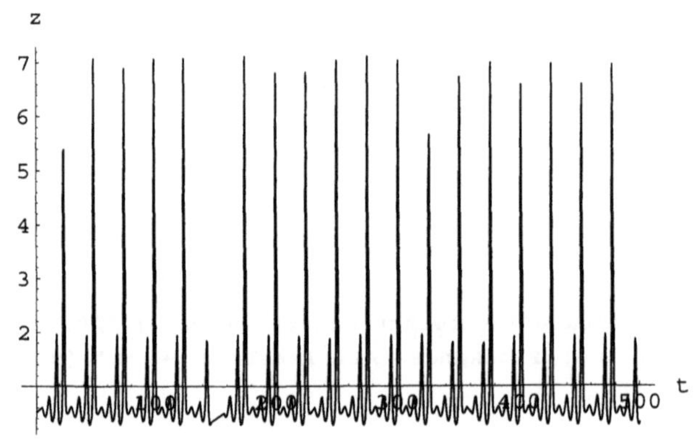

2.3 The logistic function

The logistic function $x_{t+1} = \alpha x_t(1-x_t)$ defines a data-generating process on the unit interval that becomes chaotic for values of α near 4.

```
In[16] := Clear[Logistic];

           Logistic[α_][x_] = α x (1 - x);
```

```
In[17] := Plot[Logistic[3.95][x], {x, 0, 1}];
```

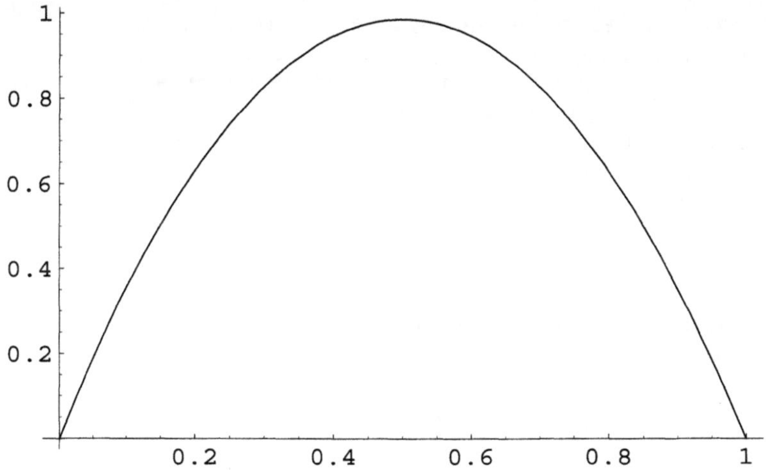

The recursive application of the logistic map for $0 < \alpha < 4$ to an initial value within the unit interval yields an orbit that remains within the unit interval.

```
In[18]:= Clear[Logisticpath];

         Logisticpath[α_, x0_, n_] := NestList[Logistic[α], x0, n]
```

We can visualize the logistic dynamics:

```
In[19]:= ListPlot[logisticchaos = Logisticpath[3.99, 0.398, 2000]];
```

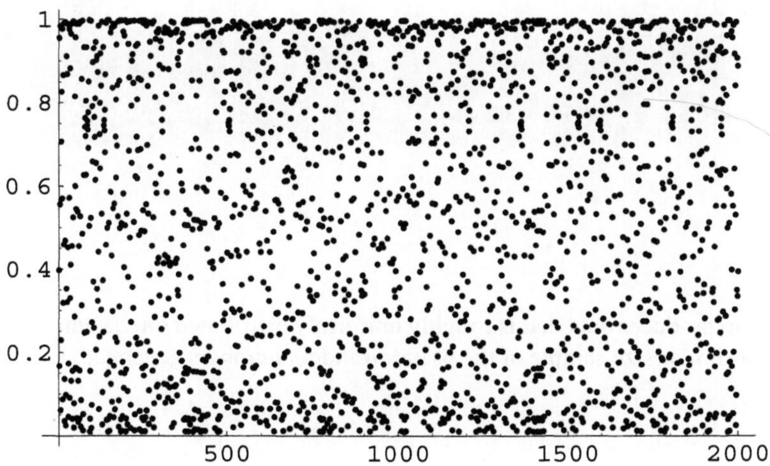


```
In[20]:= << Statistics`DataManipulation`

In[21]:= logistichistogram = BinCounts[logisticchaos, {0, 1, 0.01}]
```

```
Out[21]= {7, 67, 33, 39, 51, 31, 26, 29, 29, 17, 21, 18, 19, 17, 18, 28,
          28, 22, 11, 17, 20, 14, 19, 16, 12, 12, 14, 12, 13, 21, 20, 9, 18,
          15, 10, 13, 11, 9, 16, 10, 7, 17, 8, 16, 17, 15, 12, 11, 9, 16,
          14, 22, 17, 17, 21, 18, 14, 15, 17, 11, 11, 15, 13, 11, 14, 18, 5,
          13, 19, 15, 12, 17, 9, 15, 14, 16, 10, 14, 15, 15, 15, 16, 20, 20,
          23, 20, 21, 21, 16, 16, 22, 26, 21, 22, 32, 25, 38, 50, 65, 135}
```

```
In[22]:= BarChart[logistichistogram[[Range[5, 95]]],
           Ticks → {Table[i, {i, 5, 95, 10}], Automatic}];
```

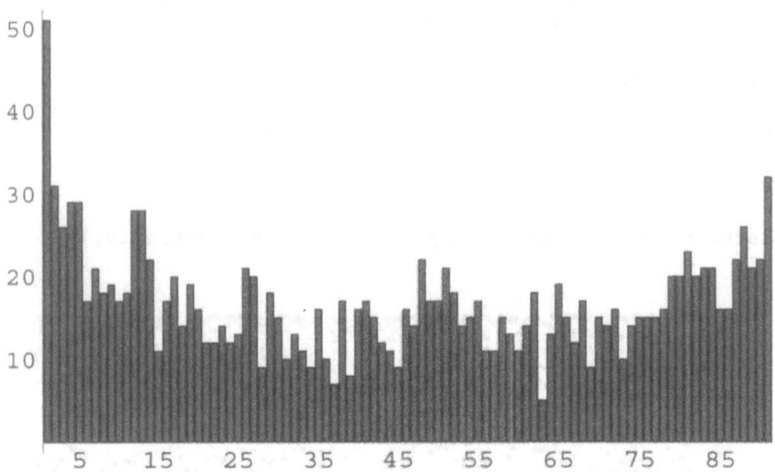

The logistic map produces data that is roughly uniformly distributed on the unit interval. We can compare it to a similar size sample of the pseudo-random numbers generated by *Mathematica*:

```
In[23]:= BarChart[
           BinCounts[randdata = Table[Random[], {2000}], {0, 1, 0.01}][[
             Range[5, 95]]], Ticks → {Table[i, {i, 0, 100, 10}], Automatic}];
```

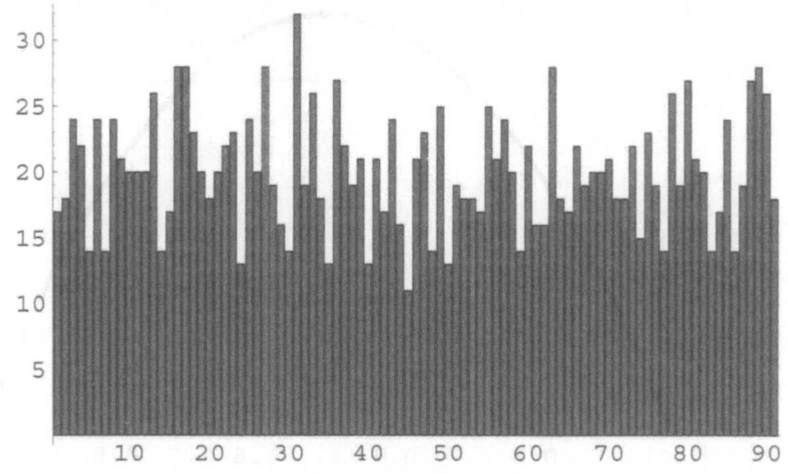

The plot of the random data looks rather like the output of the logistic map:

```
In[24]:= ListPlot[randdata];
```

But if we re-organize the logistic data into successive pairs, we see the original map:

```
In[25]:= ListPlot[Partition[logisticchaos, 2, 1]];
```

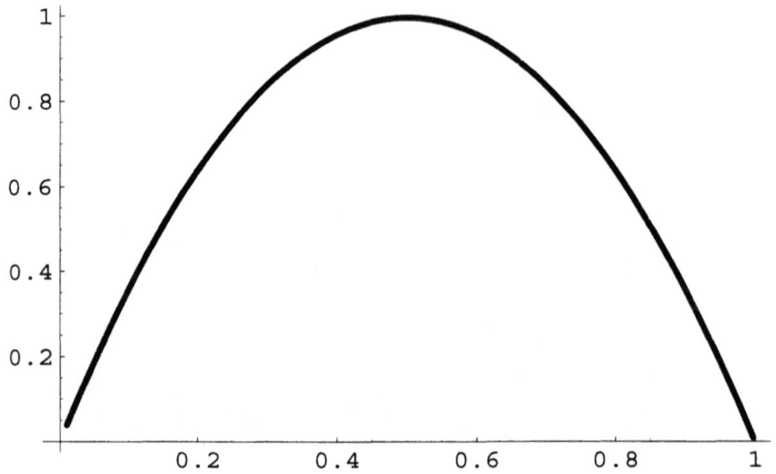

On the other hand, re-organizing the random data in this particular way reveals no particular pattern:

```
In[26]:= ListPlot[Partition[randdata, 2, 1]];
```

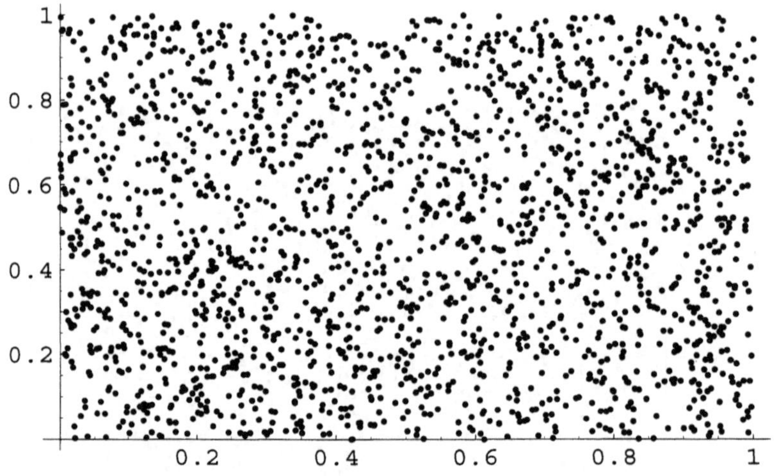

3 Predictability of Chaotic Systems

3.1 The Unpredictability of Chaotic Orbits

In stable dynamical systems, two orbits that have initial conditions close together will tend to become even closer as time unfolds. For example, consider the oscillatory system:

```
In[27]:= Clear[VanDerPolOscillator];
         VanDerPolOscillator =
           {x'[t] == μ x[t] + ω y[t] - a (x[t]^2 + y[t]^2) (x[t] - y[t]),
            y'[t] == - ω x[t] + μ y[t] - a (x[t]^2 + y[t]^2) (x[t] + y[t])}

Out[27]= {x'[t] == μ x[t] + ω y[t] - a (x[t] - y[t]) (x[t]^2 + y[t]^2),
          y'[t] == -ω x[t] + μ y[t] - a (x[t] + y[t]) (x[t]^2 + y[t]^2)}
```

The eigenvalues of the linearized system at the equilibrium $\{x == 0, y == 0\}$ are:

```
In[28]:= Flatten[
           (D[{x'[t], y'[t]}/.Solve[VanDerPolOscillator,
                        {x'[t], y'[t]}]//Simplify, #]&/@{x[t], y[t]})/.
            {x[t] → 0, y[t]- > 0}, 1]

Out[28]= {{μ, -ω}, {ω, μ}}
```

```
In[29]:= Eigenvalues[
           Flatten[
             (D[{x'[t], y'[t]}/.Solve[VanDerPolOscillator,
                          {x'[t], y'[t]}]//Simplify, #]&/@{x[t], y[t]})/.
              {x[t] → 0, y[t]- > 0}, 1]]

Out[29]= {μ - i ω, μ + i ω}
```

If $a > 0$, this system undergoes a supercritical Hopf birfurcation at $\mu = 0$.

```
In[30]:= Options[VanDerPol] = {μ → 0, ω → 1, a → 0};
         VanDerPolOrbit[{x0_, y0_}, T_, opts___] :=
           {x[t], y[t]}/.
             Flatten[
               NDSolve[
                 Flatten[{VanDerPolOscillator/.{opts}/.
                       Options[VanDerPol], {x[0] == x0, y[0] == y0}}],
                 {x[t], y[t]}, {t, 0, T}, Method → ExplicitRungeKutta]]
```

```
In[31]:= ParametricPlot[
           Evaluate[VanDerPolOrbit[{0.5, 0.5}, 100, μ → -0.05, a → 0.05]],
           {t, 0, 100}, AspectRatio → 1, PlotRange → All];
```

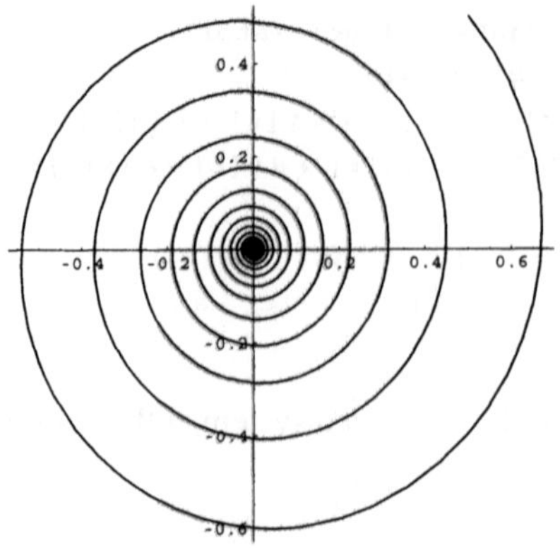

To look at what happens to nearby orbits, we can plot the difference between them:

```
In[32]:= ParametricPlot[
            Evaluate[VanDerPolOrbit[{0.1, 0.1}, 100, μ → -0.05, a → 0.05] -
              VanDerPolOrbit[{0.11, 0.09}, 100, μ → -0.05, a → 0.05]],
           {t, 0, 100}, PlotRange → All, AspectRatio → 1];
```

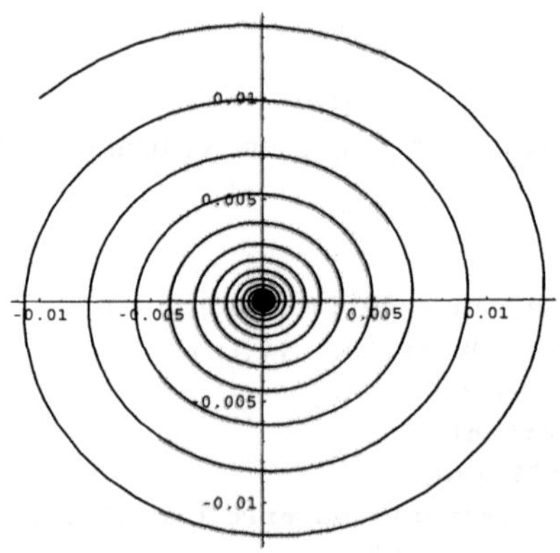

```
In[33]:= Plot[Evaluate[(Flatten[#][[1]]^2 + Flatten[#][[2]]^2)^(1/2)&[
              VanDerPolOrbit[{0.1, 0.1}, 100, μ → -0.05, a → 0.05] -
                VanDerPolOrbit[{0.11, 0.09}, 100, μ → -0.05, a → 0.05]]],
           {t, 0, 100}, PlotRange → All, AspectRatio → 1];
```

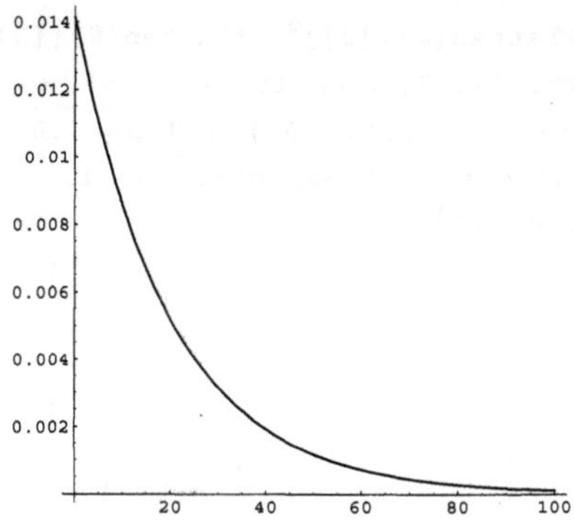

For a stable system, the distance between the orbits vanishes as time goes on. This fact has an extremely important practical implication, which is that errors in measurement of the initial conditions of a stable dynamical system make a smaller and smaller difference to the actual position of the system as time goes on. This means from a practical point of view that it is possible to predict the state of a stable dynamical system at any point in the future with arbitrarily high accuracy.

When we deal with a limit cycle in a locally unstable system, however, things are quite different:

```
In[34]:= ParametricPlot[
         Evaluate[VanDerPolOrbit[{0.1, 0.1}, 100, μ → 0.05, a → 0.05] -
            VanDerPolOrbit[{0.11, 0.09}, 100, μ- > 0.05, a → 0.05]],
         {t, 0, 100}, PlotRange → All, AspectRatio → 1,
         AxesLabel → {xdiff, ydiff}];
```

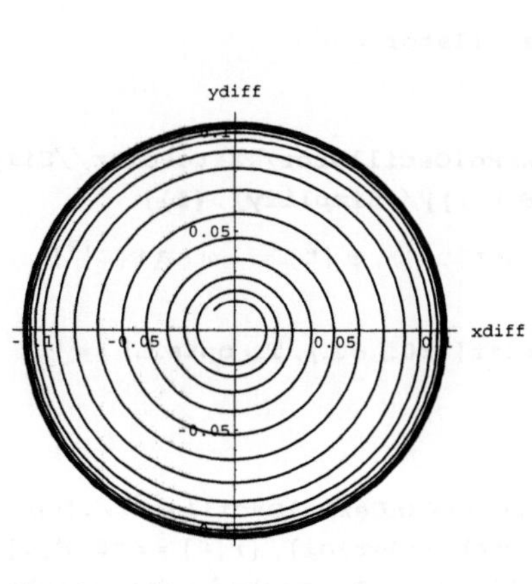

```
In[35]:= Plot[Evaluate[(Flatten[#][[1]]^2 + Flatten[#][[2]]^2)^(1/2)&[
             VanDerPolOrbit[{0.1, 0.1}, 100, μ → 0.05, a → 0.05] -
               VanDerPolOrbit[{0.11, 0.09}, 100, μ → 0.05, a → 0.05]]],
          {t, 0, 100}, PlotRange → All, AspectRatio → 1,
          AxesLabel → {t, rdiff}];
```

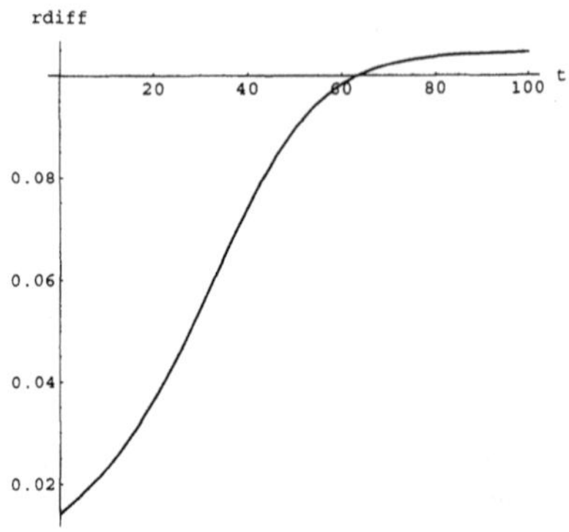

In the locally unstable case the trajectories initially diverge. (The divergence is limited in the limit cycle to their memory of the initial phase difference.)

```
In[36]:= XYtoPolar = {x[t] → r[t] Cos[θ[t]], y[t] → r[t] Sin[θ[t]],
            x'[t] → D[r[t] Cos[θ[t]], t], y'[t] → D[r[t] Sin[θ[t]], t]}

Out[36]= {x[t] → Cos[θ[t]] r[t], y[t] → r[t] Sin[θ[t]],
          x'[t] → Cos[θ[t]] r'[t] - r[t] Sin[θ[t]] θ'[t],
          y'[t] → Sin[θ[t]] r'[t] + Cos[θ[t]] r[t] θ'[t]}

In[37]:= PolarVanDerPolOscillator =
          Apply[Equal,
            Flatten[
              Solve[VanDerPolOscillator/.XYtoPolar//Simplify,
                {r'[t], θ'[t]}]//Simplify], {1}]

Out[37]= {r'[t] == r[t] (μ - a r[t]^2), θ'[t] == -ω - a r[t]^2}

In[38]:= PolarVanDerPolOrbit[{r0_, θ0_}, T_, opts___] :=
          {r[t], θ[t]}/.
            Flatten[
              NDSolve[
                Flatten[{PolarVanDerPolOscillator/.{opts}/.
                     Options[VanDerPol], {r[0] == r0, θ[0] == θ0}}],
                {r[t], θ[t]}, {t, 0, T}, Method → ExplicitRungeKutta]]
```

```
In[39]:= Plot[
           Evaluate[
             PolarVanDerPolOrbit[{Sqrt[0.1² + 0.1²], ArcTan[0.1/0.1]},
                 100, μ → -0.05, a → 0.05][[1]] -
               PolarVanDerPolOrbit[{Sqrt[0.11² + 0.09²], ArcTan[0.09/0.11]},
                 100, μ → -0.05, a → 0.05][[1]]], {t, 0, 100}, PlotRange → All,
           AspectRatio → 1, AxesLabel → {t, "rdiff"}];
```

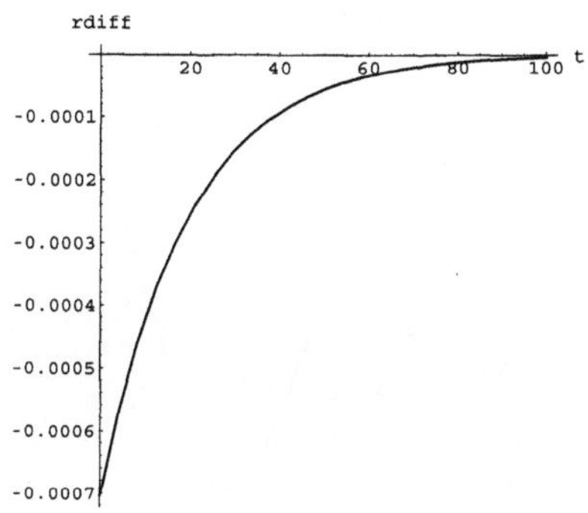


```
In[40]:= Plot[
           Evaluate[
             VanDerPolOrbit[{Sqrt[0.1² + 0.1²], ArcTan[0.1/0.1]}, 100,
                 μ → -0.05, a → 0.05][[2]] -
               VanDerPolOrbit[{Sqrt[0.11² + 0.09²], ArcTan[0.09/0.11]},
                 100, μ → -0.05, a → 0.05][[1]]], {t, 0, 100}, PlotRange → All,
           AspectRatio → 1, AxesLabel → {t, "θdiff"}];
```

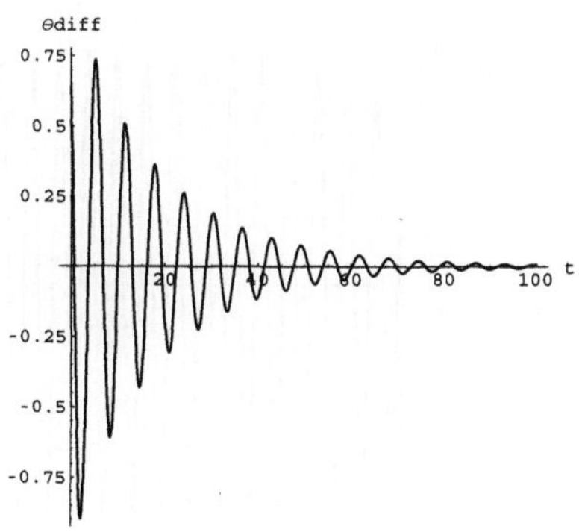

```
In[41]:= Plot[
    Evaluate[
      PolarVanDerPolOrbit[{Sqrt[0.1^2 + 0.1^2], ArcTan[0.1/0.1]},
          100, μ → 0.05, a → 0.05][[1]]-
        PolarVanDerPolOrbit[{Sqrt[0.11^2 + 0.09^2], ArcTan[0.09/0.11]},
          100, μ → 0.05, a → 0.05][[1]]], {t, 0, 100}, PlotRange → All,
    AspectRatio → 1, AxesLabel → {t, "rdiff"}];
```

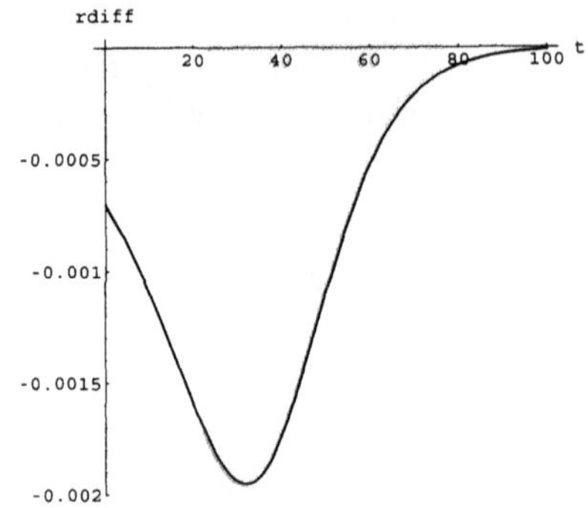


```
In[42]:= Plot[
    Evaluate[
      VanDerPolOrbit[{Sqrt[0.1^2 + 0.1^2], ArcTan[0.1/0.1]}, 100,
          μ → 0.05, a → 0.05][[2]]-
        VanDerPolOrbit[{Sqrt[0.11^2 + 0.09^2], ArcTan[0.09/0.11]},
          100, μ → 0.05, a → 0.05][[1]]], {t, 0, 100}, PlotRange → All,
    AspectRatio → 1, AxesLabel → {t, "θdiff"}];
```

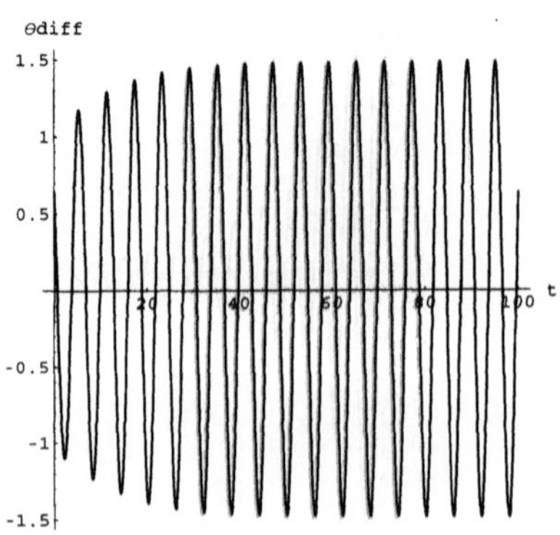

Like the limit-cycle oscillator, the orbits of chaotic dynamical systems starting from nearby initial conditions diverge. (In this case the divergence is in the phase of the system, since the limit cycle is a circle.)

Like the orbits of limit cycle systems, the orbits of chaotic dynamical systems diverge. For example, in the Røssler system:

```
In[43]:= ParametricPlot3D[
          Evaluate[RosslerAttractor[{-0.04,-0.3,0.52},900]-
             RosslerAttractor[{-0.05,-0.299,0.521},900]],{t,0,500},
          PlotRange → All, AspectRatio → 1,
          AxesLabel → {xdiff, ydiff, zdiff}, PlotPoints → 5000];
```

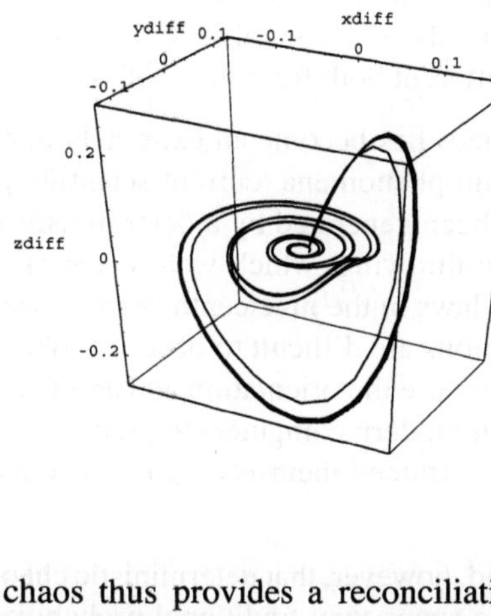

The model of deterministic chaos thus provides a reconciliation of the paradox inherent in Laplace's remark that if we knew the momentum and position of all the particles in the universe at any instant, we could use Newton's Laws to predict the entire future and retrodict the entire past. There is good reason to suppose that real economies, to the degree that they exhibit deterministic regularities, are nonlinear dynamical systems with a large number of degrees of freedom, and thus are very likely to exhibit chaotic behavior. The limits to predictability we have just explored are therefore likely to apply to economic dynamics as well. As in the case of meteorology, even if we have confidence in our ability to identify key parameters governing economic dynamics, any specific predictions we make based on these findings will deteriorate in accuracy over time.

There are, however, some aspects of economic systems that seem much more predictable than the exact orbit of the system. For example, it seems to me a much better bet to predict that capitalist economies, if they still exist one hundred years from now will have organized commodity markets, organized equity and financial markets, will exhibit characteristic instability in their growth paths, and so forth, than to try to predict the exact level of world GDP, or the interest rate or profit rate, or even what the relative size of various sectors of the economy will be. We will return to this point in our discussion of complexity.

3.2 The Statistical Predictability of Chaotic Systems

Although it is practically impossible to predict the exact evolution of chaotic systems due to sensitive dependence of the orbits on initial conditions, it is possible to make strong statistical statements about the data generated by chaotic dynamical systems. Chaotic dynamical systems move rapidly (with a relatively brief transient) to the neighborhood of their attractors. Once in the neighborhood of the attractor, the system will remain close to the attractor forever. While we cannot predict exactly where on the attractor the system will be at any future time, the density of the attractor set in the state space in a neighborhood is a reliable statistical predictor of the amount of time the system will spend in that neighborhood. If we believe we know the exact dynamical system underlying the motion of the chaotic system it is even possible to calculate this density. In this sense the statistical properties of chaotic systems are completely predictable. Stable dynamical systems, or those that have periodic attractors like limit cycles, have degenerate statistical properties. Over a long time horizon the system is certain to be close to its equilibrium or its limit cycle. (In the case of the limit cycle there is still some residual uncertainty as to the phase of the system, which "remembers" its initial state.) As we will see, the statistical properties of complex systems are quite different both from those of stable systems and chaotic systems.

In recent years deterministic chaos has become an extremely popular explanation of stochastic phenomena. Except for quantum phenomena, current scientific philosophy views most apparently stochastic data as having been generated by a deterministic chaotic system. For example, the case of coin-tossing or dice-throwing, which were taken as the models of stochastic phenomena subject to probabilistic laws in the nineteenth century, we now think of as deterministic phenomena whose initial conditions are difficult to observe. With modern technology, however, it is possible, for example, to measure the orientation and angular momentum of a coin in the air after it has been tossed, and with modern computers to predict whether it will fall on one side or the other. Some researchers have trained themselves to toss coins so that they land one way or the other with high probability.

It is very important to understand, however, that deterministic chaotic motion occupies in general a much smaller part of the state space than traditional probability density models, such as the joint uniform, the joint normal, or other commonly used models, predict. The reason for this is that the attractor of a chaotic dynamical system is typically of a much lower (and usually fractal) dimension than the state space in which it is embedded. While chaotic motions have unstable eigenvalues that generate their chaotic motion, they usually also have stable eigenvalues that move the system to a manifold containing its attractor. At the same time that the orbits of system are "spreading out" on the attractor set due to sensitive dependence on initial conditions, they are "squeezing down" onto the manifold that contains the attractor set. We have seen a schematic illustration of this phenomenon in the logistic function dynamics, where, plotted in the appropriate state space, that is, as successive pairs of observations, the actual logistic dynamics become degenerate in the two-dimensional state space.

One curious side-path in this circle of ideas is the theory of random-number generators in computers. Many random-number algorithms work in the following manner. The computer takes an initial number (the "seed"), either specified by the program, or generated quasi-"randomly" by observing, say, the state of the internal clock of the computer at the time the program is actually executed, raises it to a high power, and takes the value of the result modulo some number. It is not hard to see that this process is a non-linear map (rather similar to the logistic system), which, like the logistic system, is generating data that appears to have a close to uniform probability distribution. It is possible, however, to embed data generated by this type of quasi-random number algorithm in a higher-dimensional state space and recover the deterministic attractor that underlies it.

Stephen Wolfram, whose investigations into complex dynamics in cellular automata we will discuss in more detail, argues that the apparent stochastic character of chaotic dynamical systems is something of an illusion, because it is based on a single mechanism, the gradual revelation of the exact initial conditions of the system (Wolfram, 2002, ch 6). The chaotic dynamical system has the effect of magnifying small differences in its initial conditions; thus, observing the system at a future date is effectively discovering the higher-order digits in the decimal expansion of the numbers specifying the initial conditions. All of the "stochastic" properties of the system are already there in the initial conditions, and all the chaotic system does is to reveal them. Wolfram believes that there is another, more fundamental, deterministic source of randomness in the exact evolution of simple non-linear interactive systems such as cellular automata.

3.3 The Financial and Economic Implications of Deterministic Chaos

These general observations on the character of chaotic motions and their predictability have far-reaching implications for economics and finance which are not widely understood.

The basic point is that the marginal distributions of data generated by deterministic chaotic dynamical systems can look very much like the marginal distributions econometricians and statisticians use as "models" of stochastic variability. But someone who takes this marginal information as evidence for the hypothesis that the data is generated by a particular statistical model (joint uniform, or joint normal, for example) will believe that the joint and conditional distributions of the data will also follow the same statistical distributions. As the example of the logistic map dramatically shows, this belief can be spectacularly wrong in the case of data generated by deterministic chaos.

This point is far from abstract when we apply it to economic forecasting, or, even more practically, financial speculation. Consider two speculators trading assets in a financial market. The current "fundamental" valuation of the asset typically depends on the future path of a number of variables, some of them specific to the asset (like the quality of management of a firm) and some of them general to all assets (the interest rate, or rate of inflation, for example). If speculator A applies standard econometric analysis to the data series, he will come up with a model that closely matches the observed moments (means, variances and covariances) of the data. Speculator A, however, is actually betting in buying and selling the asset on the joint or conditional probabilities of these data. If speculator B suspects that the data are generated by a deterministic chaotic system, and has even a very rough idea of where the attractor of that system is located, she will generate a model that has the same marginal probability distributions as speculator A's, but very different conditional and joint probabilities. (In particular, speculator B may be able to rule out the possibility that the system will ever visit certain regions of the state space.) If speculator B's information is even very approximately correct, she will take money away from speculator A in the market.

The realization that the attractors of deterministic chaotic systems occupy a small subset of the state space galvanized econometricians in the 1980s and motivated a major research effort to develop methods for the detection of deterministic chaos in data (Brock and Dechert (1988)). These methods are based on the idea of embedding the data in a high-dimensional space (with many lags, for example) and actually counting how often the system visits any region (say a small hyper-cube) in this embedding space. This works well with large amounts of data, as physicists have discovered.

The attempt to apply these methods to macroeconomic time series revealed the sad fact that macroeconomic data series are too short, given their rather low quality, for these data-intensive methods to work. It may very well be that macroeconomic time series are generated by deterministic chaotic motions (together with a lot of observational noise), but we are unlikely to be able to discover the underlying structure of the system through intensive data analysis. (There is also the likely possibility that the underlying structure of the macroeconomy changes on a time scale comparable to the collection of data, which would also defeat this type of analysis.)

The picture in the case of financial data, however, is rather different. Trading in financial markets generates a very large volume of very high-quality observations, just the kind of data physicists have had success in analyzing with their powerful non-linear time-series methods. A number of researchers have claimed to find evidence of deterministic structure in financial data. The details of this research are generally not widely published, because knowledge of these structures can be used as the basis of profitable financial trading strategies. One side-effect of these developments has been the explosion in the employment of mathematical and statistical physicists by financial institutions.

4 What are complex dynamics?

4.1 Complexity as a concept

In ordinary language we call a phenomenon "complex" because it is hard to understand, predict, or explain, and seems not to follow any simple rule of behavior. The most complex systems we encounter in nature, such as the cell, the brain and nervous system, language, the capitalist social division of labor, and the universe, also have an evolutionary or adaptive character. Some influential scientists and social scientists have put forward the view that there are common properties to all these complex systems, which can be the subject of a particular science of complexity. (In some cases these claims are very strong, and in others rather weak, amounting minimally to the observation that the understanding of any of these systems requires the transcendence of the paradigm of stable linear dynamical systems analysis.)

The concept of complex dynamics is an attempt to find a mathematical class of dynamical systems that can be put forward as plausible models of complex phenomena. Dynamical systems with simple attractors, such as stable equilibrium points or limit cycles, are too simple to represent the openness and unpredictability of complex phenomena. Structural regularities in these systems are destroyed by the collapse of the whole basin of attraction of the simple stable attractor to the attractor set. Chaotic dynamical systems have some attractive properties as models of complex phenomena, including the fractal self-similar characters of their attractors, and their ability to produce scaling phenomena such as power laws. But chaotic systems are also incapable

of maintaining structural regularities, which explode with the divergence of nearby orbits in the system.
A number of scientists, working from a wide range of starting points, have focused on the idea that there must be a type of dynamics located between stable and chaotic dynamical systems, which would tend to maintain differences in initial states without either compressing or exploding them. Such systems, broadly speaking, are nonlinear systems whose linear components have neutral eigenvalues (with zero real part in the case of dynamical flows, or on the unit circle in the case of dynamical maps). The nonlinear components of such systems can continue to produce interesting complex dynamics and allow structures to evolve and interact without collapsing into stable equilibria or exploding into chaotic disorder.
One of these approaches, championed particularly by Stephen Wolfram, approaches the study of complexity through the analysis of cellular automata, which are a class of non-linear dynamical system that is particularly easy to describe. I learned about complex systems in this approach through my work with my co-author Peter Albin (Duncan K. Foley (ed.) and Peter S. Albin (1998)).

4.2 Cellular Automata

The mathematician John von Neumann initiated the theory of automata in the 1950s. Von Neumann's interest in this subject seems to have been spurred by his dissatisfaction with the theory of games he had created (with Oskar Morgenstern) as a way of understanding strategic interaction. (An interesting account of this history can be found in Mirowski (2002).) Von Neumann was particularly interested in the question of coneptualizing systems capable of self-reproduction mathematically.
An *automaton* is a mathematically well-defined set of rules through which an entity interacts with its environment. Automata can be physically realized in hardware, or simulated in software. They have played an important role in the development of economics and social science in recent years as a device for simplifying and disambiguating claims about the properties of interactive systems.
Cellular automata are a particularly simple class of automata that live on a graph or network. (In many of the examples I will show you here the graph is in fact a regular lattice, like a checkerboard, but in principle it need not be and one very interesting line of research concerns the connection between the behavior of a cellular automaton and the topology of the lattice on which it lives.) At least in the simplest cases, all the nodes of the lattice are identical "cells" which can take on a finite range of "states". To begin with I will consider cellular automata that live on a one-dimensional lattice (the integer numbers, or the integer numbers modulo some number n, which makes the integer number line effectively into a circle by making cell n the immediate left-hand neighbor of cell 1). But there are some well-known higher-dimensional cellular automata, such as John Conway's *Game of Life* which is used as a demonstration program in many software systems. The Game of Life is a two-dimensional lattice in which each node is a cell that can be in one of two states, "alive" or "dead". As time passes (usually in cellular automata in discrete fashion, like the ticking of a clock) a dead cell comes to life if it is surrounded by exactly 2 or 3 living cells, and a living cell continues to live only if it is surrounded by exactly 2 living cells. It has been shown that there is a particular starting configuration for the Game of Life that is a

universal computer, in that it will carry out any computation a general Turing machine can.

4.3 Examples of cellular automata

One-dimensional cellular automata are defined by the number of states, k, which Wolfram often calls "colors", and the radius or range of the neighborhood, r, which determines which neighboring cells affect each cell. The simplest cases is when $k = 2$, and $r = 1$, so that there are only two states, and each cell changes according the state of its immediate neighbors and itself. In this case we can describe the cellular automaton rule by a series of substitutions of the form:

```
In[44]:= TableForm[
           Reverse[{{0, 0, 0} → 0, {0, 0, 1} → 1, {0, 1, 0} → 1,
             {0, 1, 1} → 1, {1, 0, 0} → 1, {1, 0, 1} → 0,
             {1, 1, 0} → 0, {1, 1, 1} → 0}]]

          {1, 1, 1} → 0
          {1, 1, 0} → 0
          {1, 0, 1} → 0
          {1, 0, 0} → 1
Out[44]=  {0, 1, 1} → 1
          {0, 1, 0} → 1
          {0, 0, 1} → 1
          {0, 0, 0} → 0
```

specifying what state the cell should take in the next period for each of the eight possible states of its neighborhood (including itself). Wolfram proposes to assign to each rule the number which corresponds to the binary digits of the assignment, so the rule described would be 30. This system can be generalized to any number of states and any range.

We can visualize the evolution of a 1-dimensional cellular automaton by graphing its states (using colors) across a number of pixels, and then moving down as time moves forward. For example

```
In[45]:= CAPlot[data_] :=
           ListDensityPlot[Reverse[Max[data] - data],
             AspectRatio- > Automatic, Mesh- > False,
             FrameTicks- > None]
```

```
In[46]:= CAPlot[CellularAutomaton[30,
             Table[Random[Integer], {250}], 100]];
```

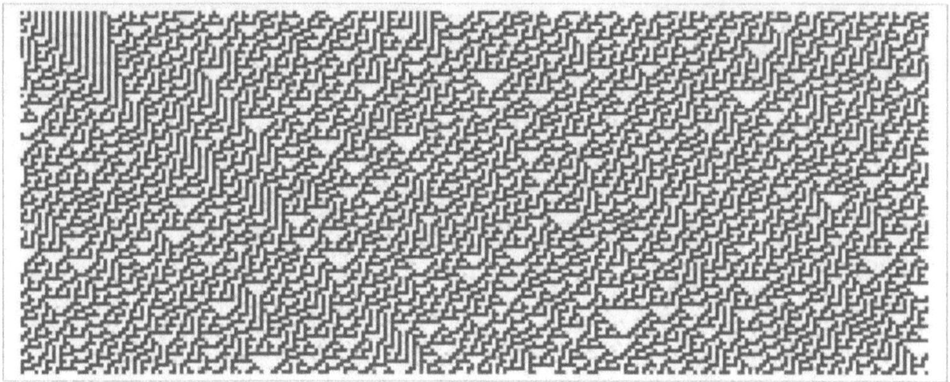

The Rule 30 cellular automaton (with two states and a range of 1) produces this type of output on random initial conditions. In fact, it produces something like this even when the initial condition is a single cell:

```
In[47]:= CAPlot[CellularAutomaton[30, {{1}, 0}, 100]];
```

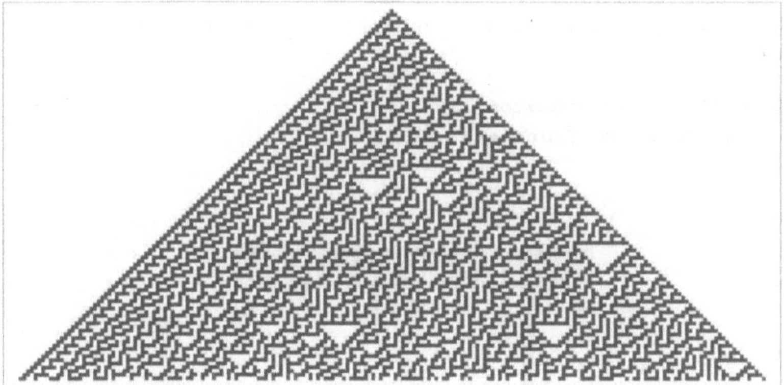

Similarly other rules can be plotted:

```
In[48]:= CAPlot[CellularAutomaton[90, {{1}, 0}, 100]];
```

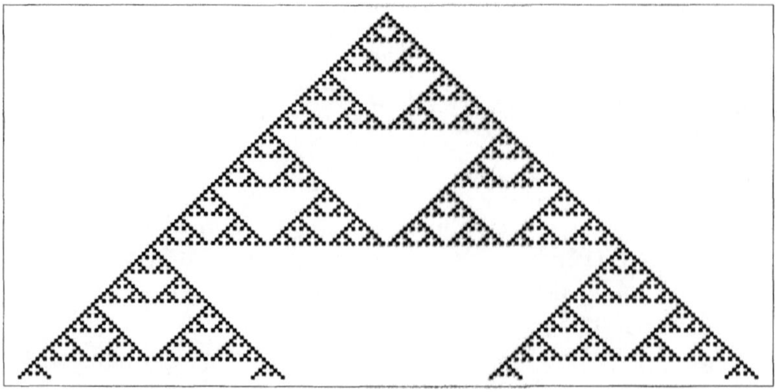

4.4 Complexity Classes in Cellular Automata

The examples of Rules 30 and 90 already suggest two quite different types of evolving patterns that cellular automaton rules can produce. Rule 30 produces a dense, apparently constantly changing, expanding pattern. (In fact, the center vertical line of the Rule 30 output interpreted as a sequence of 1s and 0s satisfies all known tests for "randomness", and is the basis of *Mathematica*'s random number generator.) Rule 90, on the other hand, produces a highly regular, repetitive pattern. These are examples of Class 3 and Class 2 cellular automata, respectively. Class 2 cellular automata produce regular, periodic patterns in both space and time that are equivalent to periodic or limit-cycle motions of dynamical systems. Class 3 cellular automata produce highly mixed, constantly varying output and are equivalent to chaotic dynamical systems. Class 1 cellular automata rapidly converge to a single state both in time and space, and are equivalent to asymptotically stable dynamical systems, as the following example shows:

```
In[49]:= CAPlot[CellularAutomaton[128,
            Table[Random[Integer], {250}], 10]];
```

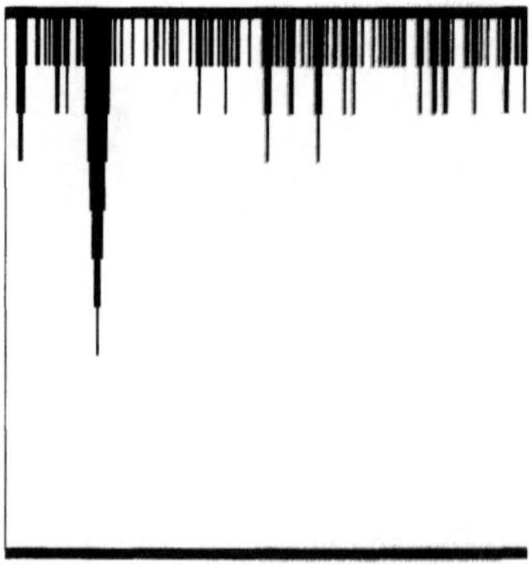

Class 4 cellular automata, however, exhibit quite a different type of behavior. It turns out that $k = 2$, $r = 1$ cellular automata are incapable of Class 4 behavior, so the "simplest" example has $k = 3, r = 1$:

```
In[50]:= CAPlot[CellularAutomaton[{2007, {3, 1}, 1},
           {Table[Random[Integer], {250}], 0}, 500]];
```

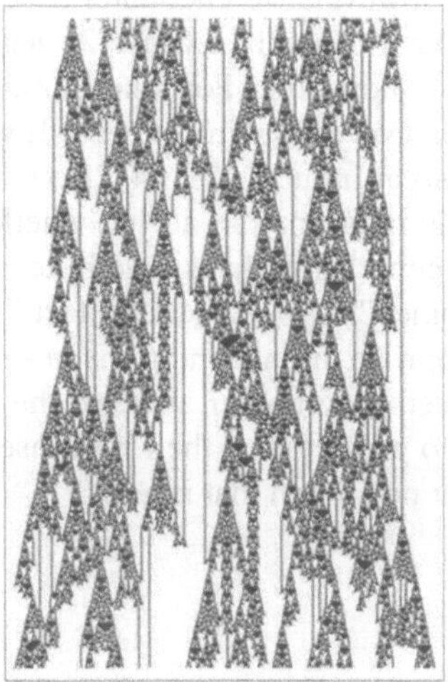

There are several remarkable and thought-provoking features of Class 4 cellular automata. First, unlike Class 1 and 2 CAs, Class 4 does not settle down into a single state or repetitive pattern. On the other hand, the structures generated by a Class 4 system are not explosive like those of Class 3, and, in particular, sometimes highly elaborate structures collapse into much smaller ones. Class 4 CAs can maintain structures for long periods of time, and allow them to interact. Thus the Class 4 cellular automaton, though it is an extremely simple construct, provides us with a very abstract model of complex interactive systems.

5 Predictability of Class 4 Cellular Automata

5.1 Computational irreducibility and universality

In the case of Class 1 and 2 cellular automata, it is a pretty safe bet to predict that they will rapidly find their absorbing state from arbitrary initial conditions. This property is quite similar to the tendency of stable dynamical systems to seek equilibrium.

In the case of Class 3 and 4 cellular automata the specific evolution of the system from given initial conditions cannot be predicted in general except by simulating its evolution in detail. In this sense Class 3 and 4 cellular automata are *computationally irreducible*: there is no shorter path to predicting their state after T periods than simulation. In the case of CAs, these simulations are not subject to error: the computer given the rules of the cellular automaton and its initial

conditions will produce exactly the same pattern every time. Wolfram puts a lot of weight on this phenomenon, which he views as an independent (and probably very important) mechanism of the generation of randomness in the real world. Whereas the apparent randomness of chaotic dynamical systems, according to Wolfram, is really no more than the gradual revelation of the higher digits of the initial conditions, the randomness of Class 3 cellular automata genuinely inheres in their structure, that is, their rules. Like chaotic dynamical systems, the evolution of Class 3 cellular automata can be described statistically.
With Class 4 cellular automata, however, we encounter a new phenomenon. For some initial conditions a Class 4 CA will, like a Class 1 or Class 2, degenerate into a single simple state or repetitive pattern in a relatively short time. For other initial conditions, however, the Class 4 seems to generate new patterns for a very long time indeed. If we regard Class 4 CAs as computer programs, and the initial conditions as input, a Class 4 CA seems to be computing some property of the input. For some inputs the program can decide whether or not that property is present in a short time, but other inputs generate perhaps indefinite computation. In fact Wolfram and his associates have shown that some Class 4 CAs are in fact "universal computers", in the sense that they can be set up with appropriate initial conditions to simulate a Turing machine, the most widely accepted model of a universal computer. One of the fundamental properties of Turing machines is that it is impossible to predict what their response to a given input will be (whether, for example, they will ever halt or not, given that input).

5.2 Statistical properties

Chaotic dynamical systems generate some patterns in data that are very difficult for traditional econometrics to handle. The Lorenz system, for example, shifts back and forth between two characteristic oscillatory modes at unpredictable intervals. Trying to "fit" this type of data econometrically begins to force the econometrician into the hypothesis of "regime shifts", and to try to fit various subsets of the sample data with different models.

Let's take a look at some simple statistics generated by our example of a complex cellular automaton. Here is the plot of the total sum of the cell states in each period in a long run of the 3-state CA presented above:

```
In[51]:= complextest = CellularAutomaton[{2007, {3, 1}, 1},
           {Table[Random[Integer], {250}], 0}, 2000];
```

```
In[52]:= ListPlot[Apply[Plus, complextest, {1}],
          AxesLabel → {t, "total activity"}, PlotJoined → True];
```

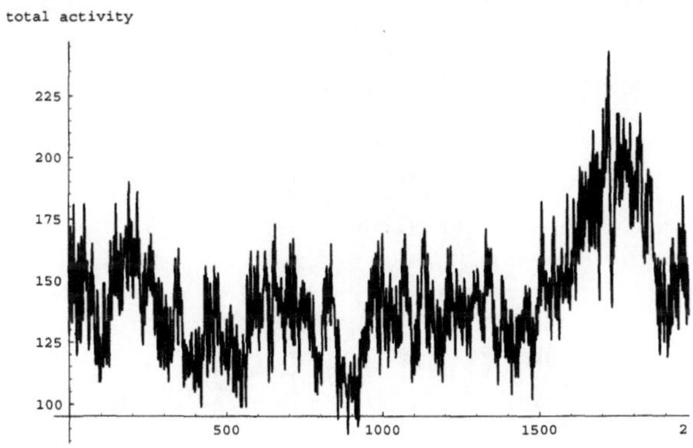

The fluctations of a statistic like this can be summed up by first differencing:

```
In[53]:= (complextestdiff =
            -Apply[Subtract,
               Partition[Apply[Plus, complextest, {1}], 2, 1],
               {1}])//Short

Out[53]= {37, -5, -18, 12, 10, 8, -10, -24, -5, 12, 1,
           <<1978>>, 9, -22, -2, 24, 7, -18, -15, -1, 4, -8, 15}

In[54]:= {Mean[#], StandardDeviation[#]}&[complextestdiff]//
          N

Out[54]= {0.022, 9.32191}
```

The statistic already shows some interesting and characteristic differences from Normally distributed random variables.

```
In[55]:= << Graphics`Graphics`

In[56]:= << Statistics`DescriptiveStatistics`

In[57]:= << Statistics`NormalDistribution`

In[58]:= Show[
           {Histogram[complextestdiff//N,
              DisplayFunction → Identity],
            Plot[
              2000 PDF[NormalDistribution[Mean[complextestdiff],
                    StandardDeviation[complextestdiff]], x],
              {x, -32., 32.}, PlotStyle → {Thickness[0.01]},
              DisplayFunction → Identity]},
          DisplayFunction → $DisplayFunction];
```

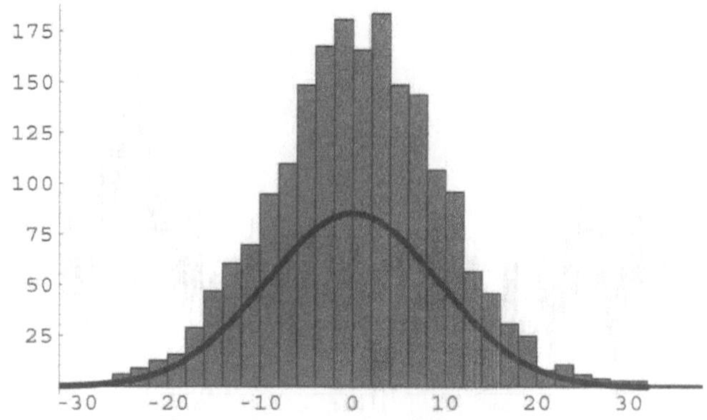

The first differences in the statistic have "fat tails" compared to the Normal distribution with the same mean and variance, as is confirmed by finding excess kurtosis:

```
In[59]:= ShapeReport[complextestdiff]//N

Out[59]= {Skewness → 0.0665474,
          QuartileSkewness → 0., KurtosisExcess → 0.342463}
```

Another characteristic of Class 4 cellular automata is "long-distance correlation", a tendency for correlations to remain robust over very long periods.

```
In[60]:= << Statistics`MultiDescriptiveStatistics`

In[61]:= AutoCovariance[data_, lag_] :=
          (Covariance[data, RotateLeft[data, lag]]/
               Variance[data])//N

In[62]:= ListPlot[
           Table[
             {lag, AutoCovariance[Apply[Plus, complextest, {1}],
                 lag]}, {lag, -200, 200}], AxesLabel → {lag, AutoCov},
           PlotJoined → True, AxesOrigin → {0, 0}]//Timing
```

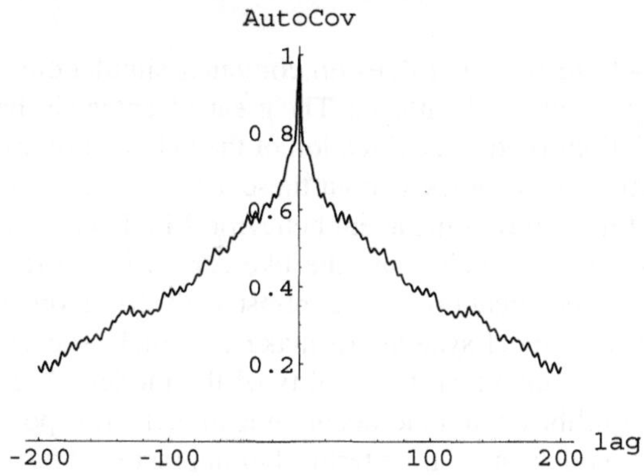

Class 4 CAs tend to produce patterns with correlations at long distances in time and space. This is another reflection of the long-lasting influence particular aspects of initial configurations can have in such systems.

5.3 Class 4 Cellular Automata as a model of the world?

Stephen Wolfram argues that Class 4 CAs, with their properties of computational irreducibility and universality, are a kind of paradigm for simple rule-based models that can generate outcomes of unlimited complexity. Wolfram (2002) explores this research program in some detail. The basic idea has already surfaced in the notion that life itself exists "at the edge of chaos". Stable dynamical systems destroy structure by collapsing it to their attractors; chaotic dynamical systems destroy structure by exploding it into indistinguishable fragments. Systems on the boundary between stability and chaos can support evolving and reproducing structures, and are therefore a candidate for modeling complex phenomena like life, or the capitalist economy and its attendant social division of labor.

6 Complexity and "Agent-Based" Modeling in Economics

6.1 Cellular Automata and Agent-Based Modeling

The cellular automaton is a paradigm of "bottom-up" modeling, in that the evolution of a cellular automaton depends only on the actual interaction of each cell with its current environment. A natural extension of this concept is the "agent-based" model, which simulates the interaction of a large number of independent agents acting independently. These agents need not always be stationary, like the cells of a cellular automaton, but may move in a kind of virtual "space" in response to signals from the environment. Rob Axtell and Josh Epstein have explored one path to this kind of model in Axtell and Epstein (1996). The model of decentralized exchange I outline below is another example of this type of modeling.

It is possible to approach any of the classic problems of economics, international trade, market equilibrium, financial stability, macroeconomic stability, and so on, through agent-based meth-

ods.
The agent-based approach, resting as it does on computer simulations, has some characteristic methodological advantages and disadvantages. The great advantage is that the simulation method puts essentially no restrictions on the specification of the behavior or information of the individual agent, since any particular hypothesis about these aspects of the model can be incorporated into the computer algorithm representing agent behavior. Liquidity constraints, limited information, bounded rationality, heterogeneity, and the like can easily be represented in agent-based models. This freedom of specification is in contrast with the frequent need for conventional closed-form analysis of dynamical systems to make extremely special assumptions about the system studied to ensure the analytical tractability of the model. A good example here is the "rational expectations" equilibrium in macroeconomic models. It is possible to state the equilibrium conditions for such models in abstract terms, but in practice it turns out to be impossible to compute equilibria except under a very restrictive range of assumptions: the existence of a representative agent with a quadratic utility function, linear production relations, and full information.
The great disadvantage of simulation methods is that it is difficult to establish how robust the conclusions of the analysis are. If we find a particular phenomenon arising in the simulations of a particular model, how sure can we be that it is typical or generalizable to a broader class of situations, including the "real world"?

6.2 Some peculiarities of economic agent-based models

Much of the existing literature on bottom-up modeling arises in the physical sciences. The cellular automaton is a good example of this. Two pervasive and almost unquestioned features of physical systems, the organization of space and the locality of information, tend to get built into these models, but there is good reason to question the relevance of both of these assumptions to models of social and economic interaction.
One of reasons for the astonishing success of physical theories is fact that physical space, at least for large scales, is organized in a mathematically tractable way. It is possible to define the mathematical distance between physical objects, for example, in an unambiguous and rigorous fashion. This organization of space is reflected in cellular automata models in the assumption that the interactions take place on a regular lattice, which is a kind of abstraction of physical space, and lends a considerable amount of structure to the system.
But in social interactions it is much harder to define a single functioning "topology" of agent-distance. Even if we are physically close to some other people, say, when we walk down the street and bump into them, we may have almost no social interaction with them in terms of the interchange of information or goods.Two firms which are located physically as neighbors may be in completely different lines of production and have much more intense interactions with physically distant firms than with each other. Different concepts of distance become salient in economic and social interactions: geographical distance is less important than transportation cost; distance in terms of information transfer may be quite different from distance in terms of movement of goods and services. One active area of research in agent-based modeling involves the relaxation of the hypothesis that economic interactions take place on a regular lattice. Duncan Watts, for example, in Watts (1999), explores a range of alternative hypotheses about the connectivity of social and economic interactions, including random graphs and "small-world" networks.

It is difficult conceive of physical systems such as elementary particles interacting at a distance. The representation of interactions in bottom-up models as entirely local, as in the case of the cellular automaton, is a natural consequence of this observation. But this may not be so compelling an assumption in the case of economic and social interactions. Agents who want to trade goods and services, for example, must find, directly or indirectly, trading partners, and one way of modeling this process is through neighbor-interaction as in the decentralized exchange model. But economic agents in a market generally also have other sources of relevant information: they read newspapers with price quotations and macroeconomic statistics in them, for example. Thus in social and economic contexts it may make sense to supplement the modeling of local interaction with the provision of global information that also influences agent behavior. The properties of even simple models like cellular automata when individual agents have a mixture of local and global information are largely unexplored.

6.3 The methodological role of agent-based models

Agent-based modeling has enormous potential in economics and the social sciences more generally. As I have already remarked, every classic problem of economics, sociology, and political science can in principle be approached with agent-based methods. This research program is in its infancy, but we know enough about how to construct and use these models that there are no fundamental obstacles in extending these methods rapidly to the whole range of issues discussed in the literature.

It would be a mistake, however, to imagine agent-based modeling, at least in its current form, replacing traditional deductive and statistical methods of modeling completely. A better goal would be to use agent-based models to supplement and complement traditional deductive and statistical methods. Because agent-based models can incorporate levels of complexity and non-linearity that are beyond the power of traditional methods, they can be used both to explore the limits of the conclusions of traditional models, and to extend their range.

There are some promising paradigms for this type of interactive investigation already in the nascent literature of agent-based models. Although it is generally impossible to solve the behavior of complex, nonlinear agent-based systems analytically, it is often possible to solve special cases in which some important nonlinearities, such as liquidity constraints, have been "turned off" in the agent-based model. The analytical investigation of these special cases can throw considerable light on the structure of the agent-based model and its relation to traditional deductive and inductive models of the same phenomenon. By the same token, turning on the nonlinearities agent-based models can represent so easily and studying the resulting outcomes, can throw important light on how robust the conclusions of traditional deductive and inductive models are.

This method of investigation is bound to be dialectical. In their earliest stages agent-based models are not going to look enough like traditional deductive models to "nest" easily with them. The agent-based models are going to have agents whose behavior is not very intelligent compared to assumptions of hyper-rationality and full information commonly adopted in the traditional literature. One of the dialectical moments in this interaction is going to be the realization from the agent-based models of the practical difficulties in terms of computation and information representation in actually implementing hyper-rational individual behavior. The opposite pole of this dialectic will be the pressure from traditional modeling techniques to incorporate more and more assumptions of rationality and information into agent-based models to explore exactly where the sources of disagreement among the modeling approaches lies. The way forward, however, is going to be through a scientific dialogue between these methods of investigation.

7 A Cellular Automaton Representation of Exchange

The purpose of these notes is to explore a direct Cellular Automaton representation of a pure exchange economy of the general type studied in Duncan K. Foley (ed.) and Peter S. Albin 1998, ch 5. As in that paper, the agents are arrayed around a circle. The state of an agent at any step is a list $\{x, y\}$representing the agent's holding of the two commodities on that round.
All agents prefer to consume the commodities in equal proportions. Each step consists of two parts: an exchange phase in which agents exchange commodities with their neighbors; and an optional consumption-reendowment phase in which the agent consumes and receives endowment. If there is no consumption-reendowment phase the model will represent the movement from an initial endowment to an equilibrium.
The exchange algorithm establishes a trade based on the relative differences in current marginal rates of substitution y/x. The agents trade in this algorithm if the logarithms of their marginal rates of substitution differ by more than a threshold value. They trade at a price which is the geometric average of their two marginal rates of substitution, an amount that is proportional to the parameter *size*.

```
In[63]:= Clear[Trade];

         Trade[{x_, y_}, {xp_, yp_}, thresh_:0.05, size_:2] :=
           If[(x > 0&&y > 0&&xp > 0&&yp > 0)&&Abs[Log[y/x] - Log[yp/xp]] > thresh,
             With[{p = N[Sqrt[y yp/(x xp)]]},
         size{1/(1 + p), -p/(1 + p)}Sign[y xp - x yp]], {0, 0}]
```

Two agents with symmetrical marginal rates of substitution will trade at a price equal to 1:

```
In[64]:= Trade[{1, 9}, {9, 1}]
Out[64]= {1., -1.}
```

If one of the agents holds the goods in the desired proportions (in this case 1:1) and the other has more of one good, the first agent benefits in the trade by getting a high price for the scarcer good:

```
In[65]:= Trade[{5, 5}, {9, 1}]
Out[65]= {1.5, -0.5}
```

If the marginal rates of substitution are very close together, no trade takes place:

```
In[66]:= Trade[{5.05, 4.95}, {4.95, 5.04}]
Out[66]= {0, 0}
```

A trade step applies Trade[] to each of the neighbors of each agent in turn. The program uses the *Mathematica* function RotateRight[] to generate a list of neighboring agents to trade:

Each agent is allowed to trade once in each round with the neighboring agent to the right and left:

```
In[67]:= Clear[TradeStep];

         TradeStep[agents_, thresh_:0.05, size_:2] :=
           Map[
             (#[[2]] + Trade[#[[2]], #[[1]], thresh, size]+
                  Trade[#[[2]], #[[3]], thresh, size])&,
             RotateRight[Partition[agents, 3, 1, 1]], {1}]
```

The endowment algorithm generates a random pattern of endowments over the agents in such a way that the holding of each agent has the same total of the two commodities. The expected value of the total endowment of the two commodities is equal, but in any run of the algorithm the total endowment of the two goods may be different. The pattern of endowments is fixed at the beginning of the process.

```
In[68]:= Clear[Endow];

         Endow[n_, x_:100] := Table[{#, x - #}&[Random[Real, {0, x}]], {n}]
```

The agents consume a fraction $1 - \alpha$ of their holdings in each round. The function Consume[] returns what is left.

```
In[69]:= Clear[Consume];

         Consume[{x_, y_}, α_:0.5] := α{x, y}
```

Combining trade, consumption and re-endowment, we get one step in the evolution of the economy:

```
In[70]:= Clear[EconStep];

         EconStep[agents_, endowment_:0, α_:1, thresh_:0.05, size_:2] :=
           Map[Consume[#, α]&, TradeStep[agents, thresh, size], {1}] + endowment
```

Successive application of EconStep[] to the list of agents' holdings generates a simulation of the trading process in the economy:

```
In[71]:= Clear[EconEvolve];

         EconEvolve[initstate_, t_, thresh_:0.05, endowment_:0, α_:1, size_:2] :=
           NestList[EconStep[#, endowment, α, thresh, size]&, initstate, t]
```

It is helpful to display the result of a simulation in graphical terms. The function EconGraphics[] produces a raster plot of the simulation using a function color[] to choose the color of each agent in each step.

```
In[72]:= Clear[EconGraphics];

         EconGraphics[color_][history_] :=
           Graphics[Raster[Map[color, Reverse[history], {2}]]]
```

The function MRSColor[] produces a color which represents the current marginal rate substitution of the agent, with and mrs of 0 corresponding to white, and an mrs of infinity corresponding to black:

```
In[73]:= Clear[MRSColor];

         MRSColor[{x_, y_}] := Which[y > 0&&x > 0, (1 + Erf[Log[y/x]])/2, y < 0, 0, x < 0, 1]
```

This function provides a visual record of the evolution of trading. Here is a simulation with no consumption, and no re-endowment, showing the process by trade tends to equalize the bid and asked prices across the agents:

```
In[74]:= Show[EconGraphics[MRSColor][econtest1 = EconEvolve[Endow[100], 200]],
           AspectRatio → Automatic]; //Timing
```

Another statistic we might want to visualize is the distribution of wealth at the Walrasian market clearing price:

```
In[75]:= Clear[WealthColor];

         WealthColor[scaling_][{x_, y_}] := (y + x)/scaling
```

The following simulation allows for consumption and re-endowment:

```
In[76]:= With[{e = Endow[100]},
           Show[EconGraphics[MRSColor][econtest2 = EconEvolve[e, 100, 0.05, 0.02 e, 0.98]],
            AspectRatio → Automatic]]//Timing
```

```
In[77]:= Show[EconGraphics[WealthColor[250]][econtest2], AspectRatio → Automatic];
```

In this situation trading continues to maintain a steady-state spatial distribution of prices:

```
In[78]:= << Graphics`Graphics`
```

We can also plot wealth at the Walrasian market clearing price as a histogram:

```
In[79]:= Histogram[Map[(#[[1]] + #[[2]])&, econtest2[[100]], {1}]];
```

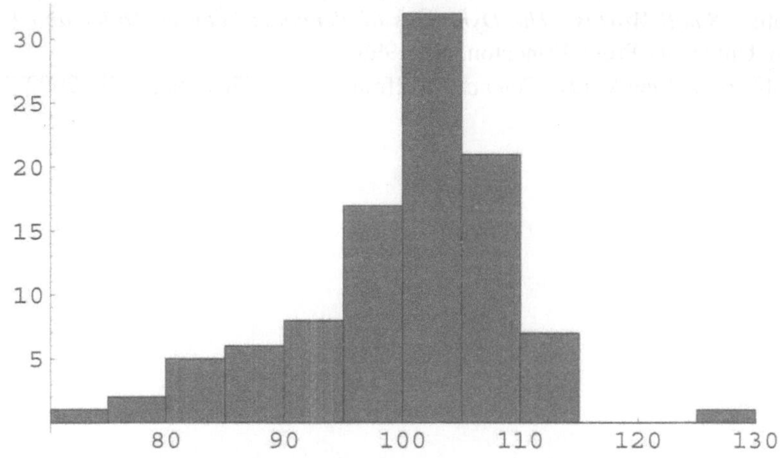

7.1 Some extensions and explorations

Here are some ideas for exploration using this basic trading setup:
1) Is it possible to alter the Trade[] algorithm to generate complex dynamics here? Why are these dynamics not complex? What is the economic significance of this observation? (Hint: perhaps agents sometimes react to encountering a very high or low mrs in a neighbor by speculating on the good.)
2) What happens if the endowments, rather than being randomly distributed around the circle of traders, are spatially correlated? Will regions of high and low average price result?
3) What happens if the agents are connected in a less regular way than the circular one-dimensional lattice? Can you represent the agents as trading on a more complicated network?
4) What would happen if there were three goods, but agents could only trade two of them at a time? Is there any way make a money commodity emerge from this model?

Bibliography

Rob Axtell and Josh Epstein. *Growing Artificial Societies.* M.I.T. Press, Cambridge, MA, 1996.

William A. Brock and W. D. Dechert. Theorems on distinguishing deterministic from random systems. In W. Barnett et al, editor, *Dynamic Econometric Modelling*, pages 247–265. Cambridge University Press, Cambridge, UK, 1988.

Duncan K. Foley (ed.) and Peter S. Albin. *Barriers and Bounds to Rationality: Essays on Economic Complexity and Dynamics in Interactive Systems.* Princeton University Press, Princeton, 1998.

James Gleick. *Chaos: Making a New Science.* Penguin Books, New York, 1988.

Philip Mirowski. *Machine Dreams: Economics Becomes a Cyborg Science.* Cambridge University Press, Cambridge, UK, 2002.

Duncan Watts. *Small Worlds: The Dynamics of Networks between Order and Randomness.* Princeton University Press, Princeton, NJ, 1999.

Stephen Wolfram. *A New Kind of Science.* Wolfram Media, Champagne, IL, 2002.

Ergodic Theory of Nonlinear Dynamics

Alfredo Medio

Department of Statistics, University of Udine, Udine, Italy

Abstract This lectures provides an introduction to ergodic theory – the study of probabilistic properties of orbits generated by continuous– or discrete–time dynamical systems. It includes some elementary measure theory, together with the basic concepts and methods of ergodic theory, such as invariant, ergodic, natural probability measures, isomorphism and metric entropy. The notion of predictability of dynamical systems and the related definition of complex or chaotic dynamics are discussed and some basic results are applied to certain types of maps commonly used in applications. Finally, the lecture discusses Bernoulli systems, the relation between deterministic chaotic systems and stochastic processes, and the notion of α–congruence.

1 The ergodic approach

A substantial part of the specialized literature studies dynamical systems mainly from a geometrical or topological point of view. The geometrical approach is intuitively appealing and lends itself to suggestive graphical representations. Therefore, it has been tremendously successful in the study of low-dimensional systems: continuous-time systems with one, two or three variables; discrete-time systems with one or two variables. For higher-dimensional systems, however, the approach has encountered rather formidable obstacles and rigorous results and classifications are few. Thus, it is sometimes convenient to change perspective and adopt a different approach, based on the concept of measure, and aimed at the investigation of the statistical properties of ensembles of orbits. This requires the use and understanding of some basic notions and results, to which we devote these lectures.

The ergodic theory of dynamical systems often parallels its geometric counterpart, re–visiting from a different prospective many of the same concepts , such as invariant, indecomposable and attracting sets, attractors, and Lyapunov characteristic exponents. We shall see that the ergodic approach is very powerful and effective for dealing with basic issues such as chaotic behaviour and predictability, and investigating the relationship between deterministic and stochastic systems.

From the point of view of ergodic theory, there is no essential difference between discrete- and continuous-time dynamical systems. Therefore, in what follows, we develop the discussion mostly in terms of maps, occasionally mentioning special problems that occur for flows.

2 Ergodic measures

2.1 Some elementary measure theory

After these preliminary considerations, we now need to define a certain number of concepts and methods which we will be used in the sequel. Ergodic theory discusses dynamical systems in terms of two fundamental mathematical objects: a *measure space* $(X, \mathcal{F}, \mu)$ and *measure-preserving* map $G : X \to X$ (or, for short, $X \hookleftarrow$). In ergodic theory, a continuous, surjective (onto), measure-preserving map G acting on a measure space is often called an *endomorphism.* If, in addition, G is one–to–one and therefore invertible, it is called an *automorphism.* In this context, G is also called *transformation.*

X is some arbitrary space. $\mathcal{F}$ is a collection of subsets of X such that:

1. $X \in \mathcal{F}$;
2. if $A \in \mathcal{F}$, then the complement of A, $X \setminus A \in \mathcal{F}$;
3. given a finite or infinite sequence $\{A_i\}$ of subsets of X such that $A_i \in \mathcal{F}$, their union $\cup_i A_i \in \mathcal{F}$.

From properties 1–3, it follows that

4. the empty set $\emptyset \in \mathcal{F}$; and
5. $\cap_i A_i \in \mathcal{F}$, i.e., $\mathcal{F}$ is closed under the operation of intersection.

The set $\mathcal{F}$ endowed with these properties is called a *σ-algebra.* If X is a metric space, the most natural choice for $\mathcal{F}$ is the so-called *Borel σ-algebra*, $\mathcal{B}$. By definition, this is the smallest σ-algebra containing open subsets of X, where 'smallest' means that any other σ-algebra that contains open subsets of X also contains any set contained in $\mathcal{B}$. In what follows, unless stated otherwise, it will always be assumed that $\mathcal{F} = \mathcal{B}$.

The third element of the triplet $(X, \mathcal{F}, \mu)$ is a *measure.* Broadly speaking, a measure belongs to the class of *set functions*, i.e., functions assigning numerical values to sets. In order for μ to be a measure, values must be assigned in a reasonable manner, in the sense that μ must satisfy the following requirements:

1. $\mu(A) \geq 0$ for all $A \in \mathcal{F}$, that is, μ must assign nonnegative values (possibly $+\infty$);
2. $\mu(\emptyset) = 0$, that is, the empty set must have zero measure;
3. if $\{A_i\}$ is a sequence of sets, then

$$\mu\left(\bigcup_{i=\mathbb{Z}_+} A_i\right) \leq \sum_{i=1}^{\infty} \mu(A_i).$$

That is to say, if a set is the union of a countable number of pieces, the value assigned to the set as a whole should be no greater than the sum of the values assigned to its subsets. If the sets are pairwise disjoint, strict equality holds.

For a set $A \in \mathcal{F}$, the quantity $\mu(A)$ is called the measure of A and the sets $A \in \mathcal{F}$ are called *measurable sets* because, for them, the measure is defined. The integral notation[1]

$$\mu(A) = \int_A \mu(dx) \quad A \in \mathcal{B}(X)$$

is often used, where the expression on the RHS is the Lebesgue integral with respect to the measure μ.

Here we are interested in finite measure spaces, such that $\mu(X) < \infty$. In particular, if we put $\mu(X) = 1$ the measure space is said to be 'normalised' or 'probabilistic' and $0 \leq \mu \leq 1$ is called a *probability measure.* The smallest closed subset of X that is μ-measurable and has a μ-null complement is called the *support of* μ and denoted by $\text{supp}(\mu)$ and we have

$$[x \in \text{supp}\ (\mu)] \iff [\mu(B_r(x)) > 0] \quad \forall r > 0$$

where $B_r(x)$ denotes a ball of radius r centered on x.

A transformation G is said to be *measurable* if $[A \in \mathcal{F}] \Rightarrow [G^{-1}A = \{x \mid G(x) \in A\} \in \mathcal{F}]$. G is said to be *measure-preserving* with respect to μ or, equivalently, μ is said to be *G-invariant*, whenever $\mu(G^{-1}(A)) = \mu(A)$ for all sets $A \in \mathcal{F}$. Thus, G-invariant measures are compatible with G in the sense that sets of a certain size (in terms of the selected measure) will be mapped by G into sets of the same size.

In the applications with which we are concerned, X denotes the state space and usually we have $X \subset \mathbb{R}^m$; the sets $A \in \mathcal{F}$ denote configurations of the state space of special interest, such as fixed or periodic points, limit cycles, strange attractors, or subsets of them. The transformation G is the law governing the time evolution of the system. We shall often refer to the quadruplet $(X, \mathcal{F}, \mu, G)$, or even to the triplets $(X, \mathcal{F}, \mu)$ or $(X, \mathcal{F}, G)$ as 'dynamical systems'. When the σ-algebra $\mathcal{F}$ has been specified but the measure μ has not, then $(X, \mathcal{F})$ is called a *measurable space.*

We concentrate the discussion on the study of invariant measures for reasons that can be explained as follows. Because we want to study the statistical, or probabilistic properties of orbits of dynamical systems, we need to calculate averages over time. As a matter of fact, certain basic quantities such as Lyapunov characteristic exponents (which measures the rate of divergence of nearby orbits), or metric entropy (which, as we shall see below, measures the rate of information generated by observations of a system) can be looked at as time averages. For this purpose, it is necessary that orbits $\{x, G(x), G^2(x), ...\}$ generated by a transformation G possess statistical regularity and certain limits exist.

For example, an interesting problem addressed by ergodic theory of dynamical systems is how often different regions of the state space are visited by orbits generated by the controlling map G.

[1] Notice that different, equivalent notations for the Lebesgue integral are in use, thus if f is an integrable function on X, we can write equivalently

$$\int f d\mu = \int_X f(x) d\mu(x) = \int_X f(x) \mu(dx)$$

where $x \in X$ and the second and third forms are used to emphasise the integrand's argument.

To formulate the problem more precisely, consider a transformation G of the space X, preserving a measure μ, and let A be an element of $\mathcal{F}$. Then we define

$$V_n(x) = \# \{i | 0 \le i < n, G^i(x) \in A\} \tag{2.1}$$

and

$$v_n(x) = \frac{1}{n} V_n(x) \quad x \in X \tag{2.2}$$

where $\#\{\cdot\}$ means 'the number of elements in the set'. Thus, $V_n(x)$ denotes the number of 'visits' of a set A after n iterations of G and $v_n(x)$ the *average* number of visits.

Now let n become indefinitely large. We would like to know whether the limit

$$\hat{v}(x) = \lim_{n \to \infty} v_n(x) \tag{2.3}$$

exists. This can be established by means of a basic result in ergodic theory, known as the *Birkhoff-Khinchin (B-K) ergodic theorem.*[2] In its generality, the B-K theorem states that, if $G : X \hookleftarrow$ preserves a probability measure μ and f is any function μ-integrable on X, then the limit

$$\lim_{n \to \infty} \frac{1}{n} \sum_{i=0}^{n-1} f[G^i(x)] = \hat{f}(x) \tag{2.4}$$

exists for μ-almost every point $x \in X$, $\hat{f}(x)$ is integrable and G-invariant, i.e., $\hat{f}(G(x)) = \hat{f}(x)$, wherever it is defined. ("μ–almost every point" means that the set of points for which limit (2.4) does not exist is negligible in the sense that the invariant measure μ assigns zero value to it.) Moreover, for each G-invariant set $A \in \mathcal{F}$, in the sense that $G^{-1}(A) = A$

$$\int_A \hat{f} d\mu = \int_A f d\mu.$$

The reader can easily verify that, if we choose $f = \chi_A$, where χ_A denotes the so-called *characteristic function*, or *indicator* of A, namely:

$$\chi_A(x) = \begin{cases} 1, & \text{if } x \in A \\ 0, & \text{if } x \notin A, \end{cases}$$

then $(1/n) \sum_{i=0}^{n-1} f[G^i(x)] = v_n(x)$ and therefore the B-K theorem guarantees the existence of limit (2.3), μ-almost everywhere.

2.2 Invariant, ergodic measures

In general, however, limit (2.4) in the B-K theorem depends on x, which means that the time average in question may be different for orbits originating from different initial states. This happens, for example, when the space X is decomposable under the action of G and there exist two subspaces X_1 and X_2, both forward invariant with respect to

[2] Proofs of the B-K rgodic theorem can be found in many texts on ergodic theory. See, for example, Katok and Hasselblatt (1995), pp. 136–7; Keller (1998), pp. 24–30.

G, i.e., when G maps points of X_1 only to X_1 and points of X_2 only to X_2. In that case, clearly we expect different *histories* of the system, and consequently different time averages and statistical properties, depending on the initial conditions.

The dynamic decomposability of the system, which is a geometric or topological fact, is reflected in the existence of a G-invariant measure μ that is decomposable in the sense that it can be represented as a weighted average of invariant measures μ_1 and μ_2. That is, we have $\mu = \alpha\mu_1 + (1-\alpha)\mu_2$, where $\alpha \in (0,1)$ and the measures μ_1 and μ_2, in turn, may or may not be decomposable.

We are not so much interested in the properties of a single orbit starting from a given initial point, but in the overall properties of ensembles of orbits originating from most initial conditions in certain regions of the space. Thus, it would be desirable that the average calculated along a certain, randomly chosen history of the system should be a typical representative of the averages evaluated over most of the other possible histories. There exists a fundamental class of invariant measures that satisfy this requirement, called *ergodic measures.*

Several equivalent characterisations of ergodicity exist, three of which we present below.

Definition 2.1. Given a dynamical system $(X, \mathcal{F}, \mu, G)$, the (normalised) G-invariant measure μ is said to be *ergodic* for G if:

1. whenever $G^{-1}(A) = A$ for some $A \in \mathcal{F}$, then either $\mu(A) = 1$ or $\mu(A) = 0$; or equivalently,
2. if f is an integrable function, G-invariant μ-almost everywhere, then f is constant μ-almost everywhere; or equivalently,
3. the function $\hat{f}$ defined in the B-K theorem is a constant, and we have

$$\lim_{n\to\infty} \frac{1}{n} \sum_{i=0}^{n-1} f[G^i(x)] = \hat{f} = \int_X f(x)\mu(dx) \tag{2.5}$$

for μ-almost every x.

The RHS of (2.5) is the expected value of the function f with respect to the measure μ and is sometimes denoted by $E\{f\}$. Intuitively, it can be interpreted as an average with respect to space, where the measure μ 'weighs' each subset of the state space X.

Property 3 of definition 2.1 states that, if μ is ergodic, then μ-almost everywhere the time average of any integrable function f is equal to its expected value. The situation is often described summarily by saying that 'the time average equals the space average'.

Again using $f = \chi_A$, where A is a measurable subset of X, the ergodicity of μ implies that the average number of visits to a region A of an infinite orbit originating from μ-almost every point is equal to the 'size' that the ergodic measure μ assigns to that region. In formal terms, we have

$$\lim_{n\to\infty} \frac{1}{n} \sum_{i=0}^{n-1} \chi_A(G^i(x)) = \int_X \chi_A(x)\mu(dx) = \int_A \mu(dx) = \mu(A) \tag{2.6}$$

for μ-almost every $x \in X$.

As we shall see, however. the set of points for which (2.5) does *not* hold may well include *almost every point* with respect to another measure, in particular with respect to the Lebesgue measure.

Remark 2.2. Ergodicity is a property of the pair (μ, G). Thus, we can (and do) use equivalently the phrase 'μ is ergodic for G' or 'G is ergodic for μ'.

Before proceeding further in our analysis, we need to discuss two special and extremely useful types of measure.

Definition 2.3. Let us fix a point $x \in X$. The *Dirac measure* centred on x is the probability measure μ that assigns value one to all the subsets A of X that contain x, and value zero to those subsets that do not contain it. Formally, we have

$$\mu(A) = \begin{cases} 1 & \text{if } x \in A \\ 0 & \text{if } x \notin A \end{cases}$$

The Dirac measure (centred on x) is also called 'Dirac delta' and is usually denoted by δ_x.

The second type is known as a k-dimensional Lebesgue measure.

Definition 2.4. Consider a set $A \subset \mathbb{R}^k$ defined by

$$A = \{x \equiv (x_1, x_2, \ldots, x_k) \in \mathbb{R}^k | a_i < x_i \leq b_i \; a_i, b_i \in \mathbb{R}, \; i = 1, 2, \ldots, k\}$$

and called a *coordinate parallelpiped* in $\mathbb{R}^k$. Then the *k-dimensional Lebesgue measure of A*, denoted by $m^k(A)$, is given by

$$m^k(A) = \operatorname{vol}^k(A)$$

where $\operatorname{vol}^k(A)$ is the k-dimensional volume of A, given by

$$\operatorname{vol}^k(A) = \prod_{i=1}^{k}(b_i - a_i).$$

The k-dimensional Lebesgue measure can be extended to arbitrary subsets of $\mathbb{R}^k$ by defining

$$m^k(A) = \inf\left\{\sum_{i=1}^{\infty} \operatorname{vol}^k(A_i) \Big| A \subset \bigcup_{i=1}^{\infty} A_i\right\}$$

where $\{A_i\}$ is a collection of coordinate parallelpidpeds covering A and the infimum is taken over all possible coverings (i.e. over all possible countable unions of coordinate parallelpepids containing A).

It is natural to think of m^1 (henceforth denoted simply by m) as the length of an interval of $\mathbb{R}$, m^2 as the area of a subset of $\mathbb{R}^2$, m^3 as the volume of a subset of $\mathbb{R}^3$ and so on and so forth.

Notice that if f is an integrable function on $X \subset \mathbb{R}^k$, then the Lebesgue integral with respect to m^k is often denoted by

$$\int_X f(x)dx$$

rather than by $\int_X f(x)m^k(dx)$. If f is also Riemann integrable, the Lebesgue integral and the Riemann integral are the same. Some examples of invariant, ergodic measures will give the rather abstract notions discussed so far a more intuitive flavour and also establish a bridge between the geometric and the ergodic approach to dynamical systems.

example 1 Consider a dynamical system in $\mathbb{R}^m$, characterised by a unique, fixed point $\bar{x}$. In this case, the Dirac measure $\delta_{\bar{x}}$ is invariant and ergodic.

example 2 Consider Figure 1 representing the state space of the system of ordinary difference equations ($\dot{x} = x - x^3; \dot{y} = -x$) with fixed points $(\bar{x}_1, \bar{y}_1 = 0, 0)$, $(\bar{x}_2, \bar{y}_2 = -1, 0)$, $(\bar{x}_3, \bar{y}_3 = 1, 0)$. In this case, the measure $\mu = \alpha\delta_{(\bar{x}_2,0)} + (1-\alpha)\delta_{(\bar{x}_3,0)}$, where $\alpha \in (0,1)$, is invariant. However, as the reader can easily establish, μ is not ergodic. It can be decomposed into the two measures $\delta_{(\bar{x}_2,0)}$ and $\delta_{(\bar{x}_3,0)}$ which are also invariant. Accordingly, the time averages of orbits starting in the basin of attraction of $(\bar{x}_2, 0)$ are different from those of orbits originating in the basin of attraction of $(\bar{x}_3, 0)$. The system is decomposable both from a geometrical and from an ergodic point of view.

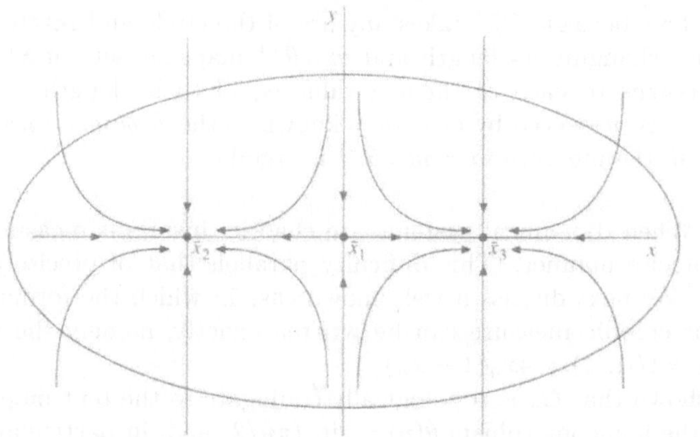

Figure 1. A decomposable invariant set.

example 3 Consider a discrete-time dynamical system characterised by a periodic orbit of period k, $\{x, G(x), ..., G^{k-1}(x)\}$. In this case, the measure

$$\sum_{i=0}^{k-1} \frac{\delta_{x_i}}{k}$$

(where $x_i = G^i(x)$ and $G^0(x) = x$) is invariant and ergodic.

example 4 Consider a continuous-time dynamical system characterised by a limit cycle of period τ, $\Gamma = \{\phi_t(x) \mid 0 \leq t < \tau\}$, where ϕ_t is the flow-map associated to the solution of the system, τ is the period of the cycle and x is any point on Γ. In this case, the following measure is invariant and ergodic:

$$\mu = \frac{1}{\tau}\int_0^\tau \delta_{\phi_t(x)}dt.$$

This means that the probability is spread evenly over the cycle Γ, which is the support of μ, according to the time parameter.

example 5 Consider the map of the circle $G_C : S^1 \to S^1$ (multiplicative notation)

$$z_{n+1} = G_C(z_n) = cz_n \quad c = e^{i2\pi\alpha} \ \alpha \in [0,1).$$

If we consider the map $\theta : \mathbb{R} \to S^1$, $\theta(x) = e^{i2\pi x}$, we can see that G_C preserves the measure $\hat{m} = m \circ \theta^{-1}$ where m is the Lebesgue measure on the interval. To prove this we must show that for any measurable subset $C \subset S^1$

$$m\left[\theta^{-1}(C)\right] = m\left(\theta^{-1}\left[G_C^{-1}(C)\right]\right).$$

But this is true because G_C^{-1} takes any arc of the circle and rotates it in a clockwise manner without changing its length and $m \circ \theta^{-1}$ maps subsets of S^1 to subsets of the interval and assigns to each of them a value equal to its length. Consequently, the measure $m \circ \theta^{-1}$ is preserved by G_C. $\hat{m}$ is known as the *Lebesgue measure on the circle*. If α is irrational, the measure $\hat{m} = m \circ \theta^{-1}$ is ergodic.

example 6 When dynamical systems are chaotic, invariant measures seldom can be defined in a precise manner. This difficulty parallels that of precisely locating chaotic invariant sets. We next discuss a well-known case in which the formula for the density of an invariant ergodic measure can be written exactly, namely the logistic map $G_4 : [0,1] \hookleftarrow$, $x_{n+1} = G_4(x_n) = 4x_n(1 - x_n)$.

It can be shown that G_4 is topologically conjugate to the tent map G_Λ (see example 7, below) via the homeomorphism $\theta(y) = \sin^2(\pi y/2)$ and, in particular, that

$$\theta \circ G_\Lambda = G_4 \circ \theta. \tag{2.7}$$

Equation (2.7) implies that, if I is a subset of $[0,1]$, the sets

$$\begin{aligned} \theta^{-1}G_4^{-1}(I) &= \{x \in [0,1] \mid G_4[\theta(x)] \in I\} \\ G_\Lambda^{-1}\theta^{-1}(I) &= \{x \in [0,1] \mid \theta[G_\Lambda(x)] \in I \end{aligned}$$

are the same, namely:

$$\theta^{-1}\left[G_4^{-1}(I)\right] = G_\Lambda^{-1}\left[\theta^{-1}(I)\right]. \tag{2.8}$$

Consider now that for any measurable subset $I \subset [0,1]$

$$G_\Lambda^{-1}(I) = I_1 \bigcup I_2$$

where I_1 and I_2 are two subsets whose lengths are equal to half the length of I. From this we conclude that G_Λ preserves the Lebesgue measure on $[0,1]$.

We can also establish that G_4 preserves the measure $m \circ \theta^{-1}$. This requires that for any measurable subset I of $[0,1]$, we have

$$m\left[\theta^{-1}(I)\right] = m\left(\theta^{-1}[G_4^{-1}(I)]\right) = m\left(G_\Lambda^{-1}\left[\theta^{-1}(I)\right]\right) \tag{2.9}$$

the last equality deriving from (2.8). But (2.9) is true because G_Λ preserves the Lebesgue measure.

Then the still unspecified G_4-invariant measure μ must satsify

$$\mu(I) = m(\theta^{-1}(I)) = \int_{\theta^{-1}(I)} dy$$

(where of course $dy = m(dy)$) for any measurable subset I of the interval. By making use of a standard change-of-variable rule (cf. Billingsley, 1965, p. 192) we have

$$\int_{\theta^{-1}(I)} dy = \int_I |(\theta^{-1})'(x)|\, dx. \tag{2.10}$$

Considering that

$$(\theta^{-1})'(x) = \frac{1}{\theta'[y(x)]}$$

we have

$$\mu(dx) = \frac{dx}{\pi\sqrt{x(1-x)}}. \tag{2.11}$$

Thus, the measure

$$\mu(I) = \int_I \frac{dx}{\pi\sqrt{x(1-x)}}$$

is invariant w.r.t. G_4.

3 Lyapunov characteristic exponents

The ideas developed in the previous section can be used to provide a measure–theoretic definition of Lyapunov characteristic exponents (LCE), a hallmark of chaos theory. We recall that, in the one–dimensional case, the LCE evaluated along an orbit of a map G, starting at the point x_0 is defined as

$$\lambda(x_0) = \lim_{n\to\infty} \frac{1}{n}\sum_{i=0}^{n-1} \ln\left|G'[G^i(x_0)]\right| \tag{3.1}$$

From our discussion of the Birkhoff-Khinchin theorem and ergodicity of measures, and putting $f(x) = \ln|G'(x)|$, we can conclude that, if G preserves a measure μ, the limit 3.1 exists μ-almost everywhere.

In general, λ depends on the initial point x_0. However, if μ is ergodic, we have

$$\lambda = \lim_{n\to\infty} \frac{1}{n} \sum_{i=0}^{n-1} \ln\left|G'[G^i(x_0)]\right| = \int \ln|G'(x)|\mu(dx) \tag{3.2}$$

where the integral is taken over the state space and it does not depend on x. In this case, therefore, LCEs evaluated along μ–almost all orbits are the same, and (for a given μ) we can talk of "the LCE of G". Equation (3.2) can be given a heuristic interpretation by saying that the LCE is the local stretching determined by the (logarithm of the) slope of the curve of the map G, weighted by the probability of that amount of stretching according to the measure μ. Sets of point of zero measure 'do not count'. All this can be illustrated by two simple examples.

example 7 The asymmetric tent map

$$G_{\hat{\Lambda}} : [0,1] \to [0,1]$$

$$G_{\hat{\Lambda}}(x) = \begin{cases} x/a & \text{for } 0 \le x \le a \\ (1-x)/(1-a) & \text{for } a < x \le 1 \end{cases}$$

Recalling the discussion of the thent map G_{Λ} in Section 2 above, we can easily show that $G_{\hat{\Lambda}}$ preserves the length of subintervals of $[0,1]$ and therefore it preserves the Lebesgue measure m. Then, putting again $m(dx) = dx$, we have

$$\begin{aligned} \lambda &= \int_0^1 \ln|G'_{\hat{\Lambda}}(x)|dx \\ &= \int_0^a \ln\left(\tfrac{1}{a}\right) dx + \int_a^1 \ln\left(\tfrac{1}{1-a}\right) dx \\ &= a\ln\left(\tfrac{1}{a}\right) + (1-a)\ln\left(\tfrac{1}{1-a}\right) \end{aligned} \tag{3.3}$$

If $a = 1/2$, we are in the case of the symmetric tent map and $\lambda = \ln 2$.

example 8 As usual G_4 denotes the logistic map with parameter value 4, i.e., $G_4(x) = 4x(1-x)$. Recalling example 6, we have for almost all points x,

$$\lambda = \int_{[0,1]} \frac{\ln|G'_4(x)|}{\pi\sqrt{[x(1-x)]}} dx = \int_{[0,1]} \frac{\ln|4-8x|}{\pi\sqrt{[x(1-x)]}} dx = \ln 2. \tag{3.4}$$

However, notice that, if we choose the special initial point $x_0 = 0$, we have $\lambda(x_0) = \lim_{n\to\infty} \frac{1}{n}\sum_{i=0}^{n-1} \ln|G'_4[G^i(x_0)]| = \ln|G'_4(x_0)| = \ln 4$.

In the general m-dimensional case, the B-K theorem cannot be applied to the analysis of LCEs as simply and directly as in the one-dimensional case. Broadly speaking, the root of the difficulty is the fact that, when G is multi-dimensional, the quantities $DG(x)$ (where D, as usual, is the partial derivative operator) are not scalars but noncommuting matrices and consequently their product along an orbit

$$DG^n(x_0) = \prod_{i=0}^{n-1} DG(x_i)$$

depends on the order in which the matrices are multiplied. If norms are taken their product is commutative but, because of the known property of norms, namely

$$\|DG^n(x_0)\| \leq \|DG(x_0)\|\|DG(x_1)\| \cdots \|DG(x_{n-1})\|,$$

we have an inequality, that is, the relation

$$\ln \|DG^n(x_0)\| \leq \sum_{i=0}^{n-1} \ln \|DG(x_i)\|$$

is not an equality. However, a celebrated theorem by Osledec (1968), known as the "multiplicative ergodic theorem", provides the necessary extension of ergodic theory to measure-preserving diffeomorphisms. For a diffeomorphism $G : M \hookleftarrow$ preserving a measure μ, and M an m-dimensional manifold, the theorem proves that, putting

$$\lambda(x, w) = \lim_{n \to \infty} \frac{1}{n} \ln \|DG^n(x)w\| \tag{3.5}$$

(where w is a vector in the tangent space at x and $\|w\| = 1$):

1. the limit (3.5) exists for μ-almost all points $x \in M$;
2. as $w \neq 0$ changes in the tangent space, $\lambda(x, w)$ takes $s \leq m$ different values;
3. if μ is ergodic, the λs are μ-almost everywhere constant, i.e., they do not depend on initial conditions (modulo sets of μ-measure zero). In this case, we can speak of *the* LCEs of the map G with respect to the G-invariant measure μ.

4 Natural, absolutely continuous, SBR measures

To establish that an invariant measure is ergodic may not be enough, however, to make it interesting. In our discussion of dynamical systems from a geometric point of view, we first of all considered the properties of invariance and indecomposability of a set under the action of a map (or a flow). We also tried to establish the conditions under which an invariant set is, in an appropriate sense, observable. In so doing, however, we encountered some conceptual difficulties. In particular, we learned that, if we define attractors as sets to which most points evolve under the action of a flow or a map, they need not be stable (in the sense of Lyapunov) or asymptotically stable sets. We shall now consider the question of observability in the light of ergodic theory.

Consider again the system described by fig. 1, p. 7. The stable fixed points $(\bar{x}_2, \bar{y}_2 = -1, 0)$ and $(\bar{x}_3, \bar{y}_3 = 1, 0)$ are observable. If we pick the initial conditions at random and plot the orbit of the system on a computer screen, we have a nonnegligible chance of 'seeing' either of them on the screen (after the transients have died out). On the contrary, the unstable fixed point $(\bar{x}_1, \bar{y}_1 = 0, 0)$ is not observable, unless we start from points on the y-axis, an unlikely event, *and* there are no errors or disturbances. It is reasonable to conclude that, although all three Dirac measures $\delta_{(\bar{x}_1,0)}, \delta_{(\bar{x}_2,0)}$ and $\delta_{(\bar{x}_3,0)}$ are invariant and ergodic, only the last two are physically relevant.

The basic reason of this fact is that the set defined by 'μ-almost every initial condition' in (2.5) and (2.6) may be too small *vis-à-vis* the state space and therefore negligible in a physical sense. In order to avoid this situation, an invariant measure μ should reflect the asymptotic behaviour of the system not just for μ-almost all points of the state space, but for a physically relevant set, that is, a set of positive k-volume and, therefore, a positive Lebesgue measure. Mathematically, this requirement takes the form

$$\mu = \lim_{n\to\infty} \frac{1}{n} \sum_{i=0}^{n-1} \delta_{G^i(x)} \quad \text{discrete time} \tag{4.1}$$

or

$$\mu = \lim_{T\to\infty} \frac{1}{T} \int_0^T \delta_{\phi_t(x)} dt \quad \text{continuous time} \tag{4.2}$$

for $x \in S$ where S is a set of positive Lebesgue measure. Measures satisfying this requirement are sometimes called *natural invariant measures* and the corresponding density (defined below) is called *natural invariant density*; the phrase *physical measure* is also used.

Whereas the properties characterising a natural measure are easily verified in the simpler cases for which the dynamics are not too complicated, in the general case including complex or chaotic systems the determination of the natural invariant measure is a difficult and not entirely solved problem. However, an invariant ergodic measure μ which is absolutely continuous with respect to the Lebesgue measure will automatically satisfy the requirement for a natural measure. To make this clear we introduce the following definition.

Definition 4.1. Given a measurable space $(X, \mathcal{F})$ and two probability measures μ_1 and μ_2, we say that μ_1 is *absolutely continuous* with respect to μ_2 (denoted sometimes as $\mu_1 \ll \mu_2$) if , for any set $B \in \mathcal{F}, [\mu_2(B) = 0] \Rightarrow [\mu_1(B) = 0]$.

Absolute continuity with respect to the Lebesgue measure m (often called simply *absolute continuity*) of a measure μ thus excludes the possibility that sets which are negligible with respect to the Lebesgue measure (and therefore negligible in a physical sense) are assigned a positive value by μ because, from definition 4.1, it follows that if $\mu \ll m$, then $[\mu(B) > 0] \Rightarrow [m(B) > 0]$. In particular, supp$(\mu)$ must have positive Lebesgue measure.

If $\mu_1 \ll \mu_2$, there exists a function ρ integrable on X with respect to μ_2, uniquely determined μ_2-almost everywhere, such that $\rho \geq 0$, $\int_X \rho \, d\mu_2 = 1$, and for any measurable set $A \in \mathcal{F}$ we have

$$\mu_1(A) = \int_A \rho(x)\mu_2(dx).$$

In this case, we say that μ_1 is a measure with *density* ρ with respect to μ_2, and we can write $\mu_1 = \rho\mu_2$. Sometimes ρ is written as $d\mu_1/d\mu_2$, the so-called *Radon-Nikodym derivative.* If μ is absolutely continuous (with respect to m), the set defined by μ-almost every initial condition must have positive Lebesgue measure. Therefore, μ reflects the asymptotic behaviour of a physically relevant set of orbits and it qualifies as a 'natural' measure.

Unfortunately, dissipative systems, which form a class of systems often studied in applications, cannot have attractors supporting invariant, absolutely continuous measures. Since, by definition, such systems contract volumes of initial conditions, their attractors must have a (k-dimensional) Lebesgue measure equal to zero.

Because experimental, or computer-generated dynamics of systems often seem to provide a natural selection among the many (even uncountably many) invariant measures, the question arises whether it is possible to define rigorously a class of invariant measures (and thereby a class of dynamical systems) possessing the desired properties of natural measures. An answer to this question is provided by the so-called SBR (Sinai-Bowen-Ruelle) measures, broadly speaking defined as those measures which are absolutely continuous *along the unstable directions.*[3] These are smooth (have densities) in the stretching directions, but are rough (have no densities) in the contracting directions. For systems possessing a SBR measure μ, there exists a subset S of the state space with positive Lebesgue measure such that, for all orbits originating in S, the SBR measure is given by the time averages (4.1) or (4.2).

Although dissipative systems cannot have absolutely continuous invariant measures, they can have SBR measures. SBR measures have been proved to exist for certain classes of systems (e.g., axiom A systems, Anosov diffeomorphisms) and also for the geometric Lorenz attractor. However, there exist counterexamples showing that they need not exist. For greater detail, besides the works quoted in ft. 3, consider Ruelle (1989) and the bibliography therein.

Another natural way of providing a selection of physical measures is based on the observation that, owing to the presence of noise due to physical disturbances or computer roundoff errors, the time evolution of a system can be looked at as a stochastic process. Under commonly verified assumptions, the latter has a unique stationary measure μ_ε which is a function of the level of noise ε. If this measure tends to a definite limit as the level of noise tends to zero, the limit, which is sometimes called the *Kolmogorov measure*, can be taken as a description of the physical measure. For some, but not all systems the Kolmogorov and the SBR measures actually coincide.

5 Attractors as invariant measures

The ideas and results discussed in the previous sections suggest a characterisation of attractors that integrates their geometric and the ergodic features. We present the issue for maps (the corresponding continuous-time version can be obtained easily with slight modifications).

[3] A rigorous definition of SBR measures can be found in Eckmann and Ruelle (1985), pp. 639–41. For a somewhat different characterisation of SBR measures, see Keller (1998), pp. 124–30.

Consider the dynamical system $(X, \mathcal{F}, \mu)$ and the map $G : X \hookleftarrow$ preserving the measure μ. Let us now define the set

$$W = \left\{ x \in X \,\middle|\, \lim_{n\to\infty} \frac{1}{n} \sum_{i=0}^{n-1} f\left[G^i(x)\right] = \int_X f(x)\mu(dx) \right\} \tag{5.1}$$

where f is any continuous function and write the following definition.

Definition 5.1. We say that *the measure μ is an attractor* if the set W defined in (5.1) has positive Lebesgue measure.

Definition 5.1 characterises an attractor as a probability measure on the state space X rather than a subset of that space. The geometric counterpart of the measure-theoretic attractor μ is the smallest closed subset of X with μ-measure one, namely the support of μ. The definition emphasises that, even if supp(μ) has zero Lebesgue measure and is therefore non-observable, for a non-negligible set of initial conditions the orbits of the system behave in a statistical regular way and the rules governing their long-run behaviour depend on the statistical properties of the attractor, as defined by the invariant measure μ.[4]

6 Predictability, entropy

The theoretical apparatus described above will allow us to discuss the question of predictability of chaotic systems in a rigorous manner. In so doing, however, we must remove a possible source of confusion. The ergodic approach analyses dynamical systems by means of probabilistic methods. One might immediately point out that the outcome of deterministic dynamical systems, such as those represented by differential or difference equations, are not random events but, under usually assumed conditions, are uniquely determined by initial values. Consequently, one might conclude, measure and probability theories are not the appropriate tools of analysis. *Prima facie*, this seems to be a convincing argument. If we know the equations of motion of a deterministic system *and we can measure its state with infinite precision*, then there is no randomness involved and the future of the system can be forecast exactly.

Infinite precision of observation is a purely mathematical expression, however, and it has no physical counterpart. When dynamical system theory is applied to real problems, a distinction must therefore be made between *states* of a system, i.e., points in a state space, and *observable states*, i.e., subsets or cells of the state space, whose (nonzero) size reflects our limited power of observation. For example, we cannot verify by observation the statement that the length of an object is π centimetres, a number with an infinitely long string of decimals, thus containing an infinite amount of information. Under normal circumstances, however, we can verify the statement that the length of the object is, say, between 3 and 4 centimetres, or between 3 and 3.2 centimetres and so on. Alternatively, we can think of the situation occurring when we plot the orbits of a system on the screen of a computer. What we see are not actual points, but 'pixels' of small but nonzero size, the smaller the greater is the resolution of the graphics environment.

[4]On this point, cf. Ornstein and Weiss (1991), pp. 79–81; MacKay (1992), p. 5.

On the other hand, in real systems perfect foresight makes sense only when it is interpreted as an asymptotic state of affairs which is approached as observers (e.g., economic agents) accumulate information and learn about the position of the system. Much of what follows concerns the conditions under which prediction is (or it is not) possible, given precise knowledge of the equations of the system, that is, given a deterministic system, but an imprecise, albeit arbitrarily accurate observation of its state.

The distinction between *state* and *observable state* is unimportant for systems whose orbit structure is simple, e.g., systems characterised by a stable fixed or periodic point or a stable limit cycle. For these systems the assumption of infinite precision of observation is a convenient simplification and all the interesting results of the investigation still hold qualitatively if that unrealistic assumption is removed. The distinction, however, is essential for complex, or chaotic systems. Indeed, one might even say that many of the characterising features of chaotic dynamics, above all their lack of predictability, can be understood only by taking into account the basic physical fact that observation can be made arbitrarily but not infinitely precise. We shall see later that the study of the dynamics of observable states provides an essential link between deterministic and stochastic systems.

After these broad considerations, we now turn to a formal treatment of the issue. Let us consider a dynamical system $(X, \mathcal{F}, \mu, G)$ where the state space is restricted to the support of an ergodic measure μ preserved by G. The idea of finite-precision observation can be given a mathematical form by defining a *finite partition* $\mathcal{P}$ of X as a collection $\{P_1, P_2, ..., P_N\}$ of disjoint nonempty sets whose union is equal to X. A partition can also be viewed as an 'observation, or information function' $\mathcal{P} : X \to \{P_1, P_2, ..., P_N\}$ such that, for each point $x \in X$, $\mathcal{P}(x)$ is the element (or cell) of the partition, in which x is contained. It G is a transformation acting on X, then for any $\mathcal{P}$, $G^{-1}(\mathcal{P}) = \{G^{-1}(P_i) | P_i \in \mathcal{P}\}$ where $G^{-1}(P_i) = \{x \in X | G(x) \in P_i\}$. $G^{-1}(\mathcal{P})$ defines another partition of X. Because G is measure-preserving, $G^{-1}(\mathcal{P})$ has the same number of elements as $\mathcal{P}$ and corresponding elements have the same measure.[5]

We also need to introduce the operation called 'joint partition' or *join*, generally defined as

$$\mathcal{P} \vee \mathcal{Q} = \{P_i \cap Q_j \big| P_i \in \mathcal{P}, Q_j \in \mathcal{Q};\ \mu(P_i \cap Q_j) > 0\}$$

where $\mathcal{P}$ and $\mathcal{Q}$ denote two partitions, with elements P_i and Q_j, respectively.

Each observation in a partitioned state space can be regarded as an experiment whose outcome is uncertain. The uncertainty of the experiment, or equivalently the amount of information contained in one observation, can be measured by means of a quantity called the *entropy of a partition* and defined as

$$H(\mathcal{P}) = -\sum_{i=1}^{N} \mu(P_i) \ln \mu(P_i) \tag{6.1}$$

where $\mu(\cup_i P_i) = \mu(X) = 1$. (If we let $\mu(P_i) = 0$ for some i, then we must add the convention $0 \ln 0 = 0$.) Equation (6.1) is the celebrated formula due to Shannon, a

[5] The reason why we iterate G backward is to deal with noninvertible maps. In particular, notice that if $\mathcal{P}$ is a partition of X and G is not invertible, $G^i(\mathcal{P})$ need not be a partition of X.

founder of the modern theory of information. It satisfies certain basic axioms deemed to be necessary for a 'good' measure of uncertainty, the presentation of which we omit here. Notice that the function $H(\mu(P_1), \ldots, \mu(P_N))$ has a unique maximum $H = \ln N$ at $\mu(P_i) = 1/N, \forall i = 1, \ldots, N)$, and a minimum $H = 0$ if for some $k, 1 \leq k \leq N, \mu(P_k) = 1$ and $\mu(P_i) = 0$ for all $i \neq k$.

When dealing with the predictability of a dynamical system we are not interested in the entropy of a partition of the state space, that is, the information contained in a single experiment, but with the entropy of the system as a whole (the rate at which replications of the experiments — i.e., repeated, finite-precision observations of the system as it evolves in time — produce information), when the number of observations becomes very large.

Because the probabilistic structures of the partitions $\mathcal{P}$ and $G^{-1}(\mathcal{P})$ are the same whenever G is measure-preserving, backward iterates of G on $\mathcal{P}$ can be regarded as replications of the same experiment.

The outcome of the 'simple experiment' $\mathcal{P}$ is the observation of the system in one of the elements of $\mathcal{P}$, whereas the outcome of the 'super experiment' defined by the partition

$$\bigvee_{i=0}^{n-1} G^{-i}(\mathcal{P}) \tag{6.2}$$

is the observation of *a sequence of n successive states* occupied by the system under repeated iterations of G, with a finite precision depending on $\mathcal{P}$.

We can evaluate the uncertainty of the super experiment (the amount of information generated by it) by applying the Shannon formula over all of the elements of (6.2), namely

$$H\left(\bigvee_{i=0}^{n-1} G^{-i}(\mathcal{P})\right). \tag{6.3}$$

If we now divide (6.3) by the number of observations n, we obtain the *average* amount of uncertainty (the average amount of information) of the super experiment. If we then increase the number of observations indefinitely, we obtain[6]

$$h(\mu, \mathcal{P}) = \lim_{n\to\infty} \frac{1}{n} H\left(\bigvee_{i=0}^{n-1} G^{-i}(\mathcal{P})\right) \tag{6.4}$$

which is the *entropy of the system with respect to the partition $\mathcal{P}$*.

The RHS of (6.4) is (the limit of) a fraction. The numerator is the entropy of a partition obtained by iterating G^{-1}, and the denominator is the number of iterations. Define $\mathcal{Q} = \bigvee_{i=0}^{n-1} G^{-i}(\mathcal{P})$. The number of elements of $\mathcal{Q}, N$, is equal to the number of possible orbits of length n observed with $\mathcal{P}$–precision, and is a non–decreasing function of n, the number of iterations of G^{-1}. Recalling that $H(\mathcal{Q}) \leq \ln N$, we have

$$\lim_{n\to\infty} \frac{H(\mathcal{Q})(n)}{n} \leq \lim_{n\to\infty} \frac{\ln N(n)}{n}$$

Intuitively, we can distinguish three main cases, namely:

[6]For a proof that this limit exists, see Billingsley (1965), pp. 81–2; Mañe (1987), p. 216.

1. Transients apart, $N(n)$ *does not grow* with n. In this case , $\lim_{n\to\infty} \ln N(n)/n = 0$ and consequently $\lim_{n\to\infty} H(\mathcal{Q})(n)/n = 0$. The entropy of the map G (with respect to the partition $\mathcal{P}$) is therefore equal to 0. This is the case for "simple" dynamical systems, i.e., systems characterized by periodic attractors (including fixed points as period–one cycles).
2. $N(n)$ grows with n but *less than exponentially* (e.g., $N(n) = an^k, a > 0, k \geq 1$). It easy to calculate that in this case, too the entropy of G with respect to $\mathcal{P}$ is zero. This case obtains for aperodic but not chaotic systems.
3. $N(n)$ grows *exponentially* with n, $\lim_{n\to\infty} \ln N(n)/n > 0$ and consequently the entropy of G may be positive. This is the case of chaotic systems for which the number of possible sequences, and consequently their dynamical complexity grows rapidly with the number of observations so as to make long–run prediction impossible.

We shall discuss examples of these three cases below.

There is a second, very illuminating representation of entropy, directly related to the notion of information and predictability. For this we need to define the following concepts and definitions:

Definition 6.1. Let $\mathcal{A}$ and $\mathcal{B}$ be two finite partitions with elements $A \in \mathcal{A}$ and $B \in \mathcal{B}$; for each $x \in X$, let $\mathcal{A}(x)$ and $\mathcal{B}(x)$ denote the *information functions* that for each $x \in X$ return the elements of $\mathcal{A}$ and $\mathcal{B}$ containing x, respectively; let $\mu(A|B) = \frac{\mu(A\cap B)}{\mu(B)}$. Then $I_{\mathcal{A},\mathcal{B}}(x) = -\ln \mu[\mathcal{A}(x)|\mathcal{B}(x)]$ is called **conditional information function.**

Consider now the partitions $\mathcal{P}$ and $\mathcal{Q}$, defined as before, and the information functions $\mathcal{P}(x)$ and $\mathcal{Q}(x)$ respectively associated with them. Intuitively: for each $x \in X$, $\mathcal{P}(x)$ gives the state of the system "today", whereas $\mathcal{Q}(x)$ gives the "past history" of x, i.e., the sequence of states generated by the iterations of G, all the states being observed with $\mathcal{P}$–precision.

It can be shown that (cf. Katok and Hasselblatt (1995), pp. 162–163) that

$$h(\mu, \mathcal{P}) = \lim_{n\to\infty} \int_X I_{\mathcal{P},\mathcal{Q}}(x)\mu(dx) = \lim_{n\to\infty} \int_X -\ln \mu[\mathcal{P}(x)|\mathcal{Q}(x)]\mu(dx) \tag{6.5}$$

Heuristically, the RHS term of 6.5 measures the expected value of the information given by the observation of present state of the system, x, conditional on the knowledge of its past history (= *ex ante* uncertainty of that observation). The informative value is zero if and only if the conditional probability of observing the system in a given subset $P_j \subset X$ is equal to 1, whereas it is equal to 0 for all $P_i, i \neq j$. In this case, we could say that knowledge of the past asymptotically removes all uncertainty and the dynamics of the system are therefore predictable. On the contrary, positive entropy means that, no matter how long we observe the evolution of the system, additional observations still have a positive information content and the system is not entirely predictable.

So far we have been talking about entropy *relative to a specific partition.* The entropy of a system is then defined to be

$$h(\mu) = \sup_{\mathcal{P}} h(\mu, \mathcal{P}) \tag{6.6}$$

where the supremum is taken over all finite partitions.

The quantity $h(\mu)$ is also known as *Kolmogorov-Sinai (K-S)* or *metric entropy*. Unless we indicate differently, by entropy we mean K-S entropy.

Remark 6.2. Metric entropy is a function of the pair (G, μ), but it is commonly (and equivalently) denoted as $h_\mu(G)$, $h_G(\mu)$ (or even $h(G)$ or $h(\mu)$), according to which of the two arguments μ or G one wishes to emphasise.

Remark 6.3. If we consider a flow as a one-parameter family of maps, then by 'metric entropy of a flow ϕ_t' we mean the number $h(\phi_1)$, that is, the entropy of the 'time-one map'. On the other hand, for every fixed $t \in \mathbb{R}$, the entropy of the flow map ϕ_t, $h(\phi_t) = |t|h(\phi_1)$.

In the mathematical literature, as well as in applications, one can find a related concept, known as *topological entropy*. Consider a transformation G of the state space X onto itself, together with a partition $\mathcal{P}$ of X. Let $N(\mathcal{P})$ be the number of elements of $\mathcal{P}$. The topological entropy of $\mathcal{P}$ is defined as

$$H_{TOP}(\mathcal{P}) = \ln N(\mathcal{P}). \tag{6.7}$$

Then the topological entropy of G with respect to $\mathcal{P}$ is:

$$h_{TOP}(G, \mathcal{P}) = \lim_{n\to\infty} \frac{1}{n} H_{TOP}\left(\bigvee_{i=0}^{n-1} G^{-i}(\mathcal{P})\right). \tag{6.8}$$

Finally, the *topological entropy* of G is defined as

$$h_{TOP}(G) = \sup_{\mathcal{P}} h_{TOP}(G, \mathcal{P}). \tag{6.9}$$

Comparing (6.2)–(6.6) and (6.7)–(6.9), the reader will notice that, in the computation of $H_{TOP}(\mathcal{P})$ and consequently of $h_{TOP}(G)$, we have not taken into account the probability of finding the system in each of the cells of the partition $\mathcal{P}$ as quantified by a G-invariant measure μ. Consequently, we have not taken into account the probability of the elements of the 'superpartition' $\vee_{i=0}^{n-1} G^{-i}(\mathcal{P})$, that is, of allowed sequence of n states.

If X is compact, there is a simple relation between topological and metric entropies, namely:

$$h_{TOP}(G) = \sup_{\mathcal{M}} h(\mu)$$

where $\mathcal{M}$ is the set of the ergodic measures invariant with respect to G. Hence, positive topological entropy indicates the presence of an invariant ergodic measure and a corresponding invariant set over which the dynamics are chaotic (unpredictable). However, when $h_{TOP}(G) > 0$ but the metric entropy with respect to the natural measure is zero, chaos may take place over a region of the state space which is *too small* to be observed. This phenomenon is nicknamed *thin chaos*.

Actual computation of the metric entropy $h(\mu)$ directly from its definition looks a rather desperate project. Fortunately, a result from Kolmogorov and Sinai guarantees that, under conditions often verified in specific problems, the entropy of a system $h(\mu)$ can be obtained from the computation of its entropy relative to a given partition, $h(\mu, \mathcal{P})$. Formally, we have the following.[7]

Theorem 6.4 (Kolmogorov-Sinai). *Let $(X, \mathcal{F}, \mu)$ be a measure space; G a transformation preserving μ, and $\mathcal{P}$ a partition of X with finite entropy. If $\vee_{i=0}^{\infty} G^{-i}(\mathcal{P}) = \mathcal{F}$ mod 0, then $h(\mu, \mathcal{P}) = h(\mu)$.*

(In this case mod 0 means: if we exclude certain sets of measure zero.) In this case, $\mathcal{P}$ is called a *generating partition* or a *generator*. Intuitively, a partition $\mathcal{P}$ is a generator if, given a transformation G acting on a state space X, to each point $x \in X$ there corresponds a unique infinite sequence of cells of $\mathcal{P}$, and vice versa. This also means that, for a generating partition $\mathcal{P}$, the knowledge of a sufficiently long "past history" of the system, observed with $\mathcal{P}$–precision, allows us to determine with arbitrarily accurate precision the initial point of that "history". In what follows, we shall repeatedly apply this powerful result.

A simple example will help clarify these ideas. Consider, again, the symmetrical tent map G_Λ on the interval $[0, 1]$ and the partition consisting of the two subintervals located, respectively to the left and to the right of the 1/2 point. Thus, we have a partition $\mathcal{P} = \{P_1, P_2\}$ of $[0, 1]$, where $P_1 = \{0 \leq x \leq 1/2\}$ and $P_2 = \{1/2 < x \leq 1\}$. (Recall that measure zero sets do not count so it does not matter where we allocate the point 1/2.) Then $G_\Lambda^{-1} P_1$ consists of the union of the two subintervals $\{0 < x \leq 1/4\}$ and $\{3/4 \leq x \leq 1\}$ and $G_\Lambda^{-1} P_2$ consists of the union of the two subintervals $\{1/4 < x \leq 1/2\}$ and $\{1/2 < x < 3/4\}$. Hence, taking all possible intersections of subintervals, the join $\{G_\Lambda^{-1}(\mathcal{P}) \vee \mathcal{P}\}$ consists of the four subintervals $\{0 \leq x \leq 1/4\}, \{1/4 < x \leq 1/2\}, \{1/2 < x < 3/4\}, \{3/4 \leq x \leq 1\}$. Repeating the same operation, after $n - 1$ iterates of the map G_Λ^{-1}, the join $\{\vee_{i=0}^{n-1} G_\Lambda^{-i}(\mathcal{P})\}$ is formed by 2^n subintervals of equal length 2^{-n}, defined by $\{x \mid (j-1)/2^n < x < j/2^n\}$, $1 \leq j \leq 2^n$. Moreover, if we use the Borel σ-algebra the selected partition is a generator for the tent map. Hence, we can apply the Kolmogorov-Sinai theorem and have

$$h(\mu) = h(\mu, \mathcal{P}).$$

Finally, taking into account the fact that the tent map preserves the Lebesgue measure m, we conclude that the K-S entropy of the map is equal to

$$h(m) = \lim_{n\to\infty} \frac{1}{n} H\left(\bigvee_{i=0}^{n-1} G_\Lambda^{-i}(\mathcal{P})\right) = \lim_{n\to\infty} \frac{1}{n}\left(-2^n[2^{-n}(\ln(2^{-n}))]\right) = \ln 2.$$

Before concluding this section, we would like to recall that entropy is closely linked with another type of statistical invariant, the Lyapunov characteristic exponents. A known result due to Ruelle establishes that for a differentiable map on a finite-dimensional

[7]For discussion and proof of the K-S theorem, see, Billingsley (1965), pp. 84–5; Mañe (1987), pp. 218–22.

manifold M, preserving an ergodic measure μ with compact support, the following inequality holds

$$h(\mu) \leq \sum_{i|\lambda_i>0} \lambda_i, \tag{6.10}$$

where λ denotes an LCE. For systems characterised by a SBR measure, strict equality holds. As we have seen before, the equality indeed holds for the logistic map (with parameter equal to 4) and for the tent map.[8]

The close relation between entropy and LCEs is not surprising. We have already observed that entropy crucially depends on the rate at which the number of new possible sequences of coarsed-grained states of the system grows as the number of observations increases. But this rate is strictly related to the rate of divergence of nearby orbits which, in turn, is measured by the LCEs. Thus, the presence of one positive LCE on the attractor signals positive entropy and unpredictability of the system.

7 Isomorphism

In the discussion of dynamical systems from a topological point of view, the notion of *topological conjugacy* plays a very important role. In ergodic theory of dynamical systems, there exists an analogous, fundamental equivalence relation between measure-preserving transformations, called *isomorphism*, which we shall use in what follows.

Definition 7.1. Let G and $\hat{G}$ be two transformations acting, respectively, on measure spaces $(X, \mathcal{F}, \mu)$ and $(\hat{X}, \hat{\mathcal{F}}, \hat{\mu})$. We say that G and $\hat{G}$ are *isomorphic* (or *metrically isomorphic*) if, excluding perhaps certain sets of measure zero, there exists a one-to-one map θ from X onto $\hat{X}$ such that

1. the following diagram commutes

$$\begin{array}{ccc} X & \xrightarrow{G} & X \\ \theta \downarrow & & \downarrow \theta \\ \hat{X} & \xrightarrow[\hat{G}]{} & \hat{X} \end{array}$$

   i.e., we have $\hat{G} \circ \theta = \theta \circ G$;
2. the map θ preserves the probability structure, so that if I and $\hat{I}$ are, respectively, measurable subsets of X and $\hat{X}$, then $m(I) = \hat{m} \circ \theta(I)$ (or $\hat{m}(\hat{I}) = m \circ \theta^{-1}(\hat{I})$).

Maps θ having the properties 1–2 are called *isomorphisms*.

Definition 7.2. Adopting the same notation as in definition 7.1, suppose the map θ is not one-to-one (and therefore not invertible). If $\hat{G} \circ \theta = \theta \circ G$ and $\hat{m}(\hat{I}) = m \circ \theta^{-1}(\hat{I})$ then we say that $\hat{G}$ is a *metric factor* of G.

Certain properties such as ergodicity and entropy are invariant under isomorphism. Two isomorphic transformations have the same entropy and consequently, if one is chaotic

[8] For technical details, see Ruelle (1989), pp. 71–7; Ornstein and Weiss (1991), pp. 78–85.

(positive entropy), so is the other. The reverse is true only for a certain class of transformations called Bernoulli which we address below.

8 Aperiodic and chaotic dynamics

As we mentioned before, it can be easily ascertained that simple systems, characterised by attractors that are fixed points or periodic orbits, all have zero entropy and their dynamics are therefore predictable. We shall then apply the ideas discussed in the previous sections to more complex systems, whose attractors are aperiodic. The asymptotic behaviour of these systems, like that of stochastic processes, can be discussed by considering densities of states, rather than orbits. However, we shall see that complex systems in this sense are not necessarily chaotic in the sense relevant to our present discussion, i.e., they are not necessarily unpredictable. To do so, we shall distinguish between two fundamental classes of behaviour: quasiperiodic (aperiodic but not chaotic) and chaotic.

8.1 Quasiperiodic dynamics

Aperiodic nonchaotic (quasiperiodic) behaviour arises in numerous applications in different areas of research. This is often the case when, for certain not unreasonable parameter configurations, a dynamical system undergoes a Neimark bifurcation. Recall that this bifurcation occurs when, owing to a change in the controlling parameter, the modulus of a pair of complex conjugate eigenvalues of the Jacobian matrix calculated at equilibrium becomes greater than one. Excepting certain special resonance cases, a Neimark bifurcation generates an invariant (stable or unstable) closed curve the dynamics on which can be represented by a map of the circle and they are periodic or quasiperiodic according to whether the rotation number is rational or irrational. We want to show that, in the quasiperiodic case, entropy is zero and the dynamics are predictable. (Of course, entropy is zero in the periodic case, too.)

Before proving this result we show that, when ρ is irrational, the maps of the circle $G_C(z) = cz$, $c = e^{i2\pi\rho}$ (multiplicative notation), and $G_\rho(x) = x + \rho \bmod 1$ (additive notation), are isomorphic and therefore have the same ergodic properties and the same entropy. Consider the following diagram

$$\begin{array}{ccc} [0,1) & \xrightarrow{G_\rho} & [0,1) \\ \theta\downarrow & & \downarrow\theta \\ S^1 & \xrightarrow[G_C]{} & S^1 \end{array}$$

where $\theta(x) = e^{i2\pi x}$. The map G_ρ preserves the Lebesgue measure (the pre-image of any subset of $[0,1)$ is an interval of the same length). Analogously, G_C preserves the 'Lebesgue measure on the circle', $\hat{m} = m \circ \theta^{-1}$ (the pre-image under G_C of any arc of S^1 is an arc of the same length). Also we can verify that for $x \in [0,1)$

$$\theta\left[G_\rho(x)\right] = G_C\left[\theta(x)\right]$$

or

$$e^{i2\pi(x+\rho)} = e^{i2\pi\rho}e^{i2\pi x}.$$

Thus the diagram commutes. Moreover, from the definition of $\hat{m}$ it is easy to see that for any measurable subset I of $[0, 1)$ we have

$$m(I) = \hat{m}\left[\theta(I)\right]$$

or, for any measurable subset of S^1

$$\hat{m}(\hat{I}) = m\left[\theta^{-1}(\hat{I})\right].$$

Therefore, G_C and G_ρ are isomorphic.

We can now use two standard results of ergodic theory and state the following:

Proposition 8.1. *In the irrational case, the map G_C is ergodic (with respect to the invariant measure $\hat{m}$).*

For a proof see, for example, Doob (1994), pp. 120–1.

Proposition 8.2. *In the irrational case, the map G_C has zero entropy.*

proof [9] First, consider that the partition $\mathcal{P}_N$ of the circle into N equal intervals is a generator and thus, for the map G_C preserving the Lebesgue measure on the circle $\hat{m}$, we have

$$h(\hat{m}, \mathcal{P}_N) = h(\hat{m}).$$

Next, consider that if ρ is irrational, the joint partition

$$\bigvee_{i=0}^{n-1} G_C^{-i}(\mathcal{P}_N)$$

contains Nn elements and therefore, for the map G_C

$$h(\hat{m}) = \lim_{n\to\infty} \frac{1}{n} H\left(\bigvee_{i=0}^{n-1} G_C^{-i}(\mathcal{P}_N)\right) \leq \frac{\ln(Nn)}{n} = 0.$$

Then, because of isomorphism, we have the following.

Proposition 8.3. *If ρ is irrational, the map G_ρ is ergodic (with respect to the Lebesgue measure) and has zero entropy.*

[9]cf. Mañe (1987), p. 222: Katok and Hasselblatt (1995), pp. 173–4.

8.2 Chaotic dynamics

Let us take first the logistic map

$$G(x) = \mu x(1-x) \qquad 1 \leq \mu \leq 4. \tag{8.1}$$

Map (8.1) and other analogous one-dimensional, unimodal maps have often been used as mathematical idealisations of problems arising in many different fields. It is known that for system (8.1) there exists a nonnegligible (positive Lebesgue measure) set of values of the parameter μ for which its dynamics are chaotic.[10] We can study the behaviour of the logistic map for $\mu = 4$, denoted G_4, by way of conjugacy with the even simpler tent map G_Λ. The tent map is one of the very few maps for which exact results are available and we used it to calculate the Lyapunov characteristic exponent for G_4 exactly. We will now show that the maps G_4 and G_Λ are isomorphic, and therefore have the same metric entropy. Using the results established in section 2.2, example 6, we can conclude that conditions 1 and 2 of definition 7.1 are verified for maps G_4 and G_Λ for $\theta(x) = \sin^2(\pi x/2)$ and that G_4 preserves the measure $m \circ \theta^{-1}$ where m is the Lebesgue measure. Therefore, we can write the following.

Proposition 8.4. *The logistic map with parameter $\mu = 4$, G_4, and the tent map G_Λ, are isomorphic.*

Because isomorphism preserves entropy, we can conclude that the logistic map has entropy equal to $\ln 2 > 0$ and its dynamics are therefore unpredictable. Notice that, in this case, the metric entropy and the unique Lyapunov characteristic exponent (for most initial conditions) are equal.

Consider now the doubling map G_D on the interval

$$G_D : [0,1] \to [0,1]$$

$$G_D(x) = \begin{cases} 2x, & \text{if } 0 \leq x \leq \frac{1}{2}, \\ 2x-1, & \text{if } \frac{1}{2} < x \leq 1 \end{cases}$$

and the following diagram

$$\begin{array}{ccc} [0,1] & \xrightarrow{G_D} & [0,1] \\ \theta \downarrow & & \downarrow \theta \\ [0,1] & \xrightarrow[G_\Lambda]{} & [0,1] \end{array}$$

where G_Λ is again the tent map. We already know that the map G_Λ preserves the Lebesgue measure and it is easy to verify that so does the map G_D.

Let $\theta = G_\Lambda$. (Notice that G_Λ plays two distinct roles in the diagram: it is one of two maps investigated and it is also the map connecting them.) G_Λ is, of course, two-to-one and it is not an isomorphism between G_D and G_Λ. However,

---

[10] cf. Jakobson (2000), p. 242, theorem 2.2.

1. the diagram commutes, that is, we have

$$G_\Lambda[G_D(x)] = G_\Lambda[G_\Lambda(x)]$$

for $x \in [0,1]$;
2. G_Λ is measure-preserving, in the sense that, for any measurable subset $I \subset [0,1]$, we have

$$m(I) = m\left[G_\Lambda^{-1}(I)\right]$$

(in view of the fact that m is G_Λ-invariant).

Therefore G_Λ is a metric factor of G_D.

Consider now, the following proposition (cf. Katok and Hasselblatt, 1995, pp. 171–2, proposition 4.3.16).

Proposition 8.5. *If the map $\hat{G}$ is a metric factor of G, according to definitions 7.1 and 7.2, then $h_{\hat{\mu}}(\hat{G}) \leq h_\mu(G)$ where, in general, $h_\mu(T)$ is the metric entropy of the map T with respect to the T-invariant probability measure μ.*

Therefore, because we know that $h_m(G_\Lambda) = \ln 2 > 0$, it must also be true that $h_m(G_D) \geq h_m(G_\Lambda) > 0$.

9 Mixing

For dynamical systems defined by measure-preserving transformations, there exists another characterisation of chaos called *mixing* that focuses on the probabilistic properties of orbits.

Definition 9.1. A dynamical system $(X, \mathcal{F}, \mu, G)$ is said to have the mixing property or, for short, to be *mixing* , if for every pair $A, B \in \mathcal{F}$,

$$\lim_{n\to\infty} \mu\left[A \cap G^{-n}(B)\right] = \mu(A)\mu(B); \tag{9.1}$$

or, equivalently,for any two square integrable functions f and g,

$$\lim_{n\to\infty} \int_X f[G^n(x)]g(x)d\mu = \int_X f(x)d\mu \int_X g(x)d\mu. \tag{9.2}$$

Sometimes we describe this situation by saying that 'the transformation G is mixing'.

An intuitive, physical interpretation of mixing is the following. Consider a cocktail shaker S full of, say, 90% cola and 10% rum, initially occupying two separate regions of the shaker. Let the transformation G denote the action of shaking. If the liquid is incompressible, we can assume that G preserves the three-dimensional Lebesgue measure, m^3. If R is the part of S originally occupied by rum, then the relative amount of rum contained in any other part A of the shaker, after k shakes is given by

$$\frac{m^3\left[G^{-k}(A) \cap R\right]}{m^3(A)}. \tag{9.3}$$

If G is mixing, (9.3) tends to $m^3(R)$ as $k \to \infty$. Metaphorically speaking, if the barman is good at shaking cocktails, then after a sufficiently large number of shakes, any portion of the shaker contents, small as you wish, should contain approximately 10% of rum.

We can also look at mixing in a different, but equivalent, way by considering the *correlation function* of the map G defined as

$$\mathrm{cor}_G(f,g;n) = \left| \int_X f[G^n(x)]g(x)\,d\mu - \int_X f(x)\,d\mu \int_X g(x)\,d\mu \right|,$$

where, again, f and g are any two square integrable functions and μ is a G-invariant measure. If G is mixing, from (9.1) and (9.2) we deduce that

$$\lim_{n\to\infty} \mathrm{cor}_G(f,g;n) = 0.$$

Thus, the mixing property implies asymptotic vanishing of correlation.

The invariant measure μ of a mixing system has an interesting stability property (cf. Cornfeld *et al.*, 1982, pp. 22–6). Let μ_0 be any arbitrary normalised measure, absolutely continuous with respect to μ (see definition 4.1) and let ρ be the Radon–Nikodyn derivative $d\mu_0/d\mu$. For any measurable set A, let us define

$$\mu_n(A) = \mu_0\left[G^{-n}(A)\right]$$

or

$$\mu_n(A) = \int_X \chi_A\left[G^n(x)\right]\,d\mu_0 = \int_X \chi_A\left[G^n(x)\right]\rho(x)\,d\mu$$

(where χ_A is the indicator function for A).

If G is mixing, because of (9.2)

$$\lim_{n\to\infty} \int_X \chi_A\left[G^n(x)\right]\rho(x)\,d\mu = \int_X \chi_A(x)\,d\mu \int_X \rho(x)\,d\mu. \tag{9.4}$$

But the first integral on the RHS is equal to $\mu(A)$ and the second is equal to one. Consequently,

$$\lim_{n\to\infty} \mu_n(A) = \mu(A).$$

Thus, for a mixing system, initial arbitrary probability distributions converge asymptotically to the invariant one.

An interesting question is whether, and under what conditions, different characterisations of chaos are equivalent. This problem is discussed in detail in Oono and Osikawa (1980). The authors find that for *endomorphisms of the interval*, all the common characterisations of chaos (including mixing, positive metric entropy and positive Lyapunov exponent) are equivalent. This result covers the simple, one-dimensional examples discussed in the previous sections but does not extend to multi-dimensional systems for which there exist counterexamples such as mixing systems with zero LCE and systems with positive LCE but not mixing.

10 Bernoulli dynamics

In the previous sections we discussed the question of predictability by means of the concept of entropy. As we shall see, however, not all systems with positive entropy are equally unpredictable. Whereas zero entropy implies that the dynamics of a system are predictable with regards to *any* possible finite partition, positive entropy simply means that the system is unpredictable with regards to *at least one* partition. However, there exist systems that are unpredictable for *any* possible partition. Among the latter there exists a special class, called Bernoulli, which is the most chaotic, or the least predictable of all, and to which we now turn our attention.

The first step in making the above informal statements more precise is to provide a unified characterisation of *abstract dynamical systems*. This will allow us to discuss the relations between deterministic chaotic systems and random, or stochastic processes more rigorously and effectively.

Let Ω be the set of all bi-infinite sequences $\omega = (\ldots, x_{-1}, x_0, x_1, \ldots)$ where the coordinate x_i of each element of Ω are points of a certain measurable space $(X, \mathcal{F})$. A natural σ-algebra $\tilde{\mathcal{F}}$ for the space Ω is defined in terms of *cylinder sets* C, thusly:

$$C = \{\omega = (\ldots, x_{-1}, x_0, x_1, \ldots) \in \Omega \mid x_{i_1} \in C_1, \ldots, x_{i_k} \in C_k\}$$

where $C_1, \ldots, C_k \in \mathcal{F}$. Suppose now that μ is a measure on $\tilde{\mathcal{F}}$, normalised so that $\mu(\Omega) = 1$[11]. In the language of probability theory, the triplet$(\Omega, \tilde{\mathcal{F}}, \mu)$ is called a (discrete-time) *stochastic process*, taking values in the state space $(X, \mathcal{F})$. If the measure $\mu(\{\omega \in \Omega \mid x_{i_1+n} \in C_1, x_{i_2+n} \in C_2, \ldots, x_{i_k+n} \in C_k\})$ does not depend on n, $-\infty < n < \infty$, we say that the process in *stationary*. In this case, the measure μ is invariant with respect to the shift map $T : \Omega \to \Omega$ defined as

$$\omega' = T(\omega),\ \omega' = (\ldots, x'_{-1}, x'_0, x'_1, \ldots)\ x'_i = x_{i+1},\ i \in \mathbb{Z}.$$

In particular, for any measurable set $C \in \tilde{\mathcal{F}}$, and any $-\infty < n < \infty$, $\mu\left[T^{-n}(C)\right] = \mu(C)$. Therefore, the quadruplet $(\Omega, \tilde{\mathcal{F}}, \mu, T)$ defines a dynamical system, and T is an automorphism of the space $(\Omega, \tilde{\mathcal{F}}, \mu)$.

An analogous argument can be developed for the set Ω_+ of one-sided infinite sequences. In this case we use a one-sided shift T_+, that is, a shift that moves a sequence one step to the left and drops the first element. In this case, T_+ is an endomorphism of the space $(\Omega_+, \tilde{\mathcal{F}}_+, \mu_+)$.

Remark 10.1. When deriving an abstract dynamical system from a (stationary) stochastic process, care must be used to distinguish the *state space of the dynamical system* (in the present notation, the space of infinite sequences Ω), on which T acts, and the *state space of the process* (in this case the space X).

---

[11] The measure space $(\Omega, \tilde{\mathcal{F}}, \mu)$ may have to be "completed" so that subsets of measure zero sets may be measurable (with zero measure). See, for example, Billingsley (1979), p.35.

In probability theory, a special role is played by stationary processes which are "completely random" in the sense that they describe sequences of independent trials[12] with the same probability of observation ρ (or the same probability density in the case of a continuous sample space). In this case, the state space of the dynamical system is a Cartesian product

$$\left(\Omega, \tilde{\mathcal{F}}, \mu\right) = \prod_{n=-\infty}^{\infty} \left(X^{(n)}, \mathcal{F}^{(n)}, \rho^{(n)}\right)$$

where $\left(X^{(n)}, \mathcal{F}^{(n)}, \rho^{(n)}\right) = (X, \mathcal{F}, \rho)$ for all n. The measure μ is the *product measure* generated by the measure ρ, sometimes denoted by $\mu = \prod_n \rho^{(n)}$.

These processes are called *Bernoulli* after the famous Swiss probabilist. Then T, the two-sided shift defined as before, is called a *Bernoulli automorphism* or *Bernoulli shift* on Ω. In an analogous manner, we can define a *one-sided Bernoulli shift*, or a *Bernoulli endomorphism* T_+ on the space of one-sided sequences Ω_+.

The simplest example of an experiment whose representation is a Bernoulli process is given by the repeated tossing of a fair coin, with 1/2 probability of heads and 1/2 probability of tails. Then the probability that an infinite sequence of tosses of the coin contains any *given* finite n-subsequence of heads and tails is equal to $(1/2)^k$. The process is commonly denoted by $B(1/2, 1/2)$. On the other hand, the Bernoulli shift $B(p_1, \ldots, p_k)$ is the mathematical description of a process consisting of spinning a roulette wheel with k slots of widths p_i, $p_i \geq 0$ and $\sum_i p_i = 1$.

Definition 10.2. A process is said to have the Bernoulli property or, for short, to be a *B-process*, if it is isomorphic to a Bernoulli process. A flow $\phi_t(x)$ is said to be a B-process if and only if the time-one map $\phi_1(x)$ is.

B-processes include both deterministic (discrete- or continuous-time) dynamical systems and stochastic processes. Examples of the former include the logistic map (for $\mu = 4$), the tent map, the Lorenz geometric model, the Shilnikov model; examples of the latter include i.i.d. processes and continuous-time Markov processes.

B-processes are characterised by a property called "Very Weak Bernoulli (VWB)". A rigorous definition of this property is beyond the scope of this lecture (see, Ornstein (1974), pp.41–44 and Ornstein and Weiss (1991), pp.58–60) and we provide only an intuitive description. Broadly speaking, a VWB is an asymptotic form of independence. For an independent process the probability of a future event, conditioned on *any* past event is the same as the unconditional probability. For a VWB process the future, conditional on the past, converges in time (in an appropriately defined metric) to the unconditional future. In other words, for B-processes, the information provided by the past regarding the long-term future becomes vanishingly small.

The crucial role played by Bernoulli dynamical systems in chaos theory can be better appreciated in the light of two well-known basic results. (For proofs see, Walters (1982), p.108; Cornfeld and Sinai (2000), p.50.)

[12]Recall that if $x_{i_1}, x_{i_2}, \ldots, x_{i_k}$ is a sequence of random variables with state space $(X, \mathcal{F})$, we say that the x_{i_j} are *independent* if for any sequence $C_1, C_2, \ldots, C_k \in \mathcal{F}$, the events $\{x_{i_1} \in C_1\}$,$\{x_{i_2} \in C_2\}$,..., $\{x_{i_k} \in C_k\}$ are independent in the sense that prob($x_{i_1} \in C_1, x_{i_2} \in C_2, \ldots, x_{i_k} \in C_k$)= prob($x_{i_1} \in C_1$)$\times$ prob($x_{i_2} \in C_2$) $\times \cdots \times$ prob($x_{i_k} \in C_k$).

Proposition 10.3. *If G is an automorphism on the measure space $(X, \mathcal{F}, \mu)$ which is chaotic in the sense that the metric entropy $h(G) > 0$, and if G_1 is a Bernoulli automorphism with $h(G_1) \leq h(G)$, then there exists a measure-preserving transformation θ such that $\theta \circ G = G_1 \circ \theta$, that is, G_1 is a (metric) factor of G.*

Proposition 10.4. *Any automorphism G_1 which is a factor of a Bernoulli automorphism G is also a Bernoulli automorphism.*

These two results indicate that although not all chaotic (positive entropy) systems are Bernoulli, there is a "Bernoulli core" in each of them[13].

We now use these general ideas and results to show that two simple maps on the interval, which we have discussed previously and which are quite commom in applications, are indeed not only chaotic but Bernoulli.

Proposition 10.5. *The symmetrical tent map $G_\Lambda : [0,1] \to [0,1]$*

$$G_\Lambda(x) = \begin{cases} 2x, & \text{if } 0 \leq x \leq \frac{1}{2}, \\ 2(1-x), & \text{if } \frac{1}{2} < x \leq 1. \end{cases}$$

is isomorphic (modulo 0) to the one-sided Bernoulli shift T_+ on the two-symbol space Σ_{2+}.

proof Consider the two subintervals $I_- = [0, 1/2)$ and $I_+ = (1/2, 1]$ and the set $I_0 = \{x \in [0,1] \mid G_\Lambda^n(x) \in I_+ \text{ or } I_- \; \forall n \geq 0\}$, that is, the set of points of the interval which are never mapped to its middle point 1/2. Let Σ_{2+} denote the space of one-sided infinite sequences of the symbols 0, 1 (i.e., $\Sigma_{2+} = \{0,1\}^{\mathbb{Z}_+}$), and define the map $\theta : I_0 \to \Sigma_{2+}$

$$\theta(x) = s \equiv (s_0 s_1 \ldots s_n \ldots)$$

where

$$s_k = \begin{cases} 0, & \text{if } G_\Lambda^k(x) \in I_-, \\ 1, & \text{if } G_\Lambda^k(x) \in I_+. \end{cases}$$

Notice that the map θ is one-to-one, "nearly onto", because the set $\Sigma_{2+} \setminus \theta(I_0)$ contains countably many points of the form $s = (s_0 s_1 \ldots s_k \, 1 \, 0 \ldots \{0\}^\infty)$, and that θ is a homeomorphism between I_0 and $\theta(I_0)$. Moreover, if T_+ denotes again the one-sided shift map on Σ_{2+}, we have $T_+ \circ \theta = \theta \circ G_\Lambda$. Let μ_1 be a (stationary) probability measure on Σ_{2+} defined by

$$\mu_1(C) = 2^{-k}$$

where C is any cylinder set

$$C = \{s \in \Sigma_{2+} \mid s_{i_1} = c_1, \ldots, s_{i_k} = c_k\}$$

[13] There exists an intermediate class of invertible transformations which are known as *Kolmogorov*, or simply *K-automorphisms*, which are unpredictable for any possible partition. Although all Bernoulli automorphisms are K, the reverse need not be true (cf. Ornstein and Weiss (1991), pp.19–20). K-automorphisms are seldom met in applications and we shall not deal with them here. There exits an analogous class of noninvertible transformations (endomorphisms) called *exact* (cf. Cornfeld *et al.* (1982), p.289).

where $c_j (j = 1, 2, \ldots, k)$ are fixed values equal to 0 or 1, and for any (i, j)

$$\text{prob } (s_{i_j} = 1) = \text{ prob } (s_{i_j} = 0) = \frac{1}{2}.$$

We shall denote this measure by $\mu_1(1/2, 1/2)$. The measure μ_1 is invariant with respect to T_+. Notice also that, because $\Sigma_{2+} \setminus \theta(I_0)$ is a countable set, $\mu_1[\theta(I_0)] = 1$ and therefore $\Sigma_{2+} \setminus \theta(I_0)$ is μ_1-negligible. In order to prove isomorphism, we look for a probability measure μ_2 on $[0, 1]$, invariant with respect to G_Λ and such that for any measurable subset $C \subset \Sigma_{2+}$ we have

$$\mu_1(C) = \mu_2 \left[\theta^{-1}(C)\right]$$

or for any measurable subset $A \subset [0, 1]$

$$\mu_2(A) = \mu_1 \left[\theta(A)\right] = \mu_1 \left[\theta(A \bigcap I_0)\right].$$

We can verify that the Lebesgue measure m which we know to be G_Λ-invariant, satisfies this condition. To see this, consider that for any "cylinder set" C defined as before, the set $\theta^{-1}(C)$ is a subinterval of $[0, 1]$ which is mapped onto $[0, 1]$ by a linear branch of G_Λ^k with slope equal to 2^k. Thus, the length of an interval $\theta^{-1}(C)$, and therefore its Lebesgue measure, is equal to 2^{-k}. Hence, setting $\mu_2 = m$, we have the desired result

$$\mu_1(C) = m \left[\theta^{-1}(C)\right].$$

For a generalization of the result just discussed and further technical details, cf. Keller (1998), pp.16–17 and 166–167, on which the present discussion is based.

Proposition 10.6. *The logistic map*

$$G_4 : [0, 1] \to [0, 1] \qquad G_4(x) = 4x(1 - x)$$

is isomorphic to the tent map. Therefore the map G_4 is Bernoulli.

proof Isomorphism is proved in proposition 8.4. The rest follows from the definitions.

Proposition 10.7. *The doubling map on the interval*

$$G_D : [0, 1] \to [0, 1]$$

$$G_D(x) = \begin{cases} 2x, & \text{if } 0 \le x \le \frac{1}{2}, \\ 2x - 1, & \text{if } \frac{1}{2} < x \le 1 \end{cases}$$

is isomorphic (modulo 0) to the one-sided Bernoulli shift on two symbols and therefore it is Bernoulli.

proof The proof is similar to that of proposition 10.5 and we abbreviate it. Let $(\Sigma_{2+}, T_+, \mu(1/2, 1/2))$ where $\mu(1/2, 1/2)$ is the same as μ_1 defined in the proof of proposition 10.5. Let $\mathcal{P} = \{P_0, P_1\}$ be a partition of $[0, 1]$ with $P_0 = [0, 1/2]$ and $P_1 = (1/2, 1]$. The map $\theta : \Sigma_{2+} \to [0, 1]$

$$\theta(s) = \bigcap_{j=0}^{\infty} G_D^{-j} P_{s_j}$$

(where $s_j = 0$ or 1) is one-to-one and invertible (modulo sets of measure zero) and the diagram

$$\begin{array}{ccc} \Sigma_{2+} & \xrightarrow{T_+} & \Sigma_{2+} \\ {\scriptstyle \theta(s)} \downarrow & & \downarrow {\scriptstyle \theta(s)} \\ [0, 1] & \xrightarrow[G_D]{} & [0, 1] \end{array}$$

commutes.

Consider now that G_D preserves the Lebesgue measure m, because the pre-image of any measurable subset I of $[0, 1]$ is the union of two subsets, the length of which is equal to half that of I. For a given sequence $\{s_j\}_0^{k-1}$, $s_j \in \{0, 1\}$, the length of the subset $I^{(k)} \subset [0, 1]$

$$I^{(k)} = \bigcap_{j=0}^{k-1} G_D^{-j} P_{s_j}$$

is equal to 2^{-k}. Also, if $C^{(k)}$ is the cylinder set defined by the same sequence, we have $\mu(C^{(k)}) = 2^{-k}$. Because $I^{(k)} = \theta(C^{(k)})$, it follows that $\mu(C^{(k)}) = m[\theta(C^{(k)})]$ (and $m(I^{(k)}) = \mu[\theta^{-1}(I^{(k)})]$. We can conclude that θ is an isomorphism between the shift map T_+ and the map G_D. Thus, G_D is Bernoulli.

11 Markov shifts

A second, basic example of dynamical systems arising in probability theory is provided by Markov shifts (cf. Cornfeld *et al.* (1982), pp.182–188). Broadly speaking, we say that a stochastic process is a *Markov process* (or *chain*) if the future of the process is independent of the past, given its present value (one might say that the process has short memory). In order to provide a more rigorous characterisation of this idea, let us consider again a stochastic process $(\Omega, \tilde{\mathcal{F}}, \mu)$ taking values on a state space $(X, \mathcal{F})$. Then, the evolution of a Markov process in time can be described in terms of a one-step *transition probability kernel* (also called *stochastic operator*)

$$P(x, A) \; x \in X \; A \in \mathcal{F}$$

where

1. for each A, $P(\cdot, A)$ is a measurable function on X; and
2. for each x, $P(x, \cdot)$ is a probability measure on $\mathcal{F}$.

We say that a probability measure ρ on $\mathcal{F}$ is invariant with respect to P, or equivalently that P preserves ρ, if we have

$$\rho(A) = \int_X P(x, A)\rho(dx).$$

A transition probability kernel P and a corresponding invariant measure ρ define a measure μ on the space of sequences Ω as follows:

$$\mu(C) = \int_{C_1} \rho(dx_i) \int_{C_2} P(x_i, dx_{i+1}) \cdots \int_{C_r} P(x_{i+r-2}, dx_{i+r-1})$$

where again

$$C = \{\omega \in \Omega | x_i \in C_1, \ldots, x_{i+r-1} \in C_r\} \in \tilde{\mathcal{F}}$$

$\omega = (\ldots, x_{-1}, x_0, x_1, \ldots)$ with $-\infty < i < \infty$ and $C_i \in \mathcal{F}$. Invariance of ρ (with respect to P) implies stationarity of the process (that is, given P and ρ, μ does not depend on the choice of i).

The shift map T on the measure space $(\Omega, \tilde{\mathcal{F}}, \mu)$ defines a dynamical system called a *Markov shift* (or *Markov automorphism*). In a perfectly analogous manner it is possible to define Markov shifts on the space Ω_+ of one-sided infinite sequences, i.e., *Markov endomorphisms*.

A special, interesting case occurs when the state space X of the stochastic process is a finite set, that is, we have $X = \{X_1, \ldots, X_m\}$. In that case the transition probability kernel reduces to a transition matrix $\Pi = (\pi_{ij})$ where $\pi_{ij} = P(X_i, \{X_j\})$, $i, j = 1, \ldots, m$. The measure ρ invariant with respect to P is now defined by a vector $\pi^T = (\pi_1, \ldots, \pi_m)$ where $\pi_k = \rho(\{X_k\})$ for $k = 1, \ldots, m$ and $\pi^T = \pi^T \Pi$.

The matrix Π is said to be a *stochastic matrix* because $\pi_{ij} \geq 0$, $\sum_{j=1}^m \pi_{ij} = 1$. Notice that the Bernoulli shift is a special case of a Markov shift with $P(x, C) = \rho(C)$ or, in the case of a finite state space, $\pi_{ij} = \pi_j$.

Let $\Pi^{(n)} = (\pi_{ij}^{(n)})$ denote the nth iterate of the matrix Π. The Markov shift is ergodic when the matrix Π is irreducible in the sense that for each pair (i, j) there exists an n such that $\pi_{ij}^{(n)} > 0$. The shift is mixing if there exists an n such that all of the elements of $\Pi^{(n)}$ are strictly positive (mixing implies irreducibility, and irreducibility plus aperiodicity implies mixing).

12 α-congruence

Equivalence implicit in isomorphism concerns the probabilistic structure of orbits, not their geometry, much of which can be distorted by the map that relates two isomorphic spaces. Therefore, geometrically different systems can be isomorphic. In order to overcome this difficulty the notion of α-congruence has been suggested. The following definition, based on Ornstein and Weiss (1991), pp.22–23 and 63, is formulated in the more general terms of flows, but can be easily adapted to discrete-time systems.

Definition 12.1. Consider two flows ϕ_t and $\tilde{\phi}_t$, defined on the same metric space M and preserving the measures μ and $\tilde{\mu}$, respectively. We say that ϕ_t and $\tilde{\phi}_t$ are *α-congruent* if they are isomorphic via a map $\theta : M \to M$ that satisfies

$$\mu\{x \mid d[x, \theta(x)] > \alpha\} < \alpha$$

where $x \in M$ and d is a fixed metric on M.

That is to say, the isomorphism θ moves points in M by less than α, except for a set of points in M of measure less than α. Thus, if α is so small that we do not appreciate distances in M smaller than α and we ignore events whose probability is smaller than α, then we consider α-congruent systems as actually indistinguishable. α-congruence is a form of equivalence stronger than isomorphism, as it requires that systems be close not only in a measure-theoretic sense but also in a geometric sense.

If we want to compare stochastic processes and deterministic systems, and the realisations of the former do not lie in the same metric space as the orbits of the latter, we need a definition of α-congruence covering the general case of two flows (or maps) acting on different abstract measure spaces (see, Ornstein and Weiss (1991), pp.22–25).

Definition 12.2. Let ϕ_t and $\tilde{\phi}_t$ be two flows acting on measure spaces M and $\tilde{M}$ and preserving the probability measures μ and $\tilde{\mu}$, respectively. Let $\mathcal{P}$ and $\tilde{\mathcal{P}}$ be two functions from M (or $\tilde{M}$) to the same metric space (X, d). We say that ϕ_t and $\tilde{\phi}_t$ are α-congruent if there exists an invertible measure-preserving map $\theta : M \to \tilde{M}$ such that

1. $\theta \circ \phi_t = \tilde{\phi}_t \circ \theta$ almost everywhere;
2. for all measurable subsets $\tilde{A} \subset \tilde{X}$, $\mu\left[\theta^{-1}(\tilde{A})\right] = \tilde{\mu}(\tilde{A})$ (therefore, ϕ_t and $\tilde{\phi}_t$ are isomorphic); and
3. $d\left(\mathcal{P}(x), \tilde{\mathcal{P}}[\theta(x)]\right) < \alpha$ except for a set of μ-measure $< \alpha$.

This defintion can be easily adapted to maps. Suppose now that we have a discrete-time deterministic system defined by (X, G, ρ) and a stochastic process defined by (Ω, T, μ) where T is the shift map. A natural choice for the function $\tilde{\mathcal{P}}$ on the space of sequences Ω is the partition of Ω giving the state of the sequence at time zero, i.e., the current state of the process, observed with a finite degree of precision. The typical choice for $\mathcal{P}$ is a partition of the state space of the deterministic dynamical system that can be interpreted as an observation (or information) function such that each element of $\mathcal{P}$ includes points of the state space which cannot be distinguished at a certain level of precision of observation. If the functions $\tilde{\mathcal{P}}$ and $\mathcal{P}$ have the same range, realisations of the stochastic process and orbits of the deterministic system, observed with finite precision, can be compared. If the stochastic process and the deterministic system thus partitioned are α-congruent, in the sense of definition 12.2, we can say that the realisations of the former and the orbits of the latter are observationally indistinguishable at a level of precision depending on α.

The following, recently established results (Radunskaya (1992)) shed some doubt on the possibility of distinguishing deterministic chaos and randomness observationally.

Proposition 12.3. *Let ϕ_t be a flow on a manifold M that is isomorphic to the Bernoulli flow of infinite entropy. Then, for any $\alpha > 0$, there is a continuous time, finite state Markov process $\mathcal{M}_t$ taking value on M which is α-congruent to ϕ_t.*

This is remarkable result but is not sufficient for our present purposes. In the study of deterministic chaotic systems, we usually consider the dynamics of the system on a compact attractor whose entropy is finite and bounded by the sum of the positive Lyapunov characteristic exponents. Therefore we are interested here in flows with finite entropy. The following result is then more relevant to our purpose.

Proposition 12.4. *Let ϕ_t be a B-flow of finite entropy on a manifold M. Let B_t^∞ be an infinite entropy B-flow on a probability space Ω. Then, for any $\alpha > 0$, there exists a continuous-time Markov process $\mathcal{M}_t$, on a finite number of states $\{s_i\} \in M \times \Omega$ such that $\mathcal{M}_t$ is α-congruent to $\tilde{\phi}_t = \phi_t \times B_t^\infty$.*

These rather abstract results can be given a striking common-sense interpretation. Let us consider an observer looking at orbits generated by a deterministic Bernoulli system with infinite entropy and let us suppose that observation takes place through a device (a viewer) that distorts by less than α, with probability greater than $1-\alpha$, where α is positive number that we can choose as small as we wish. Proposition 12.3 (infinite entropy case) tells us that the orbits as seen through the viewer are arbitrarily close to a continuous-time, finite state Markov process. In the finite entropy case, in order to compare the orbits of the deterministic system with the sample paths of the (infinite entropy) Markov process, we need to introduce some additional entropy by "sprinkling" the deterministic system with a bit of noninterfering noise. We can again use the parable of orbits observed through a slightly distorting viewer, but now the errors are random. Proposition 12.4 tells us that in this case, too, the observed orbits are most of the time arbitrarily close to the sample paths of the Markov process.

These sharp results should produce some skepticism on the possibility of rigorously testing whether a given series has been generated by a deterministic or a stochastic mechanism, for example, by estimating the value of correlation dimension or the dominant Lyapunov characteristic exponent. In view of propositions 12.3 and 12.4, if those tests are applied to a Markov process and to a deterministic Bernoulli system which are α-congruent, they should give the same results for sufficiently small values of α.

Our main concern is with the general consequences of the results above, and we leave details aside. However, a simple example of α-congruence is in order and we consider one between a discrete-time deterministic system and a discrete-time stochastic (Markov) process, using once again the tent map G_Λ, with the Lebesgue measure on the interval, which we know to be Bernoulli. For the tent map along with a partition of the state space, we can define a Markov process on k states (the number of states depending on α), such that its sample paths are α-indistinguishable from the orbits of the map[14]. For example, put $\alpha = 1/2$ and choose the partition $\mathcal{P} : [0,1] \to \{L, R\}$ where $L = \{x \in [0,1/2]\}$, $R = \{x \in (1/2,1]\}$. Then a Markov process on these two states L and R, with transition matrix

$$\begin{array}{c} \\ L \\ R \end{array} \begin{array}{c} \begin{matrix} L & R \end{matrix} \\ \begin{pmatrix} 1/2 & 1/2 \\ 1/2 & 1/2 \end{pmatrix} \end{array}$$

[14]This example has been suggested by A. Radunskaya in a private correspondence with the author.

will generate sample paths α-indistinguishable from those of the deterministic map G_Λ[15]

If we reduce α and put, say, $\alpha = 2^{-k}, k \geq 2$, and choose a partition $\mathcal{P}_k$ such that the unit interval is divided into 2^k subintervals of equal length 2^{-k} defined by

$$\left\{ x \,\middle|\, \frac{j-1}{2^k} < x < \frac{j}{2^k} \right\} \; 1 \leq j \leq 2^k$$

we can construct a 2^k state Markov process with transition matrix (omitting the state labels)

$$\begin{pmatrix} 1/2 & 1/2 & 0 & 0 & \cdots & \cdots & 0 & 0 \\ 0 & 0 & 1/2 & 1/2 & \cdots & \cdots & 0 & 0 \\ \cdots & \cdots & \cdots & \cdots & \cdots & \cdots & \cdots & \cdots \\ 0 & 0 & 0 & 0 & \cdots & \cdots & 1/2 & 1/2 \\ \cdots & \cdots & \cdots & \cdots & \cdots & \cdots & \cdots & \cdots \\ 0 & 0 & 1/2 & 1/2 & \cdots & \cdots & 0 & 0 \\ 1/2 & 1/2 & 0 & 0 & \cdots & \cdots & 0 & 0 \end{pmatrix}$$

Again, the sequences generated by the Markov process can be matched (within α) to the orbits generated by the tent map on the k-partitioned space.

Our considerations so far can be given a more or less optimistic interpretation according to one's point of view and temperament. The results discussed above indicate that we cannot hope to provide a generally valid test for distinguishing deterministic chaos and true randomness. This would certainly be impossible for Bernoulli systems and, to the extent that the conjecture that "most observable chaos is Bernoulli"[16] is correct, it would be generally impossible. Consequently, at least for a certain class of concrete dynamical systems, the possibility exists of representing them either as deterministic systems (plus perhaps some random, noninterfering disturbances), or as stochastic processes. The choice between the two is a matter of expedience rather than theory. In principle, a deterministic representation is superior for the purpose of explanation, but this is only true if the the resulting model is sufficiently simple and we can provide a physical interpretation of the state variables and the functional relationships among them.

Bibliography

Billingsley, P. 1965. *Ergodic Theory and Information.* New York: John Wiley.

Billingsley, P. 1979. *Probability and Measure.* New York: John Wiley.

Cornfeld, I. P., Fomin, S. V. and Sinai, Ya. G. 1982. *Ergodic Theory.* New York: Springer-Verlag.

[15]The partition $\tilde{\mathcal{P}}$ on the space of sequences Ω is again chosen so that for each sequence it returns its current value in the space $\{L, R\}$, endowed with the discrete metric

$$d(x,y) = \begin{cases} 0, & \text{if } x = y; \\ 1, & \text{if } x \neq y. \end{cases}$$

[16]See Ornstein and Weiss (1991), p.22.

Cornfeld, I. P. and Sinai, Ya. G. 2000. General ergodic theory of groups of measure preserving transformations, in Ya.G. Sinai (ed.), *Dynamical Stystems, Ergodic Theory and Applications.* Berlin: Springer-Verlag.

Doob, J. L. 1994. *Measure Theory.* New York: Springer-Verlag.

Eckmann, J. P. and Ruelle, D. 1985. Ergodic theory of chaos and strange attractors. *Reviews of Modern Physics*, 57:617–56.

Jakobson, M. V. 2000. Ergodic theory of one-dimensional mappings, in Ya. G. Sinai (ed.), *Dynamical Stystems, Ergodic Theory and Applications.* Berlin: Springer-Verlag.

Katok, A. and Hasselblatt, B. 1995. *Introduction to the Modern Theory of Dynamical Systems.* Cambridge: Cambridge University Press.

Keller, G. 1998. *Equilibrium States in Ergodic Theory.* Cambridge: Cambridge University Press.

MacKay, R. S. 1992. *Nonlinear dynmaics in economics: a review of some key features of nonlinear dynamical systems.* Florence: European University Institute, manuscript.

Mañe, R. 1987. *Ergodic Theory and Differentiable Dynamics.* Berlin: Springer-Verlag.

Oono, Y. and Osikawa, M. 1980. Chaos in nonlinear difference equations, I. *Progress of Theoretical Physics*, 64:54–67.

Ornstein, D. S. 1974. *Ergodic Theory, Randomness, and Dynamical Systems*, Yale Mathematical Monographs 5. New Haven and London: Yale University Press.

Ornstein, D. S. and Weiss, B. 1991. Statistical properties of chaotic systems. *Bulletin (New Series) of the American Mathematical Society*, 24:11-115.

Osledec, V. I. 1968. A multiplicative ergodic theorem. Liapunov characteristic numbers for dynamical systems. *Transactions of the Moscow Mathematical Society*, 19:197–221.

Radunskaya, A. 1992. *Alpha-Congruence of Bernoulli Flows and Markov Processes: Distinguishing Random and Deterministic Chaos*, PhD thesis. Palo Alto: Stanford University, unpublished.

Ruelle, D. 1989. *Chaotic Evolution and Strange Attractors.* Cambridge: Cambridge University Press.

Walters, P. 1982. *An Introduction of Ergodic Theory.* Berlin: Springer-Verlag.

Local Bifurcation Theory Applied to OLG Models

Marji Lines

Department of Statistics, University of Udine, Udine, Italy

Abstract In Section 1 a brief overview is given of the standard overlapping generations model as presented in Blanchard and Fischer (1989). The first step in all sections below is to develop the model structure with a minimum of functional hypotheses, followed by results under explicit forms for utility and/or production. In Section 2 the basic model is then extended to include a pay-as-you-go pension scheme and forward dynamics are determined from the backward equation of motion. In Section 3 the basic model is extended to allow for the accumulation of capital, leading to a second order relation for which fold bifurcations exist. In Section 4 a brief overview is given of a well-known OLG model in two dimensions, following Medio (1992) for which Neimark-Sacker bifurcations exist. In Section 5 an extension is given for the case of an environmental externality leading to a three dimensional system for which both fold and Neimark-Sacker bifurcations exist.

1 The Basic Diamond Model

The assumptions of Diamond's formulation (1965) of the overlapping generations (OLG) model are well-known and are presented below without much comment[1]. The single agent decides a two-period work-saving-consumption plan under uncertainty regarding the interest rate that will be prevailing in the retirement period and, therefore, regarding consumption in retirement. This issue is resolved by assuming that agents predict endowed with perfect foresight. Production is described by a competitive market algorithm under typical assumptions. By inserting the optimal choices of consumer/producers into the equilibrium condition for the goods market the equation of motion can be written in the capital intensity variable and qualitative dynamics determined.

[1]See Blanchard and Fischer (1989) and original articles by Allais (1947), Samuelson (1958), Diamond (1965), Blanchard (1985).

1.1 Worker–Capitalists

The problem facing the representative agent is:

$$\begin{aligned}
\max_{c_{1t}} W &= u(c_{1t}) + (1+\theta)^{-1} u(c_{2t+1}) \\
\text{subject to} & \\
c_{1t} + s_t &\leq w_t \\
c_{2t+1} &\leq (1 + E_t(r_{t+1}))s_t \\
c, w, u, r &\in \mathbb{R}^+ \quad s, \theta \in \mathbb{R}_0^+ .
\end{aligned} \tag{1.1}$$

and variables are defined as follows: c_{1t} is consumption in the working period at time t, c_{2t+1} is consumption in the retired period at time $(t+1)$, w_t is the wage in period t, s_t is saving in period t, r_{t+1} is the interest rate on one–period loans at time $t+1$, $E_t(r_{t+1}) = r_{t+1}$ and $(1+\theta)^{-1}$ is the subjective discount factor for future utility.

From the constrained maximization problem (1.1) optimal consumption, c_{1t}^*, and optimal saving, s_t^*, are expressed as functions of the wage and interest rate and we have

$$s_t^* = s_t^*(w_t, r_{t+1}). \tag{1.2}$$

Each member of the labor force N is characterized by the same utility function and subjective discount factor so that total saving in any period, S_t is simply the product $N_t s_t$. It is assumed that the labor force grows according to

$$N_t = N_0(1+n)^t \qquad -1 < n < 1 \tag{1.3}$$

where n is given exogenously.

1.2 Technology and Firms

Total output Y_t is produced by capital K_t and labor N_t in a relation defined by a function F that is homogeneous to the first degree, permitting output to be expressed in per capita terms (in intensive form, using lower case variables)

$$\begin{aligned}
Y_t &= F(K_t, N_t) \quad N_t \in \mathbb{R}^+, \quad K_t \in \mathbb{R}_0^+ \\
\frac{Y_t}{N_t} &= y_t = f(k_t).
\end{aligned}$$

The per capita production function is well–behaved and satisfies the Inada conditions

$$f'(k_t) > 0 \quad f''(k_t) < 0 \quad f(0) = 0 \quad \lim_{k \to 0} f'(k_t) = \infty \quad \lim_{k \to \infty} f'(k_t) = 0 \tag{1.4}$$

While production technology is well–defined in the standard model, the organization of production is typically somewhat ambiguous. In Diamond's words "Capital demanders are entrepreneurs who wish to employ capital for production in period $t+1$." (1965, p. 1130), but in later analysis, capital demanders are profit–maximizing firms. Essentially, in the current standard OLG model, production is operated by a profit–maximizing algorithm which solves the following problem where the price of output is set to unity.

$$\begin{aligned} \max_{N_t,K_t} P &= Y_t - w_t N_t - r_t K_t \\ \text{subject to} & \\ Y_t &\leq F(K_t, N_t). \end{aligned} \tag{1.5}$$

First order conditions for problem (1.5) give optimal levels of labor and capital as those for which respective prices are equivalent to respective marginal products. Given the production function these are:

$$\begin{aligned} MP_N = w_t &= f(k_t) - k_t f'(k_t) \\ MP_K = r_t &= f'(k_t) \end{aligned} \tag{1.6}$$

assuming, for simplicity, that the per-capita production function is net of depreciation. To be more exact, it is assumed that none of the capital stock carries over from one generation to the next so that, in a sense, depreciation is complete (more on this point in Section 3.)

The algorithm employs the optimal factor levels and distributes wages and interest. Under the hypothesis that capital is entirely owned by retirees, the firm algorithm is the mechanism by which output is distributed between the young (worker) and the retired (capitalist) generations. Thus is the classical antagonistic framework of heterogeneous cohorts (workers and capitalists) transformed into that of homogeneous cohorts, heterogeneous generations. This formal description is particularly useful for the study of transactions between generations (as it focuses exactly on their opposing interests), for example, the retirement scheme studied in Section 2.

1.3 Equilibrium Conditions and Equation of Motion

The equilibrium condition in the single good market, investment equals saving, is

$$K_{t+1} - K_t = N_t s_t - K_t \tag{1.7}$$

the RHS expressing net saving as the difference between worker's saving and retiree's dissaving (they consume all the current capital stock). The equation of motion for capital in intensive form is

$$k_{t+1} = \frac{s_t^*(w_t, r_{t+1})}{1+n}$$

or, substituting in the equilibrium factor prices (1.6),

$$k_{t+1} = \frac{s_t^*([f(k_t) - k_t f'(k_t)], [f'(k_t)])}{1+n}. \tag{1.8}$$

The relation between k_{t+1} and k_t defined by (1.8), known as the saving locus, determines the dynamics of the model but unless more explicit functional forms are assumed the implications of the saving locus for the dynamics are ambiguous.

1.4 Explicit Functions

The instantaneous utility function assumed for consumption here, and in the next two Sections, is the strictly concave, isoelastic function $u(\cdot) = \ln(\cdot)$, which meets the usual requirements of a utility function and guarantees that forward dynamics can be determined because the intertemporal substitution effect exactly cancels the income effect. In fact, the first order condition determines the optimal amount of consumption and saving in the first period as

$$\begin{aligned} c_{1t}^* &= \tfrac{1+\theta}{2+\theta} w_t \\ s_t^*(w_t) &= w_t - c_{1t}^* = \tfrac{1}{2+\theta} w_t \end{aligned} \tag{1.9}$$

and the future interest rate does not influence the consumption choice. Optimal saving is simply a (constant) proportion of the individual's income, the usual Keynesian hypothesis. Note that if the individual values utility in the retirement period as much as current utility ($\theta = 0$), half of wages are saved for the second period. If the future has no weight at all, $\theta \to \infty$ and $s_t^* \to 0$.

The production function is assumed to be a power function, first degree homogeneous

$$\begin{aligned} Y_t &= F(K_t, N_t) = K_t^\alpha N_t^{1-\alpha} \qquad 0 < \alpha < 1 \qquad N \in \mathbb{R}^+,\ K \in \mathbb{R}_0^+ \\ Y_t/N_t &= f(k_t) = k_t^\alpha \end{aligned} \tag{1.10}$$

resulting in a well-behaved production function in intensive form which satisfies the Inada conditions and, substituting in (1.6) gives the equilibrium factor prices as

$$\begin{aligned} w_t &= (1-\alpha)k_t^\alpha \\ r_t &= \alpha k_t^{\alpha-1}. \end{aligned} \tag{1.11}$$

Substituting optimal savings (1.9) in (1.8) we have the equation of motion

$$k_{t+1} = \nu k_t^\alpha \qquad \nu = \frac{1-\alpha}{(1+n)(2+\theta)}. \tag{1.12}$$

Local behavior is determined by the eigenvalue of the linearized model which, in one dimension, is simply the derivative of k_{t+1} with respect to k_t calculated at the equilibria and we have

$$\bar{k}_1 = 0 \qquad \left.\frac{dk_{t+1}}{dk_t}\right|_{\bar{k}_1} = \infty \qquad \bar{k}_2 = \nu^{\frac{1}{1-\alpha}} \qquad \left.\frac{dk_{t+1}}{dk_t}\right|_{\bar{k}_2} = \alpha.$$

The trivial equilibrium repels trajectories and given parameter assumptions, $\bar{k}_2$ attracts trajectories. Figure 1 presents a typical trajectory ($n = 0$, $\theta = 1$, $\alpha = 0.25$, $k_0 = 0.01$) in the (k_t, k_{t+1}) plane, with monotonic convergence to the positive steady state.

Moreover, there are no changes in stability. Partial effects of parameters on the steady state value are

$$\frac{\partial \bar{k}_2}{\partial n} < 0 \qquad \frac{\partial \bar{k}_2}{\partial \theta} < 0 \qquad \frac{\partial \bar{k}_2}{\partial \alpha} < 0$$

as may be observed in Figure 2, parameter values on the horizontal axis, steady state values on the vertical axis. The partial effect of the production parameter α (elasticity

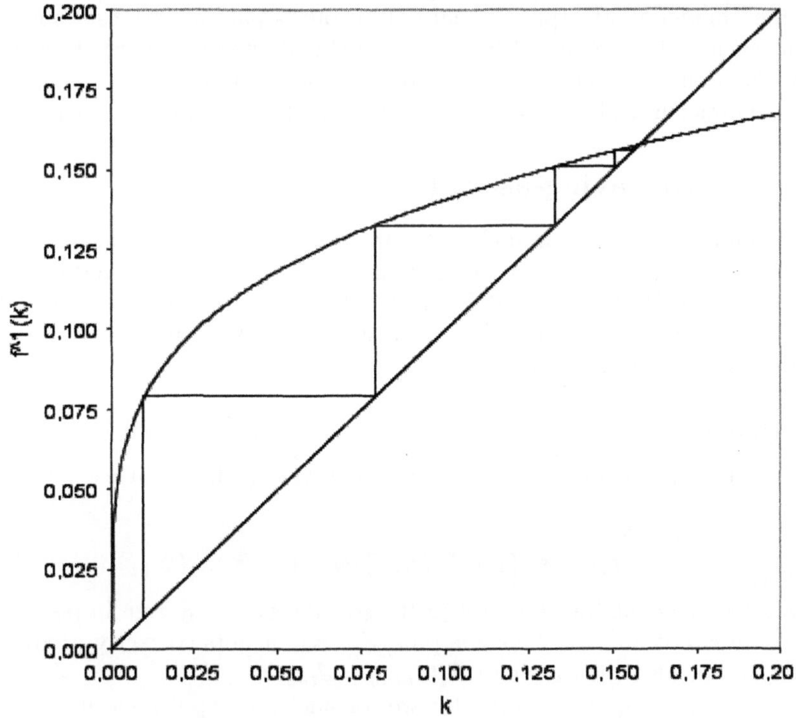

Figure 1. Monotonic convergence to $\bar{k}_2$

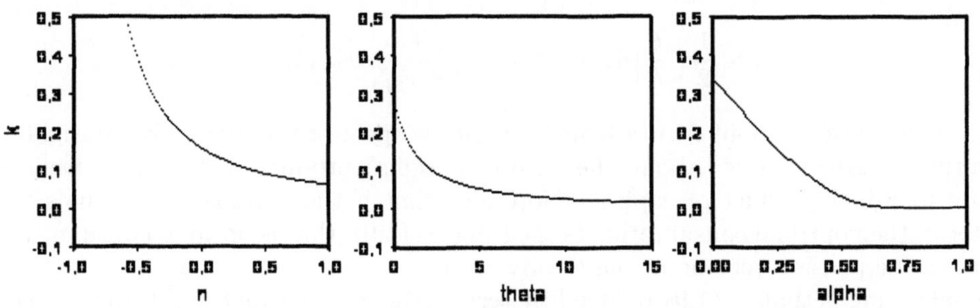

Figure 2. Equilibrium values over given parameter ranges

of production with respect to capital) may seem puzzling at first. Recall, however, that in the Diamond model all of capital's share of output is paid as interest to retirees, who use it all for consumption. Capital formation in this economy derives entirely from the saving of workers out of wages. Thus the paradox that more technologically advanced (higher α) economies have lower steady state values of (per-capita) capital.

2 Problems with Paying-as-you-go

Simple overlapping generations models are very effective in demonstrating the intertemporal tensions resulting from pay-as-you-go pension schemes. In this Section the pension-scheme framework of Blanchard and Fischer (1989) is employed to study the case for which contributions are a fixed proportion of wages. Explicit functional forms are the same as those assumed in Section 1.4.

2.1 The Model

In maximization problem (1.1) the budget constraints faced in each period are as follows:

$$\begin{aligned} c_{1t} + s_t + d_t &\leq w_t \\ c_{2t+1} &\leq (1 + E_t(r_{t+1}))s_t + (1+n)E_t(d_{t+1}) \end{aligned} \tag{2.1}$$

where d_t (d_{t+1}) is the contribution paid to the social security system in period t ($t+1$), variable range assumptions are the same plus, $d \in \mathbb{R}_0^+$, agents correctly predict not only the interest rate but also the dividend $E_t(d_{t+1}) = d_{t+1}$.

To keep the model simple and tractable we consider the hypothesis that the contribution paid for social security is a payroll tax, a fixed proportion of wages $d_t = \gamma w_t$ which, assuming the production function in (1.10) and factor prices in (1.11), gives

$$d_t = \gamma(1-\alpha)k_t^{\alpha} \tag{2.2}$$

Optimization problem (1.1), with constraints (2.1) and the natural logarithmic utility function, is solved for optimal consumption as

$$c_{1t}^* = \frac{1+\theta}{2+\theta}\left[w_t - \gamma w_t + \gamma\frac{1+n}{1+r_{t+1}}w_{t+1}\right].$$

Note that expectations about future benefits requires agents to be perfectly foresighted about future wages, that is, about the future marginal product of labor, as well as the future marginal product of capital. Note also that if the variable r_{t+1} equals the parameter n, then optimal consumption is the same as (1.9), that is optimal consumption is neutral to the pension scheme in the steady state.

Optimal saving is that of (1.9) reduced by terms related to current and future contributions:

$$s_t^* = \frac{1}{2+\theta}w_t - \frac{1}{2+\theta}d_t - \frac{(1+n)(1+\theta)}{(1+r_{t+1})(2+\theta)}d_{t+1}. \tag{2.3}$$

In the neutral case, $n = r_{t+1}$, steady state saving is $\bar{s} = \bar{w}/(2+\theta) - \bar{d}$ so that $(\partial\bar{s}/\partial\bar{d}) = -1$ and any increase in contributions for social security is counterbalanced by the exact same decrease in saving. Out of equilibrium the proportional decrease can be greater or less than one. And of course there is no reason that the population grows at the rate that invested money grows. Rather, the interesting case is that for which n is close to, or even less than, zero, as it is in many European countries.

In general the introduction of a pay-as-you-go scheme with contributions proportional to wages reduces optimal saving through two effects. The second term of (2.3) represents the reduction in saving due to the reduction in wages. Saving are reduced by an amount equal to that (discounted) part of wages deducted as a transfer to current retirees.

The third term of (2.3) represents how current agents' saving habits are influenced by the next generation's (perfectly foreseen) contributions, and several effects are at work here. This term derives from the optimal current consumption which takes into account future consumption. The proportion of retirement transfers going to future consumption is the same as the proportion of after-tax wages going to current consumption, $(1+\theta)/(2+\theta)$. That amount is then rendered a present value by making use of the predicted interest rate. Finally, the size of the transfer accruing to a single agent depends on the number of agents contributing at $(t+1)$ with respect to the number of agents retired at $t+1$, namely $(1+n)$. This term reduces saving by an amount which is larger, the higher is the growth rate, the higher is the discount rate on future consumption and the lower is the predicted interest rate. On the contrary, in economies with declining populations or higher interest rates, agents must save more to ensure the optimal retirement funds.

The effects of parameters on total optimal saving are

$$\frac{\partial s^*}{\partial n} < 0 \quad \frac{\partial s^*}{\partial r_{t+1}} > 0 \quad \frac{\partial s^*}{\partial \theta} < 0 \quad \frac{\partial s^*}{\partial \gamma} < 0.$$

where defining explicit functions allows us to give the second unambiguous result and it is clear in the last result that the tax rate reduces saving because it reduces after-tax wages.

Thus the vicious circle with negative population growth rates: more retirees with respect to workers leads to higher tax rates in order to guarantee retirees the same level of consumption as previous generations, at the same time current workers save less for their future and either the future retirees will consume less or the tax rate will have to further increase. Since capital formation in this model is financed only by workers' saving the accumulation path and steady state capital values are necessarily diminished.

2.2 Equilibria and Local Stability

With the introduction of a payroll tax on wages we have

$$k_{t+1} = \frac{s_t^* + d_t}{1+n}$$

which, after substituting for optimal saving, payroll deductions and future benefits, gives

$$k_{t+1} = \frac{1-\gamma}{(2+\theta)(1+n)} w_t - \gamma \frac{1+\theta}{(1+r_{t+1})(2+\theta)} w_{t+1}.$$

Substituting profit-maximizing values for factor prices from (1.11) and simplifying gives a much more complicated relation that that of the basic model (1.12),

$$k_t^\alpha(1-\alpha)(1-\gamma)\left(1+\alpha k_{t+1}^{\alpha-1}\right) = (1+n)\left(k_{t+1}(2+\theta)+k_{t+1}^\alpha[\alpha(2+\theta)+\gamma(1-\alpha)(1+\theta)]\right).$$

Forward dynamics are inextricable in this equation and the analysis progresses by first writing the equation of backward motion:

$$k_t = \left\{\frac{(1+n)\left(k_{t+1}(2+\theta)+k_{t+1}^\alpha[\alpha(2+\theta)+\gamma(1-\alpha)(1+\theta)]\right)}{(1-\alpha)(1-\gamma)(1+\alpha k_{t+1}^{\alpha-1})}\right\}^{\frac{1}{\alpha}}. \tag{2.4}$$

Once again, there is a trivial equilibrium at $\bar{k}_1 = 0$. Other equilibria must solve

$$-(\rho\sigma)^{-1}\bar{k}^{2\alpha-2} + \left(\alpha+\gamma(1+n)(1-\alpha)(1+\theta)\rho^{-1} - (\alpha\rho\sigma)^{-1}\right)\sigma\bar{k}^{\alpha-1} + 1 = 0$$

letting $\rho = [\alpha(1-\alpha)(1-\gamma)]^{-1}$, $\sigma = [(1+n)(2+\theta)]$ and under the parameter assumptions ρ, $\sigma > 0$. The LHS can be written as a second degree polynomial using the auxiliary variable

$$z = \bar{k}^{\alpha-1} \tag{2.5}$$

to get

$$z^2 - (\alpha\rho\sigma + \gamma(1+n)(1-\alpha)(1+\theta)\rho - \alpha^{-1})z - \rho\sigma = 0 \tag{2.6}$$

and z_2, z_3 determine the equilibria as

$$\bar{k}_{2,3} = \left(\frac{1}{z_{2,3}}\right)^{\frac{1}{1-\alpha}}. \tag{2.7}$$

The existence of real roots of (2.6) depends on the sign of the discriminant. Under the parameter assumptions the constant is negative, and Descartes' theorem guarantees that there are two real roots, one positive and one negative, let $z_2 > 0$, $z_3 < 0$. Thus we have existence of a positive, real steady state $\bar{k}_2$. A third steady state, $\bar{k}_3 = (1/z_3)^{\alpha-1}$, can be complex or real, depending on the value of α. The branch of steady states $\bar{k}_3$ will not be continuous over the parameter α (see the Appendix).

The partial effects of the parameters on the steady state value were determined by numerical simulations. Over the assumed ranges for parameters we find

$$\frac{\partial\bar{k}_2}{\partial n} < 0 \quad \frac{\partial\bar{k}_2}{\partial\theta} < 0 \quad \frac{\partial\bar{k}_2}{\partial\alpha} < 0 \quad \frac{\partial\bar{k}_2}{\partial\gamma} < 0.$$

As expected higher proportional growth rates, higher discount rates and higher payroll tax rates induce lower steady state values for per-capita capital, as does the production parameter.

Local stability is determined by the single eigenvalue of the equation of motion calculated at the steady state. Although unable to invert (2.4), numerical simulations using relevant parameter ranges suggest that the relation between k_t and k_{t+1} is one-to-one and, therefore, invertible. Then the eigenvalue determined on the basis of the backward dynamics is the reciprocal of the eigenvalue for the forward dynamics. For the trivial equilibrium we have

$$\left.\frac{\partial k_t}{\partial k_{t+1}}\right|_{\bar{k}_1} = 0 \qquad \left.\frac{\partial k_{t+1}}{\partial k_t}\right|_{\bar{k}_1} = +\infty$$

so that any positive initial value close to the origin is repelled by it.

For a given real, positive steady state k_2, $\partial k_t(\bar{k}_2)/\partial k_{t+1}$ is a long and inextricable expression. Numerical simulations, using values of $\bar{k}_2$ resulting from assuming reasonable ranges for parameters, suggest that

$$3 < \left.\frac{\partial k_t}{\partial k_{t+1}}\right|_{\bar{k}_2} < 4 \qquad 0.25 < \left.\frac{\partial k_{t+1}}{\partial k_t}\right|_{\bar{k}_2} < 0.33.$$

Once again we have monotonous dynamics. In the positive quadrant (k_t, k_{t+1}) the unique steady state at $\bar{k}_2$ is an attractor for a local neighborhood. Convergence to the steady state is monotonic and is an accumulation or a depletion path, depending on the initial conditions

$$k_0 < \bar{k}_2 \text{ accumulation path} \qquad k_0 > \bar{k}_2 \text{ depletion path.} \tag{2.8}$$

Numerical simulations support the affirmation that for initial values $0 < k_0 < 10$, $\bar{k}_2$ is indeed the unique attractor.

Appendix

The problem that arises in finding the steady state values for the equation of backward dynamics in (2.4) using (2.6) and (2.7) derives from solving models based on power functions which permit the exponent to vary over a range. For a posistive real z_2 there are no complications. For a negative real z_3, however, the fact that the exponent $1/(1-\alpha)$ takes on even and odd values as α varies means that the respective steady state values can be real, positive or negative, complex or even imaginary. The issue can be clarified by taking values over a typical range for the parameter α.

Consider the case of taking an odd root, raised to an even power, e.g., $\alpha = 0.3$ and

$$\bar{k}_3 = \left(\frac{1}{z_3}\right)^{\frac{1}{1-\alpha}} = \frac{1}{(\sqrt[7]{z_3})^{10}}.$$

Then if z is negative, $z^{1/7}$ is negative, but $z^{10/7}$ is positive, as is $\bar{k}_3$! If raised to an odd power, e.g., $\alpha = 0.32$,

$$\bar{k}_3 = \frac{1}{(\sqrt[25]{z_3})^{17}}$$

and if z is negative, so is $\bar{k}_3$.

In the case of an even root of a negative number, $\bar{k}_3$ is complex, e.g., $\alpha = 1/3 = 0.3\bar{3}$, then

$$\bar{k}_3 = \frac{1}{(\sqrt[2]{z_3})^3}$$

and in this case, $\bar{k}_3$ is either complex or imaginary if z is negative. If the imaginary number is raised to the nth even power it will become real, negative if $n/2$ is odd, positive if $n/2$ is even. (For completeness, an even root raised to an even power will always reduce to one of the above.)

If z_3 is negative, then, the analytical branch of steady states is discontinuous over α, steady states are either real, complex, or imaginary. Computer algorithms will not calculate fractional powers of negative numbers (the log or natural log will not be defined). But if α is such that $1/(1-\alpha)$ is a whole number, e.g., $\alpha = 1/2, 2/3, 3/4, \ldots$ the exponent is whole $1/(1-\alpha) = 2, 3, 4, \ldots$ respectively and $\bar{k}_3$ is real and either positive or negative (exactly the case of an odd root, 1, raised to an even or odd power). An example leading to a spurious, shadow limit set is given in Section 4, Figure 6.

3 Genuine Accumulation

The basic Diamond model is an excellent tool for studying phenomena depending on intergenerational transfers if one can assume that each retired generation consumes all of its savings or, equivalently, each new generation replaces the entire capital stock employed by the previous generation. Some alternative frameworks are developed in the literature on altruism and inheritances (see, for example, Michel and Pestieau, 1998). In what follows we take another point of view. Suppose, instead, that in the initial periods a portion of the capital stock is not assigned to retirees. Potential recipients of the non-retiree's part could be pure capitalists, entrepreneurs, speculators, or any other agents whose consumption patterns can be ignored in a first approximation (the extreme of the classical saving hypothesis) or the firm algorithm which, in addition to its other tasks, reinvests any of capital's share remaining after distribution to retirees. The homogeneous cohorts vision is maintained by the latter assumption, but violated by the former. In either case, no further assumptions are necessary, as long as the *other* owners of capital refrain from consuming, the economy will be characterized by *genuine* capital accumulation, that is, some part of capital remains from one period to the next. It will be shown how the emergence of capitalism in a context of few retirees, high discount rates and/or subsistence wages is more credibly explained in such a framework.

3.1 The Model and Equilibria

Let us relax the assumption that the value of capital stock is totally consumed at the end of every period. Then, on the RHS of the equilibrium condition (1.7), total saving is replaced by $Y_t - C_{1t}$ and K_t is replaced by $C_{2t} = S_{t-1}$ defined as total dissaving of the retired generation. Under the genuine accumulation assumption, $C_{2t} < K_t$ and the equilibrium condition is

$$K_{t+1} - K_t = Y_t - C_{1t} - C_{2t}. \tag{3.1}$$

If all of capital's share of production goes to retirees $C_{2t} = K_t$ and the model reduces to the standard version. Condition (3.1) can be written as

$$\begin{aligned} K_{t+1} - K_t &= r_t K_t + w_t N_t - N_t c_t - (1 + r_t) N_{t-1} s_{t-1} \\ &= N_t s_t + r_t K_t - (1 + r_t) N_{t-1} s_{t-1} \end{aligned} \tag{3.2}$$

making use of Euler's theorem for a first-degree homogeneous production function.

In an accumulation framework, where some capital stock remains from period to period, it is useful to explicitly introduce a depreciation or obsolescence factor so that the effects of varying the rate of depreciation can be studied directly. Introducing radioactive decay depreciation δK in equation (3.2) and expressing it in per capita terms we have

$$k_{t+1} = \frac{1+r_t-\delta}{1+n}k_t + \frac{s_t}{1+n} - \frac{1+r_t}{(1+n)^2}s_{t-1}.$$

After substituting optimal marginal products (1.11) and saving function (1.9), the equation of motion for the genuine accumulation model can be written as:

$$k_{t+1} = \beta(1-\delta)k_t + (\alpha\beta+\nu)k_t^\alpha - \beta\nu k_{t-1}^\alpha - \alpha\beta\nu k_t^{\alpha-1}k_{t-1}^\alpha \tag{3.3}$$

with $\beta = (1+n)^{-1}$, $\nu = \beta(1-\alpha)/(2+\theta)$, and given the parameter assumptions $\beta > 0$, $\nu > 0$. In comparison to (1.12) there are now terms with k_{t-1} and the equation of motion is not a simple power function. As usual, there is a trivial steady state at $\bar{k}_1 = 0$. The other equilibria can be found by solving for the auxiliary variables z as defined in (2.5) as roots of $\alpha\nu z^2 - (\alpha+n\nu)z + (n+\delta) = 0$. Then

$$\begin{aligned} \bar{k}_{2,3} &= \left(\tfrac{1}{z_{2,3}}\right)^{\frac{1}{1-\alpha}} \\ z_{2,3} &= \tfrac{1}{2\alpha\nu}\left[(\alpha+n\nu) \pm \sqrt{(\alpha+n\nu)^2 - 4(n+\delta)\alpha\nu}\right]. \end{aligned} \tag{3.4}$$

In this case the solutions for $z_{2,3}$ can be real or complex. Since roots of complex numbers are complex, a condition for the existence of a non–trivial steady state is that $z_{2,3}$ be real, that is

$$\delta < \frac{(\alpha - n\nu)^2}{4\alpha\nu}. \tag{3.5}$$

However, even if (3.5) is satisfied but the labor population is allowed to decline and $-1 < n < -\delta$, Descartes' theorem again gives $z_2 > 0$, $z_3 < 0$ and we have steady state at the origin, a positive real steady state, and a third steady state that can be either complex or real valued. For $n > -\delta$, if (3.5) is satisfied, $z_2, z_3, \bar{k}_2, \bar{k}_3 \in \mathbb{R}^+$.

There are 4 parameters involved in the determination of the steady states: α, n, θ, and δ. Surfaces for $\bar{k}_2$, the smaller value, and $\bar{k}_3$, the larger, setting $\theta = 1$, $\delta = 0.1$, are shown in Figure 3 left and right, respectively, over a wide range for the technology coefficient and labor growth rate. Note that for non-zero depreciation rates some combinations of parameters imply complex values (where surfaces are truncated), confirming that for completeness one should explicitly model depreciation. For $\delta = 0$ the surfaces are real over the ranges of parameter values considered.

3.2 Local Stability and Bifurcations

Setting $x_t = k_{t-1}$ the second order equation in (3.3) is written as the first order system:

$$\begin{aligned} k_{t+1} &= \beta(1-\delta)k_t + \big(\alpha\beta+\nu\big)k_t^\alpha - \beta\nu x_t^\alpha - \alpha\beta\nu k_t^{\alpha-1}x_t^\alpha \\ x_{t+1} &= k_t. \end{aligned} \tag{3.6}$$

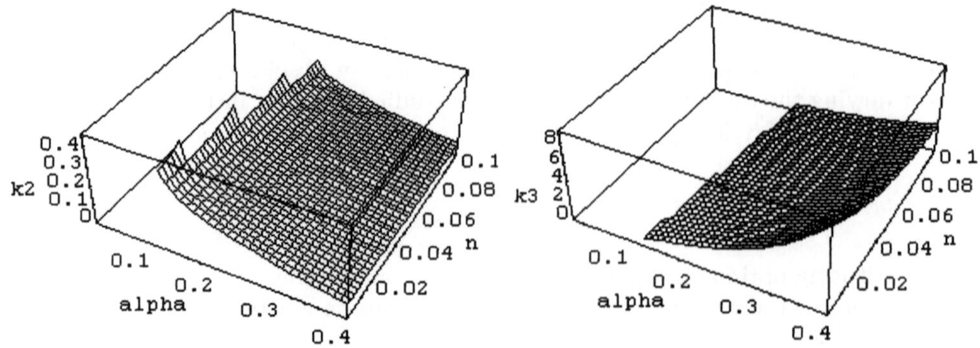

Figure 3. Steady state values in parameter space: left, $\bar{k}_2$; right, $\bar{k}_3$.

and local stability properties depend on the eigenvalues of the linearized system represented by the Jacobian matrix J

$$J = \begin{pmatrix} J_{11} & J_{12} \\ J_{21} & J_{22} \end{pmatrix}$$

where

$$\begin{aligned} J_{11} &= \beta(1-\delta) + \alpha(\alpha\beta + \nu)k_t^{\alpha-1} + \alpha\beta\nu(1-\alpha)k_t^{\alpha-2}x_t^{\alpha} \\ J_{12} &= -\alpha\beta\nu x_t^{\alpha-1} - \alpha^2\beta\nu k_t^{\alpha-1}x_t^{\alpha-1} \\ J_{21} &= 1 \\ J_{22} &= 0. \end{aligned}$$

At $(\bar{k}_1, \bar{x}_1) = (0,0)$ the Jacobian, as well as the dynamic equation of the model, are undefined. However, inserting near–zero values for k ($k = 10^{-5}$ and $k = 10^{-7}$) into the Jacobian gives one large eigenvalue ($7.2x10^5$ and $4.5x10^8$, respectively), and a second eigenvalue less than unity (0.429 for both). As for the basic Diamond model with explicit functions and the OLG with pay-as-you-go retirement scheme, the origin is locally unstable.

If the non–contraction condition given by (3.5) is satisfied and $n > -\delta$, two positive steady states exist and the Jacobian and its eigenvalues can be calculated. In Figure 4 examples of the branches of $\bar{k}_2$ and $\bar{k}_3$ are provided for $n = 0.1$, $\theta = 1$, over $\alpha \in (0.001, 0.3)$ for 4 values of the depreciation rate $\delta = 0, 0.05, 0.1, 0.15$. Higher values are the $\bar{k}_3$ stable nodes, lower values are the $\bar{k}_2$ saddles and at the point at which the two branches converge and disappear, the steady states $\bar{k}_{2,3}$ become complex. For a given value of α, if the initial values are less than the lower branch in Figure 4 the economy contracts, that is, trajectories from positive initial values tend rapidly towards negative infinity. For any given parameter set, the take–off condition for initial capital intensity in system (3.6) is $k_0, k_1 > \bar{k}_2$. If this is satisfied and initial values are below [above] those of the stable node, capital accumulates [declines] to k_3:

$$\begin{array}{c} k_0, k_1 < \bar{k}_2 \text{ contraction trap} \\ \bar{k}_2 < k_0, k_1 < \bar{k}_3 \text{ accumulation to } \bar{k}_3 \\ k_0, k_1 > \bar{k}_3 \text{ decline to } \bar{k}_3. \end{array} \tag{3.7}$$

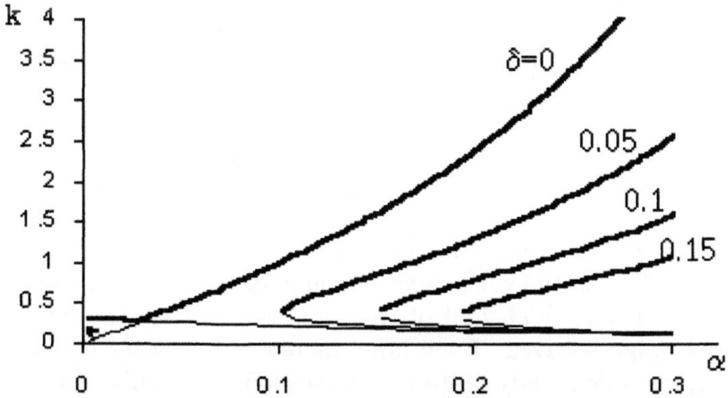

Figure 4. Analytical bifurcation diagram

Bifurcations occur where equilibria become nonhyperbolic (an eigenvalue of J is singular) as one or more parameters are varied. For a system in two dimensions there are three conditions that must be simultaneously met to ensure that both eigenvalues remain within the unit circle (see Chapter 1, Section 8) For the equilibria $\bar{k}_{2,3}$, condition (*i*) is always satisfied, eliminating the possibility of a flip bifurcation. Conditions (*ii*) and (*iii*) are not easily proven analytically. However condition (*iii*) is satisfied over the combinations of parameter ranges studied and would seem to be always satisfied over common ranges assumed in the literature for the parameters, eliminating Neimark bifurcations.

That leaves only condition (*ii*) and the possibility of a generic fold bifurcation, which was signaled in the analysis of equilibria and supported by simulations. The stability properties of the branches of steady states $\bar{k}_2$ and $\bar{k}_3$ are virtually unchanged by varying n and α over ranges typically assumed in economic models. That is not the case for δ and θ.

At $\delta = 0$ the branches observed in Figure 4 are seen as an extreme case of the fold bifurcation, actually back–to–back fold bifurcations with pieces of left hand wings of other branches visible near the origin. As the rate of depreciation increases, the range of α admitting of real, non–trivial equilibria diminishes until by a value of $\delta = 0.25$ no real steady state branches appear for the indicated range of α (e.g., steady states calculated at $\delta = \alpha = 0.3$ are complex–valued). For non–zero depreciation, if values of α are to the left of the fold bifurcation point, the unique equilibrium is the origin, a saddle point which sends trajectories to $-\infty$. For those combinations of parameter values the only dynamical behavior possible for the model economy is collapse. In order to avoid the contraction trap high depreciation rates must be accompanied by high values of α, the elasticity of output with respect to the capital input.

Numerical simulations suggest that to the right of the bifurcation point positive steady states attract over at least $(\bar{k}_2, 10^6)$. If the initial capital intensity values satisfy the take–off condition $k_0, k_1 > \bar{k}_2$, growth to a steady state is assured. Under the standard parameter set used in Figure 4, $\bar{k}_2 = 0.16$, $\bar{k}_3 = 1.15$ and initial values must be larger than one–seventh of the steady state value for take–off. An early capitalism scenario of low–α technology ($\alpha = 0.05$) and a high discount rate ($\theta = 20$) gives a similar ratio. On the other hand, a technology transfer scenario of high–α technology ($\alpha = 0.25$) combined with a medium–high discount rate ($\theta = 10$, or 8% of earnings are saved) gives $\bar{k}_2 = 0.02$ very low, and 2 orders of magnitude smaller than $\bar{k}_3 = 1.30$, making it easier to satisfy the take–off conditions. Numerical simulations suggest that over typical ranges,

$$\frac{\partial \bar{k}_2}{\partial \alpha} < 0, \frac{\partial \bar{k}_3}{\partial \alpha} > 0 \quad \frac{\partial \bar{k}_2}{\partial n}, \frac{\partial \bar{k}_3}{\partial n} < 0 \quad \frac{\partial \bar{k}_2}{\partial \theta} < 0, \frac{\partial \bar{k}_3}{\partial \theta} > 0 \quad \frac{\partial \bar{k}_2}{\partial \delta} \approx 0, \frac{\partial \bar{k}_3}{\partial \delta} < 0$$

where, in particular, the take–off value is greatly influenced by θ.

Recall that $(1+\theta)^{-1}$ is the subjective discount factor for utility in the retired phase and varies from $\theta = 0$ for which half of the wage is saved for the future, to $\theta = \infty$ for which none of the wage is saved. Even large increases in θ after $\theta = 1$ have little effect on the value of the stable steady state $\bar{k}_3$. However in the limit, $\theta = \infty$, equation (3.3) reduces to

$$k_{t+1} = \frac{1-\delta}{1+n} k_t + \frac{\alpha}{1+n} k_t^{\alpha},$$

a first order difference equation with steady states at $\bar{k}_1 = 0$, $\bar{k}_2 = ((\delta + n)/\alpha)^{\frac{1}{\alpha - 1}}$, the latter always real if $n > -\delta$. Then it can be shown that the origin is a repellor. As long as $\bar{k}_2$ is real, its eigenvalue is less than unity and it is a local attractor. As for its basin of attraction, simulations suggest that any initial value less than $\bar{k}_2$ and not exactly 0 is attracted to it, as well as all higher initial values used in simulation (up to 10^6).

That is to say, even if workers save nothing for their retirement phase, there is a real, positive, stable capital intensity to which the economy moves from any positive initial value. In such a case, workers do not save and supply funds for capital and all of capital's share goes to firms who drive the accumulation process. This aspect allows greater flexibility in the model and makes it much more suitable for explaining the early phase of capital accumulation.

Essentially, what differentiates the genuine accumulation model (3.3) from the standard model (1.12) is a relaxing of the initial conditions. It can be shown that if $k_1 \leq \nu k_0^{\alpha}$, the framework reduces to the standard model for which retirees own the whole of the capital stock. The condition is sensitive to the discount parameter, so that for high discounting (as one might expect in an early phase of capitalism), firms will almost surely be endowed with some of the capital stock and the return on this stock is entirely re-invested.

4 An OLG Model with Disutility

In this section the OLG model introduced in Grandmont (1985) and formalized in Reichlin (1986), and Medio (1992) is introduced. This model differs from the basic Diamond model of Section 1 in that the young agent defers consumption to the second period and derives disutility from work (or equivalently, utility from leisure), and that output is produced with capital formed in the previous period.

4.1 The Model

The economy, at any moment in time, is composed of a young generation that derives disutility from work $v_1(l_t)$ in the first period of its life, defers consumption and derives utility from consumption $u(c_{t+1})$ in the second period of its life. There is a single commodity that can be consumed or used in production, R_t is the interest factor $(1 + r_t)$. The agent who is young at time t faces the following optimization problem:

$$\begin{aligned} \max_{l_t} W &= u(c_{t+1}) - v(l_t) \\ &\text{subject to} \\ k_t &\leq w_t l_t \\ c_{t+1} &\leq R_{t+1} k_t \\ c, w, u, v, R, l &\in \mathbb{R}^+, \; k \in \mathbb{R}_0^+. \end{aligned} \tag{4.1}$$

in which $s_t = k_t$ is directly indicated.

This problem differs from optimization problem (1.1) in that the control variable is labor, and the objective functional includes the disutility of work but only deferred consumption. The representative young agent allocates a given amount of the total time available $\hat{l}$ (say 24 hours a day) between work l_t (and thereby consumption in old age) and leisure $\hat{l} - l_t$. The functions $u(\cdot)$ and $v(\cdot)$ are continuous on $[0, \infty]$. The utility function satisfies the usual hypotheses $u'(c_{t+1}) > 0$, $u''(c_{t+1}) < 0$. The function v describes disutilty, which not only increases in labor, but also increases at an increasing rate $v'(l_t) > 0$, $v''(l_t) > 0$ such that $\lim_{l_t \to \infty} v'(l_t) = +\infty$, $\lim_{l_t \to 0} v'(l_t) = 0$.

First-order conditions from maximization problem (4.1) are

$$\begin{aligned} u'(c_{t+1}) \frac{\partial c_{t+1}}{\partial l_t} &= v'(l_t) \\ c_{t+1} &= R_{t+1} w_t l_t. \end{aligned} \tag{4.2}$$

Substituting the constraint into the first equation of (4.2) we have the necessary and sufficient condition for the existence of an optimal path $\{c^*, l^*\}_t$

$$\mathcal{U}(c_{t+1}) = \mathcal{V}(l_t) \;\text{ where }\; \mathcal{U}(c_{t+1}) = c_{t+1} u'(c_{t+1}), \;\; \mathcal{V}(l_t) = l_t v'(l_t) \tag{4.3}$$

which determines an equation of forward motion for consumption if $\mathcal{U}^{-1}$ exists

$$c^*_{t+1} = f(l^*_t) \qquad f = \mathcal{U}^{-1}[\mathcal{V}(l_t)]. \tag{4.4}$$

Per–capita technology is assumed to be approximated by a Leontief relation in which output is produced by this period's labor, l_t, applied to the capital formed in the previous period,

$$y_t = \min[l_t, bk_{t-1}] \tag{4.5}$$

where b is the output produced per unit of capital and $b > 1$ for a viable economy. The coefficient of labor has been set at unity. Constant coefficient production is a simple relation which might be considered a short run description of the production process. Assuming full employment of all factors, $y_t = l_t = bk_{t-1}$. If the equilibrium condition in the goods market is satisfied, forward dynamics in l_t are determined by

$$l_{t+1} = b(l_t - c_t). \tag{4.6}$$

The resulting model system is given by (4.4) and (4.6).

4.2 Explicit Utility

Assume that the isoelastic utility and disutility functions are

$$u(c_{t+1}) = \frac{c_{t+1}^{\alpha}}{\alpha} \quad 0 < \alpha < 1 \quad v(l_t) = \frac{l_t^{\beta}}{\beta} \quad \beta > 1 \tag{4.7}$$

which, given first–order conditions and purely competitive market conditions, lead to forward dynamics for c_t as:

$$c_{t+1} = l_t^{\frac{\beta}{\alpha}}. \tag{4.8}$$

The model representing the economy (see Medio, 1992 for more details) is composed of equations (4.6), (4.8):

$$\begin{aligned} c_{t+1} &= l_t^{\frac{\beta}{\alpha}} \\ l_{t+1} &= b(l_t - c_t) \end{aligned} \tag{4.9}$$

System (4.9) has two steady states $(\bar{c}, \bar{l})$. The trivial $E_1 = (0,0)$ is again an unstable saddle point. It can be shown that a second equilibrium E_2 exists in the positive quadrant. The stability of this steady state is studied through the stability inequalities for a second order system of difference equations given in Chapter 1, Section 8, and the Jacobian matrix calculated at E_2 is

$$J = \begin{pmatrix} 0 & \frac{\beta}{\alpha}\frac{b-1}{b} \\ -b & b \end{pmatrix}.$$

Under the parameter assumptions, (i) and (ii) are always satisfied, eliminating flip and fold bifurcations. Setting $\mu = \beta/\alpha$, if condition (iii) is satisfied, $\mu(b-1) - 1 < 0$ and E_2 is stable. At the parameter values for which condition (iii) holds as an equality E_2 becomes unstable and a Neimark bifurcation occurs. For stability of E_2, b and μ must be close to 1. Further, we have that the smaller the production of non–replacement capital, the higher can be the ratio between the exponent of labor disutility and the exponent of consumption utility, while maintaining stability.

Let the stability frontier (where $\det J = 1$) be defined by $h_1(b, \mu) = \mu b - \mu - 1 = 0$. The change from real to complex eigenvalues occurs at what is known as the flutter condition, in this case $h_2 = \frac{b^2}{b-1} - 4\mu = 0$. The dynamics over parameter space can be summarized as in Figure 5. If b and μ are in the area labelled x, eigenvalues are real and less than 1 in absolute value (transient motion is monotonic towards the steady state). In the parameter subspace y the flutter boundary has been crossed, eigenvalues are complex with modulus less than 1 (damped oscillations towards the steady state). At values on the stability frontier h_1 a Neimark bifurcation takes place and the steady state becomes unstable. Near the bifurcation point an invariant circle appears which may be attracting or not, and whose dynamics may be periodic or quasi–periodic. In this case, numerical simulations suggest that the invariant circle is indeed attracting and that there are both types of cyclic behavior, depending on parameter values. For values further to the right of the stability frontier the invariant circle also loses stability and there is no finite attracting invariant set.

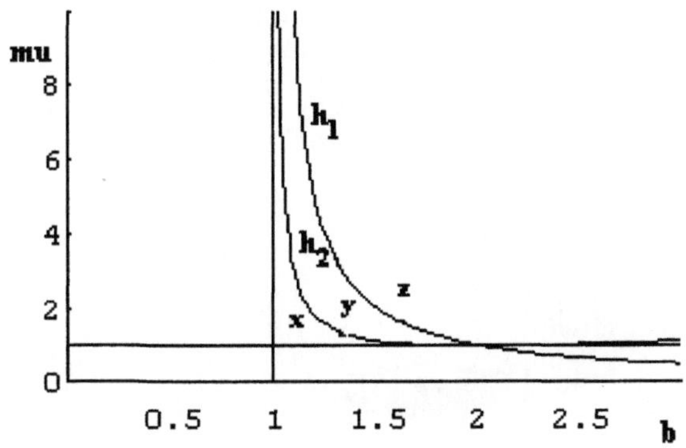

Figure 5. Dynamics over parameter space for system (4.9)

Obviously the model makes sense (and is defined) over positive values for consumption and labor. If the ranges of these variables are not constrained in simulations one may observe the spurious limit sets mentioned in the appendix to Section 2. For example, if the exponent $\beta/\alpha \equiv \mu$ is an odd power of an odd root (say $\mu = 7$), a shadow invariant curve appears in the fourth quadrant, while the relevant invariant curve is in the first, see Figure 6, where the basins of attraction are also provided.

5 A Pollution Externality

In this section the modelling of utility trade-offs is extended to include not only that between production (consumption) and leisure, but also between production (consumption) and the environment. While it is true that fossil fuels have greatly increased consumption levels, it is also apparent that the negative energy externality can no longer be ignored. The important intertemporal equilibrium aspects of these trade-offs in the context of the environment have been given much attention in the optimal growth literature in the framework of a central planner. In this section the environmental externality is introduced into the basic market economy described by the OLG model in Section 4 where there is no central planner or coordinating authority to address the tragedy of the commons.

In the model formalized in Section 5.1 individuals maximize utility by choosing their optimal labor supply and consumption, the latter being inseparable from the environ-

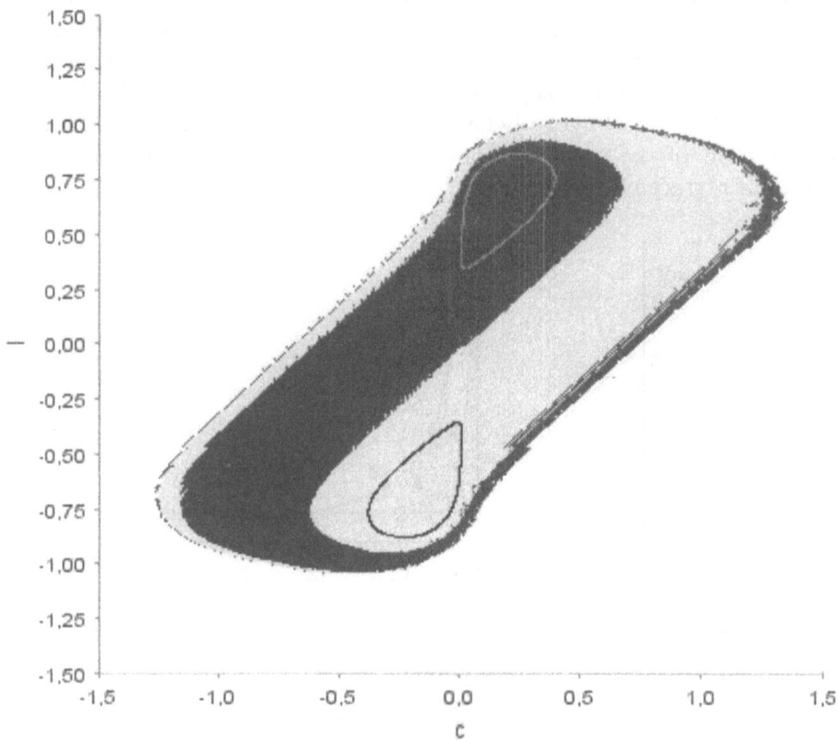

Figure 6. An invariant curve and its shadow.

mental quality, which is affected by production. The model treats a particular type of production externality, the emission of substances that in part remain and accumulate in the atmosphere. Environmental quality is measured in terms of pre-industrial levels of atmospheric concentrations following the scientific literature on global warming and the economic literature on the costs of global warming.

5.1 The Optimization Problem

As in Section 4.1 the representative agent works l_t and receives a wage per unit of labor w_t in the first period, but also derives disutility from that work $-v(l_t)$. The agent derives utility from second period consumption c_{t+1} which is inseparable from the disutility of a pollution index A_t. The maximization problem is the same as (4.1) except that utility is also a function of A_t so that welfare to be maximized is $u(c_{t+1}, A_t) - v(l_t)$.

The representative young agent allocates time available between work and leisure, taking into account the fact that utility of future consumption may be degraded by pollution. The assumption is that an agent is less inclined to work now for the sake of greater availability of goods and services in old age, if the agent expects these to be consumed in a degraded environment. The joys of travelling, of a beach-house, a motor home, a garden plot, or golf club membership, for example, are devalued by the direct effects of the pollution as well as its indirect effects on global warming.

The environmental index, A_t, represents *additional* atmospheric concentration of some greenhouse gas, such as CO_2 with respect to its pre-industrial level. When the concentration of airborne pollutants is not much higher than the pre-industrial level it may be adequate to assume that utility from consumption is independent of atmospheric pollution, but eventually the cross effects cannot be ignored. This interdependence is formalized through a variable discount rate θ, the ratio of the current pollution level A_t to the pre-industrial concentration, κ, $\theta(A_t) = A_t/\kappa$. Then, $1 + \theta(A_t)$ represents the multiples of pre-industrial concentration, the reciprocal of which is the discount factor for retirement consumption

$$\frac{u(c_{t+1})}{1+\theta(A_t)}. \tag{5.1}$$

In the case of CO_2, $\kappa = 280$ ppmv (parts per million by volume), A is currently averaging 96 (Conway, 2003), giving the discount factor around 0.75.

A common measure of changing concentrations used in the climate change literature is that of doublings of concentrations, $\log_2(1+\theta(A_t))$. There is a great deal of uncertainty associated with predicting consequences of doublings, but certainly after two doublings of pre-industrial CO_2 concentrations (to a level of 1120 ppmv, $A = 840$) the biosphere would no longer be able to absorb emissions. Much of the current policy discussion is driven by the estimate that to stabilize total CO_2 levels in a desired interval between 350 and 750ppmv ($70 < A_t < 470$), global anthropogenic emissions must drop below 1990 levels. These considerations suggest that an upper limit for A_t around 1000 is reasonable, giving a range for the environmental discount factor as $0.25 \leq (1+\theta)^{-1} \leq 1$.

In a purely competitive market economy the N (N large) individuals cannot singly affect the price, yet the price-adjustment mechanism depends on their individual choices through aggregate excess demand. In this model agents are "environment-takers", they cannot singly affect the environment, yet the accumulating pollution mechanism depends on their individual choices through the aggregate labor supply. The individual agent is aware that his/her choice has an infinitesimal effect on the atmosphere and does not consider the effect of that choice on the atmosphere in the optimization problem. Therefore the environmental index enters the problem only through the discount factor and substituting (5.1) for $u(\cdot)$ in (4.1) and using the definitions in (4.3) of $\mathcal{U}$ and $\mathcal{V}$ we have

$$\frac{\mathcal{U}(c_{t+1})}{1+\theta(A_t)} = \mathcal{V}(l_t) \qquad c_{t+1} = f(l_t, A_t) \qquad f = \mathcal{U}^{-1}[(1+\theta(A_t))\mathcal{V}(l_t)] \tag{5.2}$$

if $\mathcal{U}^{-1}$ exists.

5.2 Production and Accumulating Emissions

Per capita technology is again represented by fixed coefficient production, see (4.5), but it is further assumed that production requires the input factor energy, represented as emissions, z_t, the production externality. Per-capita output is then

$$x_t = \min[l_t, bk_{t-1}, \rho z_t]$$

where 1, b and ρ define, respectively, the per capita output produced per one unit of labor, capital and emissions, $\rho > 0$ and $b > 1$. The parameter ρ indicates how "green" is the production technology and plays an important role in the existence of sustainable equilibria. As in much of the environmental economics literature emissions are a positive function of the capital stock. Assuming full employment of all factors, production is determined as

$$x_t = l_t = bk_{t-1} = \rho z_t. \tag{5.3}$$

Other assumptions are the same as those in Section 4.1: the market is perfectly competitive, factors of production receive their marginal products, capital stock lasts only one period, equilibrium in the goods market is satisfied.

At the beginning of each period the level of additional accumulated emissions is equivalent to that part of the previous stock which has not been taken up by the natural sinks, plus current emissions. Let m indicate uptake by the ocean and marine and terrestrial biospheres as a proportion of accumulated anthropogenic emissions. Then $(1-m)$ indicates the airborne fraction emissions, that proportion of accumulated emissions which remain in the atmosphere after one period. To the airborne fraction must be added concentrations due to production. Let the population be constant at N. Current emissions are aggregated as $Z_t = z_t N_t$ and converted by the factor ϕ from gigatons of carbon emissions into ppmv concentrations. In this formulation the accumulation process of additional atmospheric concentrations is

$$A_{t+1} = (1-m)A_t + \phi N \frac{l_t}{\rho} \qquad 0 \leq m \leq 1 \tag{5.4}$$

where z_t, has been substituted by l_t/ρ using (5.3).

In environmental economic modelling, m is often hypothesized a fixed value. This assumption of constancy could be considered a linear approximation of a nonlinear relation, adequate for some ranges (such as low pollution levels), inadequate for others. For example, the IPCC (1994) report estimates that the airborne fraction of CO_2 emissions on a century time-scale varies from $15-25\%$, at 450 ppmv, to $30-40\%$, at 750 ppmv. That is, the carbon sinks are not able to uptake a constant part of emissions independently of the level of emissions. It seems plausible that at some extreme value the sinks would cease functioning altogether. A general formulation of this hypothesis is a simple threshold mechanism such as

$$m(A_t) = 1 - \frac{A_t}{\hat{A}}$$

where $\hat{A}$ represents the maximum anthropogenic additions to atmospheric concentrations for which non-atmospheric sinks and storages continue to remove a portion of emissions. When A_t reaches the maximum level ($A_t = \hat{A}$) there is no more uptake ($m = 0$), and we consider that only values of $A_t < \hat{A}$ are interesting. When there are no emissions from human activity ($A_t = 0$), the natural system is in equilibrium at its preindustrial level and the uptake is complete ($m = 1$). Under this assumption for m, the accumulation process is

$$A_{t+1} = \frac{A_t^2}{\hat{A}} + \phi N \frac{l_t}{\rho} \qquad A_t < \hat{A}. \tag{5.5}$$

5.3 The Models and Equilibrium

Two models are proposed, (5.6a) and (5.6b), differing only in the formulation of the "self-cleansing" activity of the atmosphere, respectively, proportional and threshold uptake. Combining equations (5.3), (4.7) and (5.4) or (5.5) and letting $\xi = \phi N$, we obtain

$$\begin{aligned} c_{t+1} &= f(l_t, A_t) \\ l_{t+1} &= b(l_t - c_t) \\ A_{t+1} &= g(A_t) + \xi \tfrac{l_t}{\rho} \qquad g_a = (1-m)A_t \quad g_b = \tfrac{A_t^2}{\hat{A}} \end{aligned} \tag{5.6}$$

where f is defined in (5.2). Under the assumptions on v and u indicated above, the origin is a saddle point for both models. There exists a second steady state in the positive orthant for (5.6a), and possibly two for (5.6b):

$$\begin{aligned} \bar{c} &= \mathcal{U}^{-1}[(1+\theta(\bar{A}))\mathcal{V}(\bar{l})] \\ \bar{l} &= \left(\tfrac{b}{b-1}\right)\bar{c} \\ \bar{A}_a &= \left(\tfrac{\xi}{m\rho}\right)\left(\tfrac{b}{b-1}\right)\bar{c} \\ \bar{A}_{b1,2} &= \tfrac{1}{2}\left(\hat{A} \pm \sqrt{\hat{A}^2 - 4\hat{A}\left(\tfrac{\xi}{\rho}\right)\left(\tfrac{b}{b-1}\right)\bar{c}}\right) \end{aligned} \tag{5.7}$$

where $\bar{A}_{b1,2}$ are real and positive if the discriminant is non-negative. The first two values, $\bar{c}$ and $\bar{l}$, are optimal values for the agent (*per capita*). The environmental index is instead an aggregate value and expressed in ppmv additional atmospheric concentration resulting from aggregate production.

In (5.6a) the atmosphere continues to absorb the same proportion of accumulants, independently of the level, and the steady state $(\bar{c}, \bar{l}, \bar{A})$ always exists, although some parameter sets may imply unrealistic concentrations. The higher the steady state pollution the lower are the values of steady state consumption and labor supply. Increasing the energy efficiency of production or the uptake proportion, ceteris paribus, reduces steady state pollution, that is, $\partial \bar{A}_a/\partial \rho < 0$ and $\partial \bar{A}_a/\partial m > 0$.

On the other hand, in (5.6b), with dependency between efficiency of the biosphere and level of accumulants, a positive real steady state may not exist. The discriminant for $\bar{A}_b$ depends on the relative values of the threshold and on the production coefficient for emissions. The existence of real equilibria is more likely the higher is the threshold value and the output per emission coefficient. That means the effects of the environmental parameters $\hat{A}$ and ρ are inversely related, the cleaner technology, the lower can be the maximum level of atmospheric concentrates and still maintain a steady state. A fold bifurcation is to be expected at combinations of parameter values for which the discriminant is null and $\bar{A}_{b1} = \bar{A}_{b2}$. One of the steady states is a locally stable node, the other a locally unstable saddle point. On the other side of the fold bifurcation no equilibria exist for the environmental variable and because feedback from the environment passes through the utility function influencing steady state consumption and labor, existence of equilibria in the system as a whole is precluded.

Any further analytical study of stability or bifurcation of the model with implicit utility functions runs into the problem of dimensionality. For example, demonstrating the existence of complex eigenvalues by means of the Cardano-Tartaglia formula is impossible in this case.

5.4 Explicit Utility with Linear Uptake

Substituting the isoelastic functions (4.7) in (5.2), system (5.6a) becomes

$$\begin{aligned} c_{t+1} &= l_t^{\frac{\beta}{\alpha}}(1+A_t/\kappa)^{\frac{1}{\alpha}} \\ l_{t+1} &= b(l_t - c_t) \\ A_{t+1} &= (1-m)A_t + \xi\frac{l_t}{\rho} \end{aligned} \tag{5.8}$$

Apart from the saddle point at the origin a second equilibrium exists in the positive orthant with

$$(\bar{c},\bar{l}) = \left(\left(\frac{b-1}{b}\right)^{\frac{\beta}{\beta-\alpha}}\left(1+\theta(\bar{A})\right)^{\frac{-1}{\beta-\alpha}}, \left(\frac{b-1}{b}\right)^{\frac{\alpha}{\beta-\alpha}}\left(1+\theta(\bar{A})\right)^{\frac{-1}{\beta-\alpha}}\right) \tag{5.9}$$

depending on the steady state level of additional atmospheric concentrates, $\bar{A}$, which is the solution of

$$\bar{A} = \frac{\mu(\bar{A})}{m} \quad \text{where } \mu(\bar{A}) = \left(\frac{\xi}{\rho}\right)\left(\frac{b-1}{b}\right)^{\frac{\alpha}{\beta-\alpha}}\left(1+\theta(\bar{A})\right)^{\frac{-1}{\beta-\alpha}} \tag{5.10}$$

Letting $h(\bar{A}) = \bar{A}$ and $j(\bar{A})$ be the RHS of equation (5.10) the steady state value of atmospheric pollutants is determined as the intersection of h and j, see Figure 7, left[2]. Equilibrium values $\bar{A}$ for $\rho = 0.001$, $\rho = 0.002$, $\rho = 0.02$, $\rho = 0.2$ (barely visible) are approximately 375, 245, 45 and 5 ppmv giving discounts at 0.43, 0.53, 0.83, 1, respectively. A steady state exists because $h(0) < j(0)$ and for sufficiently large A, say A_{big}, $h(A_{big}) > j(A_{big})$, so that by continuity arguments, there must be at least one intersection. The steady state is also unique, $h(\bar{A})$is positively sloped and $j(\bar{A})$ negatively sloped.

As in the two-dimensional case we can study the stability of the systems near the steady state by considering the one-dimensional center manifolds associated with a real eigenvalue $\lambda = 1$ and a real eigenvalue $\lambda = -1$, and the two-dimensional center manifold associated with the modulus of a complex conjugate eigenvalue pair $|\lambda| = 1$. Assuming that the reduced systems exists and that all parameters are fixed except the bifurcation parameter (usually ρ below), we investigate possible losses of stability by making use

[2]Unless stated otherwise, the standard parameter set for numerical analysis and simulation is $(c_0, l_0, A_0) = (0.03, 0.2, 0)$, $b = 1.3$, $\beta = 1.2$, $\alpha = 0.4$, $\rho = 0.02$, $m = 0.75$, $\hat{A} = 840$, $N = 3.5 \times 10^9$, $\phi = 0.478$ ppmv $/10^9$ tons.

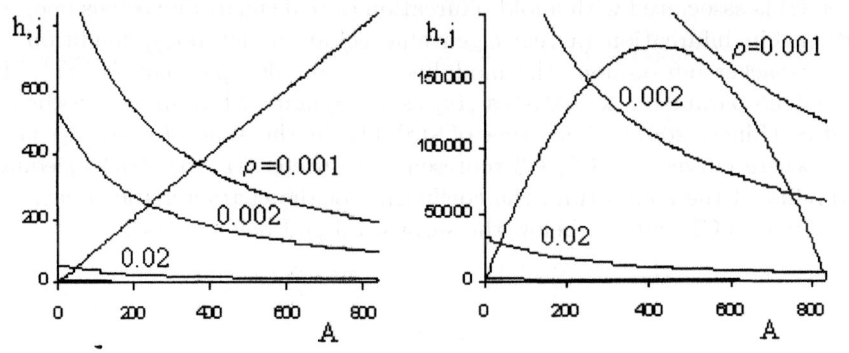

Figure 7. Existence: left, constant uptake; right, threshold uptake.

of necessary conditions (non-hyperbolicity) and numerical simulations. The Jacobian matrix of (5.6) is

$$J = \begin{pmatrix} 0 & \gamma & \delta \\ -b & b & 0 \\ 0 & \xi/\rho & \sigma \end{pmatrix}$$

where

$$\gamma = \frac{\partial f(\bar{l},\bar{A})}{\partial l_t} = \frac{\partial \mathcal{U}^{-1}[(1+\theta(\bar{A}))\mathcal{V}(\bar{l})]}{\partial l_t}$$

$$\delta = \frac{\partial f(\bar{l},\bar{A})}{\partial A_t} = \frac{\partial \mathcal{U}^{-1}[(1+\theta(\bar{A}))\mathcal{V}(\bar{l})]}{\partial A_t}$$

$$\sigma_a = 1 - m \qquad \sigma_b = \frac{2\bar{A}}{\hat{A}}$$

At the trivial steady state $(\bar{c},\bar{l},\bar{A}) = (0,0,0)$, eigenvalues of the Jacobian matrix are 0, $b > 1$ and σ. Locally then the origin is a saddle point, the unstable manifold associated with b is one-dimensional, the two-dimensional stable manifold is associated with 0 and σ, with $0 \leq \sigma_a \leq 1$, $\sigma_b = 0$.

The characteristic equation is $\lambda^3 + a_1\lambda^2 + a_2\lambda + a_3$ where $a_1 = -\text{ tr } J = -b - \sigma$, $a_2 = b(\sigma + \gamma)$, and $a_3 = -\text{ det } J = -b(\gamma\sigma - \delta\xi)$. The following stability conditions must be satisfied simultaneously in order to guarantee that the moduli of all eigenvalues are less than one and the equilibrium is locally stable. (Alternative sets of conditions for three and four dimensions are given in Farebrother (1973).)

$$\begin{aligned} 1 + a_1 + a_2 + a_3 &> 0 \qquad (i) \\ 1 - a_1 + a_2 - a_3 &> 0 \qquad (ii) \\ 1 - a_2 + a_1a_3 - a_3^2 &> 0 \qquad (iii) \\ 3 - a_2 &> 0. \qquad (iv) \end{aligned}$$

Suppose that three of these are simultaneously met. The equilibrium loses its local stability at the point in which the fourth inequality is violated. By slowly varying a single bifurcation parameter the equilibrium becomes non-hyperbolic with the bifurcation value determined when the condition is an equality. Simulations suggest that the breaking of condition (i) is associated with a fold bifurcation (a real eigenvalue equals one), condition (ii) with a flip bifurcation (a real eigenvalue equals minus one), condition (iii) with a Neimark-Sacker bifurcation (the modulus of a complex pair equals one). It can be shown that no parameter set satisfies (iv) as an equality while satisfying the first three inequalities (Lines, 2001). The area of stability in the space (a_1, a_2, a_3) is shown in Figure 8 where curves C1, C2, C3 represent conditions (i), (ii), (iii) at equality. For local stability of the equilibrium the coefficients of the characteristic equation must be above the planes C1 and C2, below the surface C3 and below $a_2 = 3$.

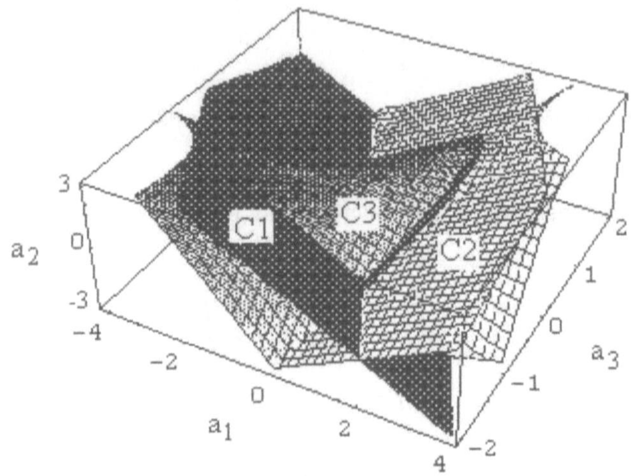

Figure 8. Stability conditions with coefficients of characteristic polynomial

For system (5.8) with steady state values (5.9) and (5.10), condition (i) is always satisfied, (ii) is satisfied for α not too near zero, (iv) is satisfied if (i) and (ii) are satisfied, leaving condition (iii) not verifiable. That is, the condition of non-hyperbolicity associated with the Neimark-Sacker bifurcation is the only relevant loss of stability. Numerical evidence suggests that the bifurcation exists for a critical value ρ_c of the technology parameter which generates a reversed supercritical scenario. In Figure 9, as the level of technology is decreased from very clean (right) to very dirty (left) we have: locally stable steady states, locally stable invariant circles, no stable equilibrium set. Under the standard set for example, the critical value is $\rho \simeq 0.03$, $\bar{A} \simeq 30$ with eigenvalues approximately $0.24, 0.65 \pm 0.80i$ that is the complex eigenvalue pair has modulus just outside the unit circle, the steady state point is unstable but a stable invariant circle exists on which orbits may be periodic or quasi-periodic. Then the existence of any locally stable steady state solution requires a minimum energy efficiency in production technology and a minimum uptake of emissions by the ocean and biosphere.

The model has a built-in stabilizing mechanism, the representative agent's perception of decreased utility on which the labor supply choice is conditioned. In the absence of a central authority or social pressure, agents respond to an increasing pollution level in the only way available to them, they reduce their labor input. For parameter values

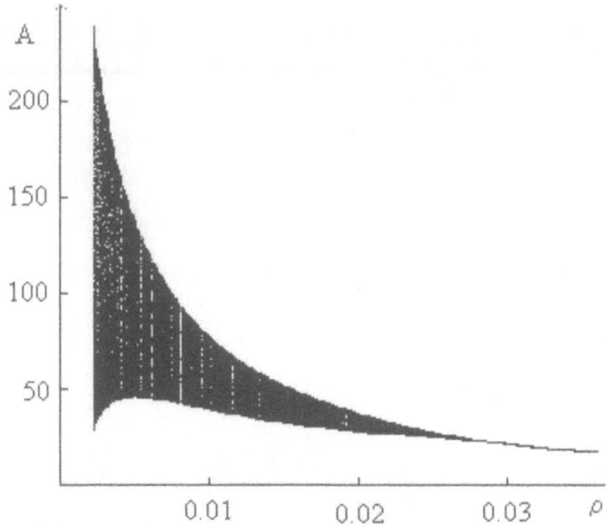

Figure 9. Bifurcation diagram, asymptotic values A_t as ρ varies.

leading to cyclical limit sets, this reaction eventually leads to lower pollution levels, which in turn eventually lead to higher optimal labor values, production increases, higher pollutant flows and again, an eventual reduction in labor and so on around the circle. The mechanism, though crude, describes the growing awareness of pollution on the part of the generation that is faced with the optimization problem. The intricate border between periodic and quasiperiodic limit sets is observable in the double parameter bifurcation diagram in Figure 10, where period 1 (upper left) represents fixed points, black (lower left) represents areas with no stable limit set, white represents areas of quasiperiodic attractors (except at the upper border where higher-order cycles may exist) and the shaded Arnol'd tongues reaching into the region of quasiperiodicity have periods of the length given in the legend.

5.5 Explicit Utility with Threshold Uptake

Substituting isoelastic utility functions (4.7) in (5.2) gives system (5.6b) as

$$\begin{aligned} c_{t+1} &= l_t^{\frac{\beta}{\alpha}}(1 + A_t/\kappa)^{\frac{1}{\alpha}} \\ l_{t+1} &= b(l_t - c_t) \\ A_{t+1} &= \frac{A_t^2}{\hat{A}} + \xi\frac{l_t}{\rho}. \end{aligned} \tag{5.11}$$

In addition to the unstable saddle point at the origin, it has zero or two steady states in the positive orthant, the first two coordinates $\bar{c}, \bar{l}$ are the same as in (5.9) and $\bar{A}$ is found as the intersection of the LHS, $h(\bar{A})$, and the RHS, $j(\bar{A})$, of the following equation:

$$\hat{A}\bar{A} - \bar{A}^2 = \hat{A}\frac{\beta}{\alpha}(\bar{A}) \tag{5.12}$$

Figure 10. Periodic orbits of up to 14 periods over values of m and ρ (r) for (5.8).

(see Figure 7, right, for the standard set as ρ varies). In this model existence of a positive steady state for the environmental index is not guaranteed. As the curve j shifts up relative to the curve h, the two equilibria move closer in value until, at the tangency, they coincide. Further shifts upward result in no real solutions for $\bar{c}$, $\bar{l}$, $\bar{A}$. In fact, using the stability conditions in (i)-(iv) to find nonhyperbolic values for steady states we have condition (i) is always satisfied for the steady state value $\bar{A}$ at the left intersection of the two curves in Figure 7, right, where it exists. When the two equilibria coincide condition (i) is broken. Condition (ii) is satisfied again if α is not too low and (iv) is satisfied for reasonable values of ρ, at least for $0 < \rho < 1$. Condition (iii) is not verifiable. The relevant stability conditions are those suggesting the Neimark and fold bifurcations. Analytical and numerical analyses suggest that the Neimark bifurcation observable in the constant uptake model (5.8) is one possible sequence for the loss of local stability in model (5.11). For the standard parameter set the critical value of $\rho \simeq 0.03$ ($\bar{A} \simeq 25$) gives eigenvalues approximately $0.06, 0.65 \pm 0.78i$ with modulus of the complex pair just outside the unit circle, the asymptotic set is an invariant circle, the bifurcation diagram is similar to that in Figure 9.

A second sequence is strongly suggested by the fact that condition (i) is no longer always satisfied and by the possible disappearance of fixed points as represented in (5.6) and Figure 7, right. A typical loss of stability in systems with quadratic nonlinearities is through a fold bifurcation, in which two branches of steady states (usually a stable node and an unstable saddle) collide and collapse. On the opposite side of the convergence, no real steady state solutions exist. This would seem to be the case for system (5.11). The non-trivial steady state values depend on technology reaching a minimum level of production per emission. For example, for the standard set except $b = 1.2$, the critical value is $\rho_c \simeq 0.00084$, with threshold value $\hat{A} = 840$, steady state $\bar{A} = 547$, and eigenvalues $1.02, 0.75 \pm 0.3i$, and it is $\rho_c \simeq 0.00284$, with threshold value $\hat{A} = 420$, steady state $\bar{A} \simeq 262$ and eigenvalues $1.01, 0, 72 \pm 0.36i$.

The existence of fold bifurcations in the threshold uptake model means that parts of the parameter space contain no real limit set and the economy soon collapses. The existence and local stability of a limit set depends on the environmental parameters ρ (output per emission) and $\hat{A}$ (maximum anthropogenic addition to concentration for which the non-atmospheric sinks and storages uptake a fraction of emissions). For a given threshold pollution level, technology must be above a minimum greenness to ensure existence. Similarly, for a given ρ, $\hat{A}$ must be sufficiently large. If steady states exist there are two values of which the smaller is stable. For some parameter sets this stable steady state appears to loose stability through a Neimark-Sacker bifurction and trajectories are attracted to invariant circles. For other parameter sets it appears that it coincides with the unstable steady state and a fold bifurcation occurs. For example, if the technology is very polluting non-trivial equilibria may not exist, while clean technology ensures a steady state value.

Bibliography

M. Allias, *Economie et Interet*, Paris: Imprimerie Nationale, 1947.

O.J. Blanchard, Debt, Deficits, and Finite Horizons. *Journal of Political Economy*, 93:223–247, 1985.

O. J. Blanchard and S. Fischer, *Lectures on Macroeconomics*. Cambridge: MIT Press, 1989.

T. J. Conway (ed), Chapter 2. Carbon Cycle Greenhouse Gases. *Climate Monitoring and Diagnostics Laboratory, Report 27.* Boulder: U.S. National Oceanic Atmospheric Administration, 2003.

P. A. Diamond, National debt in a neoclassical growth model. *American Economic Review*, 55:1126–1150, 1965.

R. W. Farebrother, Simplified Samuelson conditions for cubic and quartic equations. *The Manchester School of Economics and Social Studies*, 4:396–400, 1973.

J. M. Grandmont, On endogenous competitive business cycles. *Econometrica*, 53:995–1045, 1985.

J.T. Houghton, L.G. Meira Filho, J. Bruce, Hoesung Lee, B.A. Callander, E. Haites, N. Harris and K. Maskell (eds.), *Climate Change 1994: Ratiative Forcing of Climate*

Change and an Evaluation of the IPCC IS92 Emission Scenarios, Intergovernmental Panel of Climate Change (IPCC), Cambridge: Cambridge University Press, 1994.

M. Lines, Practical bifurcation theory for discrete systems in $\mathbb{R}^3$. *Working paper 15-2001.* Department of Statistics, University of Udine, 2001.

A. Medio, *Chaotic Dynamics: Theory and Applications to Economics.* Cambridge: Cambridge University Press, 1992.

P. Reichlin, Equilibrium cycles in an overlapping generations economy with production. *Journal of Economic Theory*, 40:89–102, 1986.

P. A. Samuelson, An Exact Consumption-Loan Model of Interest with or without the Social Contrivance of Money. *Journal of Political Economy*, 66:467–482, 1958.

Heterogeneous Agent Models: two simple examples.

Cars Hommes*

* CeNDEF, Department of Quantitative Economics, University of Amsterdam, Amsterdam, The Netherlands

Abstract These notes review two simple heterogeneous agent models in economics and finance. The first is a cobweb model with rational versus naive agents introduced in Brock and Hommes (1997). The second is an asset pricing model with fundamentalists versus technical traders introduced in Brock and Hommes (1998). Agents are boundedly rational and switch endogenously between different trading strategies, based upon an evolutionary fitness measure given by realized past profits. Evolutionary switching creates a nonlinearity in the dynamic models. Rational routes to randomness, that is, bifurcation routes to complicated dynamical behavior occur when agents become more sensitive to differences in evolutionary fitness.

Acknowledgement. I would like to thank Peter Heemeijer for his help and patience in simulating the models and preparing all figures in these notes.

1 Introduction

The key difference between economics and the natural sciences is perhaps the fact that decisions of economic agents today depend upon their expectations or *beliefs* about the future. For example, in financial markets an overoptimistic estimate of future growth of ICT industries may contribute to an excessively rapid growth of stock prices and indices and might lead to over valuation of stock markets worldwide. Any dynamic economic system is in fact an *expectations feedback* system. A theory of expectation formation is therefore a crucial part of any economic model or theory.

Since its introduction in the sixties by Muth (1961) and its popularization in macroeconomics by Lucas (1971), the rational expectations hypothesis (REH) has become the dominating expectation formation paradigm in economic theory. According to the REH all agents are rational and take as their subjective expectation of future variables the objective prediction by economic theory. In a rational expectations model agents have perfect knowledge about the (linear) market equilibrium equations and use these to derive their expectations. Although many economists nowadays view rational expectations as something unrealistic, it is still viewed as an important benchmark. Despite a rapidly growing literature on *bounded rationality*, where agents use learning models for their expectations, it seems fair to say that at this point no generally accepted alternative theory of expectations is available.

In finance, the REH is intimately related to the Efficient Market Hypothesis (EMH). There are weak and strong forms of the EMH, but when economists speak of financial markets as being efficient, they usually mean that they view asset prices and returns as the outcome of a competitive market consisting of rational traders, who are trying to maximize their expected returns. The main reason why financial markets must be efficient is based upon an *arbitrage* argument (e.g. Fama (1970)). If markets were not efficient, then there would be unexploited profit opportunities, that could and would be exploited by rational traders. For example, rational traders would buy (sell) an underpriced (overpriced) asset, thus driving its price back to the correct, fundamental value. In an efficient market, there can be *no forecastable structure* in asset returns, since any such structure would be exploited by rational traders and therefore would be doomed to disappear. Rational agents thus process information quickly and this is reflected immediately in asset prices. The value of a risky asset is completely determined by its *fundamental price*, equal to the present discounted value of the expected stream of future dividends. In an efficient market, all traders are rational and changes in asset prices are completely random, solely driven by unexpected 'news' about changes in economic fundamentals.

In contrast, Keynes already questioned a completely rational valuation of assets, arguing that investors sentiment and mass psychology ('*animal spirits*') play a significant role in financial markets. Keynes used his famous *beauty contest* as a parable to financial markets. In order to predict the winner of a beauty contest, objective beauty is not all that important, but knowledge or prediction of others' perceptions of beauty is much more relevant. Keynes argued that the same may be true for the fundamental price of an asset: '*Investment based on genuine long-term expectation is so difficult as to be scarcely practicable. He who attempts it must surely lead much more laborious days and run greater risks than he who tries to guess better than the crowd how the crowd will behave; and, given equal intelligence, he may make more disastrous mistakes*' (Keynes, 1936, p.157). In Keynes view, stock prices are thus not governed by an objective view of 'fundamentals', but by 'what average opinion expects average opinion to be'.

New classical economists have viewed 'market psychology' and 'investors sentiment' as being *irrational* however, and therefore inconsistent with the REH. For example, Friedman (1953) argued that irrational speculative traders would be driven out of the market by rational traders, who would trade against them by taking long opposite positions, thus driving prices back to fundamentals. In an efficient market, 'irrational' speculators would simply loose money and therefore fail to survive evolutionary competition.

In a perfectly rational EMH world *all* traders are rational and it is *common knowledge* that all traders are rational. In real financial markets however, traders are different, especially with respect to their expectations about future prices and dividends. A quick glance at the financial pages of newspapers is sufficient to observe that *difference of opinions* among financial analysts is the rule rather than the exception. In the last decade, a rapidly increasing number of structural heterogeneous agent models have been introduced in the economics and finance literature, see for example Arthur et al. (1997), Brock (1993, 1997), Brock and Hommes (1997, 1998), Brock and LeBaron (1996), Chiarella (1992), Chiarella and He (2000), Dacorogna et al. (1995), Day and Huang (1990), DeGrauwe et al. (1993), De Long et al. (1990ab), Farmer (1998), Farmer and Joshi (2002), de Fontnouvelle (2000), Frankel and Froot (1988), Gaunersdorfer (2000), Gaunersdorfer and Hommes (2000), Kirman (1991), Kirman and Teyssière (2000), Kurz (1997), LeBaron

(2000), LeBaron et al. (1999), Lux (1995, 1997), Lux and Marchesi (1999, 2000), Wang (1994) and Zeeman (1974), as well as many more references in these papers. Some authors even talk about a *Heterogeneous Market Hypothesis*, as a new alternative to the Efficient Market Hypothesis. In all these heterogeneous agent models different groups of traders, having different beliefs or expectations, co-exist. Two typical trader types can be distinguished. The first are rational, '*smart money*' traders or *fundamentalists*, believing that the price of an asset is determined completely by economic fundamentals. The second typical trader type are '*noise traders*', sometimes called *chartists* or *technical analysts*, believing that asset prices are not determined by fundamentals, but that they can be predicted by simple technical trading rules based upon patterns in past prices, such as trends or cycles.

In a series of papers, Brock and Hommes (1997a,b, 1998, 1999), henceforth BH, propose to model economic and financial markets as *Adaptive Belief Systems (ABS)*, where agents are heterogeneous and switch between different trading strategies. In these notes we review two simple heterogeneous agent models, the cobweb model with sophisticated rational versus simple naive traders and a standard asset pricing model with fundamentalists versus chartists. These models are discussed in detail in Brock and Hommes (1997a) and Brock and Hommes (1998); see also the survey in Hommes (2001). An ABS is an evolutionary competition between trading strategies. Different groups of traders have different expectations about future prices. For example, one group might be fundamentalists, believing that asset prices return to their fundamental equilibrium price, whereas another group might be chartists, extrapolating patterns in past prices. Traders choose their trading strategy according to an evolutionary 'fitness measure', such as accumulated past profits. Agents are boundedly rational, in the sense that most traders choose strategies with higher fitness. BH introduce the notion of *Adaptive Rational Equilibrium Dynamics (ARED)*, an endogenous coupling between market equilibrium dynamics and evolutionary updating of beliefs. Current beliefs determine today's equilibrium prices, generating new, adapted beliefs which in turn lead to new equilibrium prices tomorrow, etc.. In an ARED, equilibrium prices and beliefs co-evolve over time. Most of the heterogeneous agent literature is computationally oriented. An ABS may be seen as a tractable theoretical framework for the computationally oriented 'artificial stock market' literature, such as the Santa Fe artificial stock market of Arthur et al. (1997) and LeBaron et al. (1999). A convenient feature of an ABS is that the model can be formulated in terms of *deviations* from a benchmark fundamental. In fact, the perfectly rational EMH benchmark is nested within an ABS as a special case. An ABS may thus be used for experimental and empirical testing whether deviations from a suitable RE benchmark are significant.

The coupling between market equilibrium and updating of strategies makes the evolutionary system highly *nonlinear.* A common finding is the occurrence of a *rational route to randomness*, that is, a bifurcation route to complicated price fluctuations as traders become more sensitive to differences in evolutionary fitness. These notes are organized as follows. Section 2 reviews the cobweb model with sophisticated rational versus naive producers. Section 3 reviews the asset pricing model with heterogeneous beliefs and presents examples with two, three and four different trader types. Finally, section 4 concludes.

2 The cobweb model

The cobweb model describes fluctuations of equilibrium prices in an independent market for a non-storable consumption good. The good takes one time period to produce, so that producers must form price expectations one period ahead. Applications of the cobweb model mainly concern agricultural markets, such as the classical examples of cycles in hog or corn prices. Supply $S(p_t^e)$ is a function of producer's next period expected price, p_t^e and is derived from expected profit maximization:

$$S(p_t^e) = \text{argmax}_{q_t} \{p_t^e q_t - c(q_t)\} = (c')^{-1}(p_t^e), \tag{2.1}$$

where $c(\cdot)$ is an increasing, convex cost function. The supply curve thus coincides with the inverse of the marginal cost curve. The expected price may be some function of (publically known) past prices, that is, $p_t^e = H(\vec{P}_{t-1})$, where $\vec{P}_{t-1} = (p_{t-1}, p_{t-2}, \cdots, p_{t-L})$ denotes a vector of past prices of lag-length L, and $H(\cdot)$ is called a *predictor* or *forecasting rule.*

Consumer demand D depends upon the current market price p_t. The demand curve D may be derived from utility maximization under a budget constraint, but for our purposes it is not necessary to specify preferences explicitly. We will assume that consumer demand is decreasing in the market price. If beliefs are homogeneous, i.e., all producers use the same predictor, market equilibrium price dynamics in the cobweb model is given by

$$D(p_t) = S(H(\vec{P}_{t-1})), \qquad \text{or} \qquad p_t = D^{-1}(S(H(\vec{P}_{t-1}))). \tag{2.2}$$

The actual equilibrium price dynamics thus depends upon the demand curve D, the supply curve S as well as the predictor H used by the producers. If all producers have rational expectations or perfect foresight, that is, their prediction coincides exactly with the realized price, $H^R(\vec{P}_{t-1}) = p_t$, price dynamics become extremely simple: $p_t = p^*$ in all periods, where p^* is the (unique) price corresponding to the intersection of demand and supply. If, on the other hand, all producers use the naive predictor $H^N(\vec{P}_{t-1}) = p_{t-1}$, that is, the forecast coincides with the last observation, the price dynamics is given by $p_t = D^{-1}(S(p_{t-1}))$, which is the familiar textbook cobweb system. If demand D is decreasing and supply S is increasing, price dynamics in the cobweb model with naive expectations is simple. If $-1 < S'(p^*)/D'(p^*) < 0$ prices converge to the stable steady state p^*; otherwise, prices diverge away from the steady state and either converge to a stable 2-cycle or exhibit unbounded up and down oscillations.[1]

2.1 Heterogeneous beliefs

Brock and Hommes (1997a), henceforth BH97a, studied heterogeneity in expectation formation by introducing the concept of *Adaptive Rational Equilibrium Dynamics (ARED)*, a coupling between market equilibrium dynamics and adaptive predictor selection. The ARED is an evolutionary dynamics between competing prediction strategies.

[1]Note that for other predictors such as adaptive expectations or linear predictors with two or three lags, price fluctuations in the cobweb model can become much more complicated. In particular, chaotic price oscillations may arise even when both demand and supply are *monotonic* (Hommes (1994,1998)).

Agents can choose between different prediction strategies and update their beliefs over time according to a publically available 'fitness' or 'performance' measure such as (a weighted sum of) past realized profits. Prediction strategies with higher fitness in the recent past are selected more often than those with lower fitness. Market equilibrium in the cobweb model with heterogeneous beliefs is determined by

$$D(p_t) = \sum_{j=1}^{J} n_{j,t-1} S(H_j(\vec{P}_{t-1})), \tag{2.3}$$

where H_j, $1 \leq j \leq J$, represents the forecasting strategy of type j and $n_{j,t-1}$ is the fraction of agents using strategy j at the beginning of period t.

BH97a present a detailed analysis of the cobweb model with two trader types and linear demand and supply. Demand is linearly decreasing and given by[2]

$$D(p_t) = a - dp_t, \qquad d > 0. \tag{2.4}$$

The supply curve is linear and given by

$$S(p_t^e) = sp_t^e, \qquad s > 0, \tag{2.5}$$

or equivalently, producer's cost function is quadratic and given by $c(q) = q^2/(2s)$.

Agents can either buy a sophisticated, rational expectations (perfect foresight) forecast at positive per period information costs $C \geq 0$, or freely obtain the simple, naive forecast. The two forecasting rules are thus given by

$$H_1(\vec{P}_{t-1}) = p_t, \tag{2.6}$$

$$H_2(\vec{P}_{t-1}) = p_{t-1}. \tag{2.7}$$

Market equilibrium in the cobweb model with rational versus naive expectations and linear demand and supply is given by

$$a - dp_t = n_{t-1}^R sp_t + n_{t-1}^N sp_{t-1}, \tag{2.8}$$

where n_{t-1}^R and n_{t-1}^N denote the fractions of producers using the rational respectively naive predictor, at the beginning of period t. Notice that producers using the rational expectations predictor have perfect foresight, and therefore must have perfect knowledge about the market equilibrium equation (2.8), including past prices as well as the fractions of both groups. Consequently, rational agents have perfect knowledge about the beliefs of all other agents. The difference C between the per period information costs for rational and naive expectations represents an extra effort cost producers incur over time when acquiring this perfect knowledge. It is straightforward to solve (2.8) explicitely for the market equilibrium price

$$p_t = \frac{a - n_{t-1}^N sp_{t-1}}{d + n_{t-1}^R s}. \tag{2.9}$$

[2]See Goeree and Hommes (2000) for an analysis of the cobweb model with rational versus naive expectations in the case of nonlinear (but monotonic) demand and supply.

The cobweb model with rational versus naive expectations, may be seen as an analytically tractable, stylized two predictor model in which rational expectations represents a costly sophisticated (and stabilizing) predictor, and naive expectations represent a cheap 'habitual rule of thumb' (but potentially destabilizing) predictor. It is interesting to note that other two predictor cases, such as fundamentalists (expecting prices to return to the rational expectations fundamental steady state price p^*) versus adaptive expectations yield similar results.

To complete the model, we have to specify how the fractions of traders using rational respectively naive expectations are determined. These fractions change over time, and are updated according to a publically available 'performance' or 'fitness' measure associated to each predictor. Here, we take the most recent realized net profit as the performance measure for predictor selection.[3] For the rational expectations forecasting strategy (2.6) and linear supply (2.5), realized profit in period t is given by

$$\pi_t^R = p_t\, S(p_t) - c(S(p_t)) = \frac{s}{2} p_t^2. \tag{2.10}$$

The *net* realized profit for rational expectations is thus given by $\pi_t^R - C$, where C is the per period information cost that has to be paid for obtaining the perfect forecast. For the naive predictor (2.7) and linear supply (2.5) the realized net profit in period t is given by

$$\pi_t^N = p_t\, S(p_{t-1}) - c(S(p_{t-1})) = \frac{s}{2} p_{t-1}(2p_t - p_{t-1}). \tag{2.11}$$

The fractions of the two groups are determined by the Logit discrete choice model probabilities. Anderson, de Palma and Thisse (1992) contains an extensive discussion and motivation of discrete choice modelling in various economic contexts; BH97a provide motivation of discrete choice models for selecting prediction strategies. The fraction of agents using the rational expectations predictor in period t equals

$$n_t^R = \frac{\exp(\beta(\pi_t^R - C))}{\exp(\beta(\pi_t^R - C)) + \exp(\beta\, \pi_t^N)}, \tag{2.12}$$

and the fraction of agents choosing the naive predictor in period t is

$$n_t^N = 1 - n_t^R. \tag{2.13}$$

A crucial feature of this evolutionary predictor selection is that agents are boundedly rational, in the sense that most agents use the predictor that has the highest fitness. Indeed, from (2.12-2.13) we have for instance that $n_t^R > n_t^N$ whenever $\pi_t^R - C > \pi_t^N$, although the optimal predictor is not chosen with probability one. The parameter β is called the *intensity of choice*; it measures how fast producers switch between the two prediction strategies. Let us briefly discuss the two extreme cases $\beta = 0$ and $\beta = \infty$. For

[3] The case where the performance measure is realized net profit in the most recent past period, leads to a two-dimensional dynamic system. The more general case, with a weighted sum of past net realized profits as the fitness measure, leads to higher dimensional systems, which are not as analytically tractable as the two-dimensional case. In this more general higher dimensional case however, numerical simulations suggest similar dynamic behaviour.

$\beta = 0$, both fractions are fixed over time and equal to 1/2. The other extreme $\beta = \infty$, corresponds to the *neoclassical limit* in which agents are unboundedly rational, and *all* producers choose the optimal predictor in each period. Hence, the higher the intensity of choice the more rational, in the sense of evolutionary fitness, agents are in choosing their prediction strategies. The neoclassical limit $\beta = \infty$ will play an important role in what follows.

The timing of predictor selection in (2.12) is important. In (2.9) the old fractions n_{t-1}^R and n_{t-1}^N determine the new equilibrium price p_t. This new equilibrium price p_t is used in the fitness measures (2.10) and (2.11) for predictor choice and the new fractions n_t^R and n_t^N are updated according to (2.12) and (2.13). These new fractions are then used in determining the next equilibrium price p_{t+1}, etc.. Equilibrium prices and fractions thus co-evolve over time.

It will be convenient to define the difference m_t of the two fractions:

$$m_t \equiv n_t^R - n_t^N, \tag{2.14}$$

so $m_t = -1$ corresponds to all producers being naive, whereas $m_t = +1$ means that all producers prefer the rational expectations predictor. The evolution of the equilibrium price, p_t, and the difference of fractions, m_t, is then summarized by the following two-dimensional, non-linear dynamical system

$$p_t = \frac{a - n_{t-1}^N s p_{t-1}}{d + n_{t-1}^R s} = \frac{2a - (1 - m_{t-1}) s p_{t-1}}{2d + (1 + m_{t-1}) s}, \tag{2.15}$$

$$m_t = \tanh\left(\frac{\beta}{2}(\pi_t^R - \pi_t^N - C)\right). \tag{2.16}$$

BH97a called the coupling (2.15-2.16) between the equilibrium price dynamics and adaptive predictor selection an *Adaptive Rational Equilibrium Dynamics (ARED)* model.

For a linear supply curve, using (2.10) and (2.11) the difference in realized profits of rational and naive agents can be simplified to

$$\pi_t^R - \pi_t^N = \frac{s}{2}(p_t - p_{t-1})^2, \tag{2.17}$$

that is, the difference in realized profits is proportional to the squared prediction error of the naive forecast. In the case of a linear demand and supply the ARED thus becomes

$$p_t = \frac{2a - (1 - m_{t-1}) s p_{t-1}}{2d + (1 + m_{t-1}) s} \tag{2.18}$$

$$m_t = \tanh\left(\frac{\beta}{2}\left[\frac{s}{2}(p_t - p_{t-1})^2 - C\right]\right). \tag{2.19}$$

The reader may easily verify that the model has a unique steady state $(p^*, m^*) = (a/(d+s), \tanh(-\beta C/2))$. Notice that $p^* = a/(d+s)$ is exactly the price where demand and supply intersect. It will be convenient to rewrite (2.18-2.19) in *d*eviations from the steady state price, $x_t = p_t - p^*$, yielding[4]

$$x_t = \frac{-(1-m_{t-1})sx_{t-1}}{2d+(1+m_{t-1})s} \tag{2.20}$$

$$m_t = \tanh(\frac{\beta}{2}[\frac{s}{2}(x_t - x_{t-1})^2 - C]). \tag{2.21}$$

In the sequel we use the shorthand notation $(x_t, m_t) = F_\beta(x_{t-1}, m_{t-1})$ for the ARED-model (2.20-2.21). We are especially interested in the dynamics when the 'degree of rationality', that is, the intensity of choice, β to switch forecasting strategies, becomes high.

2.2 Local (in)stability of the steady state

We will now discuss the dynamical behaviour of prices and fractions in the cobweb model with rational versus naive expectations, starting with the stability conditions for the steady state. Recall that the model has a unique steady state $(p^*, m^*) = (a/(d+s), \tanh(-\beta C/2))$, where $p^* = a/(d+s)$ is the price where demand and supply intersect. Notice that for $C = 0$, i.e. when there are no costs for rational expectations, $m^* = 0$, so that at the steady state the fractions of the two types are equal. In contrast, for positive information costs for rational expectations, i.e. for $C > 0$ we have $m^* < 0$, so that at the steady state most agents employ the naive forecasting rule. This makes sense, because at the steady state both forecasting rules yield exactly the same forecast, and most agents then prefer the cheap, naive forecast.
The stability properties of the steady state are determined by the derivatives of supply and demand at the steady state price p^*. A straightforward computation shows that the eigenvalues of the Jacobian matrix of (2.18-2.19) evaluated at the steady state are $\lambda_1 = 0$, and

$$\lambda_2 = \frac{(1-m^*)\,S'(p^*)}{2\,D'(p^*) - (1+m^*)\,S'(p^*)} = \frac{-(1-m^*)\,s}{2\,d + (1+m^*)\,s} < 0. \tag{2.22}$$

Since m^* is less than or equal to one in absolute value, the value of the second eigenvalue lies between $S'(p^*)/D'(p^*) = -s/d$ and 0. Hence, if the familiar cobweb stability condition $|S'(p^*)/D'(p^*)| = |s/d| < 1$ is satisfied, implying that the model is stable under naive expectations, then in the cobweb model with rational versus naive expectations and linear demand and supply, the steady state is globally stable, for all β. Prices then always converge to p^*, and the difference of fractions converges to m^*. To allow for the possibility of an unstable steady state and endogenous price fluctuations in the evolutionary ARED-model, from now on we assume the following.

Assumption U. *The market is locally unstable when all producers are naive, that is,* $S'(p^*)/D'(p^*) = -s/d < -1$.

[4]Notice that (2.20) is equivalent to fixing $a = 0$ in (2.18), so that $p^* = 0$. In fact, we are just choosing the steady state price as the origin.

The stability properties of the steady state in the evolutionary ARED-model are summarized as follows.

Proposition 1. *Under assumption U, the evolutionary ARED-model satisfies:*

(*i*) *when information costs are zero* ($C = 0$), *the steady state is globally stable for all* β,

(*ii*) *when information costs are strictly positive* ($C > 0$), *there exists a critical value* β_1 *such that the steady state is (globally) stable for* $0 \leq \beta < \beta_1$ *and unstable for* $\beta > \beta_1$. *At* $\beta = \beta_1$ *the second eigenvalue satisfies* $\lambda_2 = -1$, *and* F_β *in (2.18-2.19) exhibits a period doubling bifurcation.*

For $C = 0$, the steady state difference in fractions $m^* = 0$ and the eigenvalue in (2.22) satisfies $-1 < \lambda_2 < 0$, implying that the steady state is locally stable. Global stability follows by observing that, for $C = 0$ we must have $m_t \geq 0$, for all $t \geq 1$, and then using (2.20) x_t must converge to 0, or equivalently, prices always converge to their steady state value. The second part of the proposition follows by observing that the eigenvalue $\lambda_2 = -1$ when the steady state difference in fractions $m^* = \bar{m} = -d/s$. Assumption U implies that $-1 < \bar{m} = -d/s < 0$. As the intensity of choice β increases from 0 to $+\infty$ the steady state difference in fractions m^* decreases from 0 to -1 and, for some critical value of $\beta = \beta_1$ we have $m^* = \bar{m}$ and an eigenvalue $\lambda_2 = -1$ and the second part of the proposition follows.

2.3 A rational route to randomness

According to Proposition 1, for positive information costs C, the steady state $(p^*, m^*) = (p^*, \tanh(-\beta C/2))$ becomes unstable as the intensity of choice β increases. In this subsection we investigate the dynamics for large values of the intensity of choice. It will be useful however, to consider the neoclassical limit, that is, the case $\beta = \infty$ first.

For $\beta = \infty$ and $C > 0$, the steady state difference in fractions $m^* = tanh(-\beta C/2) = -1$, that is, at the steady state all agents are naive. Furthermore, for $\beta = \infty$ in each period *all* agents choose the optimal predictor, that is, in each period $t \geq 1$ either all agents are rational or all agents are naive. In fact, for $\beta = +\infty$ the switching between forecasting strategies (2.19) simplifies to

$$m_t = \begin{cases} +1 & \text{if } \pi_t^R - \pi_t^N = \frac{s}{2}(p_t - p_{t-1})^2 > C, \\ -1 & \text{if } \pi_t^R - \pi_t^N = \frac{s}{2}(p_t - p_{t-1})^2, \leq C. \end{cases} \tag{2.23}$$

Stated differently, as long as the squared prediction error from naive expectations is sufficiently small compared to the per period information costs for rational expectations, i.e. as long as $(p_t - p_{t-1})^2 \leq 2C/s$, all agents employ the simple, cheap forecasting strategy. As long as all agents are naive, the price dynamics is governed by $p_t = D^{-1}(S(p_{t-1}))$, a linear unstable oscillation around the steady state price p^*, and prices diverge from their steady state value oscillating with increasing amplitude. The squared forecasting error from naive expectations will increase, and at some point must exceed the critical level $2C/s$, and all agents will then switch to rational expectations. When all producers become rational in period t, next periods price $p_{t+1} = p^*$ and the price immediately jumps back to the steady state price. These simple observations prove the following proposition:

Proposition 2. *For an infinite intensity of choice $\beta = \infty$ and positive information cost $C > 0$, all time paths in the ARED system (2.18-2.19) converge to the steady state $S = (p^*, -1)$, even under assumption U when the steady state is a locally unstable saddle point.*

Now suppose we add a small amount of noise to the neoclassical limit system, by adding a small random shock (e.g. a demand shock) in each period to the equilibrium pricing equation (2.18). Almost the same story as above applies, except that when all agents switch to rational expectations the system will not be driven exactly onto the steady state, but only close to the steady state. With prices close to the steady state value, all agents will then switch back to the cheap, naive forecasting rule and prices will start to oscillate and diverge, and the story repeats. The noisy neoclassical limit is thus characterized by an irregular switching between an unstable phase in which all agents are naive and prices diverge from the steady state, and a stable phase in which all agents become rational and prices return close to the steady state.

BH97a have shown that the same behavior arises in the deterministic, noise free case for a high, but finite, intensity of choice β. In fact, for high values of the intensity of choice, the dynamical behavior becomes chaotic with prices and fractions moving on a strange attractor. Figure 1 shows an example of a strange attractor, with corresponding time series of prices p_t and fractions n_t^R of rational producers. Numerical simulations suggest that for (almost) all initial states (p_0, m_0) the orbit converges to this strange attractor. Its intricate geometric shape explains why it is called a strange attractor.

Figure 2 illustrates the *r*ational route to randomness, that is, the bifurcation route from a stable steady state for low values of the intensity of choice to the complicated dynamical behavior for high values of the intensity of choice. The primary bifurcation is a period doubling bifurcation for $\beta \approx 0.77$, in which the steady state becomes unstable and a stable 2-cycle is created. As the intensity of choice increase more bifurcations occur and the dynamical behavior becomes more and more complicated. The Lyapunov exponent plot in Figure 2 shows that for large values of the intensity of choice the largest Lyapunov exponent becomes positive and therefore the dynamics becomes chaotic.

For a high intensity of choice price fluctuations are characterized by an irregular switching between a stable phase, with prices close to the steady state, and an unstable phase with fluctuating prices, as illustrated in Figure 1. There is a strikingly simple economic intuition explaining this switching behavior when the intensity of choice is large. Suppose we take an initial state close to the (locally unstable) steady state. Most agents will use the cheap, naive forecasting rule, because it does not pay to buy a costly, sophisticated forecasting rule that yields an almost identical forecast. With most agents using the cheap, naive predictor prices diverge from the steady state, start fluctuating, and net realized profits from the naive predictor decrease. At some point, it becomes profitable to buy the rational expectations forecast, and when the intensity of choice to switch pre-

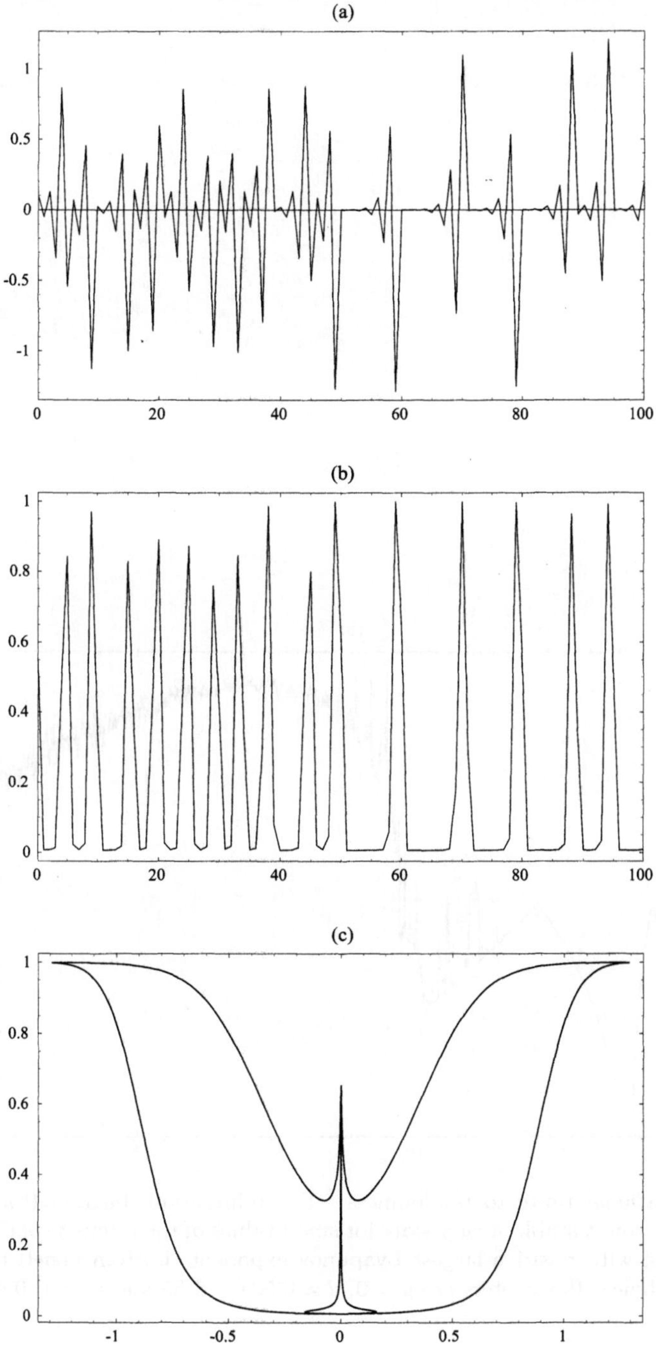

Figure 1. Chaotic time series of deviations x_t from the steady state price (top pannel) and fractions n_t^R of rational agents (middle pannel) and corresponding strange attractor in the (x, n^R)-phase space (bottom pannel). Parameters are: $\beta = 5$, $a = 0$, $d = 0.5$, $s = 1.35$ and $C = 1$.

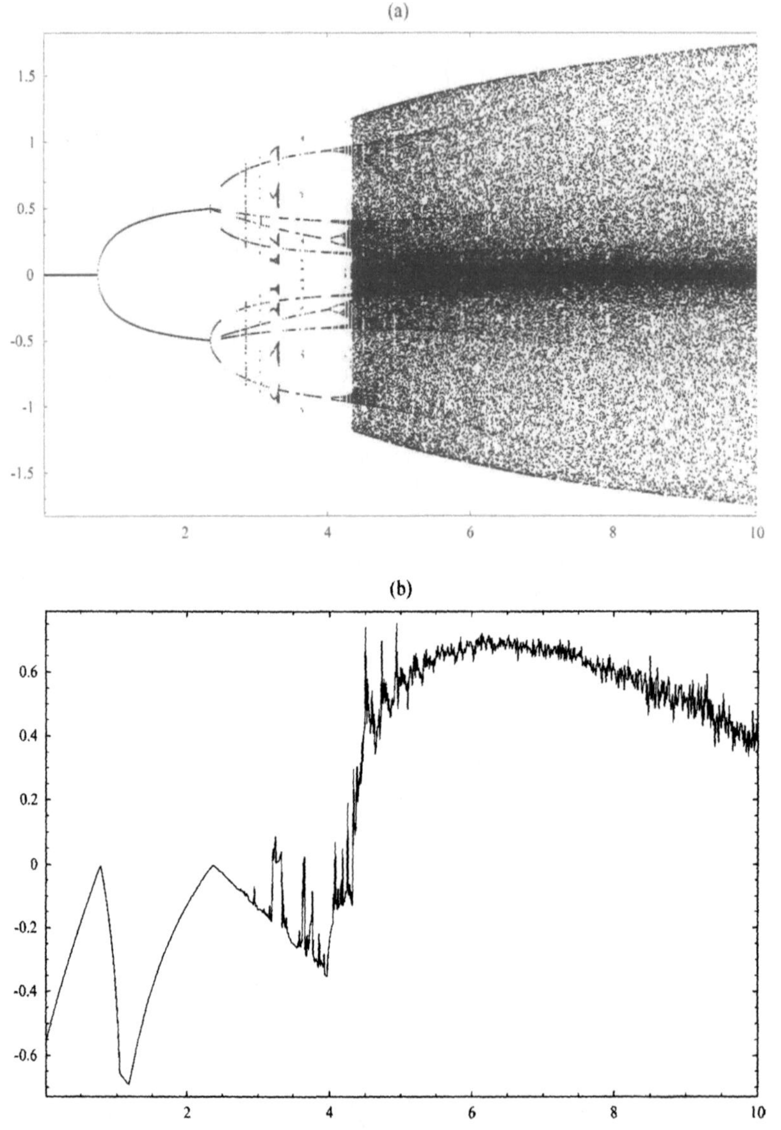

Figure 2. A rational route to randomness. The bifurcation diagram (top panel) shows a bifurcation route from a stable steady state for small values of the intensity of choice β to chaotic price fluctuations, with positive largest Lyapunov exponent (bottom panel) for high values of the intensity of choice. Parameters are $a = 0$, $d = 0.5$, $s = 1.35$ and $C = 1$, $0 \leq \beta \leq 10$.

dictors is high, most agents will then switch to rational expectations. As a result, prices are driven back close to the steady state, and the story then repeats. Irregular, chaotic price fluctuations thus result from a (boundedly) rational choice between cheap 'free riding' and costly sophisticated prediction. In fact, the above economic mechanism already suggests that for a large intensity of choice, the ARED-cobweb model will be close to a so-called homoclinic orbit associated to the unstable, saddle point steady state.

2.4 Homoclinic points and the unstable manifold of the steady state

A key feature of chaotic dynamical behavior in two- and higher dimensional systems is the existence of so-called *homoclinic points.* This concept was introduced already by Poincaré (1890), in his prize winning essay on the stability of the three-body system. Let us briefly discuss this important notion.

Recall that after the primary bifurcation in the ARED-model, the steady state S loses its stability and becomes a saddle point. In deviations x from the steady state price p^*, the steady $S = (0, m^*) = (0, tanh(-\beta C/2))$. The *stable manifold* and the *unstable manifold* of the steady state are defined as

$$W^s(S) = \{ (x,m) \mid \lim_{n\to\infty} F_\beta^n(x,m) = S \},$$
$$W^u(S) = \{ (x,m) \mid \lim_{n\to-\infty} F_\beta^n(x,m) = S \}.$$

A *transversal homoclinic point* $Q \neq S$, associated to the saddle S, is an intersection point of the stable and unstable manifold of S. It was already pointed out by Poincaré that the existence of a homoclinic intersection implies that the geometric structure of both the stable and unstable manifold is quite complicated, and the system exhibits some form of sensitive dependence on initial conditions. It is now well-known that a system having a homoclinic point is in fact chaotic. See Palis and Takens (1993) for an extensive mathematical treatment.

The unstable manifold of the steady state plays a crucial role for understanding the global characteristics of the evolutionary dynamics. Figure 3 illustrates the geometric shape of the unstable manifold of the steady state for diffent values of the intensity of choice β. Using (2.20-2.21), the reader may easily verify that all points $(0, m)$ are mapped exactly onto the steady state $(0, m^*)$ in the next period. This implies that the steady state S has an eigenvalue 0 and the stable manifold of the steady state S must contain the vertical line segment $p = p^*$, or in deviations, the vertical segment $x = 0$. For $\beta > \beta_1$, the steady state is locally unstable and has a second eigenvalue $\lambda_2 < -1$. Therefore, the unstable manifold has two different branches, each branch spiralling around one of the two points of the (un)stable period 2 orbit, as illustrated in Figure 3. Moreover, when the intensity of choice becomes large, each branch of the unstable manifold moves closer to the vertical line segment $x = 0$ of the stable manifold. For β large, the ARED-system is thus close to having a homoclinic orbit.

The geometric explanation for the dynamic complexity of the ARED-dynamics, based upon the shape of the unstable manifold of the steady state, bears a close similarity to the economic mechanism underlying complicated price fluctuations. On the one hand, for high values of the intensity of choice the system is driven towards the steady state

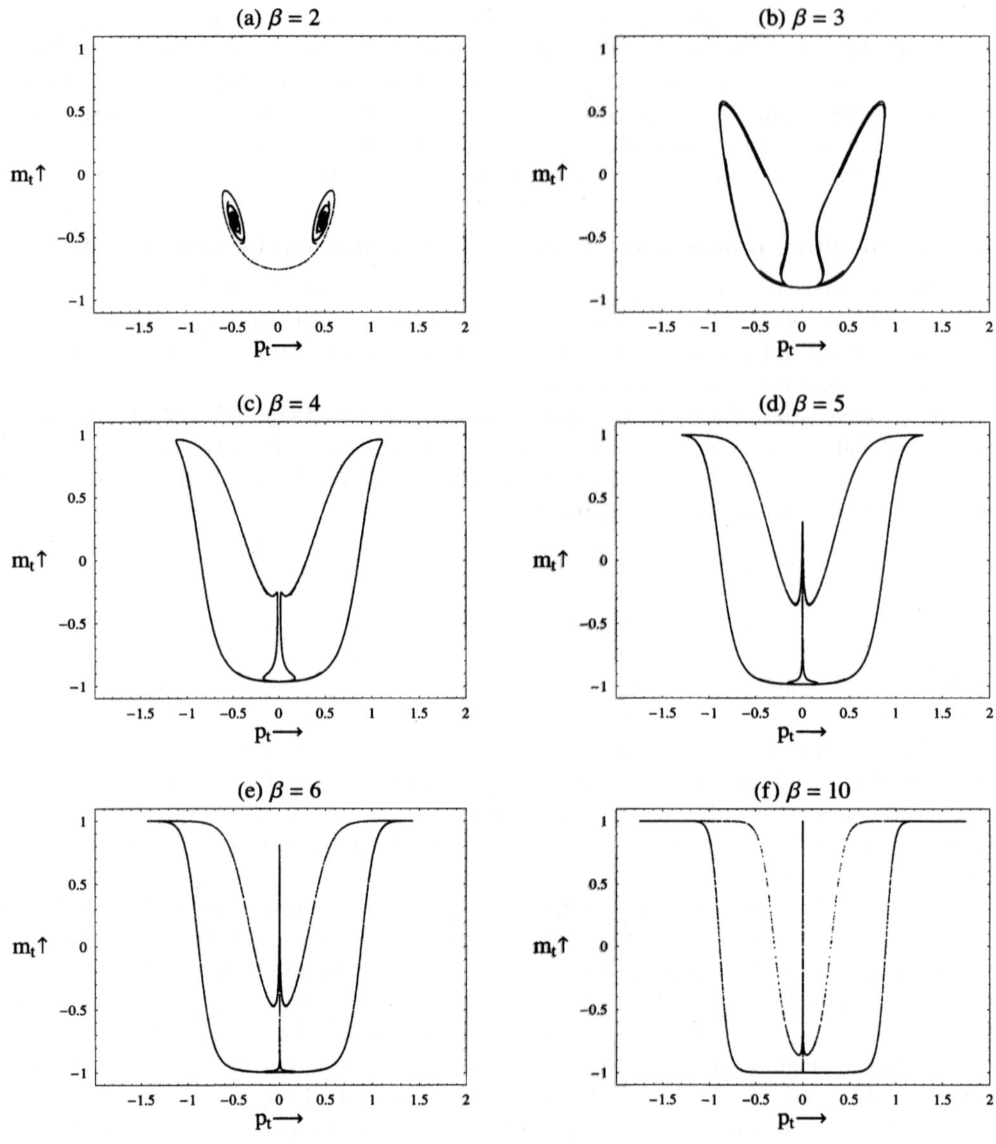

Figure 3. The unstable manifold of the steady state, for different values of the intensity of choice β. The stable manifold contains the vertical line segment $p = p^*$, or equivalently $x = 0$. The two branches of the unstable manifold spiral around the two points of the (un)stable 2-cycle. As the intensity of choice increases, the unstable manifold moves closer to the vertical line segment $x = 0$ contained in the stable manifold. For large β-values the ARED system is therefore close to a homoclinic tangency between the stable and the unstable manifold of the steady state.

by a stabilizing force when most agents become rational. On the other hand, once prices are close to their steady state, due to information costs for rational expectations most agents switch to cheap naive expectations, leading to market instability and diverging prices. Price fluctuations on the strange attractors are thus characterized by an irregular switching between a destabilizing force of cheap free riding and a costly, but stabilizing force of sophisticated prediction.

For a large value of the intensity of choice (corresponding to a high degree of rationality) the ARED system does not settle down to simple (periodic) behavior, but chaotic price fluctuations on a *strange attractor* arise. Applying the mathematical theory of homoclinic bifurcations (see e.g. Palis and Takens (1993)) BH97a have shown that the ARED system exhibits complicated dynamical behavior for a large set of parameter values:

Theorem. *Under assumption U, i.e. when the market is unstable under naive expectations, if information cost C for rational expectations is strictly positive, the ARED-model (2.18-2.19) has strange attractors for a set of β-values of positive Lebesgue measure.*

Adaptive rational equilibrium dynamics is a way of modeling evolutionary competition in a market with heterogeneous traders. The example of the cobweb model with rational versus naive expectations shows that differences in fitness may lead to market instability and endogenous fluctuations. In the next subsection we discuss a financial market applications of the evolutionary framework.

3 An asset pricing model

In this section we discuss a second application of the evolutionary framework proposed in Brock and Hommes (1997a). This application has been coined *Adaptive Belief Systems (ABS)*, and has been introduced in Brock (1997) and Brock and Hommes (1997b,1998), henceforth BH98. An ABS is in fact a standard discounted value asset pricing model derived from mean-variance maximization, extended to the case of *heterogeneous beliefs.*

Agents can either invest in a risk free asset or in a risky asset. The risk free asset is perfectly elastically supplied and pays a fixed rate of return r; the risky asset, for example a large stock or a market index, pays an uncertain dividend. Let p_t be the price per share (ex-dividend) of the risky asset at time t, and let y_t be the stochastic dividend process of the risky asset. Wealth dynamics is given by

$$\mathbf{W}_{t+1} = (1+r)W_t + (\mathbf{p}_{t+1} + \mathbf{y}_{t+1} - (1+r)p_t)z_t, \tag{3.1}$$

where bold face variables denote random variables at date $t+1$ and z_t denotes the number of shares of the risky asset purchased at date t. Let E_t and V_t denote the conditional expectation and conditional variance based on a publically available information set such as past prices and past dividends. Let E_{ht} and V_{ht} denote the 'beliefs' or forecasts of trader type h about conditional expectation and conditional variance. Agents are assumed to be myopic mean-variance maximizers so that the demand z_{ht} of type h for the risky asset solves

$$Max_{z_t}\{E_{ht}[\mathbf{W}_{t+1}] - \frac{a}{2}V_{ht}[\mathbf{W}_{t+1}]\}, \tag{3.2}$$

where a is the risk aversion parameter. The demand z_{ht} for risky assets by trader type h is then

$$z_{ht} = \frac{E_{ht}[\mathbf{p}_{t+1} + \mathbf{y}_{t+1} - (1+r)p_t]}{aV_{ht}[\mathbf{p}_{t+1} + \mathbf{y}_{t+1} - (1+r)p_t]} = \frac{E_{ht}[\mathbf{p}_{t+1} + \mathbf{y}_{t+1} - (1+r)p_t]}{a\sigma^2}, \tag{3.3}$$

where the conditional variance $V_{ht} = \sigma^2$ is assumed to be equal and constant for all types.[5] Let z^s denote the supply of outside risky shares per investor, assumed to be constant, and let n_{ht} denote the fraction of type h at date t. Equilibrium of demand and supply yields

$$\sum_{h=1}^{H} n_{ht} \frac{E_{ht}[\mathbf{p}_{t+1} + \mathbf{y}_{t+1} - (1+r)p_t]}{a\sigma^2} = z^s, \tag{3.4}$$

where H is the number of different trader types. BH98 focus on the special case of zero supply of outside shares, i.e. $z^s = 0$, for which the market equilibrium pricing equation becomes[6]

$$(1+r)p_t = \sum_{h=1}^{H} n_{ht} E_{ht}[\mathbf{p}_{t+1} + \mathbf{y}_{t+1}]. \tag{3.5}$$

3.1 The EMH benchmark with rational agents

Let us first discuss the EMH-benchmark with rational expectations. In a world where all traders are identical and expectations are *homogeneous* the arbitrage market equilibrium equation (3.5) reduces to

$$(1+r)p_t = E_t[\mathbf{p}_{t+1} + \mathbf{y}_{t+1}], \tag{3.6}$$

where E_t denotes the common conditional expectation of all traders at the beginning of period t, based on a publically available information set I_t such as past prices and dividends, i.e. $I_t = \{p_{t-1}, p_{t-2}, \ldots; y_{t-1}, y_{t-2}, \ldots\}$. This arbitrage market equilibrium equation (3.6) states that today's price of the risky asset must be equal to the sum of tomorrow's expected price and expected dividend, discounted by the risk free interest rate. It is well known that, using the arbitrage equation (3.6) repeatedly and assuming that the *transversality condition*

$$\lim_{t\to\infty} \frac{E_t[\mathbf{p}_{t+k}]}{(1+r)^k} = 0 \tag{3.7}$$

[5] Gaunersdorfer (2000) investigates the case with time varying beliefs about variances and shows that the results are quite similar to those for constant variance.

[6] Brock (1997) motivates this special case by introducing a risk adjusted dividend $y^{\#}_{t+1} = y_{t+1} - a\sigma^2 z^s$ to obtain the market equilibrium equation (3.5). In general however, the equilibrium equation (3.5) ignores a risk premium $a\sigma^2 z^s$ for investors holding the risky asset. Since dividends and a risk premium affect realized profits and wealth, in general they will affect the fractions n_{ht} of trader type h. The question how exactly the risk premium affects evolutionary competition should be investigated in future work, by taking z^s as a bifurcation parameter. The market equilibrium pricing equation (3.5) in fact represents the case of risk neutral investors.

holds, the price of the risky asset is uniquely determined by

$$p_t^* = \sum_{k=1}^{\infty} \frac{E_t[\mathbf{y}_{t+k}]}{(1+r)^k}. \tag{3.8}$$

The price p_t^* in (3.8) is called the EMH fundamental rational expectations (RE) price, or the *fundamental price* for short. The fundamental price is completely determined by economic fundamentals and given by the discounted sum of expected future dividends. In general, the properties of the fundamental price p_t^* depend upon the stochastic dividend process y_t. We focus on the case of an IID dividend process y_t, with constant mean $E[y_t] = \bar{y}$. We note however that any other random dividend process y_t may be substituted in what follows[7]. For an IID dividend process y_t with constant mean, the fundamental price is constant and given by

$$p^* = \sum_{k=1}^{\infty} \frac{\bar{y}}{(1+r)^k} = \frac{\bar{y}}{r}. \tag{3.9}$$

There are two crucial assumptions underlying the derivation of the RE fundamental price. The first is that expectations are *homogeneous*, all traders are *rational* and it is *common knowledge* that all traders are rational. In such an ideal, perfectly rational world the fundamental price can be derived from economic fundamentals. Conditions under which a RE price can be derived can be relaxed, to include for example noise traders or limited heterogeneity of information. In general however, in a world with *heterogeneous* traders having different beliefs or expectations about future prices and dividends, derivation of a RE fundamental price requires perfect knowledge about the beliefs of *all* other traders. In a real market understanding the beliefs and strategies of all other, competing traders is virtually impossible, and therefore in a heterogeneous world derivation of the RE-fundamental price becomes impossible. The second crucial assumption underlying the derivation of the fundamental price is the transversality condition (3.7), requiring that the long run growth rate of prices (and risk adjusted dividends) is smaller than the risk free growth rate r. In fact, in addition to the fundamental solution (3.8) so-called *speculative bubble solutions* of the form

$$p_t = p_t^* + (1+r)^t (p_0 - p_0^*) \tag{3.10}$$

also satisfy the arbitrage equation (3.6). It is important to note that along the speculative bubble solution (3.10), traders have rational expectations. Solutions of the form (3.10) are therefore called *rational bubbles.* These rational bubble solutions are explosive and do *not* satisfy the transversality condition. In a perfectly rational world, traders realize that speculative bubbles cannot last forever and therefore they will never get started and the finite fundamental price p_t^* is uniquely determined. In a perfectly rational world, all traders thus believe that the value of a risky asset equals its fundamental price forever. Changes in asset prices are solely driven by unexpected changes in dividends and random

[7]Brock and Hommes (1997b) for example discuss a non-stationary example, where the dividend process is a geometric random walk .

'news' about economic fundamentals. In a heterogeneous evolutionary world however, the situation will be quite different, and we will see that evolutionary forces may lead to endogenous switching between the fundamental price and the rational self fulfilling bubble solutions.

3.2 Heterogeneous beliefs

In the asset pricing model with heterogeneous beliefs, market equilibrium in (3.5) states that the price p_t of the risky asset equals the discounted value of tomorrow's expected price plus tomorrow's expected dividend, *averaged* over all different trader types. In such a *heterogeneous* world temporary upward or downward bubbles with prices deviating from the fundamental may arise, when the fractions of traders believing in those bubbles is large enough. Once a (temporary) bubble has started, evolutionary forces may reinforce deviations from the benchmark fundamental. We shall now be more precise about traders' expectations (forecasts) about future prices and dividends. It will be convenient to work with

$$x_t = p_t - p_t^*, \tag{3.11}$$

the *deviation* from the fundamental price. We make the following assumptions about the beliefs of trader type h:

B1 $V_{ht}[\mathbf{p}_{t+1} + \mathbf{y}_{t+1} - (1+r)p_t] = V_t[\mathbf{p}_{t+1} + \mathbf{y}_{t+1} - (1+r)p_t] = \sigma^2$, for all h, t.

B2 $E_{ht}[\mathbf{y}_{t+1}] = E_t[\mathbf{y}_{t+1}]$, for all h, t.

B3 All beliefs $E_{ht}[\mathbf{p}_{t+1}]$ are of the form

$$E_{ht}[\mathbf{p}_{t+1}] = E_t[\mathbf{p}^*_{t+1}] + f_h(x_{t-1}, ..., x_{t-L}), \qquad \text{for all } h, t. \tag{3.12}$$

According to assumption B1 beliefs about conditional variance are equal and constant for all types, as discussed above already. Assumption B2 states that expectations about future dividends $\mathbf{y}_{t+1}$ are the same for all trader types and equal to the conditional expectation. All traders are thus able to derive the fundamental price p_t^* in (3.8) that would prevail in a perfectly rational world. According to assumption B3, traders nevertheless believe that in a heterogeneous world prices may *deviate* from their fundamental value p_t^* by some function f_h depending upon past deviations from the fundamental. Each forecasting rule f_h represents the *model of the market* according to which type h believes that prices will deviate from the commonly shared fundamental price. For example, a forecasting strategy f_h may correspond to a technical trading rule, based upon short run or long run moving averages, of the type used in real markets.

Strictly speaking (3.12) is not a technical trading rule, because it uses the fundamental price in its forecast. Including price forecasting rules depending upon past prices only, not using any information about fundamentals, yields similar results. We will use the short hand notation

$$f_{ht} = f_h(x_{t-1}, ..., x_{t-L}) \tag{3.13}$$

for the forecasting strategy employed by trader type h. An important and convenient consequence of the assumptions B1-B3 concerning traders' beliefs is that the heterogeneous agent market equilibrium equation (3.5) can be reformulated in deviations from the benchmark fundamental. In particular substituting the price forecast (3.12) in the market equilibrium equation (3.5) and using the facts that the fundamental price p_t^* satisfies $(1+r)p_t^* = E_t[p_{t+1}^* + y_{t+1}]$ and the price $p_t = x_t + p_t^*$ yields the equilibrium equation in deviations from the fundamental:

$$(1+r)x_t = \sum_{h=1}^{H} n_{ht} E_{ht}[\mathbf{x}_{t+1}] \equiv \sum_{h=1}^{H} n_{ht} f_{ht}, \tag{3.14}$$

with $f_{ht} = f_h(x_{t-1}, ..., x_{t-L})$. An important reason for our model formulation in terms of deviations from a benchmark fundamental is that in this general setup, the benchmark rational expectations asset pricing model is *nested* as a special case, with all forecasting strategies $f_h \equiv 0$. In this way, the adaptive belief systems can be used in empirical and experimental testing whether asset prices deviate significantly from anyone's favorite benchmark fundamental.

3.3 Evolutionary dynamics

The evolutionary part of the model describes how beliefs are updated over time, that is, how the fractions n_{ht} of trader types in the market equilibrium equation (3.14) evolve over time. Fractions are updated according to an *evolutionary fitness* or performance measure. The fitness measures of all trading strategies are publically available, but subject to noise. Fitness is derived from a random utility model and given by

$$\tilde{U}_{ht} = U_{ht} + \epsilon_{ht}, \tag{3.15}$$

where U_{ht} is the *deterministic part* of the fitness measure and ϵ_{ht} represents noise. Assuming that the noise ϵ_{ht} is IID across $h = 1, ...H$ drawn from a double exponential distribution, in the limit as the number of agents goes to infinity, the probability that an agent chooses strategy h is given by the well known *discrete choice model* or 'Gibbs' probabilities[8]

$$n_{ht} = \frac{exp(\beta U_{h,t-1})}{Z_{t-1}}, \qquad Z_{t-1} = \sum_{h=1}^{H} exp(\beta U_{h,t-1}), \tag{3.16}$$

where Z_{t-1} is a normalization factor in order for the fractions n_{ht} to add up to 1. The crucial feature of (3.16) is that the higher the fitness of trading strategy h, the more traders will select strategy h. The parameter β in (3.16) is called the *intensity of choice*, measuring how sensitive the mass of traders is to selecting the optimal prediction strategy. The intensity of choice β is inversely related to the variance of the noise terms ϵ_{ht}. The extreme case $\beta = 0$ corresponds to the case of infinite variance noise, so that differences in fitness cannot be observed and all fractions (3.16) will be fixed over time and equal to $1/H$. The other extreme case $\beta = +\infty$ corresponds to the case without noise, so that the deterministic part of the fitness can be observed perfectly and in each period, *all* traders choose the optimal forecast. An increase in the intensity of choice β represents

[8]See Manski and McFadden (1981) and Anderson, de Palma and Thisse (1993) for extensive discussion of discrete choice models and their applications in economics.

an increase in the degree of rationality w.r.t. evolutionary selection of trading strategies. The timing of the coupling between the market equilibrium equation (3.5) or (3.14) and the evolutionary selection of strategies (3.16) is crucial. The market equilibrium price p_t in (3.5) depends upon the fractions n_{ht}. The notation in (3.16) stresses the fact that these fractions n_{ht} depend upon *past* fitness $U_{h,t-1}$, which in turn depend upon past prices p_{t-1} and dividends y_{t-1} in periods $t-1$ and further in the past as will be seen below. After the equilibrium price p_t has been revealed by the market, it will be used in evolutionary updating of beliefs and determining the new fractions $n_{h,t+1}$. These new fractions $n_{h,t+1}$ will then determine a new equilibrium price p_{t+1}, etc.. In the ABS, market equilibrium prices and fractions of different trading strategies thus co-evolve over time.

A natural candidate for evolutionary fitness is accumulated *realized profits*, as given by

$$U_{ht} = (p_t + y_t - Rp_{t-1})\frac{E_{h,t-1}[\mathbf{p}_t + \mathbf{y}_t - Rp_{t-1}]}{a\sigma^2} - C_h + wU_{h,t-1} \qquad (3.17)$$

where $R = 1 + r$ is the gross risk free rate of return, C_h represents an average per period *cost* of obtaining forecasting strategy h and $0 \leq w \leq 1$ is a *memory* parameter measuring how fast past realized fitness is discounted for strategy selection. The cost C_h for obtaining forecasting strategy h will be zero for simple, habitual rule of thumb forecasting rules, but may be positive for more sophisticated forecasting strategies. For example, costs for forecasting strategies based upon economic fundamentals may be positive representing investors' effort for information gathering and market research, whereas costs for technical trading rules may be (close to) zero. The first term in (3.17) represents last period's realized profit of type h given by the realized excess return of the risky asset over the risk free asset times the demand for the risky asset by traders of type h. In the extreme case with no memory, i.e. $w = 0$, fitness U_{ht} equals net realized profit in the previous period, whereas in the other extreme case with infinite memory, i.e. $w = 1$, fitness U_{ht} equals total wealth as given by accumulated realized profits over the entire past. In the intermediate case, the weight given to past realized profits decreases exponentially with time.

Fitness can now be rewritten in deviations from the fundamental as

$$U_{ht} = (x_t - Rx_{t-1})(\frac{f_{h,t-1} - Rx_{t-1}}{a\sigma^2}) - C_h + wU_{h,t-1}. \qquad (3.18)$$

3.4 Forecasting rules

To complete the model we have to specify the class of forecasting rules. Brock and Hommes (1998) have investigated evolutionary competition between *simple linear* forecasting rules with only *one lag*, i.e.

$$f_{ht} = g_h x_{t-1} + b_h. \qquad (3.19)$$

It can be argued that, for a forecasting rule to have any impact in real markets, it has to be simple. For a complicated forecasting rule it seems unlikely that enough traders will coordinate on that particular rule so that it affects market equilibrium prices. Although the linear forecasting rule (3.19) is extremely simple, it represent a number of important cases. For example, when both the trend parameter and the bias parameter $g_h = b_h = 0$ the rule reduces to the forecast of *fundamentalists*, i.e.

$$f_{ht} \equiv 0, \tag{3.20}$$

believing that the market price will be equal to the fundamental price p^*, or equivalently that the deviation x from the fundamental will be 0. Other important cases covered by the linear forecasting rule (3.19) are the pure *trend followers*

$$f_{ht} = g_h x_{t-1}, \qquad g_h > 0, \tag{3.21}$$

and the pure *biased belief*

$$f_{ht} = b_h. \tag{3.22}$$

Notice that the simple pure bias forecast (3.22) represents *any* positively or negatively biased forecast of next periods price that traders might have. Instead of these extremely simple habitual rule of thumb forecasting rules, some economists might prefer the rational, *perfect foresight* forecasting rule

$$f_{ht} = x_{t+1}. \tag{3.23}$$

We emphasize however, that the perfect foresight forecasting rule (3.23) assumes perfect knowledge of the heterogeneous market equilibrium equation (3.5), and in particular perfect knowledge about the beliefs of *all* other traders. Although the case with perfect foresight certainly has theoretical appeal, its practical relevance in a complex heterogeneous world should not be overstated since this underlying assumption seems highly unrealistic.[9]

3.5 Simple examples

This section presents simple, but typical examples of ABS, with two, three resp. four competing *linear* forecasting rules (3.19), where the parameter g_h represents a perceived *trend* in prices and the parameter b_h represents a perceived upward or downward *bias*[10].

---

[9] In the cobweb model with rational versus naive agents of the previous section, the implicitly defined heterogeneous market equilibrium equation (2.8) remains tractable and can be solved explicitly for the unique market equilibrium price (2.9). In general however, with one type of agents having rational expectations or perfect foresight a *temporary equilibrium* model with heterogeneous beliefs such as the asset pricing market equilibrium equation in (3.24) becomes an *implicitly defined* dynamical system with x_t on the LHS and x_{t+1} and e.g. x_{t-1} on the RHS. Typically such implicitly defined evolutionary systems cannot be solved explicitely and often they are not even well-defined.

[10] Brock, Hommes and Wagener (2004) recently introduced the notion of *Large Type Limit (LTL)* to study the model with a large number of different belief types.

The ABS then becomes (in deviations from the fundamental):

$$
\begin{aligned}
(1+r)x_t &= \sum_{h=1}^{H} n_{ht}(g_h x_{t-1} + b_h) + \epsilon_t && (3.24)\\
n_{h,t} &= \frac{exp(\beta U_{h,t-1})}{\sum_{h=1}^{H} exp(\beta U_{h,t-1})} && (3.25)\\
U_{h,t-1} &= (x_{t-1} - R x_{t-2})\left(\frac{g_h x_{t-3} + b_h - R x_{t-2}}{a\sigma^2}\right) + w U_{h,t-2} - C_h, && (3.26)
\end{aligned}
$$

where ϵ_t is a small noise term representing uncertainty about economic fundamentals, e.g. random outside supply of the risky asset. In order to keep the analysis of the dynamical behavior tractable, BH98 have mainly focused on the case where the memory parameter $w = 0$, so that evolutionary fitness is given by last period's realized profit. Here, we review examples with two, three and four forecasting rules stating the most important bifurcation results without; for proofs, the interested reader is referred to Brock and Hommes (1998). A common feature of all examples is that, as the intensity of choice to switch prediction or trading strategies increases, the fundamental steady state becomes locally unstable and non-fundamental steady states, cycles or even chaos arise.

Costly fundamentalists versus trend followers The simplest example of an ABS only has *two* trader types, with forecasting rules

$$
\begin{aligned}
f_{1t} &= 0 && \text{fundamentalists} && (3.27)\\
f_{2t} &= g x_{t-1}, \quad g > 0, && \text{trend followers} && (3.28)
\end{aligned}
$$

that is, the first type are fundamentalists predicting that the price will equal its fundamental value (or equivalently that the deviation will be zero) and the second type are pure trend followers predicting that prices will rise (or fall) by a constant rate. In this example, the fundamentalists have to pay a fixed per period positive cost C_1 for information gathering; in all other examples discussed below information costs will be set to zero for all trader types.

For small values of the trend parameter, $0 \leq g < 1+r$, the fundamental steady state is always stable. Only for sufficiently high trend parameters, $g > 1+r$, trend followers can *destabilize* the system. For trend parameter, $1+r < g < (1+r)^2$ the dynamic behavior of the evolutionary system depends upon the intensity of choice to switch between the two trading strategies[11]. For low values of the intensity of choice, the fundamental steady state will be stable. As the intensity of choice increases, the fundamental steady state becomes unstable due to a *pitchfork bifurcation* in which two additional non-fundamental steady states $-x^* < 0 < x^*$ are created. The evolutionary ABS may converge to the positive non-fundamental steady state, to the negative non-fundamental steady state, or,

[11] For $g > (1+r)^2$ the system may become *globally unstable* and prices may diverge to infinity. Imposing a stabilizing force, for example by assuming that trend followers condition their rule upon deviations from the fundamental e.g. as in Gaunersdorfer et al. (2000), leads to a bounded system again, possibly with cycles or even chaotic fluctuations.

in the presence of noise, switch back and forth between the high and the low steady state. As the intensity of choice increases further, the two non-fundamental steady states also become unstable due to a Hopf-bifurcation, and limit cycles or even strange attractors can arise around each of the (unstable) non-fundamental steady states, as illustrated in Figure 4. The evolutionary ABS may cycle around the positive non-fundamental steady state, cycle around the negative non-fundamental steady state or, driven by the noise, switch back and forth between cycles around the high and the low steady state.

This example shows that, in the presence of information costs and with zero memory, when the intensity of choice in evolutionary switching is high fundamentalists can *not* drive out pure trend followers and persistent deviations from the fundamental price may occur. Brock and Hommes (1999) show that this result also holds when the memory in the fitness measure increases. In fact, an increase in the memory of the evolutionary fitness leads to bifurcation routes very similar to bifurcation routes due to an increase in the intensity of choice.

Figure 5 illlustrates that the asset pricing model with costly fundemtalists versus cheap trend following exhibits a rational route to randomness, i.e. a bifurcation route to chaos as the intensity of choice to switch strategies increases.

Fundamentalists versus opposite biases In the cobweb model with rational versus naive expectations in the previous section as well as in the two type asset pricing model with fundamentalists versus trend followers rational routes to randomness occur due to information costs for the sophisticated forecasting strategy. The second example of an ABS is an example with *three* trader types without any information costs. The forecasting rules are

$$f_{1t} = 0 \qquad \text{fundamentalists} \tag{3.29}$$

$$f_{2t} = b \qquad b > 0, \qquad \text{positive bias (optimists)} \tag{3.30}$$

$$f_{3t} = -b \qquad -b < 0, \qquad \text{negative bias (pessimists).} \tag{3.31}$$

The first type are fundamentalists again, but as stated above there will be *no* information costs for fundamentalists or other types. The second and third types have a purely *biased* belief, expecting a constant price above respectively below the fundamental price.

For low values of the intensity of choice, the fundamental steady state is stable. As the intensity of choice increases the fundamental steady becomes unstable due to a *Hopf* bifurcation and the dynamics of the ABS is characterized by cycles around the unstable steady state. This example shows that, even when there are *no* information costs for fundamentalists, they cannot drive out other trader types with opposite biased beliefs. In the evolutionary ABS with high intensity of choice, fundamentalists and biased traders co-exist with fractions varying over time and prices cycling around the unstable fundamental steady state. Moreover, Brock and Hommes (1998, p.1259, lemma 9) show that as the intensity of choice tends to infinity the ABS converges to a (globally) stable cycle of period 4. Average profits along this 4-cycle are equal for all three trader types. Hence, if the initial wealth is equal for all three types, then in this evolutionary system in the long run accumulated wealth will be equal for all three types. This example suggests

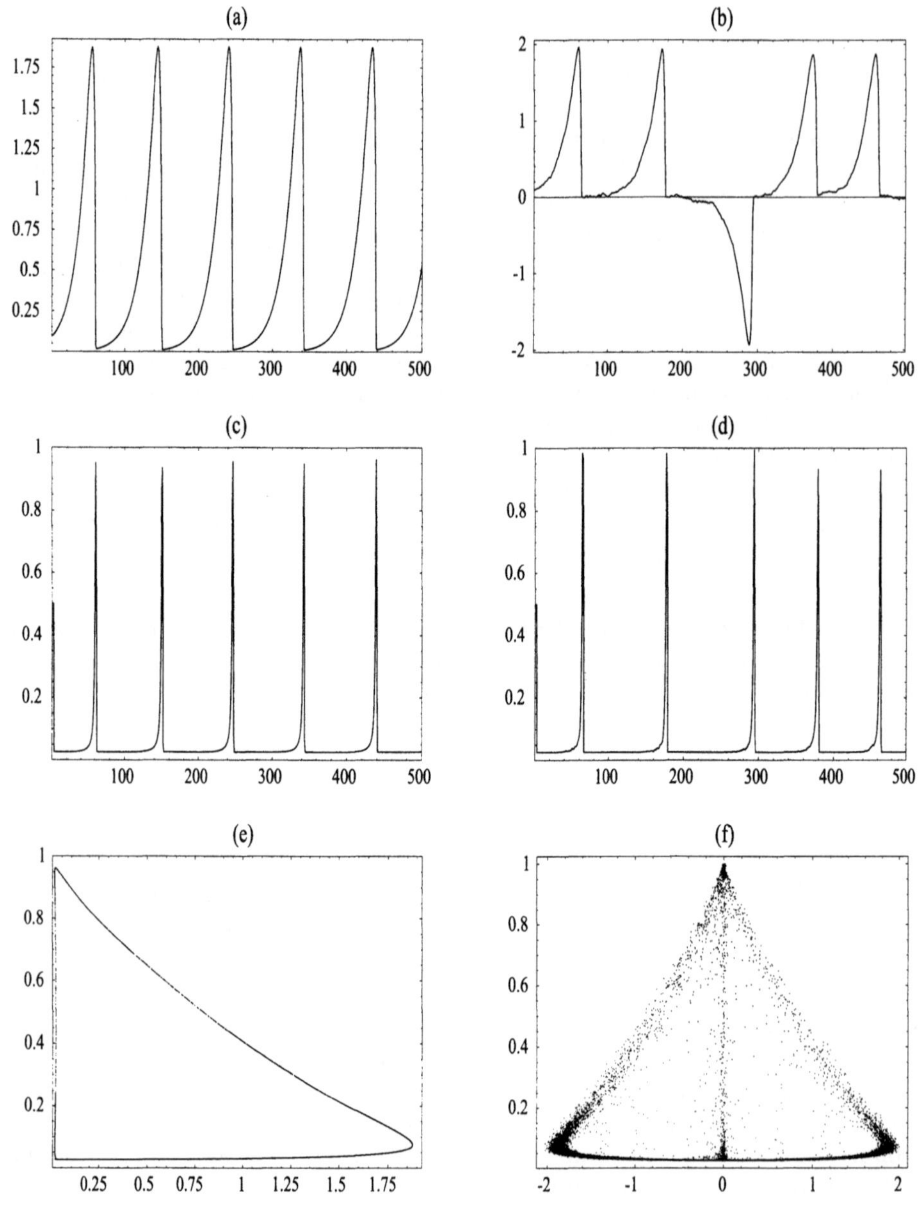

Figure 4. Time series of prices (deviations from the fundamental steady state) and fractions and attractors in the phase space for 2-type model with costly fundamentalists versus trend followers. The left panel shows chaotic dynamics without noise and the right panel illustrates the model buffeted with small noise (SD=0.01 of noise term ϵ_t in (3.24)). Without noise (left panel) the system settles down to the attractor with prices above the fundamental value. In the presence of (small) noise, the system switches back and forth between the two co-existing attractors with prices jumping between above and below fundamental values. Parameters are: $\beta = 3.6$, $g = 1.2$, $R = 1.1$ and $C = 1$.

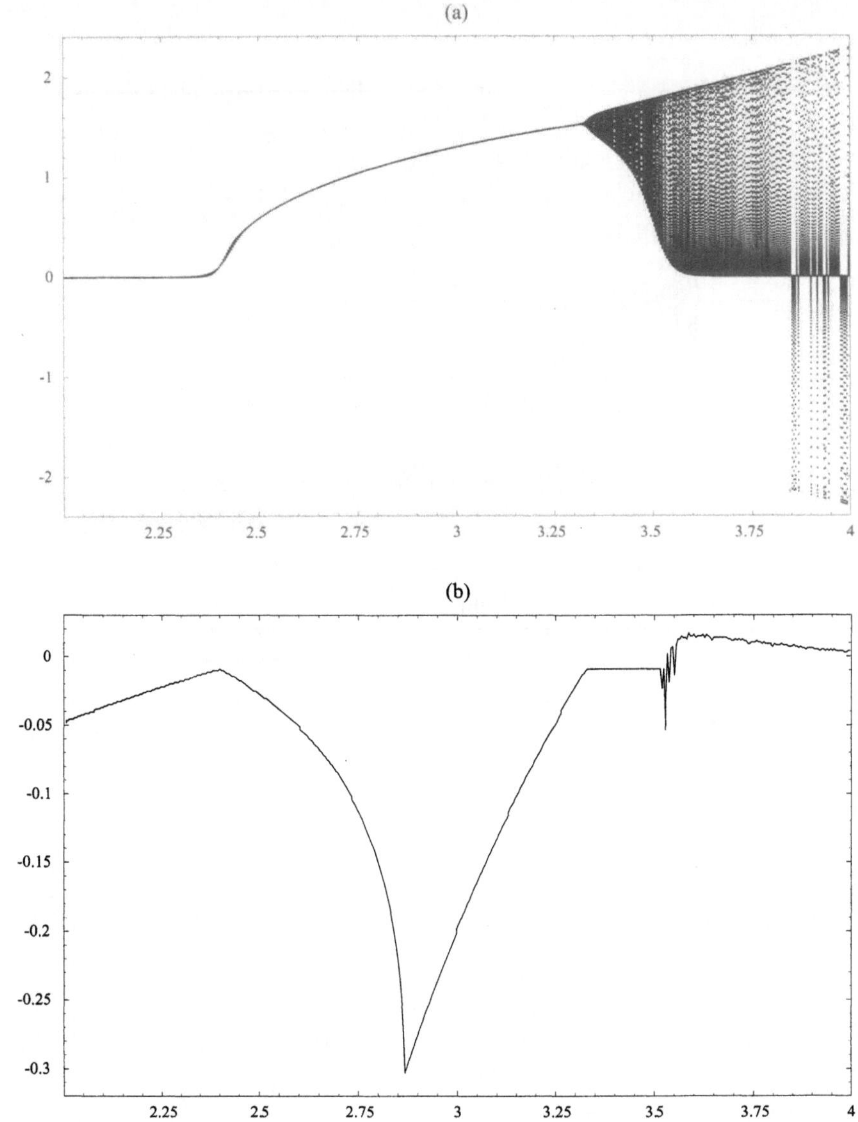

Figure 5. Bifurcation diagram (top) and largest Lyapunov exponent plot (bottom) for 2-type model with costly fundamentalist versus trend followers. In both plots the model is buffeted with very small noise ($SD = 10^{-6}$ for the noise term ϵ_t in (3.24)), to avoid that for large β-values the system gets stuck in the locally unstable steady state. Parameters are: $g = 1.2$, $R = 1.1$, $C = 1$ and $2 \leq \beta \leq 4$. A pitchfork bifurcation of the fundamental steady state, in which two stable non-fundamental steady states are created, occurs for $\beta \approx 2.37$. The non-fundamental steady states become unstable due to a Hopf-bifurcation for $\beta \approx 3.33$, and (quasi-)periodic dynamics arises. For large values of β the largest Lyapunov exponent becomes positive indicating chaotic price dynamics.

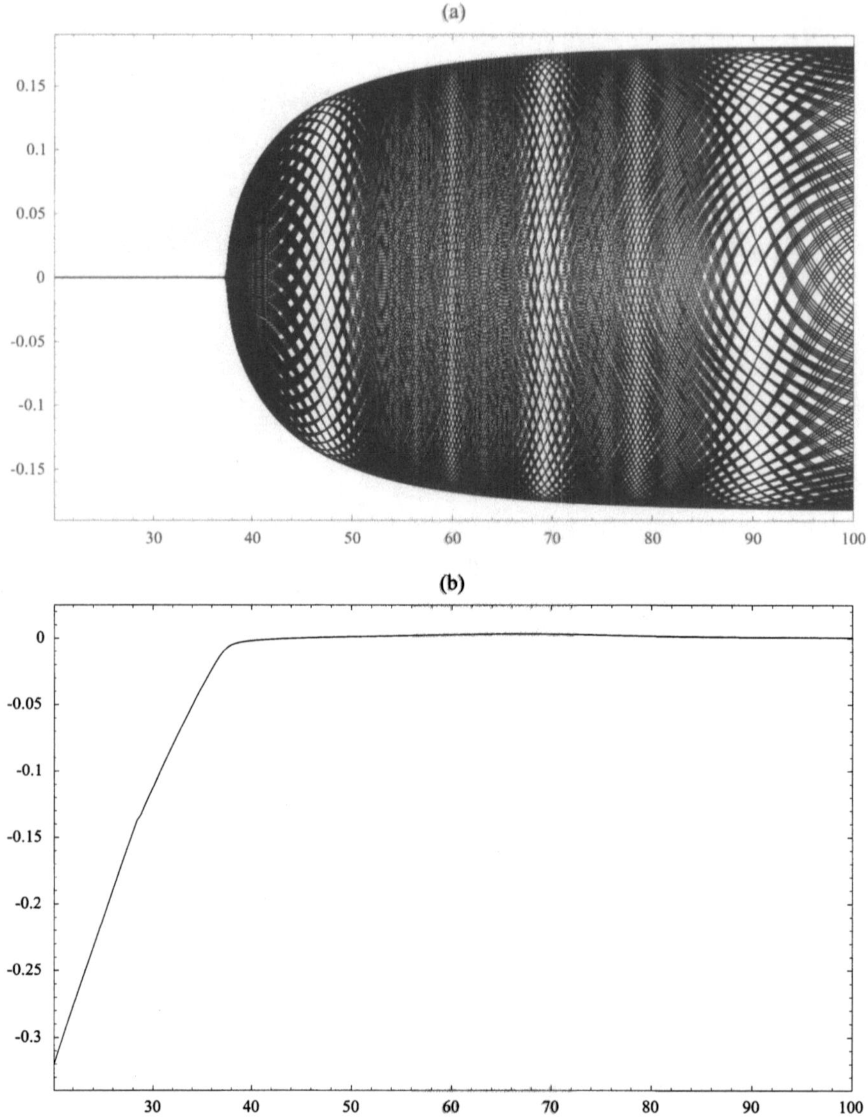

Figure 6. Bifurcation diagram and largest Lyapunov exponent plot for 3-type model. In both plots the model is buffeted with very small noise ($SD = 10^{-6}$ for the noise term ϵ_t in (3.24)), to avoid that for large β-values the system gets stuck in the locally unstable steady state. Belief parameters are: $g_1 = 0$, $b_1 = 0$; $g_2 = 0$, $b_2 = 0.2$ and $g_3 = 0$, $b_3 = -0.2$; other parameters are $r = 0.1$, $20 \leq \beta \leq 100$, $w = 0$ and $C_h = 0$ for all $1 \leq h \leq 3$ The 3-type model with fundamentalists versus opposite biases exhibits a Hopf bifurcation for $\beta \approx 37.4$. For large values of β periodic and quasi-periodic dynamics occurs, but chaos with positive largest Lyapunov exponent does not arise.

that the Friedman argument that smart-fundamental traders will automatically drive out simple habitual rule of speculative traders should be considered with care.

In this example with three trader types, cycles can occur but chaos does not arise. This is illustrated in Figure 6 showing a bifurcation diagram and a plot of the largest Lyapunov exponent. In the three type example with fundamentalists versus opposite biases, even in the presence of (small) noise, price fluctuations will be fairly regular and therefore returns will be predictable. This predictability will disappear however when we combine trend following with biased beliefs.

3.6 Fundamentalists versus trend and bias

The third example of an ABS is an example with *four* trader types, with linear forecasting rules (3.19) with parameters $g_1 = 0$, $b_1 = 0$; $g_2 = 0.9$, $b_2 = 0.2$; $g_3 = 0.9$, $b_3 = -0.2$ and $g_4 = 1 + r = 1.01$, $b_4 = 0$. The first type are fundamentalists again, without information costs, and the other three types follow a simple linear forecasting rule with one lag. The dynamical behaviour is illustrated in Figures 7 and 8.

For low values of the intensity of choice, the fundamental steady state is stable. As the intensity of choice increases, as in the previous three type example, the fundamental steady becomes unstable due to a *Hopf* bifurcation and a stable invariant circle around the unstable fundamental steady state arises, with periodic or quasi-periodic fluctuations. As the intensity of choice further increases, the invariant circle breaks into a strange attractor with chaotic fluctuations. In the evolutionary ABS fundamentalists and chartists co-exist with fractions varying over time and prices moving chaotically around the unstable fundamental steady state. Figure 8 shows that in this 4-type example with fundamentalists versus trend followers and biased beliefs a rational route to randomness occurs, with positive largest Lyapunov exponents for large values of β.

The (noisy) chaotic price fluctuations are characterized by an irregular switching between phases of close-to-the-EMH-fundamental-price fluctuations, phases of 'optimism' with prices following an upward trend, and phases of 'pessimism', with (small) sudden market crashes, as illustrated in Figure 7. Recall from subsection 3.1 that the asset pricing model with homogeneous beliefs, in addition to the benchmark fundamental price, has rational bubble solutions as in (3.10). One might say that in the ABS prices are characterized by an evolutionary switching between the fundamental value and these temporary speculative bubbles. In the purely deterministic chaotic case, the timing and the direction of the temporary bubbles seem hard to predict. However, once a bubble has started, in the deterministic case, the length of the bubble seems to be predictable in most of the cases. In the presence of noise, as in figure 7 (top right), the timing, the direction and the length of the bubble all seem hard to predict.

In order to investigate this (un)predictability issue further, we employ a so called *nearest neighbor forecasting method* to predict the returns, at lags 1 to 20 for the purely chaotic as well as for several noisy chaotic time series, as illustrated in figure 9.[12] Nearest neighbor forecasting looks for past patterns close to the most recent pattern, and then yields as the prediction the average value following all nearby past patterns. It follows essentially from Takens' embedding theorem that this method yields good forecasts for

[12] I would like to thank Sebastiano Manzan for providing this figure.

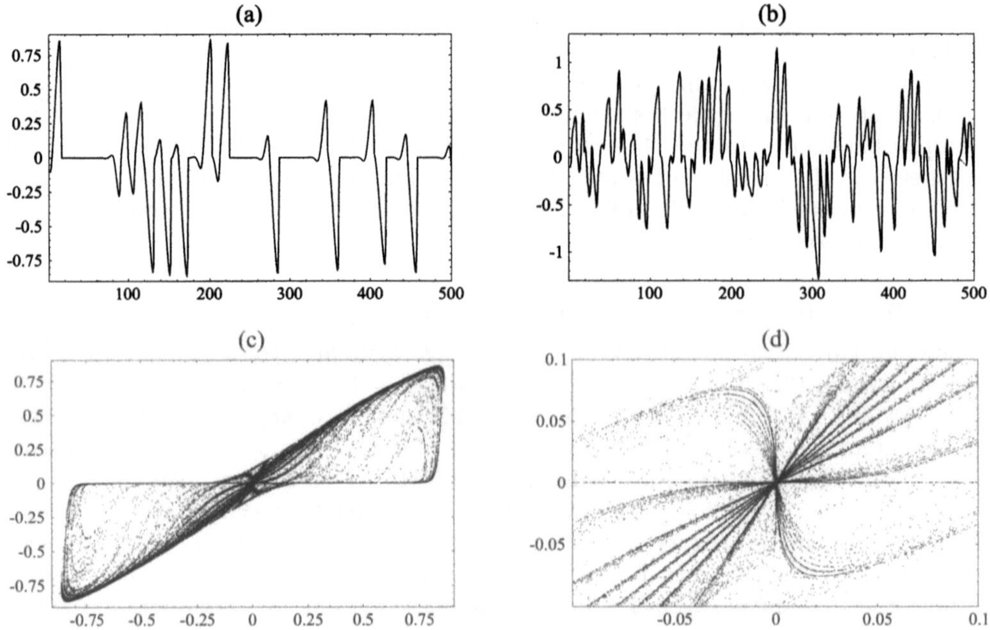

Figure 7. Chaotic (top left) and noisy chaotic (top right) time series of asset prices in adaptive belief system with four trader types. Strange attractor (bottom left) and enlargement of strange attractor (bottom right). Belief parameters are: $g_1 = 0$, $b_1 = 0$; $g_2 = 0.9$, $b_2 = 0.2$; $g_3 = 0.9$, $b_3 = -0.2$ and $g_4 = 1 + r = 1.01$, $b_4 = 0$; other parameters are $r = 0.01$, $\beta = 90.5$, $w = 0$ and $C_h = 0$ for all $1 \leq h \leq 4$.

deterministic chaotic systems[13]. Figure 9 shows that as the noise level increases, the forecasting performance of the nearest neighbor method quickly deteriorates. Hence, in our simple nonlinear evolutionary ABS with noise it is hard to make good forecasts of future returns. Our simple nonlinear ABS with small noise thus captures some of the intrinsic unpredictability of asset returns also present in real markets.

This 4-type example shows that when memory is zero, even when there are *no* information costs for fundamentalists, they cannot drive out other simple trader types and fail to stabilize price fluctuations towards its fundamental value. As in the three type case, the opposite biases create cyclic behavior but apparently the additional trend parameters turn these cycles into unpredictable chaotic fluctuations.

[13]See Kantz and Schreiber (1997) for a recent and extensive treatment of nonlinear time series analysis and forecasting techniques.

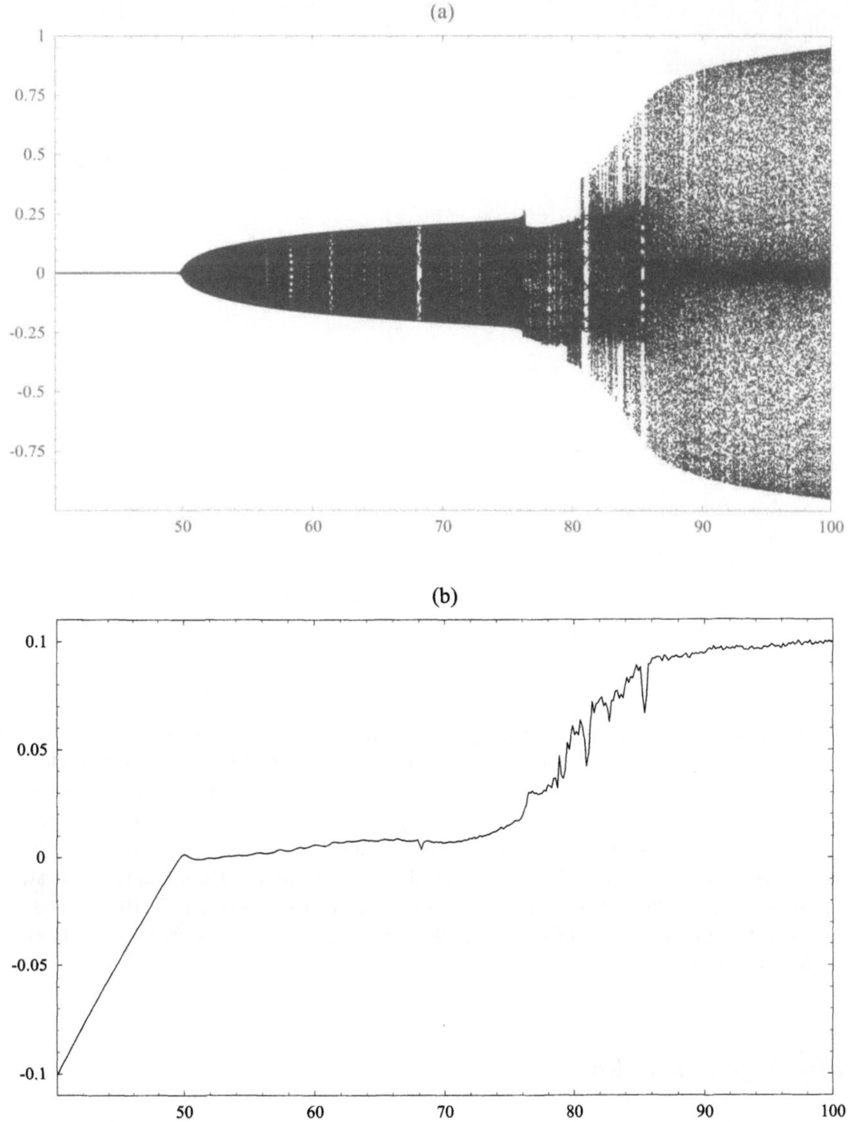

Figure 8. Bifurcation diagram and largest Lyapunov exponent plot for 4-type model. In both plots the model is buffeted with very small noise ($SD = 10^{-6}$ for noise term ϵ_t in (3.24)), to avoid that for large β-values the system gets stuck in the locally unstable steady state. Belief parameters are: $g_1 = 0$, $b_1 = 0$; $g_2 = 0.9$, $b_2 = 0.2$; $g_3 = 0.9$, $b_3 = -0.2$ and $g_4 = 1 + r = 1.01$, $b_4 = 0$; other parameters are $r = 0.01$, $\beta = 90.5$, $w = 0$ and $C_h = 0$ for all $1 \leq h \leq 4$. The 4-type model with fundamentalists versus trend followers and biased beliefs exhibits a Hopf bifurcation for $\beta = 50$. A rational route to randomness occurs, with positive largest Lyapunov exponents, when the intensity of choice becomes large.

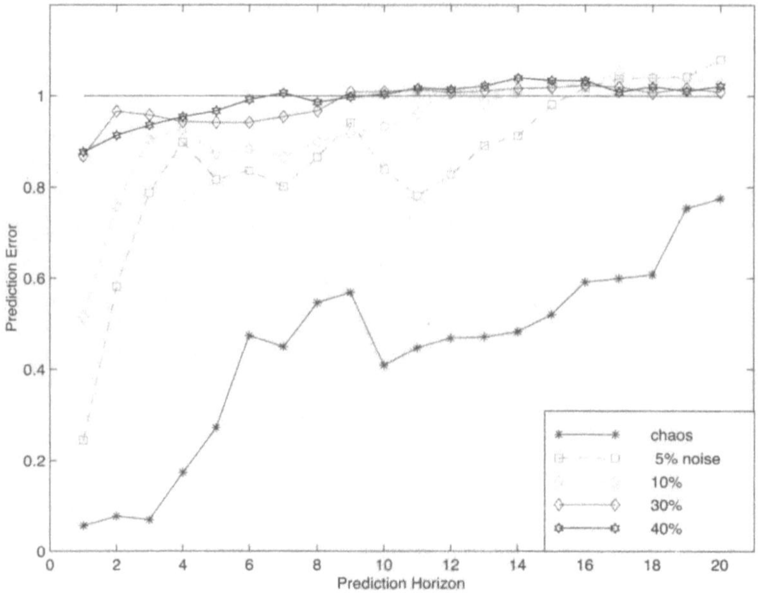

Figure 9. Forecasting errors for nearest neighbor method applied to chaotic returns series as well as noisy chaotic returns series, for different noise levels, in ABS with four trader types. All returns series have close to zero autocorrelations at all lags. The benchmark case of prediction by the mean 0 is represented by the horizontal line at the normalized prediction error 1. Nearest neighbor forecasting applied to the purely deterministic chaotic series leads to much smaller forecasting errors (lowest graph). A noise level of say 10% means that the ratio of the variance of the noise term ϵ_t and the variance of the deterministic price series is 1/10. As the noise level slowly increases, the graphs are shifted upwards. Small dynamic noise thus quickly deteriorates forecasting performance.

4 Concluding remarks

We have reviewed two simple heterogeneous agent models. In both the cobweb model and the asset pricing model we have focussed on the case of linear demand and supply curves. Heterogeneity and evolutionary updating of trading strategies creates an important *nonlinearity* in the model. In particular, when agents are highly sensitive to differences in evolutionary fitness the nonlinear evolutionary switching mechanism causes complicated, unpredictable price fluctuations. In the cobweb model, due to costs for information gathering, perfectly rational agents can not drive out boundely rational agents using simple habitual rule of thumb trading strategies. In the asset pricing model, even without information costs for fundamentalist traders, prices need not converge to the RE fundamental benchmark. Our evolutionary framework thus explains excess volatility and persistent deviations from the fundamental benchmark. More work is needed to investigate how general these phenomena are, for example with respect to introducing more memory in the evolutionary fitness measures.

Is a significant part of changes in stock prices driven by 'Keynesian animal spirits'? For many decades already, this question has lead to heavy debates among economic academics as well as financial practitioners. In the evolutionary adaptive belief systems discussed here, price changes are explained by a *combination* of economic fundamentals and 'market psychology'. Negative economic 'news' (e.g. on inflation or interest rates) may act as a trigger event for a decline in stock prices, which may become reinforced by investors sentiment and evolutionary forces. Price movements are driven by an interaction of fundamentalism and chartism, the two most important trading strategies in financial practice.

Our evolutionary ABS may be seen as, what Sargent (1999) calls an *approximate rational expectations equilibrium.* Traders are boundedly rational and use relatively simple strategies. The class of trading rules is disciplined by evolutionary forces based upon realized profits or wealth. A convenient feature of our theoretical setup is that the benchmark rational expectations model is *nested* as a special case. This feature gives the model flexibility with respect to experimental and empirical testing. It is worthwhile noting that Baak (1999) and Chavas (2000) have run empirical tests for heterogeneity in expectations in agricultural data and indeed find evidence for the presence of boundedly rational traders in the cattle market. It may seem even more natural that heterogeneity and evolutionary switching between different trading strategies play an important role in financial markets. Understanding the role of market psychology seems to be a crucial part of understanding the huge changes in stock prices observed so frequently these days. But much more insight into 'financial psychology' is needed, before 'market sentiment' based policy advice can be given. Theoretical analysis of stylized evolutionary adaptive market systems, as discussed here, and its empirical and experimental testing may contribute in providing such insight.

Bibliography

[1] Anderson, S., de Palma, A. and Thisse, J., (1993), Discrete choice theory of product differentiation, MIT Press, Cambridge.

[2] Arthur, W.B., Holland, J.H., LeBaron, B., Palmer, R. and Taylor, P., (1997) Asset pricing under endogenous expectations in an artificial stock market, in Arthur, W., Lane, D. and Durlauf, S., (eds.) The economy as an evolving complex system II, Addison-Wesley.

[3] Baak, S.J. (1999), Tests for bounded rationality with a linear dynamic model distorted by heterogeneous expectations, Journal of Economic Dynamics and Control 23, 1517-1543.

[4] Brock, W.A., (1993) Pathways to randomness in the economy: emergent nonlinearity and chaos in economics and finance, Estudios Económicos 8, 3-55.

[5] Brock, W.A., (1997), Asset Price Behavior in Complex Environments, in: Arthur, W.B., Durlauf, S.N., and Lane, D.A., eds., The Economy as an Evolving Complex System II, Addison-Wesley, Reading, MA, 385–423.

[6] Brock, W.A., and Hommes, C.H., (1997a) A rational route to randomness, Econometrica 65, 1059-1095.

[7] Brock, W.A., and Hommes, C.H., (1997b) Models of complexity in economics and finance, In: Hey, C. et al. (eds.), System Dynamics in Economic and Financial Models, Chapter 1, Wiley Publ., pp. 3-41.

[9] Brock, W.A., and Hommes, C.H., (1998), Heterogeneous beliefs and routes to chaos in a simple asset pricing model, *J*ournal of Economic Dynamics and Control 22, 1235-1274.

[9] Brock, W.A., and Hommes, C.H., (1999), Rational Animal Spirits, In: Herings, P.J.J., Laan, van der G. and Talman, A.J.J. eds., *T*he Theory of Markets, North-Holland, Amsterdam, 109–137.

[10] Brock, W.A., Hommes, C.H., and Wagener, F.O.O. (2004), Evolutionary dynamics in markets with many trader types, *J*ournal of Mathematical Economics, forthcoming.

[11] Brock, W.A. and LeBaron, (1996), A structural model for stock return volatility and trading volume, Review of Economics and Statistics 78, 94-110.

[12] Chavas, J.P., (2000) On information and market dynamics: The case of the U.S. beef market, *J*ournal of Economic Dynamics and Control, 24, 833-853.

[13] Chiarella, C., (1992), The dynamics of speculative behaviour, Annals of Operations Research 37, 101-123.

[14] Chiarella, C. and He, T. (2000), Heterogeneous beliefs, risk and learning in a simple asset pricing model, Computational Economics, forthcoming.

[15] Dacorogna, M.M., Müller, U.A., Jost, C., Pictet, O.V., Olsen, R.B. and Ward, J.R., (1995), Heterogeneous real-time trading strategies in the foreign exchange market, *E*uropean Journal of Finance 1, 383-403.

[16] Day, R.H. and Huang, W. (1990) Bulls, bears and market sheep, *J*ournal of Economic Behavior and Organization 14, 299-329.

[17] DeGrauwe, P., DeWachter, H. and Embrechts, M., (1993) Exchange rate theory. Chaotic models of foreign exchange markets, Blackwell.

[18] De Long, J.B., Shleifer, A., Summers,L.H. and Waldmann, R.J., (1990a) Noise trader risk in financial markets, *J*ournal of Political Economy 98, 703-738.

[19] De Long, J.B., Shleifer, A., Summers,L.H. and Waldmann, R.J., (1990b) Positive feedback investment strategies and destabilizing rational speculation, *J*ournal of Finance 45, 379-395.

[20] Fama, E.F., (1970) Efficient capital markets: a review of theory and empirical work, Journal of Finance 25, 383-423.

[21] Farmer, J.D., (1998), Market force, ecology, and evolution, Santa Fe Institute working paper 98-12-117.

[22] Farmer, J.D. and Joshi, S., (2002), The price dynamics of common trading strategies, *J*ournal of Economic Behaviour and Organization 49, 149-171.

[23] de Fontnouvelle, P., (2000), Information dynamics in financial markets, *M*acroeconomic Dynamics 4, 139-169.

[24] Frankel, J.A. and Froot, K.A., (1988) Chartists, Fundamentalists and the Demand for Dollars, *G*reek Economic Review 10, 49–102.

[25] Friedman, M., (1953) The case of flexible exchange rates, In: Essays in positive economics, Univ. Chicago Press.

[26] Gaunersdorfer, A., (2000) Endogenous fluctuations in a simple asset pricing model with heterogeneous beliefs, *Journal of Economic Dynamics and Control* 24, 799-831.

[27] Gaunersdorfer, A. and Hommes, C.H., (2000), A nonlinear structural model for volatility clustering, CeNDEF working paper 00-02, University of Amsterdam.

[28] Gaunersdorfer, A., Hommes, C.H., and Wagener, F.O.J., (2000) Bifurcation routes to volatility clustering, CeNDEF working paper 00-04, University of Amsterdam.

[29] Goeree, J.K. and Hommes, C.H., (2000), Heterogeneous beliefs and the non-linear cobweb model, *Journal of Economic Dynamics and Control* 24, 761-798.

[30] Hommes, C.H., (1994) Dynamics of the cobweb model with adaptive expectations and nonlinear supply and demand, *Journal of Economic Behavior & Organization* 24, 315-335.

[31] Hommes, C. H., (1998) On the Consistency of Backward-Looking Expectations: The Case of the Cobweb, *Journal of Economic Behavior and Organization*, 33, 333-362.

[32] Hommes, C.H., (2001), Financial markets as nonlinear adaptive evolutionary systems, *Quantitative Finance* 1, 149-167.

[33] Kantz and Schreiber (1997), Nonlinear time series analysis, Cambridge University Press, Cambridge.

[34] Keynes, J.M., (1936) The general theory of unemployment, interest and money, Harcourt, Brace and World.

[35] Kirman, A., (1991) Epidemics of opinion and speculative bubbles in financial markets, In M. Taylor (ed.), Money and financial markets, Macmillan.

[36] Kirman, A. and Teyssière, G., (2002), Microeconomic models for long memory in the volatility of financial time series, *Studies in Nonlinear Dynamics & Econometrics*, 5, 281-302.

[37] Kurz, M., (ed.) (1997), Endogenous economic fluctuations, Springer Verlag.

[38] LeBaron, B., (2000), Agent based computational finance: suggested readings and early research, *Journal of Economic Dynamics and Control* 24, 679-702.

[39] LeBaron, B., Arthur, W.B. and Palmer, R. (1999) Time series properties of an artificial stock market, *Journal of Economic Dynamics and Control* 23, 1487–1516.

[40] Lucas, R.E., (1971) Econometric testing of the natural rate hypothesis, In: O. Eckstein (ed.) The econometrics of price determination Conference. Board of Governors of the Federal Reserve System and Social Science Research Council.

[41] Lux, T., (1995) Herd Behavior, Bubbles and Crashes, *The Economic Journal* 105, 881–896.

[42] Lux, T., (1997) Time variation of second moments from a noise trader/infection model, *Journal of Economic Dynamics and Control* 22, 1-38.

[43] Lux, T. and Marchesi, M. (1999) Scaling and criticality in a stochastic multi-agent model of a financial market, *Nature* Vol. 397, February 1999, 498–500.

[44] Lux, T. and Marchesi, M. (2000) Volatility clustering in financial markets: a microsimulation of interacting agents, *International Journal of Theoretical and Applied Finance*, 3, 675–702.

[45] Manski, C. and McFadden, D., (1981), Structural analysis of discrete data with econometric applications, MIT Press, Cambridge.

[46] Muth, J.F., (1961) Rational expectations and the theory of price movements, Econometrica 29, 315-335.

[47] Palis, J. and Takens, F., (1993) Hyperbolicity & sensitive chaotic dynamics at homoclinic bifurcations, Cambridge University Press.

[48] Poincaré, H. (1890) "Sur le Problème des Trois Corps et les Equations de la Dynamique" Mémoire couronné du prise de S.M. le roi Oscar II de Surde), Acta Mathematica 13, 1-270.

[49] Sargent, Thomas J., (1999) The Conquest of American Inflation, Princeton: Princeton University Press.

[50] Wang, J., (1994), A model of competitive stock trading volume, Journal of Political Economy 102, 127-168.

[51] Zeeman, E.C., (1974) The unstable behavior of stock exchange, Journal of Mathematical Economics 1, 39-49.

Complex Oligopoly Dynamics

Tonu Puu
CERUM, Umeå University, SE-90187 Umeå, Sweden

Abstract The probably simplest conditions under which the Cournot duopoly model results in complex dynamics, are isoelastic demand and constant marginal costs. One advantage of this combination is that it is possible to solve for the reaction functions in simple closed form. The model is also studied in an adaptive format, in which case the flip bifurcation of the Cournot equilibrium, leading to a period-doubling cascade to chaos, is replaced by a subcritical Neimark bifurcation. The structure of the Arnol'd periodicity tongues, as well as the chaotic areas in parameter space are studied, as is multistability of attractors.

1 Introduction

The formal theory of duopoly goes as far back as to 1838, when Augustin Cournot treated the case where there is no retaliation at all, so that in every step each duopolist assumes the latest step taken by the competitor to remain his last. The process was assumed to lead to a steady state, nowadays called Cournot equilibrium, though it by no means is certain that it is stable. As a matter of fact, the following discussion will show how cycles and chaos may arise from very simple Cournot adjustment procedures.

Exactly a Century later, in 1938, Heinrich von Stackelberg made some ingenious extensions of the Cournot model assuming that any of the competitors might try to become a "leader", by taking the reactions of the other competitor according to Cournot in explicit consideration when devising his own actions. The tenability of such a situation would, of course, depend on whether the other competitor was content with adhering to his Cournot-like behaviour, i.e., being a "follower".

He might take up the challenge by trying to become a leader himself. The outcome of such warfare would depend on long term production conditions for the competitors, and on their current financial strengths. In the end one of the duopolists might ultimately force the other out of the market, thus becoming a monopolist. They may agree on collusive behaviour, provided law admits this usually forbidden solution. They may also return to the Cournot equilibrium, or to a Stackelberg equilibrium, provided the duopolists tacitly agree to form a leader-follower pair.

At the event of game theory, duopoly was one of the obvious fields of application, and the theory was recast in terms of probabilistic strategies. This, however, falls outside the scope of the present discussion, because the points we want to make do not need anything but the classical deterministic models that arouse in the Century 1838-1941.

It had long been realised that the Cournot model may lead to cyclic behaviour, and David Rand in 1978 conjectured that under suitable conditions the outcome would be chaotic. His purely mathematical treatment does, however, not include any substantial economic assumptions under which this becomes true. In what follows we supply such very simple substantial assumptions.

There exist, of course, other circumstances, such as marginal revenue curves with rising sections and hence several local equilibria, which also fulfil Rand's conjecture, and which have been proposed in the literature. One such case, with the demand function kinked in the Joan Robinson sense, was dealt with by Tord Palander and Abraham Wald both in 1936, and is easily modified to a format that increases complexity beyond that discovered by these authors, so as to even result in chaos. The disadvantage of these cases, however, is that solutions for the "reaction functions" of the duopolists become discontinuous, thus involving some extra mathematical complication.

The model we suggest is much simpler and yields simple explicit solutions for the reaction functions, so that we can easily focus on the dynamics of the process. It was suggested first by the present author in 1991, though, a more complicated version was suggested as a not analysed example by Dana and Montrucchio already in 1986.

2 The Model

Assume an isoelastic demand function, such that price, denoted p, is reciprocal to total demand. Provided demand equals supply it is made up of the supplies of the two competitors, denoted x and y. Thus:

$$p = \frac{1}{x+y} \tag{2.1}$$

This demand function is not non-problematic, because it does not yield a reasonable solution to the collusive case, the reason being that when the possibility of making total supply zero is considered, price can go to infinity and total revenue remain constant. On the other hand, total costs would vanish, and the collusive duopolists could get the entire revenue without incurring any costs. Such a solution is purely formal and does not have any economic substance. This absurdity does not occur with any of the other solutions, as the presence of a positive supply by the competitor always keeps the price finite. We could also easily remedy this technical problem by adding any positive constant in the denominator of (1). As this would not change any substantial conclusions, but has the cost of making all formulas much more messy, we abstain from this, and just point out the little complication.

Suppose next that the duopolists produce with constant marginal costs, denoted a and b respectively. The profits of the two firms become:

$$U(x,y) = \frac{x}{x+y} - ax \tag{2.2}$$

$$V(x,y) = \frac{y}{x+y} - by \tag{2.3}$$

The first firm maximizes $U(x, y)$ with respect to x, the second $V(x, y)$ with respect to y. Equating the partial derivatives to zero, we can solve for the reaction functions:

$$x = \sqrt{\frac{y}{a}} - y \tag{2.4}$$

$$y = \sqrt{\frac{x}{b}} - x \tag{2.5}$$

A check of the second order conditions, in fact, testifies that we always deal with local profit maxima, provided quantities are positive as indeed they should be. The reaction functions are displayed in Fig. 1. Their general outline is that they start at the origin, have unique maxima, and drop to zero again. The off origin intersection is unique.

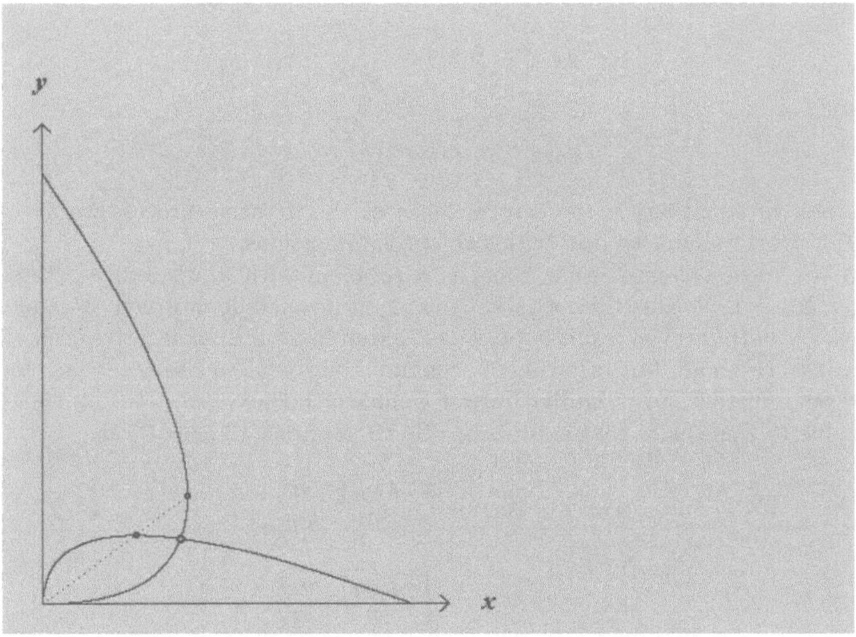

Figure 1. Reaction curves and the Cournot point.

We can easily solve for the output quantities at the Cournot point, taking (2.4)-(2.5) as a simultaneous system of equations:

$$\overline{x} = \frac{b}{(a+b)^2} \tag{2.6}$$

$$\overline{y} = \frac{a}{(a+b)^2} \tag{2.7}$$

This point, of course, is the intersection of the reaction curves as shown in Fig. 1. The profits of the duopolists at the Cournot point can be calculated by substituting back from (2.6)-(2.7) in (2.2)-(2.3):

$$\overline{U} = \frac{b^2}{(a+b)^2} \tag{2.8}$$

$$\overline{V} = \frac{a^2}{(a+b)^2} \tag{2.9}$$

3 The Iterative Process

Let us now turn to the dynamics. Once we are interested in the process of adjustment, we have to lag the variables. So. (2.4)-(2.5) must be written:

$$x_{t+1} = f(y_t) := \sqrt{\frac{y_t}{a}} - y_t \tag{3.1}$$

$$y_{t+1} = g(x_t) := \sqrt{\frac{x_t}{b}} - x_t \tag{3.2}$$

This pair of equations is the central piece of the iterative process we are going to study. However, we have to deal with two special questions:

First, we must recognize that there is a problem with (3.1)-(3.2) as stated, when $ay_t > 1$ or $bx_t > 1$, because then $x_{t+1} < 0$ or $y_{t+1} < 0$ would be returned. Mathematically such negative outputs even result in positive maximum profits, as negative costs dominate over negative revenues, but in terms of economics this is of course nonsense, and has to be ruled out. Further, any negative output would in the next iteration return a complex number due to the square root expression. So we rephrase (3.1)-(3.2) as:

$$x_{t+1} = F(y_t) := \begin{cases} f(y_t) & ay_t \le 1 \\ 0 & ay_t > 1 \end{cases} \tag{3.3}$$

$$y_{t+1} = G(x_t) := \begin{cases} g(x_t) & bx_t \le 1 \\ 0 & bx_t > 1 \end{cases} \tag{3.4}$$

It is a matter of the parameters a and b whether the entire orbit can be calculated, using the regular branches of the reaction functions (3.1)-(3.2) only, or whether the zero branches of (3.3)-(3.4) have to be included as well. To be precise, it is a matter of the marginal cost ratio b/a alone. As we will find later, many other properties too depend on this ratio, and, as a matter of fact, the whole process could have been cast in terms of just one ratio parameter. But for the sake of symmetry we yet keep both.

The maximum points for $f(y)$, $g(x)$ can be easily calculated from (3.1)-(3.2) through taking the derivatives, equating to zero, and solving. Substituting back in (3.1)-(3.2), we then easily obtain the respective maximum values: $f\left(\frac{1}{4a}\right) = \frac{1}{4a}$ and $g\left(\frac{1}{4b}\right) = \frac{1}{4b}$. As we see, the maxima are located on the diagonal in phase space as shown in Fig. 1. Whether the process visits the zero branches or not is a matter of whether these maximum values, iterated in the other reaction function of the pair (3.1)-(3.2), lead to values that exceed the values for which (3.1)-(3.2) would return a negative value. As we see $g\left(\frac{1}{4a}\right) = \frac{1}{2\sqrt{ab}} - \frac{1}{4a}$ and $f\left(\frac{1}{4b}\right) = \frac{1}{2\sqrt{ab}} - \frac{1}{4b}$. In order to avoid the zero branches, these values must be less than the values for which the reaction functions (3.1)-(3.2) become zero, i.e. $\frac{1}{a}$ and $\frac{1}{b}$ respectively. Accordingly:

$$\left(\frac{a}{b} \leq 6.25\right) \wedge \left(\frac{b}{a} \leq 6.25\right) \tag{3.5}$$

must hold in order that the process (3.1)-(3.2) be well defined even without the zero branches.

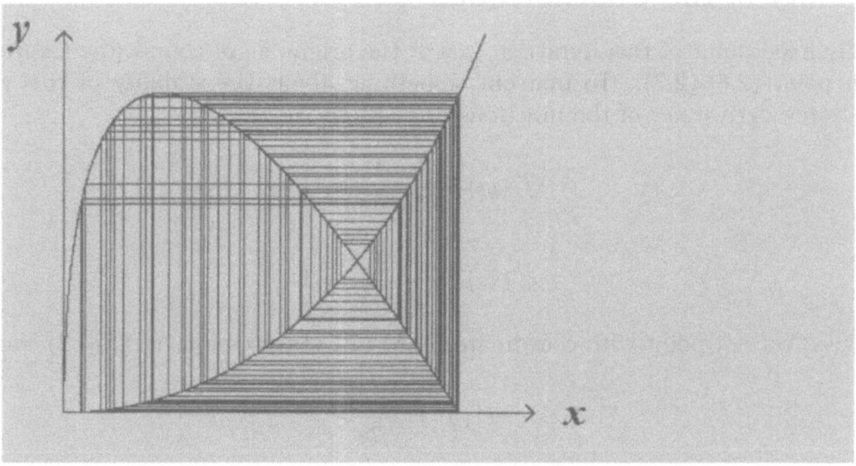

Figure 2. Chaotic Cournot duopoly adjustments.

There is also a second issue which we have to settle. In earlier literature great emphasis was put on whether duopolists react simultaneously or sequentially according to a pair of reaction functions such as (3.1)-(3.2). In order to deal with this, first note that, substituting (3.2) in (3.1), or substituting (3.1) in (3.2), we obtain

$$x_{t+2} = f\left(g\left(x_t\right)\right) = f \circ g\left(x_t\right) \tag{3.6}$$

$$y_{t+2} = g\left(f\left(y_t\right)\right) = g \circ f\left(y_t\right) \tag{3.7}$$

These are independent iterations, each in one phase variable alone, though based on a period twice as long as the fundamental period introduced from the outset. Given we have initial phase variable values for two subsequent periods, we can compute the complete trajectory for each variable. Obviously the functions $f \circ g$ and $g \circ f$ are autonomous iterations, so we get the same trajectories whether the firms adjust simultaneously or in sequence. The difference between simultaneous and sequential adjustment hence only lies in the way of pairing the two iteration series together. There also is a difference in terms of the freedom to choose initial conditions. If the adjustment is sequential, then the second iterate can be calculated from only one initial condition, and we cannot choose all initial points in the phase space as depicted in Fig. 1, just points located on the graphs of the reaction functions.

This being said, it should be noted that the system may itself settle on successive adjustment, even if we assume simultaneous. The union of the graphs of the reaction functions in Fig. 1 is an example of an invariant set. Any iteration starting on any of these leads to a trajectory which never leaves the union set. Moreover, it is attractive from a basin of nonzero area measure.

4 Stability of the Cournot Point

The only fixed point of this iteration, except the origin, is, of course, the Cournot equilibrium point (2.6)-(2.7). To find out something about the stability of this point we calculate the derivatives of the functions (3.1)-(3.2):

$$f'(y_t) = \frac{1}{2}\frac{1}{\sqrt{ay_t}} - 1 \tag{4.1}$$

$$g'(x_t) = \frac{1}{2}\frac{1}{\sqrt{bx_t}} - 1 \tag{4.2}$$

At the Cournot point with coordinates (2.6)-(2.7), expressions (4.1)-(4.2) simplify to:

$$f'(\overline{y}) = \frac{b-a}{2a} \tag{4.3}$$

$$g'(\overline{x}) = \frac{a-b}{2b} \tag{4.4}$$

Loss of stability for the Cournot point occurs when:

$$|f'(\overline{y}) \cdot g'(\overline{x})| = \left|\frac{b-a}{2a} \cdot \frac{a-b}{2b}\right| = 1 \tag{4.5}$$

Expanding (4.5), we get:

$$(a-b)^2 = 4ab \tag{4.6}$$

Observe that this condition can be solved for the ratio:

$$\left(\frac{a}{b} = 3 \pm 2\sqrt{2}\right) \vee \left(\frac{b}{a} = 3 \pm 2\sqrt{2}\right) \tag{4.7}$$

Thus, whenever any ratio of the marginal costs of the duopolists falls outside the interval bounded by the two values specified in (4.7), the Cournot point will not be stable. The two roots happen to be reciprocal, so there is nothing odd in stating this condition for any of the ratios. As we already noted in (3.5) other critical conditions as well depend on the ratio of marginal costs only, so there is just one single free control parameter.

5 Periodic Points and Chaos

As this control parameter passes either of the critical values specified in equation (4.7), the fixed point is replaced by a two period cycle. This should be so understood that x and y each oscillate between two values. The two variables themselves, of course, take on different pairs of values in the oscillatory process.

After the first cycle appears, there is a period doubling cascade to chaos. In Fig. 2 we display the cobweb of a chaotic process of adjustments in the same type of diagram as displayed in Fig. 1.

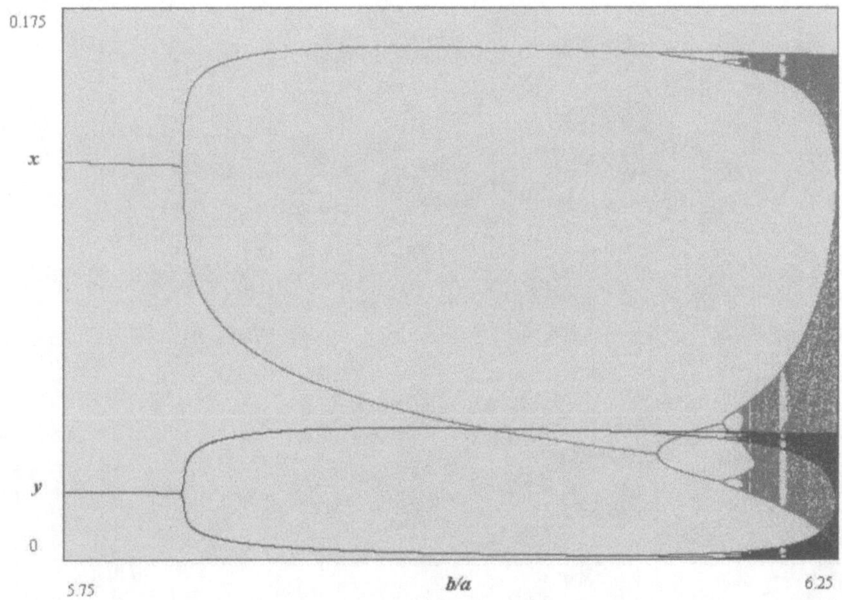

Figure 3. Bifurcation diagram. Amplitudes plotted versus marginal cost ratio.

In Fig. 3 we illustrate the bifurcation diagram. As we see from (4.7), interesting things begin to happen when the ratio b/a exceeds the critical value $3 + 2\sqrt{2} \approx 5.8584$, or falls short of its reciprocal. Until then there is just a stable fixed point. On the other hand, the smooth functions (3.1)-(3.2) alone are relevant if and only if b/a does not exceed the value 6.25, or fall short of its reciprocal, as we see from (3.5). Outside this range, the zero branches of the reaction functions start being visited, and new phenomena come into play. To avoid this we limit the bifurcation diagram to the range of marginal cost ratios between 5.75 and 6.25.

In this range we see the fixed point undergoing a period doubling bifurcation cascade to chaos. We depict the asymptotic behaviour of both the x variable (brighter shade) and the y variable (darker shade). against the marginal cost ratio b/a. As already noted, the behaviour of the system is symmetric as to this ratio and its reciprocal a/b. So shifting to the latter ratio would give the same bifurcation diagram. Further, for the same reason, we need not extend the parameter ratio axis to the origin, because its leftmost part would only be a reciprocity compressed mirror image of the information already shown.

The general appearance of the bifurcation diagram is very like that of the extensively studied logistic map. There is the period doubling cascade to chaos, as well as the windows of order in the chaotic region.

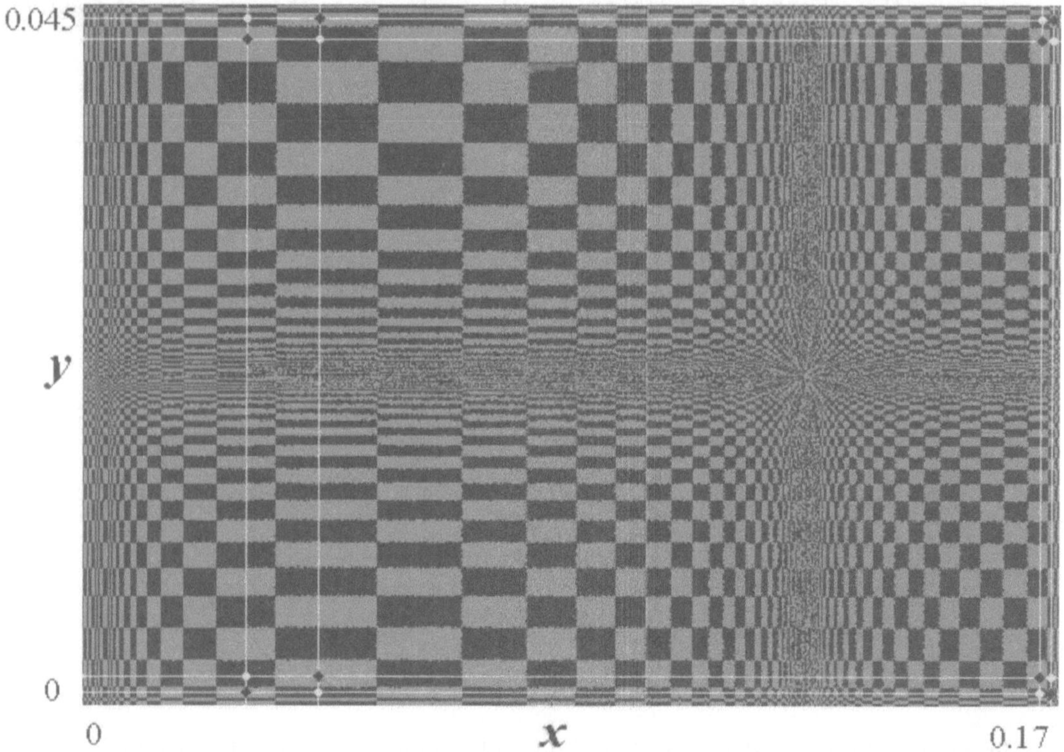

Figure 4. Two coexistent 4-period cycles and their basins of attraction. Parameter value $b/a = 6.15$.

That much for the independent iterations (3.6)-(3.7). If we study the phenomena for both variables in the phase space shown in Fig. 1, then they combine to produce coexistent cycles. Figs. 4-5 show two such cases. In Fig. 4, we took a parameter ratio $b/a = 6.15$, which, as we can see in Fig. 3 produces 4-period cycles in each variable alone. They obviously combine to produce two different coexisting 8-period cycles. The

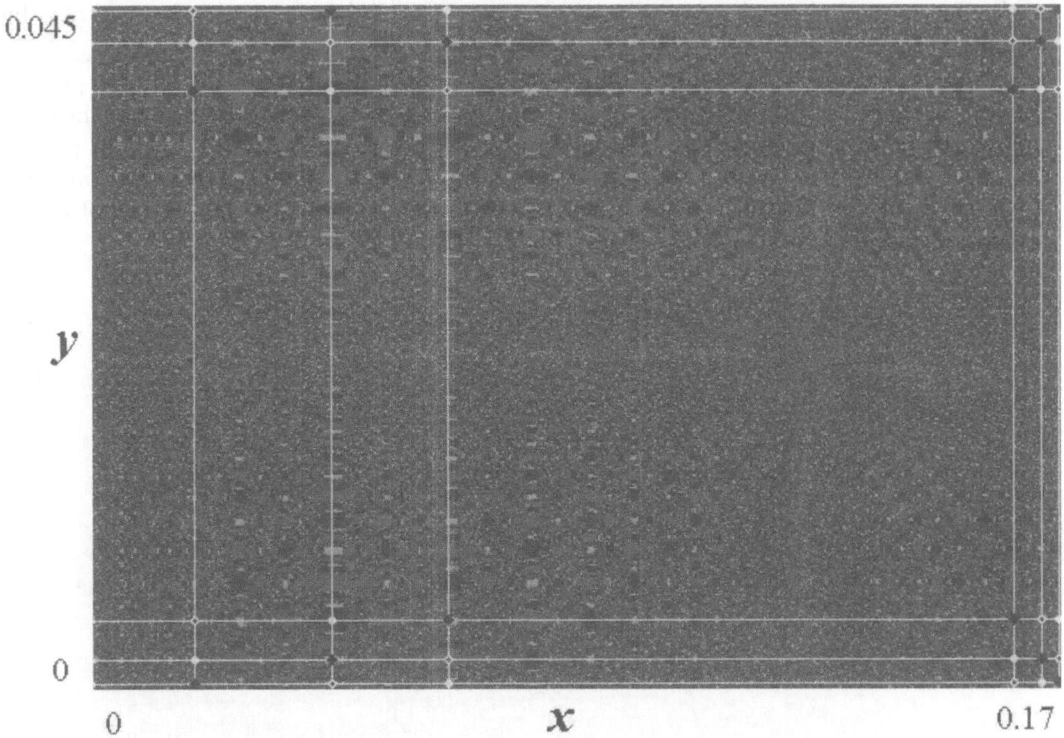

Figure 5. Three coexistent 12-period cycles and their basins of attraction. Parameter value $b/a = 6.212$.

locations of the four independent periodic points in each variable alone are indicated by the four horizontal and vertical lines, whose intersections produce a 4 by 4 lattice. As we see the periodic points are located on this 16-point lattice. The cycles are indicated by the dark and bright dots. As we see there is a deformed chequerboard pattern of fragmented attraction basins corresponding to these coexistent cycles.

The case in Fig. 5 is taken for $b/a = 6.212$, which comes from the largest window of order we see in Fig. 3. In this window (3.6)-(3.7) produce 6-period cycles for each variable alone. These are again indicated by the six horizontal and vertical lines. Their intersection forms a 6 by 6 lattice. Located on it are three different sets of dots indicated by different characters, in all three coexisting 12-period cycles. Corresponding to the cycles are three attraction basins drawn in different shade. As we see the basins are now even more fragmented as compared to the previous picture.

We see that in each case, if there are n-period cycles for each variable alone (n even), then they combine to produce $n/2$ different coexisting $2n$-period cycles. That this always is the case with maps such as (3.1)-(3.2) has been rigorously proved. See Bischi,

Mammana, and Gardini, where the corresponding results for odd-period n can also be found.

The bifurcation sequence leading to chaos, obviously has been of the flip, or period-doubling type. In the sequel we will encounter different types of bifurcations when the Cournot point loses stability. Another typical feature of the (3.1)-(3.2) type of map is the character of the fragmented attraction basins, which entirely consist of rectangular areas, getting smaller and smaller in the neighbourhood of the (unstable) Cournot point, so producing a very complex fragmentation, particularly close to this point.

Figure 6. Four piece chaotic attractor. Parameter value $b/a = 6.2$.

As we see in both Figs. 4-5, the periodic points cluster in four rectangles close to the corners of phase space. When the process is chaotic, these become chaotic rectangles dense of attractor points. We see such a case in Fig. 6. Eventually, as the parameter ratio grows towards 6.25, these grow, and finally merge into one single chaotic rectangle.

6 Adaptive Expectations

As mentioned, the iterations considered up to now are actually two independent ones. To make the map really two-dimensional, and bring in a little variation, we next assume that the duopolists do not immediately jump to their new optimal positions, but adjust their previous decisions in the direction of the new optimum. Assume:

$$x_{t+1} = \phi(x_t, y_t) := (1-\gamma)\, x_t + \gamma \left(\sqrt{\frac{y_t}{a}} - y_t \right) \tag{6.1}$$

$$y_{t+1} = \psi(x_t, y_t) := \delta \left(\sqrt{\frac{x_t}{b}} - x_t \right) + (1-\delta)\, y_t \tag{6.2}$$

With the adjustment speeds unitary, we are back at the case already treated. In the contrary case, with those speeds zero, the duopolists never revise any decision taken. Intermediate values, between zero and unity, bring in a host of new possibilities.

Again we must deal with the problems arising when the expressions within large parentheses become negative. So, we redefine the system as:

$$x_{t+1} = \Phi(x_t, y_t) := \begin{cases} \phi(x_t, y_t) & a y_t \le 1 \\ (1-\gamma)\, x_t & a y_t > 1 \end{cases} \tag{6.3}$$

$$y_{t+1} = \Psi(x_t, y_t) := \begin{cases} \psi(x_t, y_t) & b x_t \le 1 \\ (1-\delta)\, y_t & b x_t > 1 \end{cases} \tag{6.4}$$

It is easily checked that the adaptive system (6.1)-(6.2), or (6.3)-(6.4), has the same fixed points as the original system without adaptation (3.1)-(3.2), i.e. the, always unstable, origin, and the Cournot equilibrium point, whose coordinates were given in (2.6)-(2.7). The Cournot point may again be stable, or it may lose stability. The stability of various solutions, such as the Cournot fixed point, and the cycles, now depend, not only on the marginal cost ratio b/a, but on the adjustment speeds γ, δ as well.

7 The Neimark Bifurcation

Compared to the previous model, the stability loss will now be through a Neimark-Sacker bifurcation. We can study the stability around any point in phase space by linearising the system (6.1)-(6.2). The matrix of the linearised system then becomes:

$$J(x_t, y_t) = \begin{bmatrix} 1-\gamma & \gamma \left(\frac{1}{2\sqrt{a y_t}} - 1 \right) \\ \delta \left(\frac{1}{2\sqrt{b x_t}} - 1 \right) & 1-\delta \end{bmatrix} \tag{7.1}$$

Considering the Cournot point, we substitute for the phase variables from (2.6)-(2.7). The matrix then becomes:

$$J(\overline{x}, \overline{y}) = \begin{bmatrix} 1-\gamma & \gamma \frac{b-a}{2a} \\ \delta \frac{a-b}{2b} & 1-\delta \end{bmatrix} \tag{7.2}$$

At the threshold of loss of stability for the Cournot point the determinant of the matrix (7.2) becomes unitary. Putting $|J(\overline{x}, \overline{y})| = 1$, and simplifying, we get the condition:

$$(a-b)^2 = 4ab \left(\frac{1}{\gamma} + \frac{1}{\delta} - 1 \right) \tag{7.3}$$

Note that, with the adjustment speeds unitary, condition (7.3) becomes identical with (4.6), as it indeed should.

The characteristic equation is now easily obtained from the Jacobian matrix (7.2) by putting:

$$\begin{vmatrix} 1-\gamma-\lambda & \gamma\frac{b-a}{2a} \\ \delta\frac{a-b}{2b} & 1-\delta-\lambda \end{vmatrix} = 0 \tag{7.4}$$

where λ are the eigenvalues. Written out (7.4) becomes:

$$\lambda^2 - (2-\gamma-\delta)\,\lambda + (1-\gamma)\,(1-\delta) + \gamma\delta\frac{(a-b)^2}{4ab} = 0 \tag{7.5}$$

We easily recognize the coefficient of the linear term as the negative of the trace, and the constant term as the determinant of the Jacobian matrix (7.2).

Solving (7.5) we obtain the eigenvalues:

$$\lambda_{1,2} = \frac{1}{2}(2-\gamma-\delta) \pm \frac{1}{2}\sqrt{\gamma^2+\delta^2-\gamma\delta\frac{a^2+b^2}{ab}} \tag{7.6}$$

To see whether they are real or complex on the bifurcation curve, we substitute from (7.3) for the quotient under the root sign in (7.6), obtaining:

$$\lambda_{1.2} = \frac{1}{2}(2-\gamma-\delta) \pm \frac{1}{2}\sqrt{(\gamma+\delta)\,(\gamma+\delta-4)} \tag{7.7}$$

As the remaining parameters are adjustment speeds and only can take values in the unit interval, i.e. $0 \le \gamma, \delta \le 1$, we conclude that the expression under the root sign must be negative at the moment of bifurcation. The eigenvalues are hence complex conjugates, and the bifurcation accordingly of the Neimark-Sacker type.

At the moment of bifurcation the complex eigenvalues cross the unit circle in the complex plane, so we can also write (7.7) as:

$$\lambda_{1,2} = \cos\theta \pm i\sin\theta \tag{7.8}$$

where, as usual, $i = \sqrt{-1}$, and

$$\cos\theta = \frac{1}{2}(2-\gamma-\delta) \tag{7.9}$$

$$\sin\theta = \frac{1}{2}\sqrt{(\gamma+\delta)\,(4-\gamma-\delta)} \tag{7.10}$$

The bifurcation can be to a periodic or to a quasiperiodic/chaotic orbit, depending on whether θ is a rational or an irrational multiple of 2π.

From numerical work we will find that the Neimark bifurcation for the present model is of the subcritical type, not of the supercritical. The subcritical bifurcations are more difficult to understand than the supercritical, and the theorem about bifurcation of the fixed point to a closed invariant curve, whenever strong resonance is absent, does no longer apply. As a consequence, the fixed point may bifurcate to a periodic orbit, not only at the sparse rational points on the bifurcation curve, but over entire intervals on it.

As a matter of fact the Arnol'd tongues protrude through the bifurcation curve, and are thick already at the moment of the Neimark bifurcation. In the supercritical bifurcation, the attractive invariant curve is born the moment the fixed point is destabilized. In the subcritical, the fixed point is destabilized by an unstable invariant curve (or some other unstable set) collapsing around the fixed point and so destabilizing it. This means that the unstable set was created through another bifurcation, together with a stable one, even before the Neimark bifurcation. After the unstable set destabilzes the fixed point, its stable companion attracts the phase points which formerly went to the fixed point. See Guckenheimer and Holmes or Kuznetsov for more detail on subcritical Neimark bifurcations.

Meanwhile, between the two bifurcations, we can find coexistence of fixed point and some other attractor, something which does not occur with a supercritical bifurcation.

Though the periodic Arnol'd tongues do not grow out from the Neimark bifurcation curve, we can still locate the periodic tongues by substituting various rational multiples of 2π for θ in the eigenvalues. So, put:

$$\theta = 2\pi \frac{m}{n} \tag{7.11}$$

in (7.9), and solve for:

$$\gamma + \delta = 2\left(1 - \cos\left(2\pi \frac{m}{n}\right)\right) \tag{7.12}$$

Taking first $m = 1$, we get: for $n = 1$, $\gamma + \delta = 0$, for $n = 2$, $\gamma + \delta = 4$, for $n = 3$, $\gamma + \delta = 3$, and for $n = 4$, $\gamma + \delta = 2$. We find that there is no strong resonance, except the only possibility $\gamma = \delta = 1$ for the non-adaptive case. Though, we cannot invoke the theorem that the bifurcation necessarily is to a closed invariant curve, this gives an indication that the lowest resonance we may find is $n = 4$. The next higher harmonics are $\gamma + \delta = \left(5 - \sqrt{5}\right)/2 \approx 1.382$ for $n = 5$, and $\gamma + \delta = 1$ for $n = 6$, which are perfectly in the admissible parameter range.

In Fig. 7, we display the bifurcation diagram, which confirms that the corresponding resonance tongues indeed are located as expected from the above calculations. However, note that we have three parameters, the marginal cost ratio, b/a, and the adjustment speeds γ and δ. In order to make it possible to draw a plane diagram, we must reduce their number to two. Numerical experiment indicates that the best choice is to put $\gamma = \delta$, and to use this along with the marginal cost ratio b/a.

In the picture we can identify, from right to left, the tongues of periodicities $n = 4$ and higher, quite as we can infer from the above calculations. The biggest tongues are indicated through numbers. There is one series running from 4 to 8, the following ones are too thin for numbering. However, we also note larger tongues numbered, 9, 11, 13, and 15, interspersed between the tongues we already spoke of.

The reason for this is that in the above calculations we took $m = 1$, so the resonances represented were $1:4$, $1:5$, $1:6$, etc. But these are the same as $2:8$, $2:10$, $2:12$, etc., so it is not surprising that we can find resonances $2:9$, $2:11$, etc. in between. Actually, with equal adjustment speeds, equation (7.12) reads $\gamma = \delta = 1 - \cos\left(2\pi m/n\right)$,

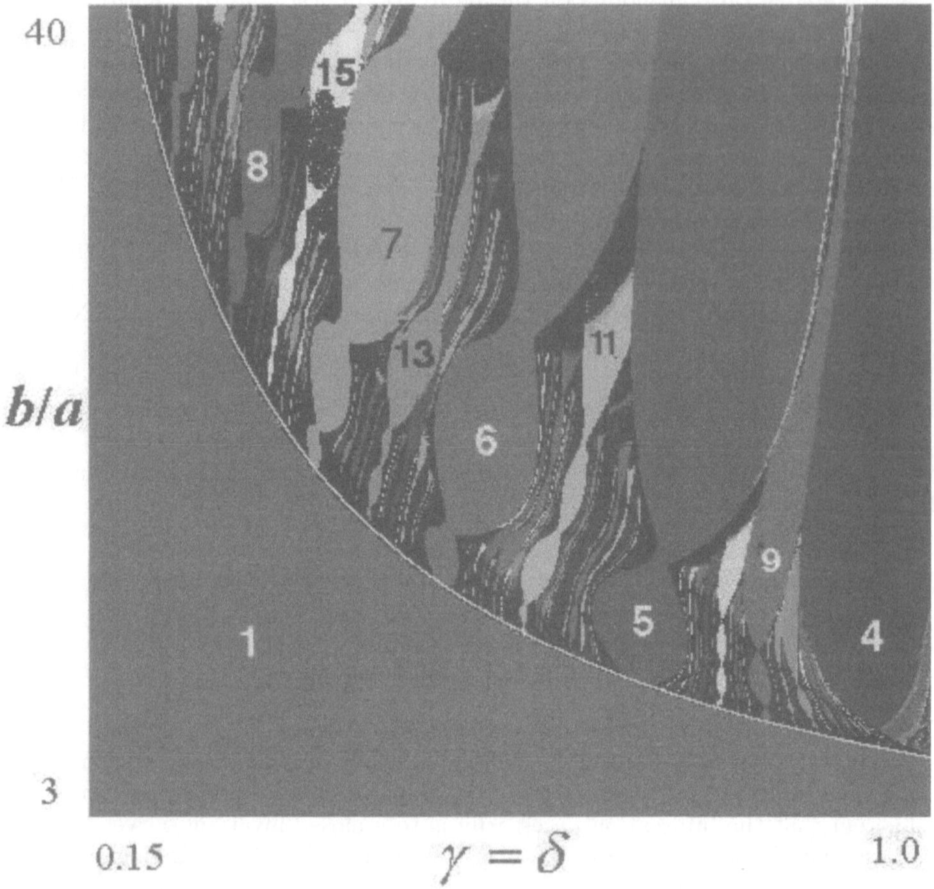

Figure 7. Neimark bifurcation curve and periodic Arnol'd tongues.

so for $m = 1, n = 4$ we have $\gamma = \delta = 1$, and for $m = 1, n = 5$, $\gamma = \delta \approx 0.691$. Calculating $\gamma = \delta = 1 - \cos(4\pi/9) \approx 0.826$ for $m = 2, n = 9$, we find that indeed the $2:9$ tongue fits between the $1:4$ and $1:5$ tongues.

In all, we checked for the 45 lowest periods in Fig. 7. As the tongues get thinner and thinner, we conjecture that in this manner we have obtained most of the information about periodicities. It should be said that we used the system (6.3)-(6.4), including the zero branches in calculating the periodicities. The "bowel like" structure in the upper parts of the picture is probably due to the application of the zero branches. Note also that the tongues penetrate through the bifurcation curve, as expected with subcriticality.

As a companion to Fig. 7, we also present Fig. 8, which displays the areas of positive Lyapunov exponents in the parameter plane in bright shade. Note how this picture of

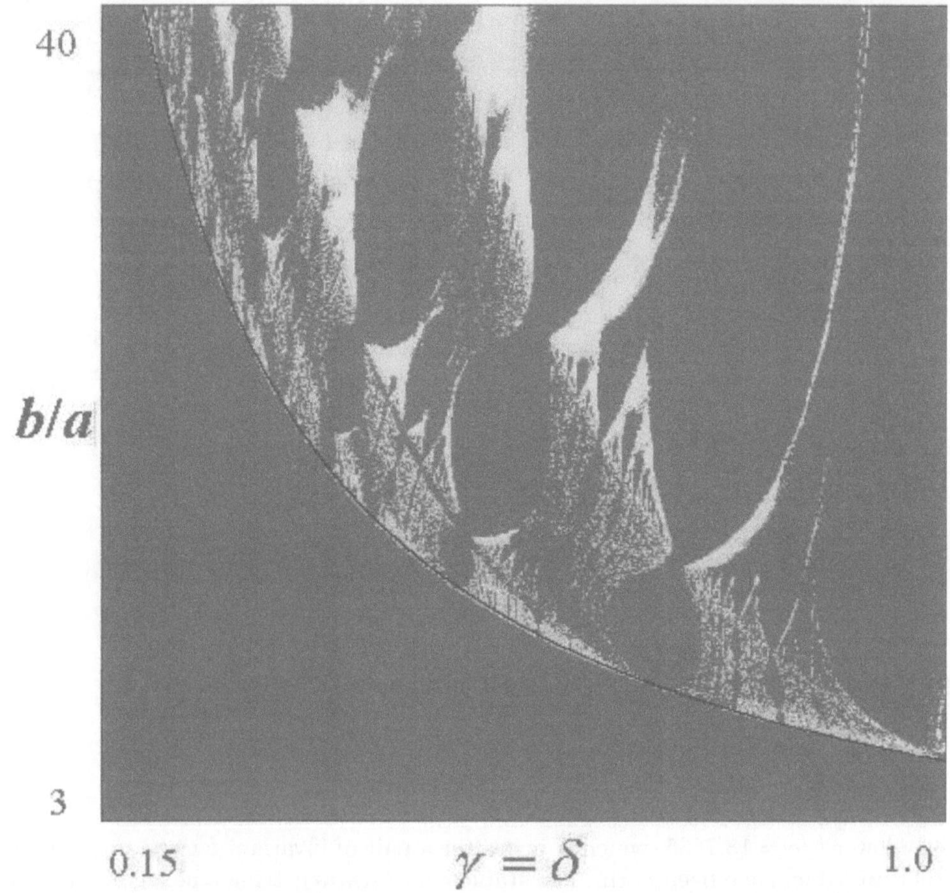

Figure 8. Areas of positive (bright) and negative (dark) Lyapunov exponents.

the chaotic region fits into the areas where no periodic tongues are present in Fig. 7. We use two different bright shades, depending on whether the Lyapunov exponent is only positive, or larger than 0.01, in order to distinguish quasiperiodic and high period cycles from chaotic motion (white). Also note that the area for positive Lyapunov exponents, quite as the low periodic tongues in Fig. 7 did, protrudes right through the Neimark bifurcation curve.

In Figs. 9-10 we illustrate the coexistence of the fixed point and another attractor just before the Neimark bifurcation. As we know, the 6-period tongue starts out at the parameter value $\gamma = \delta = 0.5$. To get the corresponding value for the marginal cost ratio we substitute this in (7.12), whence we can solve for $b/a = 4\sqrt{3} + 7 \approx 13.9282$.

As we see in Fig. 7, the stable fixed point for parameter combinations just under the bifurcation curve, seems to coexist with another attractor. So, for Fig. 9 we choose a

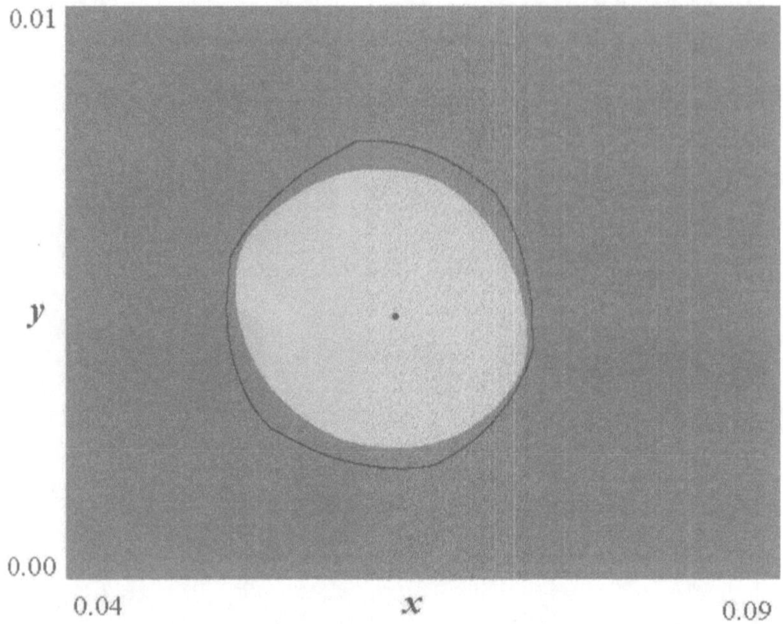

Figure 9. Coexistent fixed point and invariant curve. Parameters $\gamma = \delta = 0.5$, $a/b = 13.7635$.

slightly lower $b/a = 13.7635$, which is just after a pair of invariant curves, one stable and another unstable, have been born. The stable curve starts getting a hexagonal feature as we are in the 6-period range, the unstable one is the boundary of the basin of attraction for the fixed point (bright shade).

Fig. 10 is drawn much closer to the Neimark bifurcation curve. We put $b/a = 13.9245$. As we see the basin of attraction for the fixed point has shrunk together around the fixed point, so as to annihilate its stability in the next moment. Moreover, we see that the closed invariant curve has undergone a global saddle-node bifurcation to a 6-period cycle, as indicated by Fig. 7, where the 6-period tongue penetrates through the bifurcation curve.

We finish this discussion by displaying a chaotic attractor in the shape of a "leaf" in Fig. 11, where there is no longer any coexistence with a fixed point. The parameter values are $\gamma = \delta = 0.9$, $b/a = 6.9262$.

8 Critical Lines and Absorbing Area

We can now investigate the case with the method of critical lines and absorbing areas. See Abraham, Gardini, and Mira or Mira, Gardini, Barugola, and Cathala about this remarkable method. A very simple introduction can also be found in Puu (2000, 2003).

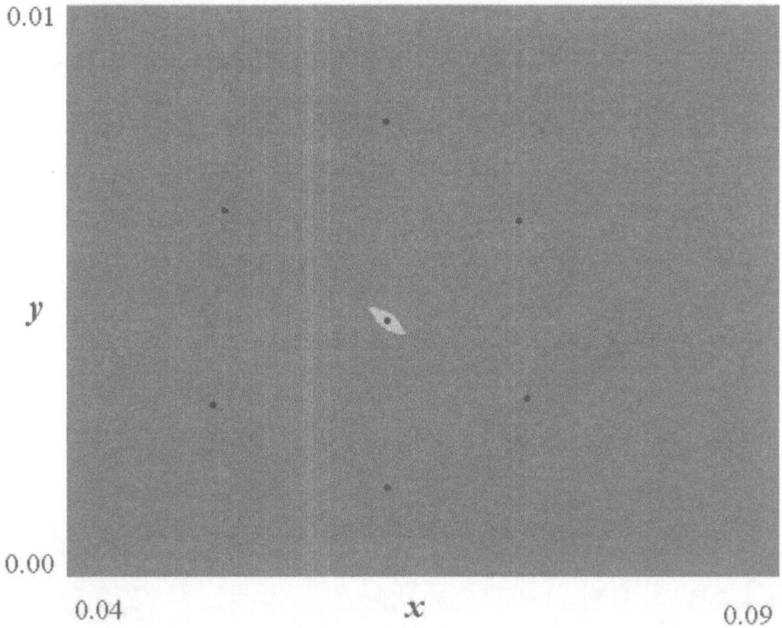

Figure 10. Coexistent fixed point and 6-period orbit. Parameters $\gamma = \delta = 0.5$, $a/b = 13.9245$.

To outline the shapes of attractors once the Cournot equilibrium loses stability and is replaced by an invariant curve or its further bifurcations (of which the chaotic cases are the most interesting in terms of geometry) we need the critical line L_{-1}.

We obtain the equation for L_{-1}, putting the determinant of the Jacobian matrix (7.1) equal to zero. Observe that we take the general matrix (7.1), not the one at the Cournot point (7.2). Also note that we put the determinant equal to zero, not to unity as in deriving the Neimark bifurcation curve (7.3), the reason being that now we just want to locate the curve along which the map folds the plane.

So, putting the determinant of (7.1) equal to zero, and deleting the time period index for the phase variables, we obtain the following expression:

$$\left(\frac{1}{2\sqrt{ay}} - 1\right)\left(\frac{1}{2\sqrt{bx}} - 1\right) = \frac{(1-\gamma)(1-\delta)}{\gamma\delta} \tag{8.1}$$

It is easy to see that this implicit equation represents a pair of hyperbolas in the x, y-plane. Their exact forward images according to (6.1)-(6.2) are too complex to write down, but they can be easily traced by the computer. Further, the numerical case illustrated in Fig. 11 has $\gamma = \delta = 0.9$. Hence the right hand side of is (8.1) is small, of the order of magnitude 0.01. If it were zero then either of the brackets on the left would have to

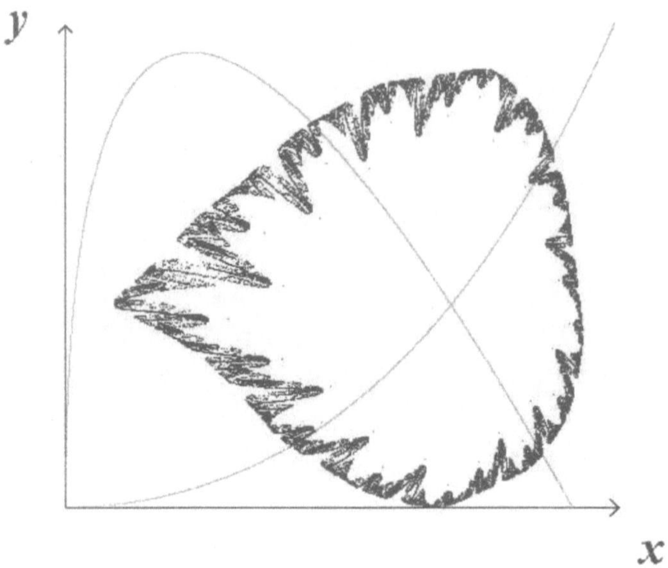

Figure 11. Fractal attractor of the adaptive model. Parameters: $\gamma = \delta = 0.9$, $a/b = 6.9262$.

be zero. The pair of hyperbolas then becomes a cross of straight lines. This is almost true with small but nonzero right hand sides, at least with a certain distance from the intersection of this "cross" (the hyperbola asymptotes).

In Figs. 12-13, the relevant part of L_{-1}, i.e., that which intersects the attractor, is a vertical line segment as far as we can see in these pictures. It corresponds to the second bracket in (8.1) being zero, i.e., to $x = \frac{1}{4b}$. As we remember from Section 3, this coordinate value represents the maximum of the reaction function for the second firm.

In Fig 12 we also show 17 of the forward iterates of this segment, which obviously suffice to outline the outward boundary of the attractor. As we know, the case is that illustrated in Fig. 11. We can easily recognize the attractor which has been superposed in gray shade and note how well it is wrapped up by the train of critical lines. We also show the reaction functions and the unstable Cournot point at their intersection.

By using 55 critical lines as illustrated in Fig. 13, we can outline the inner boundary of the attractor as well, and other structures, such as densifications of attractor points.

More accurate and efficient would have been to exclude the middle part of the segment displayed, which, as we see, coincides with the "hole" in the attractor, but we skip this computational complication.

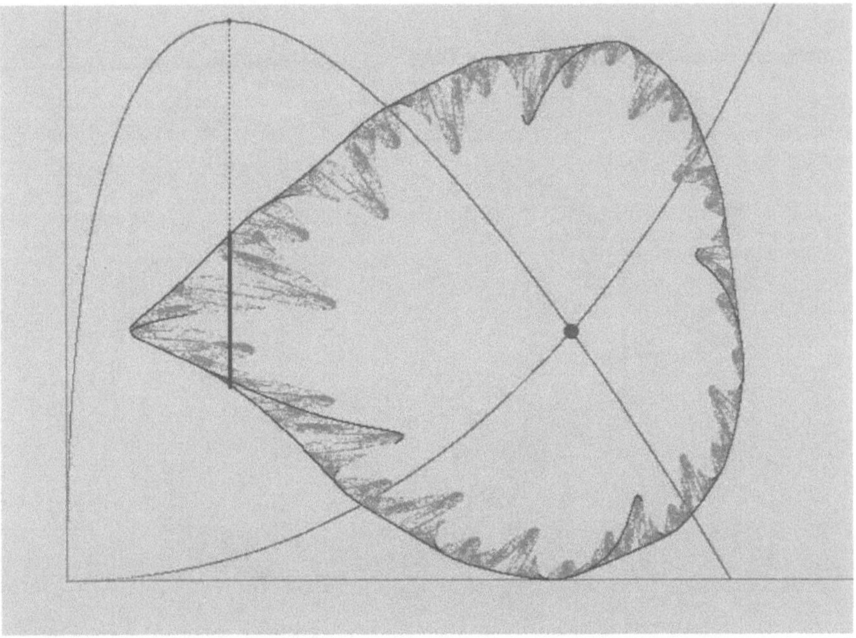

Figure 12. Chaotic attractor and absorbing area with 17 critical lines.

9 Conclusion

More interesting possibilities arise when we admit three oligopolists. Then the Neimark bifurcation occurs already in the non-adaptive setup of the model. The model was extended in this way in Puu (1996), and further studied in Agliari, Gardini, and Puu (2000). A less technical account was given in Puu (2000, 2003). The big problem in the case of three competitors is visualization techniques, particularly the use of the critical "line", i.e., surface method, which is only in its infancy. Things are simplified if two of the three competitors are assumed to be identical. In that case it was proved that the process converges to an invariant plane where the two identical competitors behave identically, and, after any transient has settled, phase space remains two dimensional.

One of the most interesting issues in connection with oligopoly models of this type are the border collision bifurcations which precede the subcritical Neimark bifurcation, as this is mathematically fairly unexplored ground. A first study can be found in Agliari, Gardini, and Puu (2004a). This describes one scenario, but there are other, as exemplified in a forthcoming article Agliari, Gardini, and Puu (2004b). The whole issue can be seen to be much more complex than may be expected.

The ultimate purpose of discussing oligopoly with an increasing number of competitors would be to find out if there is a clear road monopoly - oligopoly - perfect competition, where stability in some sense increases with the number of competitors. It is interest-

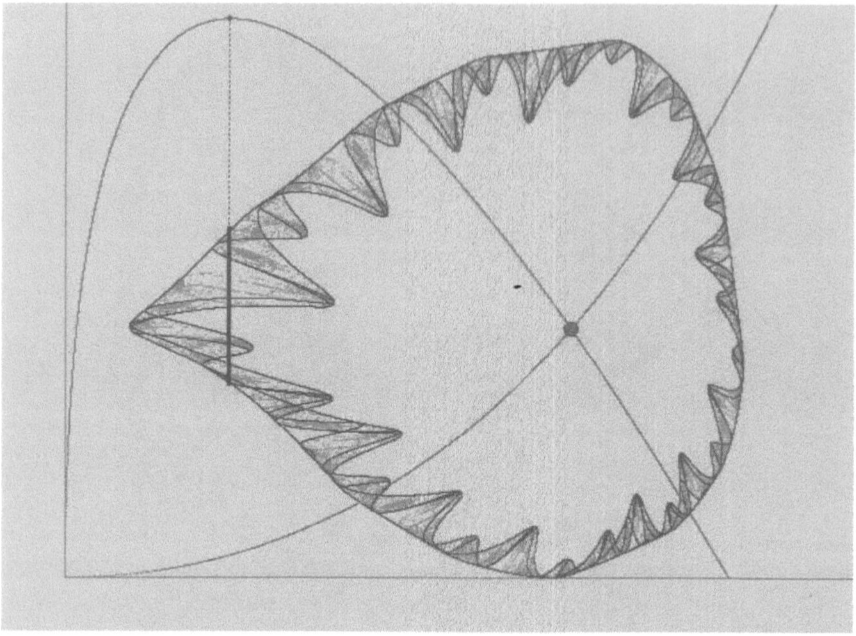

Figure 13. Chaotic attractor and absorbing area with 55 critical lines.

ing to note that Agiza (1998) and Ahmed and Agiza (1998), using the present model, unexpectedly reported destabilization with an increasing number of competitors.

The present author, however, feels that one can not just let the number of competitors increase. A fair comparison would be between few big and many small firms. However, with constant marginal costs all firms are potentially infinitely big in terms of production capacity. Hence, one should incorporate capacity constraints, as already Edgeworth in 1897 insisted on. A first attempt in this direction can be found in Puu and Norin (2003), where the capacity constraint is modelled in terms a smooth marginal cost function which starts out as if the firm operated under constant returns, but eventually bends up to reach infinity at some finite output. It remains to study what the result of an increasing number of competitors is when capacity constraints are incorporated. A study for three competitors may be found in Puu and Ruiz Marin (2004).

Understanding nonlinear dynamical systems is largely a matter of experimental work at the computer. The interested reader should contact me for details of how to write computer programs that produce some of the pictures that illustrate this chapter.

Bibliography

R.H. Abraham, L. Gardini, and C. Mira, *Chaos in Discrete Dynamical Systems.* New York: Springer-Verlag, 1997.

H.N. Agiza, Explicit stability zones for Cournot game with 3 and 4 competitors. *Chaos, Solitons, & Fractals*, 9:1955-1966, 1998.

A. Agliari, L. Gardini and T. Puu, The dynamics of a triopoly Cournot game. *Chaos, Solitons & Fractals*, 11:2531-2560, 2000.

A. Agliari and T. Puu, A Cournot duopoly model with bounded demand: in T. Puu and I. Sushko (Eds.) *Oligopoly and Complex Dynamics: Tools and Models*, New York: Springer-Verlag, 2002.

A. Agliari, L. Gardini and T. Puu, Global bifurcations in duopoly when the Cournot Point is destabilized through a Subcritical Neimark bifurcation. *International Game Theory Review*, (forthcoming), 2004a.

A. Agliari, L.Gardini, and T. Puu, Some global bifurcations related to the apperance of closed invariant curves. *Mathematics and Computers in Simulations (submitted)*, 2004b.

E. Ahmed and H.N. Agiza, Dynamics of a Cournot game vith n competitors. *Chaos, Solitons, & Fractals*, 10:1179-1184, 1998.

G.-I. Bischi, C. Mammana, and L. Gardini, Multistability and cyclic attractors in duopoly games. *Chaos, Solitons, & Fractals*, 11:543-564, 2000.

A. Cournot, *Récherces sur les principes mathématiques de la théorie des richesses*, Paris, 1838.

R.A. Dana and L. Montrucchio, Dynamic Complexity in Duopoly Games. *Journal of Economic Theory*, 40: 40-56, 1986.

F.Y. Edgeworth, La teoria pura del monopolio. *Giornale degli Economisti*, 15:13-31, 1897.

J. Guckenheimer, and P. Holmes, *Nonlinear Oscillations, Dynamical Systems, and Bifurcations of Vector Fields*, Berlin: Springer-Verlag, 1986.

Y.A. Kuznetsov, *Elements of Applied Bifurcation Theory* (Berlin: Springer-Verlag, 1995.

Mira, C., Gardini, L., Barugola, A. and Cathala, J.-C., *Chaotic Dynamics in Two-Dimensional Noninvertible Maps*, Singapore: World Scientific, 1996.

T.F. Palander, Instability in competition between two sellers: in *Abstracts of papers presented at the research conference on economics and statistics held by the Cowles Commission at Colorado College*, Colorado College Publications, General Series No. 208, Studies Series No. 21, 1936.

T. Puu, 1991, Chaos in duopoly pricing. *Chaos, Solitons & Fractals* 1:573-81, republished in J.B.Rosser (Ed.), *Complexity in Economics*, Edward Elgar Publishing Inc., 2004.

T. Puu, Complex dynamics with three oligopolists. *Chaos, Solitons, and Fractals*, 7:2075-2081, 1996.

T. Puu, The chaotic duopolists revisited. *Journal of Economic Behavior and Organization*, 33:385-394, 1998.

T. Puu and A. Norin, Cournot duopoly when the competitors operate under capacity constraints, *Chaos, Solitons & Fractals*, 18: 577-592, 2003.

T. Puu, *Attractors, Bifurcations, & Chaos - Nonlinear Phenomena in Economics*, Berlin: Springer-Verlag, 2000, 2003.

T. Puu, L. Gardini and I. Sushko,Cournot duopoly with kinked linear demand according to Palander and Wald,: in T. Puu and I. Sushko (Eds.) *Oligopoly and Complex Dynamics: Tools and Models*, Berlin: Springer-Verlag, 2002.

T. Puu and M. Ruiz Marin, The dynamics of a triopoly Cournot game when the competitors operate under capacity constraints. (forthcoming), 2004.

D. Rand, Exotic phenomena in games and duopoly models, *Journal of Mathematical Economics*, 5:173-184, 1978.

H. von Stackelberg, Probleme der unvollkommenen Konkurrenz. *Weltwirtschaftliches Archiv*, 48:95-114, 1938.

I. Sushko, L. Gardini and T. Puu, Duopoly with piecewise linear discontinuous reaction functions,: in T. Puu and I. Sushko (Eds.) *Oligopoly and Complex Dynamics: Tools and Models*, Berlin: Springer-Verlag, 2002.

A. Wald, Über einige Gleichungssysteme der mathematischen Ökonomie, *Zeitschrift für Nationakökonomie* 637-670, 1939.

Coexisting Attractors and Complex Basins in Discrete-time Economic Models

Gian Italo Bischi [†] and Fabio Lamantia [‡]

[†] Istituto di Scienze Economiche, University of Urbino, Urbino, Italy

[‡] S.A. Department, University of Calabria, Arcavacata di Rende (CS), Italy

Abstract In this lesson we consider discrete time dynamical systems with coexisting attractors, and we analyze the problem of the structure of the boundaries that separate their basins of attraction. This problem may become particularly challenging when the discrete dynamical system is represented by the iteration of a noninvertible map, because in this case nonconnected basins can be obtained, formed by several (even infinitely many) disjoint portions. Measure theoretic attractors, known as Milnor attractors, are also described, together with riddled basins, an extreme form of complex basin's structure that can be observed in the presence of such attractors. Some tools for the study of global bifurcations that lead to the creation of complex structures of the basins are described, as well as some applications in discrete time models taken from economic dynamics.

1 Introduction

Many mathematical models of social, economic and financial systems are characterized by the interaction among boundedly rational agents, that try to obtain their goals by adaptive processes, based on "trial and error" or "learning by doing" methods. This implies that the mathematical modelling of these processes, where decisions are repeatedly taken over time, are formulated as deterministic discrete time dynamical systems, i.e. their time evolution is expressed by the repeated application (iteration) of a map $T : S \rightarrow S$, where $S \subseteq \mathbb{R}^n$. If the state of the economic system is described by a vector $x \in S$, starting from an initial condition $x_0 \in S$ the time evolution of the system is expressed by a sequence of states $x(t)$, $t \in \mathbb{N}$, obtained *inductively* by the iteration of a map defined by $x' = T(x)$, where the right hand side represents the state at the time period t, and the left hand side represents the state at the time $(t+1)$.

It is worth to notice that discrete time dynamical systems are sometimes obtained through some discretization procedure applied to continuous time models, as often happens in physics or biology. Instead, economic time is often intrinsically discrete, because decisions in economics cannot be continuously revised. As trivial example to illustrate this point, let us consider a farmer that decides how much wheat has to be sowed: such a decision cannot be revised until next sowing season.

The dynamic models in economics are generally nonlinear, and it is now well known that even one-dimensional discrete nonlinear dynamical systems may exhibit complex asymptotic behaviors, due to the existence of chaotic attractors.

Moreover, nonlinearity may also imply that several equilibria may coexist. For example, dynamic games often have several equilibria (see, among others, Binmore, 1992, Weibull, 1995) and in many models with expectations and learning several rational expectations equilibria are present, or rational equilibria coexist with non rational ones (Guesnerie and Woodford, 1993). In these cases, an adaptive process may become an equilibrium selection device, as it allows one to distinguish between stable and unstable equilibria. However, in many models with evolutive (or learning) mechanism, a situation denoted as "multistability" is present, i.e. several attractors exist, each with its own basin of attraction. Consequently, selection criteria based on local stability are not sufficient to identify the long run evolution of the system, and the dynamic process becomes path-dependent: the long run dynamics depend on the starting condition, and a thorough knowledge of the basins and their structure becomes crucial for the researcher to be able to predict which one of the multiple equilibria is more likely to be observed (see e.g. Lorenz, 1992, Soliman, 1999, Barucci et al., 1999, Bischi and Kopel, 2001, Bischi et al., 2003a,b, Agliari et al., 2002, Bischi et al., 2004).

This leads to the question of the delimitation of the basins of attraction and their changes as the parameters of the model vary. This issue cannot be studied by local methods (i.e. based on linear approximations around the attractors) but through a global study of the map, often requiring an interplay among analytical, geometric and numerical methods (see e.g. Brock and Hommes, 1997, Bischi et al., 2000a, Puu, 2000, Agliari et al., 2002). The existence of complex topological structure of the basins becomes particularly intriguing when dealing with discrete dynamical systems represented by the iteration of noninvertible maps (see Mira et al., 1996, Abraham et al., 1997, and references therein). Moreover the complexity related to the structure of the basins is not related, in general, to the existence of chaotic attracting sets, in the sense that simple attractors (e.g. stable steady states) may have basins with a complicated topological structure whereas complex attractors, e.g. strange attractors, may exist whose basins have simple boundaries.

In the last two decades, the literature on economic dynamics has mainly been devoted to the study of the attractors and their qualitative changes (bifurcations) leading to more and more complex kinds of asymptotic dynamics (fixed points, cycles, quasi-periodic orbits, chaotic attractors). Such routes to more and more complex behaviors, as some parameters are varied, have been characterized by sequences of local bifurcations (such as the well known period doubling route to chaos) and by global bifurcations, typically homoclinic bifurcations. Instead, the complexity related to the structure of basins leads to a different kind of sensitivity with respect to slight changes of initial conditions. In fact, if a point is far from the basin boundaries, a slight perturbation has no effect on the long run behavior, whereas if a point is very close to a basin boundary (and many point are in such a situation in the presence of complex basin boundaries) a small perturbation has a high probability to cause a crossing of the boundary and consequently the long run evolution will be very different, i.e. the trajectory may go to a completely different region of the phase space (it may even diverge). This kind of sensitivity is different from the sensitive dependence on initial conditions which characterizes a chaotic attractor. In fact, in this case, even if two initially very close chaotic trajectories quickly depart as time increases (at an exponential rate), such trajectories are finally trapped inside the same compact invariant set (the chaotic attractor).

Both the questions outlined above require an analysis of the global dynamical properties of the dynamical system, that is, an analysis which is not based on the linear approximation of the map. When the map is noninvertible the global dynamical properties can be usefully characterized by the method of critical sets, a powerful tool introduced in the seventies (see Gumovski and Mira, 1980, Mira et al. 1996, Abraham et al. 1997) but only recently employed in the study of dynamic modelling of economic and financial systems (see e.g. Bischi et al., 1999a, Kopel et al., 2000, Puu 2000, Bischi and Kopel, 2001, Bischi et al., 2003a,b, Dieci et al., 2001, Chiarella et al., 2001, 2002). Indeed, several discrete time models of economic systems are represented by the iteration of a noninvertible map, i.e. a point transformation T which maps distinct points into the same point. Loosely speaking, this can be expressed by saying that the map "folds and pleats" the state space. As we shall describe in the following, the folding action associated with the application of a noninvertible map, as well as the "unfolding" associated with the geometric action of the inverses, can be described by using the formalism of critical sets. The repeated application of a noninvertible map repeatedly folds the state space along the critical sets and their images, and often this allows one to define a bounded region where asymptotic dynamics are trapped. Instead, the repeated application of the inverses "repeatedly unfolds" the state space, so that a neighborhood of an attractor may have preimages far from it. This may give rise to complicated topological structures of the basins, whose detection can be explained on the basis of the global properties of the dynamical system, as explained below.

The lesson is organized as follows. In section 2 we recall some definitions and properties concerning discrete dynamical systems represented by noninvertible maps. In section 3 we consider the problem of the delimitation of the basins in one-dimensional discrete dynamical systems, and we give some examples of global bifurcations that cause the creation of nonconnected basins. In section 4 we consider two-dimensional discrete dynamical systems, recalling some recent examples of two-dimensional dynamic models taken from the economic literature. In section 5 we consider the case of dynamical systems that have invariant submanifolds of lower dimension with respect to the state space, where chaotic Milnor attractors are embedded, and we analyze the related phenomena of chaos synchronization and riddled basins. We also show how such particular dynamic situations arise in competition models.

2 Some basic definitions and properties

In this section we give some basic definitions and properties, and a minimal vocabulary, about discrete dynamical systems, with a particular emphasis on the ones represented by the iteration of noninvertible maps. A map $T : S \to S$, $S \subseteq \mathbb{R}^n$, defined by $x' = T(x)$, transforms a point $x \in S$ into a unique point $x' \in S$. The point x' is called the *rank-1 image* of x, and a point x such that $T(x) = x'$ is a *rank-1 preimage* of x'. A *discrete-time dynamical system* is defined inductively by the difference equation

$$x(t+1) = T(x(t)) \tag{2.1}$$

where x represents the state of a system, and T can be seen as a "unit time advancement operator" $T : x(t) \to x(t+1)$. Starting from an *initial condition* $x_0 \in S$, the repeated application (*iteration*) of T uniquely defines a *trajectory*

$$\tau(x_0) = \{x(t) = T^t(x_0), t = 0, 1, 2, ...\}, \tag{2.2}$$

where T^0 is the identity map and $T^t = T(T^{t-1})$.

A set $A \subset \mathbb{R}^n$ is *trapping* if it is mapped into itself, $T(A) \subseteq A$, i.e. if $x \in A$ then $T(x) \in A$. A trapping set is *invariant* if it is mapped onto itself: $T(A) = A$, i.e. all the points of A are images of points of A.

A closed invariant set A is an *attractor* if it is *asymptotically stable,* that is

(i) it is *Lyapunov stable,* i.e. for every neighborhood W of A there exists a neighborhood V of A such that $T^t(V) \subset W$ $\forall t \geq 0$

(ii) a neighborhood U of A exists such that $T^t(x) \to A$ as $t \to +\infty$ for each $x \in U$.

The *basin* of an attractor A is the set of all points that generate trajectories converging to A

$$\mathcal{B}(A) = \{x \, | T^t(x) \to A \quad \text{as} \quad t \to +\infty\} \tag{2.3}$$

Let $U(A)$ be a neighborhood of an attractor A whose points converge to A. Of course $U(A) \subseteq \mathcal{B}(A)$, and also the points that are mapped into U after a finite number of iterations belong to $\mathcal{B}(A)$. Hence, the basin of A is given by

$$\mathcal{B}(A) = \bigcup_{n=0}^{\infty} T^{-n}(U(A)) \tag{2.4}$$

where $T^{-1}(x)$ represents the set of the *rank-1* preimages of $\mathbf{x}$ (i.e. the points mapped into x by T), and $T^{-n}(x)$ represents the set of the *rank-n* preimages of x (i.e. the points mapped into x after n applications of T).

Let $\mathcal{B}$ be a basin of attraction and $\partial\mathcal{B}$ its boundary. From the definition it follows that $\mathcal{B}$ is trapping with respect to the forward iteration of the map T and invariant with respect to the backward iteration of all the inverses T^{-1}, that is, $T(\mathcal{B}) \subseteq \mathcal{B}$ and $T^{-1}(\mathcal{B}) = \mathcal{B}$. The same relations hold for the points located along the boundary, i.e.

$$T(\partial\mathcal{B}) \subseteq \partial\mathcal{B}, T^{-1}(\partial\mathcal{B}) = \partial\mathcal{B}. \tag{2.5}$$

This implies that if an unstable fixed point or cycle belongs to $\partial\mathcal{B}$ then $\partial\mathcal{B}$ must also contain all its preimages of any rank. Moreover, if a saddle-point, or a saddle-cycle, belongs to $\partial\mathcal{B}$, then $\partial\mathcal{B}$ must also contain the whole stable set (see Gumowski and Mira 1980, Mira et al. 1996).

From (2.4) and (2.5) follows that in order to study the extension of a basin and structure of its boundaries one has to consider the backward iteration of T. So, the invertibility of T and the properties of the inverse relation T^{-1} must be considered. We recall that if $x \neq y$ implies $T(x) \neq T(y)$ for each x, y in S, then T is an *invertible map* in S, because the inverse mapping that gives $x = T^{-1}(x')$ is uniquely defined; otherwise T is said to be a *noninvertible map*, because points x exist that have several *rank-1* preimages, i.e. the inverse relation $x = T^{-1}(x')$ may be multivalued. So, noninvertible means "many-to-one", that is, distinct points $x \neq y$ may have the same image, $T(x) = T(y) = x'$. Geometrically, the action of a noninvertible map T can be expressed by saying that it "folds and pleats" the space S, so that the two distinct points are mapped into the same point. This is equivalently stated by saying that several inverses are defined in some points of S, and these inverses "unfold" S.

For a noninvertible map S can be subdivided into regions Z_k, $k \geq 0$, whose points have k distinct *rank-1* preimages. Generally, as the point x' varies in $\mathbb{R}^n$, pairs of preimages appear or disappear as this point crosses the boundaries separating different regions. Hence, such boundaries are characterized by the presence of at least two coincident (merging) preimages. This leads to the definition of the critical sets, one of the distinguishing features of noninvertible maps (Gumowski and Mira, 1980, Mira et al., 1996):

Definition. The *critical set* CS of a continuous map T is defined as the locus of points having at least two coincident *rank-1* preimages, located on a set CS_{-1} called *set of merging preimages.*

The critical set CS is generally formed by $(n-1)$-dimensional hypersurfaces of $\mathbb{R}^n$, and portions of CS separate regions Z_k of the phase space characterized by a different number of *rank-1* preimages, for example Z_k and Z_{k+2} (this is the standard occurrence). As we shall see below, the critical set CS is the n-dimensional generalization of the notion of local minimum/maximum value of a one-dimensional map, and of the notion of *critical curve* LC of a noninvertible two-dimensional map[1]. The set CS_{-1} is the generalization of the notion of critical point (when it is a local extremum point) of a one-dimensional map, and of the *fold curve* LC_{-1} of a two-dimensional noninvertible map.

From the definition given above it is clear that the relation $CS = T(CS_{-1})$ holds, and the points of CS_{-1} in which the map is continuously differentiable are necessarily points where the Jacobian determinant of T, denoted by $\det DT$, vanishes:

$$CS_{-1} \subseteq J_0 = \{p \in \mathbb{R}^n \mid \det DT(p) = 0\} \tag{2.6}$$

In fact, in any neighborhood of a point of CS_{-1} there are at least two distinct points which are mapped by T in the same point. Accordingly, the map is not locally invertible in points of CS_{-1}, and (2.6) follows from the implicit function theorem.

In order to explain the geometric meaning of the critical sets, let us consider a portion of CS, say $\widehat{CS}$, which separates two regions Z_k and Z_{k+2} of the phase space S, and let $\widehat{CS}_{-1}$ be the corresponding locus of merging preimages, i.e. $\widehat{CS} = T\left(\widehat{CS}_{-1}\right)$. This means that two inverses of T exist, say T_1^{-1} and T_2^{-1}, which are defined in the region Z_{k+2} (and have respective ranges in the regions R_1 and R_2 separated by $\widehat{CS}_{-1}$) that merge on $\widehat{CS}_{-1}$ (i.e. they give merging preimages on $\widehat{CS}_{-1}$) and no longer exist in the region Z_k. Now, let $U \subset S$ be a ball which intersects $\widehat{CS}_{-1}$ in $D = U \cap \widehat{CS}_{-1}$. Then $T(D) \subseteq \widehat{CS}$, and $T(U)$ is "folded" along $\widehat{CS}$ into the region Z_{k+2}. In fact, considering the two portions of U separated by $\widehat{CS}_{-1}$, say $U_1 \in R_1$ and $U_2 \in R_2$, we have that $T(U_1) \cap T(U_2)$ is a nonempty set included in the region Z_{k+2}, which is the region whose points p' have *rank-1* preimages $p_1 = T_1^{-1}(p') \in U_1$ and $p_2 = T_2^{-1}(p') \in U_2$. This means that two points $p_1 \in U_1$ and $p_2 \in U_2$, located at opposite sides with respect to

[1]This terminology, and notation, originates from the notion of critical points as it is used in the classical works of Julia and Fatou.

$\widehat{CS}_{-1}$, are mapped in the same side with respect to $\widehat{CS}$, in the region Z_{k+2}. This is also expressed by saying that the ball U is "folded" by T along CS on the side with more preimages (see Figure 1, obtained by the noninvertible map (2.11)). The same concept can be equivalently expressed by stressing the "unfolding" action of T^{-1}, obtained by the application of the two distinct inverses in Z_{k+2} which merge along CS. Indeed, if we consider a ball $V \subset Z_{k+2}$, then the set of its *rank-1* preimages $T_1^{-1}(V)$ and $T_2^{-1}(V)$ is made up of two balls $T_1^{-1}(V) \in R_1$ and $T_2^{-1}(V) \in R_2$. These balls are disjoint if $V \cap \widehat{CS} = \emptyset$ (Figure 1b).

It is worth to notice that in the case of piecewise differentiable maps the set of points where the map is not differentiable may belong to CS_{-1}, i.e. the images by T of such points may separate regions characterized by a different number of *rank-1* preimages (see e.g. Mira, 1987). For example, in one-dimensional continuous piecewise differentiable maps critical points may be located at the kinks where local maxima and minima are formed by two branches that join with slopes of opposite sign, such as the well known tent map or other piecewise linear maps. Moreover, piecewise continuous maps may have points of CS_{-1} at the discontinuities and, differently from the case of continuous maps, the corresponding portions of CS may separate regions that differ by an odd number of preimages (see again Mira, 1987). In any case, the importance of the set CS lies in the fact that its points separate regions Z_k characterized by different number of preimages[2].

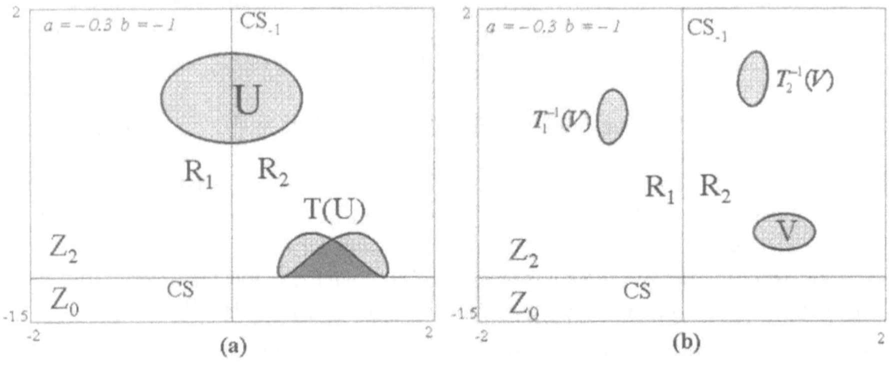

Figure 1.

2.1 Some examples in dimension one and two

As a first illustration, we consider a one-dimensional quadratic map, the logistic map (Figure 2a)

$$x' = f(x) = \mu x(1 - x). \tag{2.7}$$

[2]This property may also be shared by points where some inverses are not defined due to a vanishing denominator, as shown in Bischi et al., 1999b, 2003c.

This map has a unique critical point $c = \mu/4$, which separates the real line into the two subsets: $Z_0 = (c, +\infty)$, where no inverses are defined, and $Z_2 = (-\infty, c)$, whose points have two *rank-1* preimages. These preimages can be computed by the two inverses

$$x_1 = f_1^{-1}(x') = \frac{1}{2} - \frac{\sqrt{\mu(\mu - 4x')}}{2\mu}; \quad x_2 = f_2^{-1}(x') = \frac{1}{2} + \frac{\sqrt{\mu(\mu - 4x')}}{2\mu}. \tag{2.8}$$

If $x' \in Z_2$, its two *rank-1* preimages, computed according to (2.8), are located symmetrically with respect to the point $c_{-1} = 1/2 = f_1^{-1}(\mu/4) = f_2^{-1}(\mu/4)$. Hence, c_{-1} is the point where the two merging preimages of c are located. As the map (2.7) is differentiable, at c_{-1} the first derivative vanishes[3].

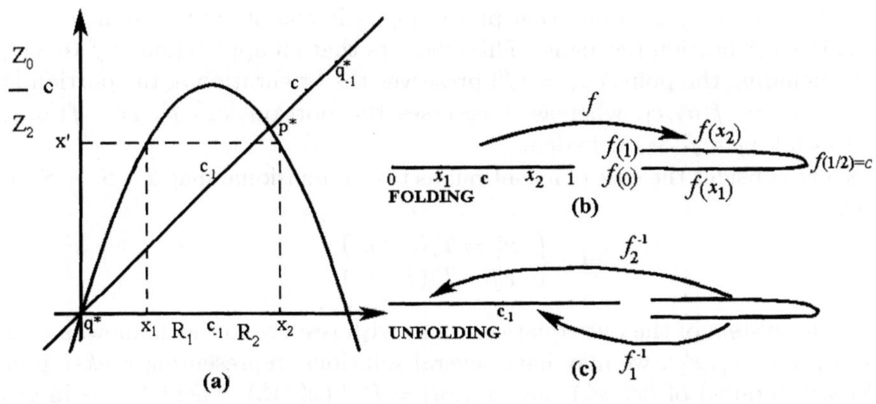

Figure 2.

In order to explain the geometric action of a critical point in a continuous map, let us consider again the logistic map and notice that as x moves from 0 to 1 the corresponding image $f(x)$ spans the interval $[0, c]$ twice, the critical point c being the turning point. In other words, if we consider how the segment $\gamma = [0, 1]$ is transformed by the map f we can say that it is *folded and pleated* to obtain the image $\gamma' = [0, c]$. Such folding gives

[3]We remark that in general the condition of vanishing derivative is not sufficient to define c_{-1}, since such condition may be also satisfied by points which are not local extrema (e.g. the inflection points with horizontal tangent).

a geometric reason why two distinct points of γ, say x_1 and x_2, located symmetrically with respect to the point $c_{-1} = 1/2$, are mapped into the same point $x' \in \gamma'$ (see Figure 2b). The same arguments can be explained by looking at the two inverse mappings f_1^{-1} and f_2^{-1} defined in $(-\infty, \mu/4]$ according to (2.8). We can consider the range of the map f formed by the superposition of two half-lines $(-\infty, \mu/4]$, joined at the critical point $c = \mu/4$ (Figure 2c), and on each of these half-lines a different inverse is defined. In other words, instead of saying that two distinct maps are defined on the same half-line we say that the range is formed by two distinct half lines on each of which a unique inverse map is defined. This point of view gives a geometric visualization of the definition of the critical point c as the point in which two distinct inverses merge. The action of the inverses, say $f^{-1} = f_1^{-1} \cup f_2^{-1}$, causes an unfolding of the range by mapping c into c_{-1} and by opening the two half-lines one on the right and one on the left of c_{-1}, so that the whole real line $\mathbb{R}$ is covered. So, the map f folds the real line, the two inverses unfold it (see Figure 2).

Another interpretation of the folding action of the unimodal map f is the following. Since $f(x)$ is increasing for $x \in [0, 1/2)$ and decreasing for $x \in (1/2, 1]$, its application to a segment $\gamma_1 \subset [0, 1/2)$ is orientation preserving, whereas its application to a segment $\gamma_2 \subset (1/2, 1]$ is orientation reversing. This suggests that an application of f to a segment $\gamma_3 = [a, b]$ including the point $c_{-1} = 1/2$ preserves the orientation of the portion $[a, c_{-1}]$, i.e. $f([a, c_{-1}]) = [f(a), c]$, whereas it reverses the portion $[c_{-1}, b]$, i.e. $f([c_{-1}, b]) = [f(b), c]$, so that $\gamma_3' = f(\gamma_3)$ is folded.

Let us now consider the case of a continuous two-dimensional map $T : S \to S$, $S \subseteq \mathbb{R}^2$, defined by

$$T : \begin{cases} x_1' = T_1(x_1, x_2) \\ x_2' = T_2(x_1, x_2) \end{cases} , \tag{2.9}$$

If we solve the system of the two equations (2.9) with respect to the unknowns x_1 and x_2, then, for a given (x_1', x_2'), we may have several solutions, representing *rank-1* preimages (or backward iterates) of (x_1', x_2'), say $(x_1, x_2) = T^{-1}(x_1', x_2')$, where T^{-1} is in general a multivalued relation.

In this case we say that T is noninvertible and the critical set, formed by critical curves LC (from the French "Ligne Critique"), constitutes the set of boundaries that separate regions of the plane characterized by a different number of *rank-1* preimages. Along LC at least two inverses give merging preimages, located on the set denoted by LC_{-1} , following the notations of Gumowski and Mira, 1980, Mira et al., 1996.

For a continuous and (at least piecewise) differentiable noninvertible map of the plane, the set LC_{-1} is included in the set where the Jacobian determinant $\det DT(x_1, x_2)$ changes sign, since T is locally an orientation preserving map near points (x_1, x_2) such that $\det DT(x_1, x_2) > 0$ and orientation reversing if $\det DT(x_1, x_2) < 0$. Of course, $LC = T(LC_{-1})$.

In order to understand this point, let us recall that when an affine transformation $x' = Ax + b$, where $A = \{a_{ij}\}$ is a 2×2 matrix and $b \in \mathbb{R}^2$, is applied to a figure of the plane, then the area of the transformed figure grows, or shrinks, by a factor $\rho = |\det A|$, and if $\det A > 0$ then the orientation of the figure is preserved, whereas if $\det A < 0$ then the orientation is reversed. This property also holds for the linear approximation of (2.9) in a neighborhood of a point $p = (x_1, x_2)$, given by an affine map with $A = DT$, DT being the Jacobian matrix evaluated at the point p

$$DT\,(p) = \begin{bmatrix} \partial T_1/\partial x_1 & \partial T_1/\partial x_2 \\ \partial T_2/\partial x_1 & \partial T_2/\partial x_2 \end{bmatrix} \tag{2.10}$$

A qualitative visualization is given in Figure 3a.

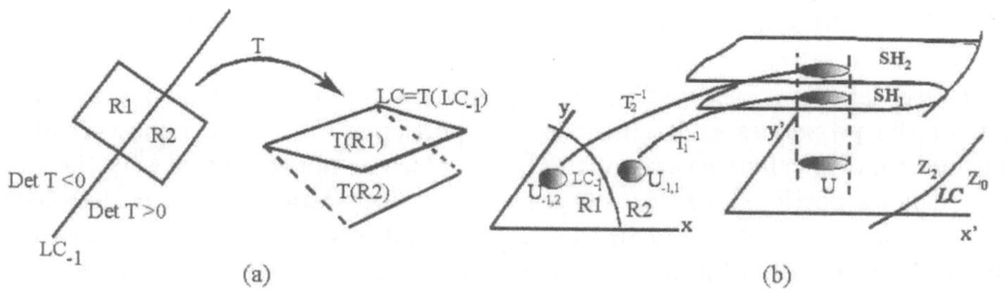

Figure 3.

In order to give a geometrical interpretation of the action of a multi-valued inverse relation T^{-1}, it is useful to consider a region Z_k as the superposition of k sheets, each associated with a different inverse. Such a representation is known as *Riemann foliation* of the plane (see Mira et al., 1996). Different sheets are connected by folds, and the projections of such folds on the phase plane are arcs of LC. This is shown in the qualitative sketch of Figure 3b, where the case of a $Z_0 - Z_2$ noninvertible map is considered. This graphical representation of the unfolding action of the inverses gives an intuitive idea of the mechanism which causes the creation of nonconnected basins for noninvertible maps of the plane.

To give an example, let us again consider a quadratic map $T : (x, y) \rightarrow (x', y')$, extensively studied in Mira et al., 1996, and Abraham et al., 1997, defined by

$$T : \left\{ \begin{array}{l} x' = ax + y \\ y' = b + x^2 \end{array} \right. \tag{2.11}$$

Given x' and y', if we try to solve the algebraic system with respect to the unknowns x and y we get two solutions, given by

$$T_1^{-1}: \begin{array}{l} x = -\sqrt{y'-b} \\ y = x' + a\sqrt{y'-b} \end{array} \quad ; \qquad T_2^{-1}: \begin{array}{l} x = \sqrt{y'-b} \\ y = x' - a\sqrt{y'-b} \end{array} \tag{2.12}$$

if $y' \geq b$, and no solutions if $y' < b$. So, (2.11) is a $Z_0 - Z_2$ noninvertible map, where Z_0 (region whose points have no preimages) is the half plane $Z_0 = \{(x,y)\,|y<b\}$ and Z_2 (region whose points have two distinct *rank-1* preimages) is the half plane $Z_2 = \{(x,y)\,|y>b\}$. The line $y=b$, which separates these two regions, is LC, and the locus LC_{-1} of points having two merging *rank-1* preimages is located on the line $x=0$ (see Figure 1). Being (2.11) a continuously differentiable map, the points of LC_{-1} necessarily belong to the set of points at which the Jacobian determinant vanishes, i.e. $LC_{-1} \subseteq J_0$, where $J_0 = \{(x,y)\,|\det DT(x,y) = -2x = 0\}$. In this case LC_{-1} coincides with J_0 (the vertical axis $x=0$) and the critical curve LC is the image by T of LC_{-1}, i.e. $LC = T(LC_{-1}) = T(\{x=0\}) = \{(x,y)\,|y=b\}$.

As stressed above, a study of the basins of attraction of a map T requires a global analysis of the properties of its inverses. In particular, if T is a noninvertible map, complicated topological structures of the basins, such as nonconnected sets (i.e. formed by many disjoint portions) and/or sets with fractal boundaries, are often observed[4].

The route to more and more complex basin boundaries, as some parameter is varied, is characterized by global bifurcations, also called *contact bifurcations*, due to contacts between the critical set and the basins' boundaries. Some particular examples in dimension one and two will be given below. However, the origin of complex topological structures of the basins, like those formed by nonconnected sets, can be heuristically explained on the basis of the geometrical properties of a noninvertible map. For example, suppose that p is a fixed point of T. Since $T(p)=p$, one of the preimages of p is p itself, but if T^{-1} is multivalued. in p, i.e. $p \in Z_k$ with $k \geq 2$, then other preimages of the fixed point p exist. If the fixed point is stable, and $U(p)$ is a neighborhood of p that belongs to its basin of attraction, then the basin of p must also include all the *rank-1* preimages of the points of $U(p)$, which may be disjoint from $U(p)$, due to the unfolding action of the inverses defined in $U(p)$ (see Figure 3b). Moreover, if also such disjoint preimages belong to regions where some inverses exist, higher rank preimages of $U(p)$ belong to the basin of p, and so on. This may give rise to a so called "arborescent sequence" of (countable) infinitely many nonconnected portions of the basin.

Hence if a parameter variation causes a crossing between a basin boundary and a critical set which separates different regions Z_k, so that a portion of a basin enters a region where an higher number of inverses is defined, then new components of the basin may suddenly appear at the contact. This is the basic mechanism which causes the creation of more and more complex structures of the basins, as we shall see in the examples given in the following sections.

[4]For the map (2.11) several studies and graphical representations of the basins and their qualitative changes are given in Mira et al., 1994, Mira and Rauzy, 1995, Mira et al., 1996, Abraham et al., 1997.

3 Basin boundaries and contact bifurcations in one-dimensional noninvertible maps

In this section, we consider continuous one-dimensional maps. Before describing the contact bifurcations, let us take a look at iterated invertible maps. If $f : I \to I$ is a continuous and increasing function, then the only invariant sets are the fixed points. When many fixed points exist, say $x_1^* < x_2^* < ... < x_k^*$, they are alternatively stable and unstable: the unstable fixed points are the boundaries that separate the basins of the stable ones (see Figure 4a). Starting from an initial condition where the graph of f is above the diagonal, i.e. $f(x_0) > x_0$, the generated trajectory is an increasing sequence converging to the stable fixed point on the right. Starting from an initial condition such that $f(x_0) < x_0$, the trajectory is a decreasing sequence converging to the fixed point on the left (see Figure 4a, where p^* is a stable fixed point, and its basin is bounded by two unstable fixed points q^* and r^*, with $q^* < p^* < r^*$). If $f : I \to I$ is a continuous and decreasing map, the only possible invariant sets are one fixed point and cycles of period 2. In fact f^2 can only have fixed points (since $f^2 = f \circ f$ is an increasing map), that include the fixed points of f and periodic points of period 2 of f. The periodic points of the 2-cycles must be located at opposite sides with respect to the unique fixed point, the unstable ones being boundaries of the basins of the stable ones (see Figure 4b, where a stable fixed point x^* exists, and its basin is bounded by the periodic points α_1, α_2 of an unstable cycle of period 2). If the fixed point x^* is stable and no cycles exist, then x^* is globally stable.

So, if the map is invertible, the basins of the attracting sets have always quite simple structures: for stable fixed points they are formed by a unique open interval that includes the fixed point, for stable two cycles they are formed by two open intervals each one including one periodic point. In general, this is not true if the map is noninvertible. In fact, in this case nonconnected portions of the basins may exist, given by open intervals that do not include any point of the related attractor.

As a first example, let us consider the logistic map (2.7), that is, as we showed, a noninvertible $Z_0 - Z_2$ map whose graph is represented again in Figure 5. For $\mu < 4$ every initial condition $x_0 \in (0,1)$ generates bounded sequences, converging to a unique attractor A[5], whereas initial conditions out of the interval $[0,1]$ generate sequences diverging to (minus) infinity. The boundary that separates the basin of the attractor A, $\mathcal{B}(A)$, from the basin of diverging trajectories, $\mathcal{B}(\infty)$ - marked by bold lines in Figure 5a - , is formed by the unstable fixed point $q^* = 0$ and its *rank-1* preimage (different from itself), $q_{-1}^* = 1$. Observe that, of course, a fixed point is always preimage of itself, but in this case also another preimage exists because $q^* \in Z_2$. If $\mu < 4$, like in Figure 5a, $q_{-1}^* > c = \mu/4$, where c is the critical point (maximum) that separates Z_0 and Z_2. Hence, $q_{-1}^* \in Z_0$, and consequently no preimages of higher order exist. If we increase μ, at $\mu = 4$ we have $q_{-1}^* = c = 1$, and a contact between the critical point and the basin boundary occurs. This is a global bifurcation, which changes the structure of the basin. For $\mu > 4$, we have $q_{-1}^* < c$, and the portion (q_{-1}^*, c) of $\mathcal{B}(\infty)$ enters Z_2. This implies that new

[5]The attractor A may be the fixed point $x^* = (\mu - 1)/\mu$ or a more complex attractor, periodic or chaotic, located around x^*, see Devaney, 1987.

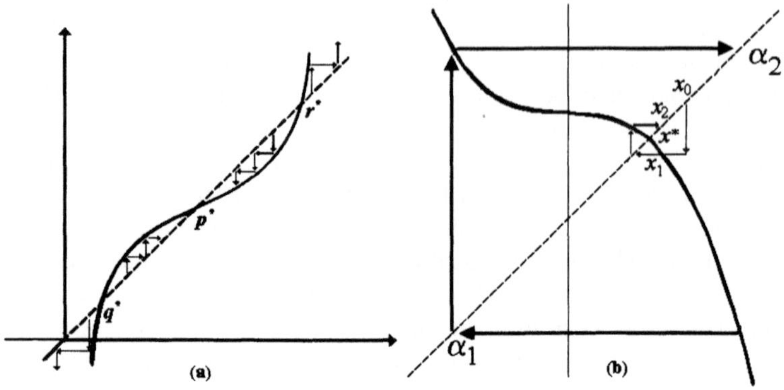

Figure 4.

preimages of that portion are created, which belong to $\mathcal{B}(\infty)$ according to (2.4). The two *rank-1* preimages of (q^*_{-1}, c) are located in a neighborhood I_0 of the critical point $c_{-1} = 1/2$, as shown in Figure 5b. Points of I_0 exit the interval $(0, 1)$ after one iteration, thus giving unbounded sequences. As $I_0 \in Z_2$, it also has two *rank-1* preimages, that are *rank-2* preimages of (q^*_{-1}, c). These preimages are given by the two smaller intervals denoted by $I^{(1)}_{-1}$ and $I^{(2)}_{-1}$ in Figure 5b, and are located symmetrically with respect to $c_{-1} = 1/2$. Points belonging to $I^{(1)}_{-1}$ and $I^{(2)}_{-1}$ exit the interval $(0, 1)$ after two iterations of (2.7). Even these two smaller – nonconnected – portions of $\mathcal{B}(\infty)$ are in Z_2. Hence, each of them has two preimages, which again result in nonconnected portions of $\mathcal{B}(\infty)$. Obviously, this process gives rise to a infinite sequence of preimages whose points generate unbounded sequences. So, after the contact between the critical point c and the basin boundary q^*_{-1}, infinitely many nonconnected portions of $\mathcal{B}(\infty)$ are created inside $(0, 1)$ (only a few of them are shown in Figure 5b). The union of all these preimages is an open set whose closure is $[0, 1]$. Its complement in $[0, 1]$ has zero Lebesgue measure and is a Cantor set (see Guckenheimer and Holmes, 1983, Devaney, 1987). After this bifurcation the attractor at finite distance no longer exists, and the generic trajectory is divergent. This global bifurcation is called *final bifurcation* in Mira et al., 1996 or in Abraham et al., 1997, and *boundary crisis* in Grebogi et al., 1983.

A similar situation occurs for a unimodal $Z_0 - Z_2$ map where the attractor at infinity

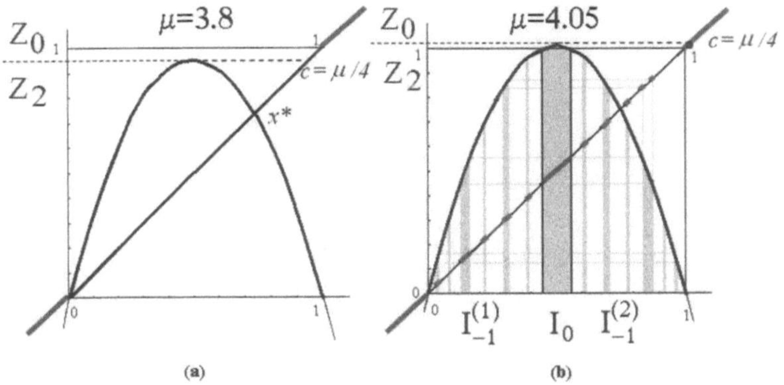

Figure 5.

is replaced by an attracting fixed point, like the one shown in Figure 6. As in the previous example, we have an attractor A, which may be the fixed point x^* (or some other invariant set around it), with a simply connected basin bounded by the unstable fixed point q^* and its *rank-1* preimage q^*_{-1}. Note that in this case, differently from the previous one, initial conditions taken in the complementary of $\mathcal{B}(x^*)$ generate trajectories converging to the stable fixed point z^*. This means that the basin $\mathcal{B}(z^*)$ is formed by the union of two nonconnected portions: $B_0 = (-\infty, q^*) \subset Z_2$, a connected set containing z^* called *immediate basin*, and $B_1 = \left(q^*_{-1}, +\infty\right) = f^{-1}(B_0) \subset Z_0$. In Figure 6 the two nonconnected portions of the basin $\mathcal{B}(z^*)$ are marked by bold lines. Now suppose that some parameter variation makes the critical point c (maximum value) increase until it crosses the basin boundary q^*_{-1}. Then the interval (q^*_{-1}, c), which is part of B_1, enters Z_2, and infinitely many nonconnected portions of $\mathcal{B}(z^*)$ emerge in the interval (q^*, q^*_{-1}). Note that the total basin can still be expressed as the union of all the preimages of any rank of the immediate basin B_0, and the boundary $\partial\mathcal{B}(z^*)$ is the set of infinitely many preimages of any rank of q^*.

Changing the right branch of the map depicted in Figure 6 by folding it upwards, another critical point (a minimum) is created (Figure 7). This map is now a $Z_1 - Z_3 - Z_1$ noninvertible map, where Z_3 is the portion of the codomain bounded by the relative minimum value $c_{\min}$ and relative maximum value $c_{\max}$. In the Figure 7a we have three

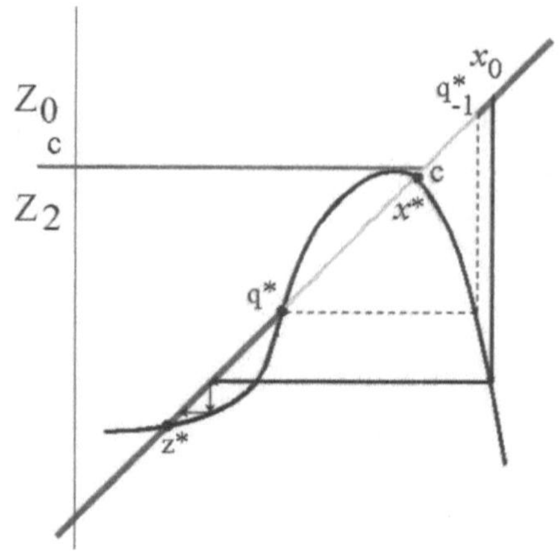

Figure 6.

attractors: the fixed point z^*, with $\mathcal{B}(z^*) = (-\infty, q^*)$, the attractor A around x^*, with basin $\mathcal{B}(A) = (q^*, r^*)$ bounded by two unstable fixed points, and $+\infty$ (i.e. positively diverging trajectories) with basin $\mathcal{B}(+\infty) = (r^*, +\infty)$. In this case all the basins are immediate, each given by an open interval. Both basin boundaries q^* and r^* are in Z_1, so they are the only preimages of themselves (like for an invertible map). However, the situation drastically changes if the minimum value $c_{\min}$ moves downwards below q^* (as in Figure 7b). After the global bifurcation, when $c_{\min} = q^*$, the portion $(c_{\min}, q^*)$ enters Z_3, so new preimages $f^{-k}(c_{\min}, q^*)$ appear with $k \geq 1$. These preimages constitute an infinite (countable) set of nonconnected portions (or *holes*) of $\mathcal{B}(z^*)$ nested inside $\mathcal{B}(A)$, represented by the thick portions of the diagonal in Figure 7b, bounded by the infinitely many preimages of any rank, say q^*_{-k}, $k \in \mathbb{N}$, of q^*, that accumulate in a left neighborhood of the fixed point r^*. In fact, as r^* is a repelling fixed point for the forward iteration of f, it is an attracting fixed point for the backward iteration of the same map.

To conclude, we stress that in the context of noninvertible maps it is useful to define the *immediate basin* $\mathcal{B}_0(A)$, of an attracting set A, as the widest connected component of the basin which contains A. Then the total basin can be expressed as $\mathcal{B}(A) = \bigcup_{n=0}^{\infty} T^{-n}(\mathcal{B}_0(A))$.

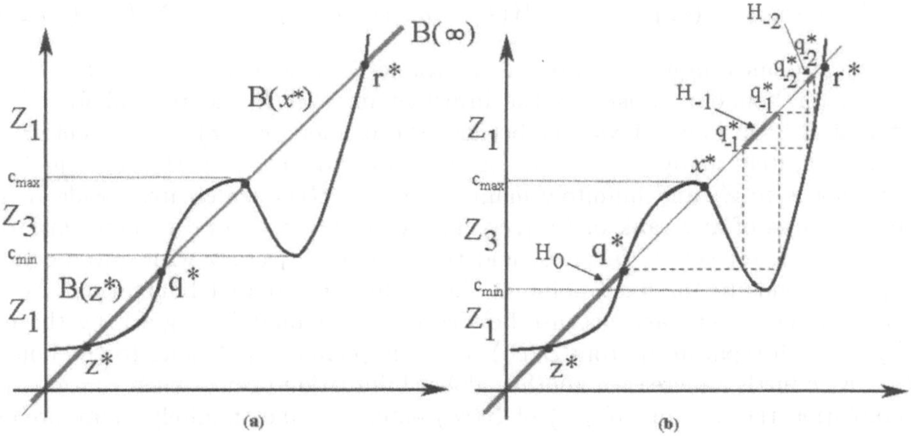

Figure 7.

The previous example shows that a contact between a critical point and a basin boundary marks the transition from simple connected to nonconnected basins: infinitely many nonconnected portions are suddenly created, given by the preimages of any rank of the portion H_0 of $\mathcal{B}(z^*)$ included into Z_3, say $H_{-i} = T^{-i}(H_0)$, $i = 1, 2, \ldots$.

Several examples where the multiplicity of preimages leads to basins with complex structures are given on Mira et al., 1994, Mira and Rauzy, 1995, Mira et al., 1996, chap. 5, Abraham et al., 1997, Bischi et al., 2003a,b[6], Bischi et al., 2004).

To conclude this section, we briefly describe a unimodal map, i.e. a map with a unique critical point c which separates Z_0 from Z_2, with two inflection points, like in the graphs shown in Figure 8 (this example is taken from Gumowski and Mira, 1980).

This map has four fixed points, $q < s < r < p$, with q and r unstable and s stable. The fixed point p belongs to the trapping interval $R = [r, r_{-1}]$ and the restriction of the map to R behaves like a logistic map. In Figure 8 three attractors are present: the infinity, the stable fixed point s and the attractor I included inside the absorbing

[6] Where an evolutionary game is studied, described by the map

$$x(t+1) = x(t) + x(t)(1 - x(t))\frac{2}{\pi}\arctan\left[\frac{\lambda\pi}{2}\left(A - B(x_{1,t} + 1) - \frac{C}{1 + \beta x_{1,t}}\right)\right]$$

whose graph is very similar to the one shown in fig. 7.

interval R, which may be the fixed point p, a cycle around it or a chaotic attractor. The respective basins are:

$$\mathcal{B}(\infty) = (-\infty, q) \cup (q_{-1}, +\infty) \qquad \mathcal{B}(s) = (q, r) \cup (r_{-1}, q_{-1}); \qquad \mathcal{B}(I) = (r, r_{-1});$$

If the critical point c moves upwards as a parameter is varied, when $c = r_{-1}$ the final bifurcation (or boundary crisis) of the invariant interval R occurs, and for $c > r_{-1}$ the interval R is no longer invariant because the portion (r_{-1}, c) of $\mathcal{B}(s)$ enters R, as well as its infinitely many preimages. In fact, after this contact, the segment (r_{-1}, c) of $\mathcal{B}(s)$ belongs to Z_2 and infinitely many "holes" of $\mathcal{B}(s)$ are created inside R, given by the preimages of any rank of (r_{-1}, c). Inside R only a chaotic repellor, given by a zero-measure Cantor set Λ, survives, and the generic trajectory with initial condition $x_0 \in (q, q_{-1})$ tends to the fixed point s. Thus, after the contact bifurcation, the basin $\mathcal{B}(s)$ has a fractal boundary because besides the outer boundary, given by the points q and q_{-1} which separate it from $\mathcal{B}(\infty)$, also the points of Λ belong to the boundary of $\mathcal{B}(s)$. As c further increases, another global bifurcation occurs when $c = q_{-1}$. After this bifurcation the portion (q_{-1}, c) of $\mathcal{B}(\infty)$ enters Z_2 and infinitely many preimages of it enter inside R. These constitute a set of infinitely many holes of $\mathcal{B}(\infty)$ nested inside $\mathcal{B}(s)$. At this stage, two sets of positive measure, made up of infinitely many disjoint subsets of $\mathcal{B}(\infty)$ and $\mathcal{B}(s)$, are nested inside R: In fact, both $(q_{-1}, c) \in \mathcal{B}(\infty)$ and $(r_{-1}, q_{-1}) \in \mathcal{B}(s)$ are inside Z_2 and have infinitely many preimages inside R. The boundary which separates $\mathcal{B}(s)$ and $\mathcal{B}(\infty)$ inside R is the chaotic repeller Λ (see Mira et al., 1996 for a more detailed discussion of this example). The above discussion has only been based on qualitative consideration related to a graph, without any analytic representation of the function. The simplest map whose graph has a shape similar to the one shown in Figure 8 is a quartic map (i.e. a polynomial of degree 4) which has only a critical point (i.e. $f'(x)$ is a cubic polynomial with only one real root) and two inflection points (i.e. $f''(x)$ is a quadratic polynomial with two real roots). An example of a map having such properties is $x' = f(x) = x(1-x)\left(\mu x^2 + (4-\mu)x + 3\right)$. As μ is increased, all the situations described above are obtained (an exercise left to the reader).

4 Basin boundaries and their bifurcations in two-dimensional noninvertible maps

As shown for one dimensional maps, even for higher dimensional maps the global bifurcations that lead to basins formed by nonconnected sets can be explained in terms of contacts between basins boundaries and critical sets. We now consider some examples, taken from recent models of economic dynamics, where two-dimensional iterated maps are used to describe the interaction among economic agents. In these examples we stress that the route to more and more complex basin boundaries, as some parameter is varied, is characterized by global bifurcations due to contacts between critical curves and the invariant sets that constitute the basins' boundaries in two-dimensional maps, such as the stable sets of saddle points or cycles, or unstable closed invariant orbits.

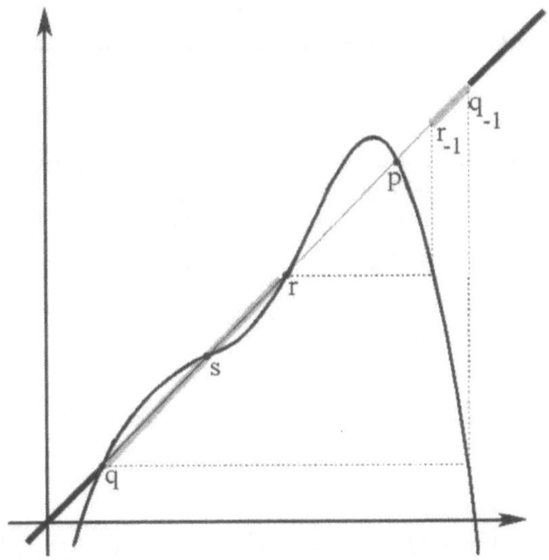

Figure 8.

For two-dimensional maps, such kinds of bifurcations can be very rarely studied by analytical methods, since the analytical equation of a singularity is not known in general. Hence the analysis is mainly performed by geometrical and numerical methods.

4.1 A Cournot duopoly game with best reply, naive expectations and adaptive behavior

We consider a Cournot duopoly game where at each time period t two firms decide their next period productions on the basis of *best reply* functions expressed as $q_i(t+1) = r_i(q_j(t))$, $i, j = 1, 2$, $i \neq j$. We assume that competitors exhibit some kind of inertia, adjusting their previous production quantities in the direction of the Best Response, according to the following adjustment mechanism

$$\begin{aligned} q_1(t+1) &= q_1(t) + \lambda_1 \left(r_1(q_2(t)) - q_1(t)\right) \\ q_2(t+1) &= q_2(t) + \lambda_2 \left(r_2(q_1(t)) - q_2(t)\right) \end{aligned} \tag{4.1}$$

where the parameters $\lambda_i \in [0, 1]$, $i = 1, 2$, represent the *speeds of adjustment.* Following Kopel, 1996, we assume in (4.1) reaction functions in the form of logistic maps $r_i(q_j) = \mu_i q_j (1 - q_j)$, so that the time evolution of the game is obtained by the iteration of the two-dimensional map $T:(q_1,q_2)\to(q_1',q_2')$ defined by

$$T:\begin{cases} q_1'=T_1(q_1,q_2)=(1-\lambda_1)\,q_1+\lambda_1\mu_1 q_2\,(1-q_2)\\ q_2'=T_2(q_1,q_2)=(1-\lambda_2)\,q_2+\lambda_2\mu_2 q_1\,(1-q_1)\end{cases}. \tag{4.2}$$

The fixed points of map (4.2), located at the intersections of the two reaction curves, coincide with the Nash equilibria of the duopoly game (see again Kopel, 1996). If we assume that $\mu_1=\mu_2=\mu$, the fixed points can be expressed by simple analytical expressions: besides $O=(0,0)$ we have $S=\left(1-\frac{1}{\mu},1-\frac{1}{\mu}\right)$, that for $\mu>1$ represents a symmetric Nash equilibrium, since it is characterized by identical quantities of the two firms. Two further Nash equilibria, given by

$$E_1=\left(\frac{\mu+1+\sqrt{(\mu+1)(\mu-3)}}{2\mu},\frac{\mu+1-\sqrt{(\mu+1)(\mu-3)}}{2\mu}\right) \tag{4.3}$$

and

$$E_2=\left(\frac{\mu+1-\sqrt{(\mu+1)(\mu-3)}}{2\mu},\frac{\mu+1+\sqrt{(\mu+1)(\mu-3)}}{2\mu}\right), \tag{4.4}$$

are created at $\mu=3$. For $\mu>3$ they are located in symmetric positions with respect to the diagonal Δ of equation $q_1=q_2$. Each of them represents a nonsymmetric Nash equilibrium: In E_1 firm 1 produces more than firm 2 in exactly the same way as firm 2 produces more than firm 1 in E_2. A study of the local stability of the equilibria reveals that O is stable for $\mu<1$, S is stable for $1<\mu<3$ and for $\mu>3$ a range of parameters μ, λ_1, λ_2 exists such that S is a saddle point and E_i, $i=1,2$, are both stable. Moreover, the map (4.2) can generate diverging trajectories, that is, an attractor at infinite distance exists (see Bischi and Kopel, 2001). This naturally leads to the question of the delimitation of the basins of attraction. Numerically computed basins of attraction are shown in Figures 10 and 11, where the dark grey region represents $\mathcal{B}(\infty)$, and the complementary set is subdivided into the basins of the stable Nash equilibria E_1 and E_2, represented by white and light grey regions respectively. These Figures show that the structure of the basins may be quite different as the values of the parameters vary, and we try to understand the basic mechanisms that cause such qualitative changes.

As argued in the previous sections, a study of the inverses of the map become important in order to understand the structure of the basins and their qualitative changes. Indeed, the map (4.2) is a noninvertible map, because given a point $q'=(q_1',q_2')\in\mathbb{R}^2$ its *rank-1* preimages $T^{-1}(q')$ may be more than one, i.e., T^{-1} is a multivalued relation. Such preimages can be computed by solving the following algebraic system obtained from (4.2) with respect to the quantities q_1 and q_2:

$$\begin{cases}(1-\lambda_1)q_1+\lambda_1\mu_2 q_2(1-q_2)=q_1'\\ (1-\lambda_2)q_2+\lambda_2\mu_1 q_1(1-q_1)=q_2'\end{cases} \tag{4.5}$$

This is a fourth degree algebraic system, which may have four, two or no real solutions. According to the number of distinct *rank-1* preimages associated with each point of $\mathbb{R}^2$,

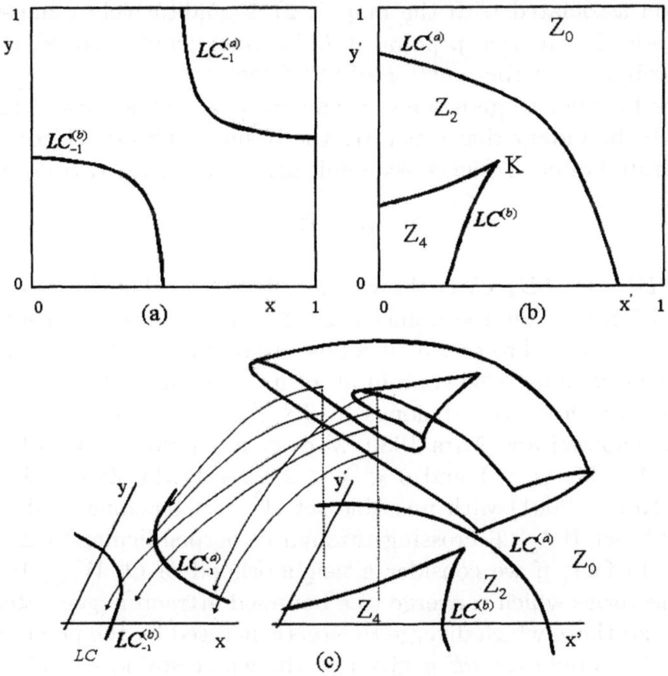

Figure 9.

the plane can be subdivided into regions, denoted by Z_k, $k = 0, 2, 4$, whose points have k distinct preimages, hence the map (4.2) is a noninvertible map of $Z_0 - Z_2 - Z_4$ type.

Being (4.2) a continuously differentiable map, the set LC_{-1} belongs to the set of points in which the Jacobian determinant vanishes, which can be computed by solving the equation

$$\left(q_1 - \frac{1}{2}\right)\left(q_2 - \frac{1}{2}\right) = \frac{(1-\lambda_1)(1-\lambda_2)}{4\lambda_1\lambda_2\mu_1\mu_2} \tag{4.6}$$

This equation represents an equilateral hyperbola, whose two branches are denoted by $LC_{-1}^{(a)}$ and $LC_{-1}^{(b)}$ in Figure 9a. It follows that also $LC = T(LC_{-1})$ is the union of two branches, say $LC^{(a)} = T(LC_{-1}^{(a)})$ and $LC^{(b)} = T(LC_{-1}^{(b)})$. $LC^{(a)}$ separates the region Z_0, whose points have no preimages, from the region Z_2, whose points have two distinct *rank-1* preimages. $LC^{(b)}$ separates the region Z_2 from Z_4, whose points have four distinct preimages (see Figure 9b). Notice that any point of $LC^{(a)}$ has two coincident *rank-1* preimages which are located at a point of $LC_{-1}^{(a)}$, and any point of $LC^{(b)}$ has two coincident *rank-1* preimages which are located at a point of $LC_{-1}^{(b)}$ plus two further distinct *rank-1* preimages, called *extra preimages* (see e.g. Mira et al. 1996). The

Riemann foliation associated with the map (4.2) is qualitatively represented in Figure 9c. It can be noticed that a cusp point of LC exists, denoted by K, characterized by three merging preimages at the junction of two folds.

The first task in order to gain some insight into the robustness of the model is the delimitation of the boundary that separates the basin of infinity, $\mathcal{B}(\infty)$, from the set of points that generate bounded (hence economically meaningful) trajectories, denoted by

$$\mathcal{B} = \mathbb{R}^2 \setminus \overline{\mathcal{B}(\infty)} \tag{4.7}$$

where $\overline{\mathcal{B}(\infty)} = \mathcal{B}(\infty) \cup \partial\mathcal{B}(\infty)$ is the closure of $\mathcal{B}(\infty)$. The boundary $\partial\mathcal{B} = \partial\mathcal{B}(\infty)$ behaves as a repelling set for the points near it, since it acts like a watershed for the trajectories of the map T. From (2.5) it follows that if an unstable fixed point or cycle belongs to $\partial\mathcal{B}$ then $\partial\mathcal{B}$ must also contain all of its preimages of any rank. Moreover, if a saddle-point, or a saddle-cycle, belongs to $\partial\mathcal{B}$, then $\partial\mathcal{B}$ must also contain the whole stable set (see Gumowski and Mira 1980, Mira et al. 1996). Let us first consider the case $\lambda_1 = \lambda_2 = \lambda$. For $\mu > 1$ and $0 < \lambda < 2/(\mu+1)$ the fixed point O is a saddle (see Bischi and Kopel, 2001) with unstable set $W^u(O)$ reaching S along the diagonal Δ and local stable set $W^s_{loc}(O)$ crossing through O perpendicular to Δ. The stable set $W^s_{loc}(O) \subseteq \partial\mathcal{B}$. In fact, if we consider a neighborhood of O, $W^s_{loc}(O)$ is a separatrix between the trajectories which converge to a bounded attractor (generated by the points above $W^s_{loc}(O)$) and those which diverge to $-\infty$ (generated by the points below $W^s_{loc}(O)$, see Figure 10a). The boundary $\partial\mathcal{B}$ is given by the whole stable set $W^s(O)$, obtained by taking the preimages of any rank of $W^s_{loc}(O)$

$$\partial\mathcal{B} = W^s(O) = \bigcup_{k\geq 0} T^{-k}\left(W^s_{loc}(O)\right)$$

In the symmetric case of homogeneous players, i.e. $\mu_1 = \mu_2 = \mu$ and $\lambda_1 = \lambda_2 = \lambda$, the preimages of O can be analytically computed, and their coordinates allow us to obtain a rough estimate of the extension of $\mathcal{B}$. Indeed, the diagonal Δ is a trapping submanifold for the map T, i.e., $T(\Delta) \subseteq \Delta$[7]. The trajectories, embedded into the one-dimensional submanifold Δ, are governed by the restriction of the two-dimensional map T to Δ, $f = T|_\Delta : \Delta \to \Delta$, where the map f, which is obtained by setting $q_1 = q_2 = q$ and $q_1' = q_2' = q'$ in (4.2), is given by

$$q' = f(q) = (1 + \lambda(\mu - 1))\, q - \lambda\mu q^2 \tag{4.8}$$

So, if $O \in Z_2$ (like in Figure 10a) its two *rank-1* preimages are O itself (being O a fixed point) and

$$O_{-1}^{(1)} = \left(\frac{1 + \lambda(\mu-1)}{\lambda\mu}, \frac{1 + \lambda(\mu-1)}{\lambda\mu}\right) \in \Delta. \tag{4.9}$$

that can be computed by solving the equation (4.8) with $q' = 0$. The condition $O \in Z_2$ can be analytically determined because in the case of homogeneous players also the cusp

[7]This means nothing more than if two firms start with equal quantities $q_1(0) = q_2(0)$ and behave identically, then their choices will be the same for each future time period.

point K of LC_{-1} belongs to the diagonal Δ, and its coordinates can be analytically computed (see Bischi and Kopel, 2001):

$$K = LC^{(b)} \cap \Delta = (k, k) \quad \text{with} \quad k = \frac{(\lambda(\mu+1)-1)(\lambda\mu+3(1-\lambda))}{4\lambda\mu} \tag{4.10}$$

If $0 < \lambda < 1/(\mu+1)$ then $O \in Z_2$, otherwise $O \in Z_4$, i.e., it has four *rank-1* preimages (see Figure 10b). In this case, two of them, O and $O_{-1}^{(1)}$, belong to Δ, and the other two, say $O_{-1}^{(2)}$ and $O_{-1}^{(3)}$, are located in symmetric positions with respect to Δ and belong to the line Δ_{-1}, of equation $q_1 + q_2 = 1 + \frac{1}{\mu}\left(1 - \frac{1}{\lambda}\right)$. Indeed, the preimages of the points of Δ are located on Δ or on Δ_{-1}, as it can be seen by setting $q_1' = q_2'$ in (4.5) and adding or subtracting the two symmetric equations. In particular, with $q_1' = q_2' = 0$ we get the solution

$$O_{-1}^{(2)} = \left(\frac{\lambda(\mu+1)-1+\sqrt{\lambda^2\mu^2+2\lambda\mu(1-\lambda)-3(\lambda^2+1)+6\lambda}}{2\lambda\mu},\right. \\ \left.\frac{\lambda(\mu+1)-1-\sqrt{\lambda^2\mu^2+2\lambda\mu(1-\lambda)-3(\lambda^2+1)+6\lambda}}{2\lambda\mu}\right) \tag{4.11}$$

and the symmetric solution $O_{-1}^{(3)}$ is obtained from $O_{-1}^{(2)}$ by swapping the two coordinates.

So, if $0 < \lambda < 1/(\mu+1)$, the stable set $W^s(O)$ consists of two smooth arcs connecting O and $O_{-1}^{(1)}$, symmetric with respect to Δ, as in Figure 10a. If $\lambda > 1/(\mu+1)$ then $W^s(O)$ has a similar shape, with the symmetric arcs connecting O and $O_{-1}^{(1)}$ which pass through the points $O_{-1}^{(2)}$ and $O_{-1}^{(3)}$, as shown in Figure 10b, obtained for $\mu = 3.4$ and $\lambda = 0.5$. It is also important to notice that even after the bifurcation occurring at $\lambda(\mu+1) = 2$, when O is transformed from a saddle point into an unstable node with the simultaneous creation of a saddle cycle C_2 of period 2, the boundary $\partial\mathcal{B}$ remains practically the same. In fact, in this case $\partial\mathcal{B} = \overline{W^s(C_2)}$, which continues to include O and its preimages of any rank.

The "size" of the basin $\mathcal{B}$ of bounded trajectories, as well as the influence of parameters λ and μ on it, can be estimated knowing the coordinates of O and $O_{-1}^{(1)}$. In fact, in the case of homogeneous behavior, the length of the segment $OO_{-1}^{(1)}$, given by $l(OO_{-1}^{(1)}) = \sqrt{2}\left[1+\lambda(\mu-1)\right]/\lambda\mu$ is a decreasing function of both parameters λ and μ, and it goes to infinity as $\lambda \to 0^+$, i.e. the basin of bounded trajectories tends to include the whole diagonal in such a limiting case. It is also interesting to note that in the other limiting case, $\lambda \to 1^-$, we get $O_{-1}^{(1)} \to (1,1)$, $O_{-1}^{(2)} \to (1,0)$, $O_{-1}^{(3)} \to (0,1)$. Hence in the case of instantaneous adjustment ($\lambda = 1$), the basin of the bounded trajectories becomes the square $(0,1) \times (0,1)$. This result also holds for $\mu_1 \neq \mu_2$, as proved in Bischi et al., 2000b.

Many of the arguments given above continue to hold in the case of different speeds of adjustment $\lambda_1 \neq \lambda_2$. However, a simple analytical expression of the preimages of O cannot be obtained, since in this case they are given by the solution of the fourth degree nonsymmetric algebraic system (4.5). The diagonal Δ is no longer invariant and the basins are no longer symmetric with respect to Δ.

Let us move now to the problem of the delimitation of the basins $\mathcal{B}(E_1)$ and $\mathcal{B}(E_2)$ of the two stable equilibria E_1 and E_2 respectively. The boundary of each of these two basins is formed by an "outer portion", which separates them from $\mathcal{B}(\infty)$, and an "inner portion", separating $\mathcal{B}(E_1)$ and $\mathcal{B}(E_2)$, which contains the saddle point S as well as its whole stable set $W^s(S)$. In fact, just after the pitchfork bifurcation, occurring at $\mu = 3$, at which the two stable fixed points E_1 and E_2 are created, the symmetric equilibrium $S \in \Delta$ is a saddle, provided that $0 < \lambda < \frac{2}{\mu-1}$, and the two branches of unstable set $W^u(S)$ departing from it reach the two stable nodes E_1 and E_2. Hence the local stable set $W^s_{loc}(S)$ belongs to the boundary that separates the two basins, as well as its preimages of any rank:

$$W^s(S) = \bigcup_{k \geq 0} T^{-k}\left(W^s_{loc}(S)\right) = \partial\mathcal{B}(E_1) \cap \partial\mathcal{B}(E_2) \tag{4.12}$$

Also in this case, in order to study the shape of $W^s(S)$, and the global bifurcations which change its structure, we first consider the symmetric case of homogeneous players. In this case, because of the symmetry of the map (4.2), the local stable set of S belongs to the invariant diagonal Δ. Indeed, as far as $\lambda(\mu+1) < 1$ the whole stable set belongs to Δ and is given by $W^s(S) = OO^{(1)}_{-1}$, where $O^{(1)}_{-1}$ is given in (4.9) and $OO^{(1)}_{-1}$ is the segment joining O with $O^{(1)}_{-1}$. In fact, as argued above, if $\lambda(\mu+1) < 1$ then the cusp point K of the critical curve $LC^{(b)}$ has negative coordinates and, consequently, the whole segment $OO^{(1)}_{-1}$ belongs to the region Z_2. This implies that the two preimages of any point of $OO^{(1)}_{-1}$ belong to Δ, and can be computed by the restriction (4.8). This proves that the segment $OO^{(1)}_{-1}$ is backward invariant, i.e.. $T\left(OO^{(1)}_{-1}\right) = OO^{(1)}_{-1}$. In this case, the structure of the basins $\mathcal{B}(E_i)$, $i = 1, 2$, is very simple: $\mathcal{B}(E_1)$ is the portion of $\mathcal{B}$ below the diagonal Δ and $\mathcal{B}(E_2)$ is the portion of $\mathcal{B}$ above it. This situation is shown in Figure 10a. The line Δ of equal quantities is the only boundary between the two basins, hence any bounded trajectory starting with $q_1(0) > q_2(0)$ converges to the Nash equilibrium E_1 and any bounded trajectory starting with $q_1(0) < q_2(0)$ converges to the Nash equilibrium E_2. In economic terms this means that an initial difference in the quantities uniquely determines which of the equilibria is selected in the long run. If player 1 offers a larger quantity than player 2, then E_1 is selected, and vice-versa. Moreover, if $q_1(0) > q_2(0)$ ($q_1(0) < q_2(0)$) then $q_1(t) > q_2(t)$ ($q_1(t) < q_2(t)$) for any t, i.e. any initial order of the quantities of the two players is maintained during the whole time evolution of the duopoly game. In particular, both of the basins $\mathcal{B}(E_1)$ and $\mathcal{B}(E_2)$ are simply connected sets[8].

Their structure becomes much more complex for $\lambda(\mu+1) > 1$. This is shown in Figure 10b, obtained with $\mu = 3.4$ as in Figure10a, but $\lambda = 0.5 > 1/(\mu+1)$. In order to understand the bifurcation occurring at $\lambda(\mu+1) = 1$, we consider the critical curves of the map (4.2). In fact, at $\lambda(\mu+1) = 1$ a contact between $LC^{(b)}$ and the fixed point O occurs, due to the merging between O and the cusp point K. For $\lambda(\mu+1) > 1$ the portion KO of the segment $OO^{(1)}_{-1}$ belongs to the region Z_4 where four inverses of T exist. This implies that besides the two *rank-1* preimages on Δ the points of KO

[8]If condition $\lambda(\mu+1) < 1$ holds, this simple structure of the basins is conserved even if E_i are no longer stable and more complex bounded attractors exist around them.

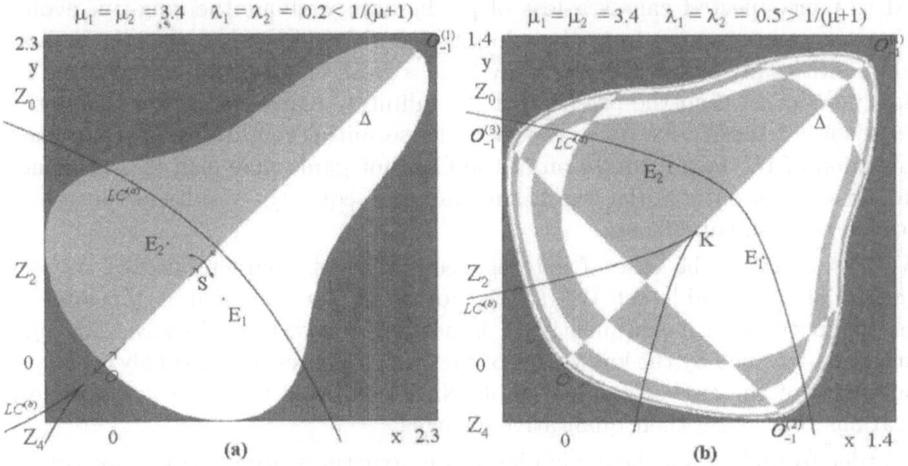

Figure 10.

have two further preimages located on the segment $O_{-1}^{(2)}O_{-1}^{(3)}$ of the line Δ_{-1}. Since $OO_{-1}^{(1)} = W_{loc}^s(S) \subset \partial\mathcal{B}(E_1) \cap \partial\mathcal{B}(E_2)$, also all the preimages of this segment belong to the boundary which separates $\mathcal{B}(E_1)$ from $\mathcal{B}(E_2)$. Furthermore, also the segment $O_{-1}^{(2)}O_{-1}^{(3)}$ has *rank-1* preimages, because portions of it are included in the regions Z_2 and Z_4. These are preimages of *rank-2* of $OO_{-1}^{(1)}$ and, consequently, belong to $W^s(S)$ according to (4.12). This repeated procedure, based on the iteration of the multivalued inverse of T, leads to the construction of the stable set $W^s(S)$ which is formed by the union of infinitely many arcs which accumulate on the boundary $\partial\mathcal{B}$. In fact the invariant set $\partial\mathcal{B}$, being a repelling set for the forward iteration of T, behaves as an attracting set for the iteration of the inverses of T.

The results given above can be summarized by the following proposition:

Proposition. *If $\mu_1 = \mu_2 = \mu$ and $\lambda_1 = \lambda_2 = \lambda$, the common boundary $\partial\mathcal{B}(E_1) \cap \partial\mathcal{B}(E_2)$ which separates the basin $\mathcal{B}(E_1)$ from the basin $\mathcal{B}(E_2)$ is given by the stable set $W^s(S)$ of the saddle point S. If $\lambda(\mu+1) < 1$ then $W^s(S) = OO_{-1}^{(1)}$, where $O = (0,0)$ and $O_{-1}^{(1)}$ is given by (4.9), and the two basins are simply connected sets; if $\lambda(\mu+1) > 1$ then the two basins are nonconnected sets, formed by infinitely many simply connected components.*

We would like to emphasize that the bifurcation occurring at $\lambda(\mu+1) = 1$ is a global bifurcation, i.e. it cannot be revealed by a study of the linear approximation of the dynamical system. The occurrence of such a bifurcation has been characterized by a contact between the stable set of S and a critical curve, and for this reason has been called *contact* bifurcation in Mira et al., 1996.

The occurrence of the bifurcation which transforms the basins from simply connected to nonconnected causes a loss of predictability about the long-run evolution of our Cournot game starting from given initial quantities of the two players. In fact, if the initial quantities are sufficiently far away from a Nash equilibrium, for example near the boundary $\partial\mathcal{B}$ of $\mathcal{B}$, then the presence of the infinitely many components of both basins causes a sort of sensitivity with respect to these initial conditions. Even a very small perturbation of the initial condition of the Cournot game may lead to a crossing of the boundary which separates the two basins and, consequently, results in the convergence to a different Nash equilibrium.

We now move to the case of heterogeneous players, characterized by $\lambda_1 \neq \lambda_2$. In this case the local stable set $W^s_{loc}(S)$ is not along the diagonal Δ, because T is no longer symmetric and, consequently, Δ is no longer invariant. However, by numerical investigations, guided by the knowledge of the critical curves, we can analyze the structure of the basins of the two coexisting stable Nash equilibria and we can characterize the bifurcations that cause their qualitative changes.

In order to understand how complex basin structures are obtained, we start from a situation in which $W^s(S)$ has a simple shape, like the one shown in Figure 11a, obtained with $\mu = 3.6$, $\lambda_1 = 0.55$ and $\lambda_2 = 0.7$. The introduction of an asymmetry in the adaptive behavior of the players has a negligible effect on the local stability properties, since the eigenvalues of the two fixed points are exactly the same and are very close to the ones obtained in the homogeneous case with the same value for μ and with $\lambda = (\lambda_1 + \lambda_2)/2$. On the other hand, it causes an evident asymmetry of the basins of attraction. As shown in Figure 11a, when $\lambda_2 > \lambda_1$ the extension of $\mathcal{B}(E_2)$ is in general greater than the extension of $\mathcal{B}(E_1)$, and the complementary situation is obtained if λ_1 and λ_2 are swapped. Furthermore, even in situations characterized by a simple structure of the basins' boundaries, like the one shown in Figure 11a where both basins are connected sets, the statement that the initial order of the quantities is maintained along the whole trajectory is no longer true. In fact, in the case of different speeds of adjustment, say $\lambda_i > \lambda_j$, the typical occurrence is that the smaller basin $\mathcal{B}(E_j)$ is surrounded by points of $\mathcal{B}(E_i)$. Hence, the adjustment dynamic in our Cournot game may lead to convergence to E_i in the long run, even if players start with quantities which are closer to E_j.

In the situation shown in Figure 11a, the smaller basin $\mathcal{B}(E_1)$ is a simply connected set. The basin $\mathcal{B}(E_2)$ is a multiply connected set, due to the presence of a big "hole" (or "island", following Mira et al., 1994) nested inside it, whose points belong to $\mathcal{B}(E_1)$. Furthermore, $W^s(S)$, i.e. the boundary which separates the two basins, is entirely included inside the regions Z_2 and Z_0. However, the fact that in Figure 11a a portion of $W^s(S)$ is close to LC suggests the occurrence of a global bifurcation. In fact, if the parameters are changed, so that a contact between $W^s(S)$ and LC occurs, this contact marks a bifurcation which causes qualitative changes in the structure of the basins. If a portion of $\mathcal{B}(E_1)$ enters Z_4 after a contact with $LC^{(b)}$, new *rank-1* preimages of that portion will appear near $LC^{(b)}_{-1}$, and such preimages must belong to $\mathcal{B}(E_1)$. Indeed, this is the situation shown in Figure11b, obtained after a small change of λ_1. The portion of $\mathcal{B}(E_1)$ inside Z_4 is denoted by H_0. It has two *rank-1* preimages, denoted by $H^{(1)}_{-1}$ and $H^{(2)}_{-1}$, which are located at opposite sides with respect to $LC^{(b)}_{-1}$ and merge on it (in fact, by definition, the *rank-1* preimages of the arc of $LC^{(b)}$ which bound H_0 must merge along $LC_{-1}^{(b)}$). The set $H_{-1} = H_{-1}^{(1)} \cup H_{-1}^{(2)}$ constitutes a nonconnected portion of $\mathcal{B}(E_1)$. Moreover, since H_{-1} belongs to the region Z_4, it has four *rank-1* preimages, denoted by $H_{-2}^{(j)}$, $j = 1, ..., 4$, which constitute other four "islands" of $\mathcal{B}(E_1)$, or "holes" of $\mathcal{B}(E_2)$. Points of these "islands" are mapped into H_0 in two iterations of the map T. Indeed, infinitely many higher rank preimages of H_0 exist, thus giving infinitely many smaller and smaller disjoint "islands" of $\mathcal{B}(E_1)$. Hence, at the contact between $W^s(S) = \partial\mathcal{B}(E_1)$ and LC the basin $\mathcal{B}(E_1)$ is transformed from a simply connected into a nonconnected set, constituted by infinitely many disjoint components. The larger connected component of $\mathcal{B}(E_1)$ which contains E_1 is the *immediate basin* $\mathcal{B}_0(E_1)$, and the whole basin is given by the union of the infinitely many preimages of $\mathcal{B}_0(E_1)$.

Such contact bifurcations can only be revealed numerically, since the equations of the curves involved in the contact cannot be analytically expressed in terms of elementary functions. This happens frequently in nonlinear dynamical systems of dimension greater than one, where the study of global bifurcations is generally obtained through an interplay between theoretical and numerical methods, and the occurrence of these bifurcations is shown by computer-assisted proofs, based on the knowledge of the properties of the critical curves and their graphical representation (see e.g. Mira et al., 1996, for many examples). This "modus operandi" is typical in the study of the global bifurcations of nonlinear two-dimensional maps.

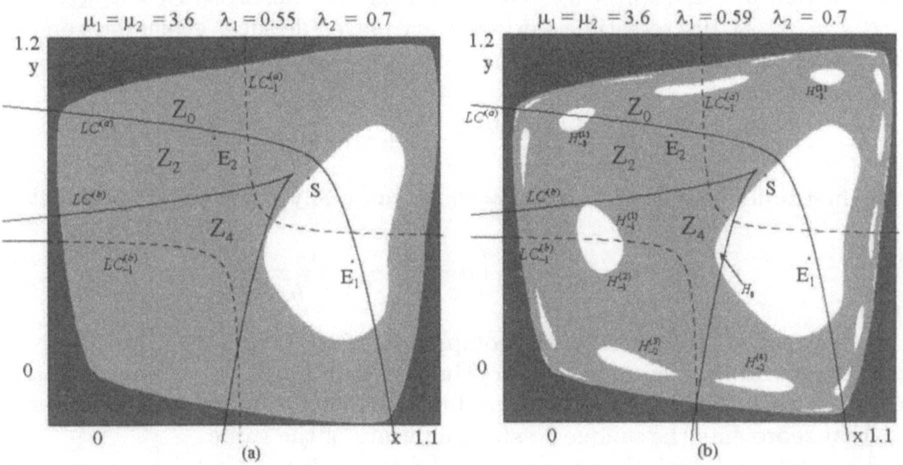

Figure 11.

An extension of such methods to the study of higher dimensional noninvertible maps is not easy in general. Indeed, some non-trivial practical problems arise, related to the obvious reason that the computer screen is two-dimensional, so the visualization of objects in a phase spaces of dimension greater than two, and the detection of contacts among these objects as their shapes change, may become a very difficult task. For example, in Agiza et al., 1999, a repeated Cournot game is considered, whose time evolution is obtained by the iteration of the three-dimensional map $T : (q_1, q_2, q_3) \rightarrow (q_1', q_2', q_3')$

$$T : \begin{cases} q_1' = (1-\lambda_1)\, q_1 + \lambda_1 \mu_1 \left[q_2 (1-q_2) + q_3 (1-q_3) \right] \\ q_2' = (1-\lambda_2)\, q_2 + \lambda_2 \mu_2 \left[q_3 (1-q_3) + q_1 (1-q_1) \right] \\ q_3' = (1-\lambda_3)\, q_3 + \lambda_3 \mu_3 \left[q_1 (1-q_1) + q_2 (1-q_2) \right] \end{cases} \tag{4.13}$$

which can be seen as the extension of the game illustrated above to the case of three players. In Agiza et al., 1999, two-dimensional sections are employed in order to visualize the basins of coexisting attractors, but this method is not useful to detect the contact bifurcations which cause changes in the structure of the basins. The same game has been re-examined in Bischi et al., 2001, where enhanced graphical methods have been used to modulate the opacity of the outer objects in order to visualize objects which are nested inside them. Moreover, the critical sets, which are now two-dimensional surfaces embedded in a three-dimensional phase space, have been represented like semi-transparent veils, so that their contacts with portions of basin boundaries, also given by two-dimensional surfaces, can be detected.

4.2 A duopoly game with gradient dynamics

In this section we consider a Cournot duopoly game, proposed by Bischi and Lamantia, 2002a, where two firms produce quantities q_1 and q_2 in a market characterized by a linear demand function $p = a - b(q_1 + q_2)$ with nonlinear cost functions $C_i = c_i q_i / (1 + \gamma_{ij} q_j)$ $i = 1, 2,\ j \neq i$. At discrete time periods each player decides, given the competitor's action, its own production in order to maximize the expected profit

$$\pi_i(q_1, q_2) = q_i \left[a - b\,(q_1 + q_2) \right] - \frac{c_i q_i}{1 + \gamma_{ij} q_j}\ ;\ i, j = 1, 2,\ i \neq j \tag{4.14}$$

From the first order conditions $\partial \pi_i / \partial q_i = 0$, we can easily get the reaction functions[9]

$$q_i = r_i(q_j) = \frac{1}{2b} \left(a - b q_j - \frac{c_i}{1 + \gamma_{ij} q_j} \right). \tag{4.15}$$

For a given expected production of the competitor, r_i represents the "Best Reply" of the quantity-setting firm i according to its optimization problem. In Bischi and Lamantia, 2002a, it is proved that these two reaction functions have a unique positive intersection, say E_*, that represents the unique Nash equilibrium of the game.

Although fully rational players are assumed to reach the Nash equilibrium immediately (in one shot), an important issue in economic literature concerns the outcome of the game when agents are not fully rational. In Bischi and Lamantia, 2002a, a repeated Cournot duopoly game is proposed where two boundedly rational players update their production strategies at discrete time periods by an adjustment mechanism based on a local estimate of the marginal profit $\partial \pi_i / \partial q_i$: At each time period t a firm decides to increase (decrease) its production for period $t+1$ if it perceives positive (negative)

[9]A simple check of the second derivatives testifies that these solutions indeed represent local profit maxima, provided that the quantities are non negative.

marginal profit on the basis of information held at time t, according to the following dynamic adjustment mechanism (see e.g. Bischi and Naimzada, 2000)

$$q_i(t+1) = q_i(t) + \alpha_i(q_i(t))\frac{\partial \pi_i}{\partial q_i}(q_1(t), q_2(t)) \quad ; \qquad i = 1,2 \tag{4.16}$$

where $\alpha_i(q_i)$ is a positive function which gives the extent of production variation of *ith* firm following a given profit signal. A Nash equilibrium, defined by the first order conditions $\partial\pi_i/\partial q_i = 0$, is a stationary point of the dynamical system. We assume linear functions $\alpha_i(q_i) = v_i q_i$, $i = 1, 2$, since this assumption captures the fact that *relative* production variations are proportional to marginal profits, i.e. $\frac{q_i(t+1)-q_i(t)}{q_i(t)} = v_i\frac{\partial \pi_i}{\partial q_i}$, where v_i is a positive *speed of adjustment*. With these assumptions, together with the profit functions given in (4.14), we obtain a discrete dynamical system of the form $(q_1(t+1), q_2(t+1)) = T(q_1(t), q_2(t))$, with the map $T : \mathbb{R}^2 \to \mathbb{R}^2$ given by

$$T : \begin{cases} q_1' = q_1 + v_1 q_1 \left[a - 2bq_1 - bq_2 - \frac{c_1}{1+\gamma_{12}q_2}\right] \\ q_2' = q_2 + v_2 q_2 \left[a - 2bq_2 - bq_1 - \frac{c_2}{1+\gamma_{21}q_1}\right] \end{cases} \tag{4.17}$$

Besides the equilibrium point E_*, located at the intersections of the reaction curves (4.15), the map (4.17) has three boundary equilibria located along the coordinate axes:

$$E_0 = (0,0), \quad E_1 = (\frac{a-c_1}{2b}, 0), \quad E_2 = (0, \frac{a-c_2}{2b}). \tag{4.18}$$

The fixed points E_1 and E_2 can be denoted as *monopoly equilibria* provided that $c_i < a$, $i = 1, 2$. It is worth to note that the coordinate axes $q_i = 0$, $i = 1, 2$, are invariant submanifold, i.e. if $q_i = 0$ then $q_i' = 0$. This means that starting from an initial condition on a coordinate axis (*monopoly case*) the dynamics are trapped into the same axis for each t, thus giving *monopoly dynamics*, governed by the restriction of the map T to that axis. Such a restriction is given by the following one-dimensional map, obtained from (4.17) with $q_i = 0$

$$q_j = (1 + v_j(a - c_j))q_j - 2bv_j q_j^2 \qquad j \neq i\ . \tag{4.19}$$

This map is conjugate[10] to the standard logistic map (2.7) through the linear transformation

$$q_j = \frac{1 + v_j(a - c_j)}{2bv_j}x \tag{4.20}$$

from which we obtain the relation $\mu = 1 + v_j(a - c_j)$.

If $\gamma_{12} = \gamma_{21} = 0$ the map (4.17) reduces to the one studied in Bischi and Naimzada, 2000, where it is shown that unbounded trajectories are obtained if the initial condition is taken sufficiently far from the Nash equilibrium[11], hence E_* cannot be globally stable.

[10] See Devaney, 1987.

[11] From an economic point of view, diverging trajectories do not represent interesting evolutions, as they can be interpreted as an irreversible departure from optimality.

As in the previous model, we denote by $\mathcal{B}$ the set of points which generate feasible trajectories and by $\mathcal{B}(\infty)$ the set of initial conditions whose trajectories diverge. A feasible trajectory may converge to the Nash equilibrium E_*, to another more complex attractor inside $\mathcal{B}$ or to a one-dimensional invariant set embedded inside a coordinate axis, when one competitor exits the market. However, when the Nash equilibrium exists the coordinate axes are transversely unstable, so they behave as repelling sets with respect to trajectories approaching them from the interior of the nonnegative orthant, and consequently evolutions of the duopoly game toward monopoly situations are excluded.

Let us first consider the dynamics of T restricted to the invariant axis $q_2 = 0$. From the one-dimensional restriction defined in (4.19), we can deduce that bounded trajectories along that invariant axis are obtained for $v_1(a - c_1) \leq 3$ (corresponding to $\mu \leq 4$ in (4.20)), provided that the initial conditions are taken inside the segment $\omega_1 = OO_{-1}^{(1)}$, where $O_{-1}^{(1)}$ is the *rank-1* preimage of the origin O computed according to the restriction (4.19), i.e.

$$O_{-1}^{(1)} = \left(\frac{v_1(a - c_1)}{2bv_1}, 0\right) \tag{4.21}$$

and divergent trajectories along the invariant q_1 axis are obtained starting from an initial condition out of the segment ω_1. Analogously, when $v_2(a - c_2) \leq 3$, bounded trajectories along the invariant q_2 axis are obtained provided that the initial conditions are taken inside the segment $\omega_2 = OO_{-1}^{(2)}$, where

$$O_{-1}^{(2)} = \left(0, \frac{v_2(a - c_2)}{2bv_2}\right). \tag{4.22}$$

and, also in this case, divergent trajectories along the q_2 axis are obtained starting from an initial condition out of the segment ω_2.

Consider now the region bounded by the segments ω_1 and ω_2 and their *rank-1* preimages, say ω_1^{-1} and ω_2^{-1} respectively. Such preimages can be analytically computed as follows. Let $X = (x, 0)$ be a point of ω_1. Its preimages are the real solutions (q_1, q_2) of the algebraic system obtained from (4.17) with $(q_1', q_2') = (x, 0)$:

$$\left\{\begin{array}{l} q_1 \left[1 + v_1 \left(a - 2bq_1 - bq_2 - \frac{c_1}{1+\gamma_{12}q_2}\right)\right] = x \\ q_2 \left[1 + v_2 \left(a - 2bq_2 - bq_1 - \frac{c_2}{1+\gamma_{21}q_1}\right)\right] = 0\,. \end{array}\right. \tag{4.23}$$

It is an easy exercise to show that the preimages of the points of ω_1 are either located on the same invariant axis $q_2 = 0$ or on the curve of equation

$$q_2 = r_2(q_1) + \frac{1}{2bv_2}. \tag{4.24}$$

where r_2 is the reaction function defined in (4.15). Analogously, the preimages of a point $Y = (0, y)$ of ω_2 belong to the same invariant axis $q_1 = 0$ or to the curve of equation

$$q_1 = r_1(q_2) + \frac{1}{2bv_1}. \tag{4.25}$$

where r_1 is the reaction function defined in (4.15). The curve (4.24) intersects the q_2 axis in the point $O_{-1}^{(2)}$ and the curve (4.25) intersects the q_1 axis in the point $O_{-1}^{(1)}$. Moreover, the two curves intersect at a point $O_{-1}^{(3)}$, which is another *rank-1* preimage of $O = (0,0)$. These four *rank-1* preimages of the origin are the vertexes of a "quadrilateral" $OO_{-1}^{(1)}O_{-1}^{(3)}O_{-1}^{(2)}$, whose sides are ω_1, ω_2 and their *rank-1* preimages located on the curves of equation (4.24) and (4.25) respectively, denoted by ω_1^{-1} and ω_2^{-1} in Figures 12a, b. It is evident that the sides $O_{-1}^{(2)}O_{-1}^{(3)}$ and $O_{-1}^{(3)}O_{-1}^{(1)}$, given by ω_1^{-1} and ω_2^{-1} of equation (4.24) and (4.25) respectively, are parallel translations of the reaction curves R_2 and R_1, shifted of $\frac{1}{2bv_i}$, $i = 2, 1$, respectively. All the points outside this quadrilateral cannot generate feasible trajectories. In fact, the points located on the right of ω_2^{-1} are mapped into points with negative q_1 after one iteration, as can be easily deduced from the first component of (4.17), and the points located above ω_1^{-1} are mapped into points with negative q_2 after one iteration, as can be deduced from the second component of (4.17).

For $\gamma_{12} = \gamma_{21} = 0$ the curves ω_1^{-1} and ω_2^{-1} reduce to straight lines, as already proved in Bischi and Naimzada, 2000. This situation is shown in Figure12a, obtained with $v_1 = 0.2$, $v_2 = 0.25$, $c_1 = 3$, $c_2 = 4$ and $\gamma_{12} = \gamma_{21} = 0$. With this set of parameters the Nash equilibrium E_* is stable, and the set $\mathcal{B}$ coincides with the basin of E_*. As it can be seen in Figure 12a, where the numerically computed basin of E_* is represented by the white region and the basin of infinity by the grey one, the boundary $\partial\mathcal{B}$ is formed by ω_1, ω_2 and their *rank-1* preimages ω_1^{-1} and ω_2^{-1} of equations (4.24) and (4.25) respectively, which are parallel to the reaction curves R_2 and R_1 (shown in Figure 12). In Figure 12b one of the spillover parameters is positive, namely $\gamma_{21} = 3$, and the other parameters are the same as in Figure 12a. It can be noticed that in this case the upper boundary, belonging to the curve ω_1^{-1}, is concave.

The simple shape of $\partial\mathcal{B}$ shown in Figure 12 is due to the fact that only preimages of *rank-1* of ω_i exist. In fact, ω_1^{-1} and ω_2^{-1} are entirely included inside a region of the plane whose points have no preimages. The situation is different when the values of the parameters are such that some portions of these curves belong to regions whose points have preimages, which constitute preimages of rank higher than one of the segments ω_i. In this case the set $\mathcal{B}$ has a more complex topological structure. Also in this case, the transitions between qualitatively different structures of the basins can be described in terms of contacts between $\partial\mathcal{B}$ and arcs of *critical curves.* In fact, the map defined in (4.17) is noninvertible, since given a point $(q_1', q_2') \in \mathbb{R}^2$ its preimages, computed by solving the sixth degree algebraic system (4.17), may be up to six. For instance, as shown above, the origin $O = (0,0)$ can have four *rank-1* preimages, given by O itself and $O_{-1}^{(i)}$, $i = 1, 2, 3$.

For a given set of parameters, the critical curves of the map (4.17) can be easily obtained numerically. For example, for the set of parameters used to obtain Figure 13a, i.e. $v_1 = 0.25$, $v_2 = 0.3$, $c_1 = 4$, $c_2 = 3$ and $\gamma_{12} = 2$, $\gamma_{21} = 4$, the numerically computed set of points at which the Jacobian vanishes is formed by the union of two branches, denoted by $LC_{-1}^{(a)}$ and $LC_{-1}^{(b)}$ in Figure 13a., where $LC^{(b)}$ separates the region Z_0, whose points have no preimages, from the region Z_2, whose points have two distinct *rank-1*

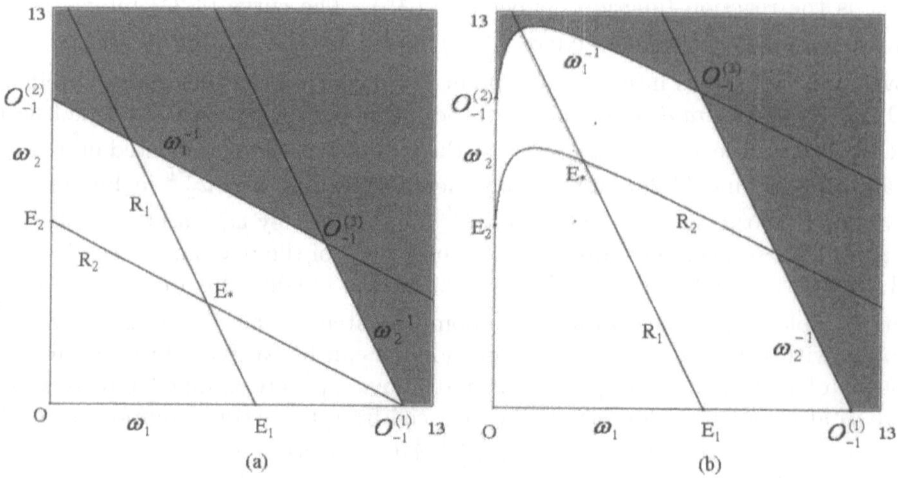

Figure 12.

preimages, and $LC^{(a)}$ separates the region Z_2 from Z_4, whose points have four distinct preimages.

The curve $LC_{-1}^{(b)}$ intersects the q_i axis at the point of maximum of the restriction (4.19), given by $M_{-1}^i = \frac{1+v_i(a-c_i)}{4bv_i}$, and the curve $LC^{(b)}$ intersects the q_i axis at the corresponding maximum value $M^i = \frac{[1+v_i(a-c_i)]^2}{8bv_i}$ of the restriction (4.19).

In Figure 13a $\mathcal{B}$ is a simply connected set, with the boundary $\partial\mathcal{B}$ having the "quadrilateral shape" described above, because the preimages ω_i^{-1}, $i = 1, 2$, of the invariant axes, are entirely included inside the region Z_0, so that no preimages of higher rank exist. The situation would be different if some portions of these lines were inside the regions Z_2 or Z_4. Indeed, the fact that a portion of $LC^{(b)}$ is close to $\partial\mathcal{B}$ suggests that a contact bifurcation may occur if some parameter is varied. In fact, if a portion of $\mathcal{B}(\infty)$ enters Z_2 after a contact of $\partial\mathcal{B}$ with $LC^{(b)}$, then new preimages of that portion will appear near $LC_{-1}^{(b)}$ and such preimages must belong to $\mathcal{B}(\infty)$. This is the situation illustrated by Figure 13b, obtained after an increase of the spillover parameters, i.e. $\gamma_{12} = 3$ and $\gamma_{21} = 7$. In fact, after a contact between $\partial\mathcal{B}$ and $LC^{(b)}$, a portion of $\mathcal{B}(\infty)$, say H_0 (bounded by a portion of ω_1^{-1} and LC) which was in region Z_0 before the bifurcation, enters inside Z_2. The points belonging to H_0 have two distinct preimages, located at opposite sides with respect to the line LC_{-1}, with the exception of the points of the curve $LC^{(b)}$ inside $B(\infty)$ whose preimages, according to the definition of LC, merge on $LC_{-1}^{(b)}$. Since H_0 is part of $\mathcal{B}(\infty)$ also its preimages belong to $\mathcal{B}(\infty)$. In other words, the *rank-1* preimages of H_0 are formed by two areas joining along LC_{-1} and constitutes a *hole* of $\mathcal{B}(\infty)$ nested inside $\mathcal{B}$. This is the largest hole appearing in Figure 13b, and is called the *main hole.* It lies inside region Z_2, hence it has 2 preimages, which are smaller holes bounded by preimages of rank 3 of ω_1. Even these are both inside Z_2, so each of them has two further preimages inside Z_2, and so on. Now the boundary $\partial\mathcal{B}$ is formed by the union of an external part, given by the coordinate axes and their *rank-1* preimages (4.24) and (4.25), and the boundaries of the holes, which are sets of preimages of higher rank of ω_1. So, the global bifurcation just described transforms a *simply connected* basin into a *multiply connected* one, with a countable infinity of holes inside, called *arborescent sequence of holes* (see Mira et al., 1994, Mira et al., 1996, Abraham et al., 1997).

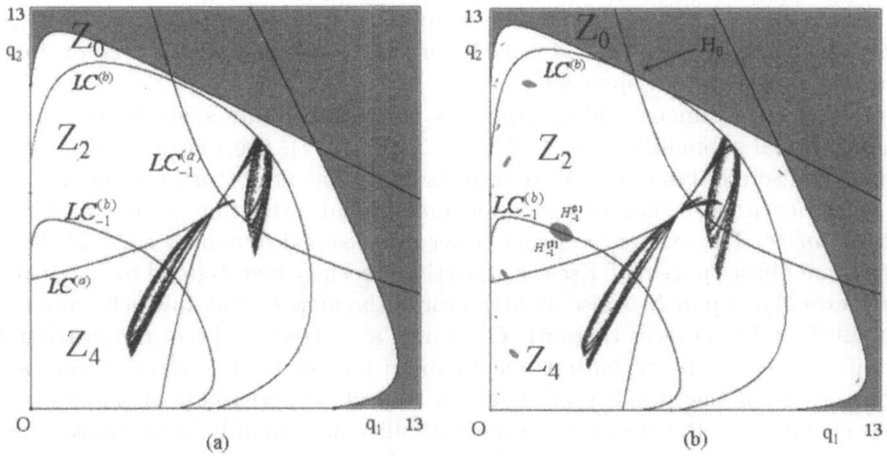

Figure 13.

5 Symmetric dynamical systems, Milnor attractors and riddled basins

In this section we consider an extension of the notion of attractor, known as *Milnor attractor* (after Milnor, 1985), whose basin of attraction may assume a structure, called *riddled basin*, characterized by an extreme form of complexity, according to the following definitions (see Alexander et al., 1992, Ashwin et al., 1996, Buescu, 1997). The more general notion of Milnor attractor has been introduced to evidence the existence of invariant sets which "attract" many points even if they are not attractors in the usual topological sense.

A closed invariant set $\mathcal{A}$ is said to be a *weak attractor in Milnor sense* (or simply *Milnor attractor*) if its stable set $\mathcal{B}(\mathcal{A})$, i.e. the set of points whose ω-limit sets of x belongs to $\mathcal{A}$[12],has positive Lebesgue measure.

If $\mathcal{A}$ is a Milnor attractor, then its stable set $\mathcal{B}(A)$ is called "riddled basin" if it is such that any neighborhood of it contains points whose trajectory converge to another attrac-

[12]The $\omega-$limit set of x is the set of accumulation points of $T^t(x)$, as $t \to \infty$.

tor. In other words, a riddled basin does not include any open subset, so it corresponds to an extreme form of uncertainty.

This section is mainly devoted to riddled basins, as well as to the global bifurcations leading to their creation.

Note that an attractor in the usual (topological) sense is also a Milnor attractor, but the converse is not true. In fact, a topological attractor is such that its basin $\mathcal{B}(\mathcal{A})$ contains an open neighborhood of $\mathcal{A}$, whereas for a Milnor attractor initial conditions arbitrarily close to $\mathcal{A}$ can generate trajectories that are locally repelled out from $\mathcal{A}$. In this case $\mathcal{B}(\mathcal{A})$ is called "realm of attraction" (Milnor, 1985) reserving the term "basin" when $\mathcal{B}(\mathcal{A})$ is an open set. However, since the term basin is more standard in the literature, we shall use such term even when $\mathcal{A}$ is a Milnor (but not topological) attractor, for which $\mathcal{B}(\mathcal{A})$ is not, in general, an open set.

Restricting an n-dimensional dynamical system with phase space S to an invariant lower dimensional submanifold $N \subset S$, (i.e. $T(N) \subseteq N$), the map $g = T|_N : N \to N$ determines a discrete dynamical system in its own. The trajectories embedded into N, whose dynamics are governed by the lower dimensional restriction g, are called *synchronized trajectories*. The existence of such lower dimensional dynamics embedded into the n-dimensional phase space of T rises the question, recently investigated by many authors, if an attractor A_N of g in N is also an attractor of the map T, and in which sense (see e.g. Buescu, 1997, and references therein). Of course, an attractor A_N of the restriction g is stable with respect to perturbations on N, so an answer to this question can be given through a study of the stability of A_N with respect to perturbations transverse to N (*transverse stability*). Results on transverse stability have mainly been studied when the dynamics restricted to the invariant submanifold are chaotic. In this case the question of transverse stability is related to the phenomenon of *chaos synchronization* (i.e. when trajectories starting out of N are attracted toward a chaotic attractor $A_N \subseteq N$).

These phenomena have recently raised interest in many fields, ranging from electrical engineering and communication systems to ecology and chemistry (see e.g. Fujisaka and Yamada, 1983, Ferretti, 1988, Pecora and Carrol, 1990, Ashwin et al., 1996, Buescu, 1997). Applications in economic modelling have recently been proposed in Bischi et al., 1999a, Bischi and Gardini, 1998, 2000, Kopel et al., 2000, Bischi and Lamantia, 2002b.

The particular feature of the invariance of a submanifold of lower dimension is a standard occurrence if the map T has some symmetry property, a situation that often occurs in applications. Measure theoretic, but not stable in Lyapunov sense, attractors appear quite naturally in this context, together with new and striking phenomena, like on-off intermittency and riddled basins, and also new kinds of bifurcations, like riddling (or bubbling) bifurcations and blowout bifurcations.

Maps with symmetry properties arise quite naturally in dynamical models of competition. In fact, when two competitors behave identically, the state variables that represent the competitors' choices can be swapped without changing the dynamical system. This means that the system has a symmetry property and, consequently, an invariant submanifold.

Let us consider, for example, the case of two competitors that choose their actions, measured by $x_1(t)$ and $x_2(t)$ respectively, at discrete time periods, and assume that this process is modelled by the iterations of a two-dimensional map $T : S \to S$, $S \subseteq \mathbb{R}^2$. In the case of identical competitors, the map T must remain the same under the exchange of the players, i.e. $T \circ P = P \circ T$, where $P : (x_1, x_2) \to (x_2, x_1)$ denotes the reflection through the diagonal $\Delta = \{(x_1, x_2) \in \mathbb{R}^2 | x_1 = x_2\}$. This symmetry property implies that the diagonal is mapped into itself by T, i.e. $T(\Delta) \subseteq \Delta$.

In this case, the *synchronized trajectories* are embedded into Δ, i.e. are characterized by identical choices $x_1(t) = x_2(t)$ for every t. This invariance property translates the obvious statement that identical players, starting with identical initial strategies $x_1(0) = x_2(0)$, behave identically for each $t \geq 0$, even if each of them behaves chaotically, and the common behavior of the two players is summarized by the dynamics of the simpler one-dimensional map $g = T|_\Delta : \Delta \to \Delta$.

An important question is whether trajectories starting with initial condition outside of Δ, i.e. when $x_1(0) \neq x_2(0)$, will evolve toward synchronization, i.e. $|x_1(t) - x_2(t)| \to 0$ as $t \to +\infty$, so that the long-run behavior is governed by the one-dimensional attractors of the restriction g. Of course, the attracting sets of the map g are stable with respect to perturbations along Δ, hence an answer to the question addressed above requires a local study of the stability with respect to perturbations transverse to Δ (*transverse stability*). When the attractors of g embedded inside Δ are chaotic, they may be Milnor (but not topological) attractors of the two-dimensional dynamical system, and their basins may be riddled.

In Bischi et al., 1999a, Kopel et al., 2000, the one-dimensional restriction $g : \Delta \to \Delta$ has been considered as the model of a *representative agent* whose dynamics summarize the common behavior of the two synchronized competitors, so the study of the asymptotic synchronization has been related to the common assumption, often made in economic modeling, that the behavior of a system with many identical agents can be summarized by that of a "representative agent", a point that has been recently criticized by some authors (see Kirman, 1992, Aoki, 1996).

5.1 Some basic definitions and results

Let A_Δ be a chaotic attractor (with absolutely continuous invariant measure on it) of g, the restriction to Δ of the bidimensional map T. The key property for the study of the transverse stability of A_Δ is that it includes infinitely many periodic orbits which are unstable in the direction along Δ. For any of these cycles it is easy to compute the associated eigenvalues. In fact, due to the symmetry of the map, the Jacobian matrix of T, computed at any point of Δ, say $DT(x, x) = \{T_{ij}(x)\}$, is such that $T_{11} = T_{22}$ and $T_{12} = T_{21}$. The two orthogonal eigenvectors of such a symmetric matrix are one parallel to Δ, say $\mathbf{v}_\parallel = (1, 1)$, and one perpendicular to it, say $\mathbf{v}_\perp = (1, -1)$, with related eigenvalues given by

$$\lambda_\parallel(x) = T_{11}(x) + T_{12}(x) \quad \text{and} \quad \lambda_\perp(x) = T_{11}(x) - T_{12}(x)$$

respectively. Of course, $\lambda_\parallel(x) = g'(x)$. Since the product of matrices with the structure of $DT(x, x)$ has the same structure as well, a k-cycle $\{x_1, ..., x_k\}$ embedded into Δ has eigenvalues $\lambda_\parallel^k = \prod_{i=1}^k \lambda_\parallel(x_i)$ and $\lambda_\perp^k = \prod_{i=1}^k \lambda_\perp(x_i)$, with eigenvectors $\mathbf{v}_\parallel$ and $\mathbf{v}_\perp$ respectively. So, for a chaotic set $A_\Delta \subset \Delta$, infinitely many transverse Lyapunov exponents can be defined as

$$\Lambda_{\perp} = \lim_{N\to\infty} \frac{1}{N} \sum_{i=0}^{N} \ln |\lambda_{\perp}(x_i)| \tag{5.1}$$

where $\{x_i = g^i(x_0), i \geq 0\}$ is a trajectory embedded in A_Δ. If x_0 belongs to a k-cycle then $\Lambda_\perp = \ln |\lambda_\perp^k|$, so that the cycle is transversely stable if $\Lambda_\perp < 0$, whereas if x_0 belongs to a generic aperiodic trajectory embedded inside the chaotic set A_Δ then $\Lambda_\perp$ is the *natural transverse Lyapunov exponent* $\Lambda_\perp^{nat}$. By the term "natural" we mean the Lyapunov exponent associated to the natural, or SBR (Sinai-Bowen-Ruelle), measure, i.e., computed for a typical trajectory taken in the chaotic attractor A_Δ. Since infinitely many cycles, all unstable along Δ, are embedded inside a chaotic attractor A_Δ, a spectrum of transverse Lyapunov exponents can be defined (see Buescu, 1997)

$$\Lambda_\perp^{\min} \leq ... \leq \Lambda_\perp^{nat} \leq ... \leq \Lambda_\perp^{\max} \tag{5.2}$$

The meaning of the inequalities in (5.2) can be intuitively understood on the basis of the property that $\Lambda_\perp^{nat}$ expresses a sort of "weighted balance" between the transversely repelling and transversely attracting cycles (see Nagai and Lai, 1997). If $\Lambda_\perp^{\max} < 0$, i.e. all the cycles embedded in A_Δ are transversely stable, then A_Δ is asymptotically stable, in the usual Lyapunov sense, for the two-dimensional map T. However, it may occur that some cycles embedded in the chaotic set A_Δ become transversely unstable, i.e. $\Lambda_\perp^{\max} > 0$, while $\Lambda_\perp^{nat} < 0$. In this case, A_Δ is no longer Lyapunov stable, but it continues to be an attractor in the weaker Milnor sense. The transition from asymptotic stability to attractivity only in Milnor sense, marked by a change of sign of $\Lambda_\perp^{\max}$ from negative to positive, is denoted as *riddling bifurcation* in Lai and Grebogi, 1996 (or *bubbling bifurcation* in Venkataramani, 1996).

Even if the occurrence of such bifurcation is detected through the study of the transverse Lyapunov exponents, its effects depend on the action of the nonlinearities far from Δ, that is, on the global properties of the dynamical system. In fact, after the riddling bifurcation two possible scenarios can be observed, according to the fate of the trajectories that are locally repelled along (or near) the local unstable manifolds of the transversely repelling cycles:

(**L**) they can be reinjected towards Δ, so that the dynamics of such trajectories are characterized by some bursts far from Δ before synchronizing on it (a very long sequence of such bursts, which can be observed when $\Lambda_\perp$ is close to zero, has been called *on-off intermittency* in Ott and Sommerer, 1994);

(**G**) they may belong to the basin of another attractor, in which case the phenomenon of *riddled basins* is obtained (see Alexander et al., 1992).

Some authors call *local riddling* the situation (**L**) and, by contrast, *global riddling* the situation (**G**) (see Ashwin et al., 1996, Maistrenko et al., 1997). When also $\Lambda_\perp^{nat}$ becomes positive, due to the fact that the transversely unstable periodic orbits embedded into A_Δ have a greater weight as compared with the stable ones, a *blowout bifurcation* occurs, after which A_Δ is no longer a Milnor attractor, because it attracts a set of points of zero measure, and becomes a *chaotic saddle.* In particular, for $\lambda_\perp^{\min} > 0$ all the cycles embedded into Δ are transversely repelling, and A_Δ is called *normally repelling chaotic saddle.*

Also the macroscopic effect of a blowout bifurcation is strongly influenced by the behavior of the dynamical system far from the invariant submanifold Δ: trajectories starting close to the chaotic saddle may be attracted by some attracting set far from Δ or remain inside a two-dimensional compact set located around the chaotic saddle A_Δ, thus giving on-off intermittency.

So, the effects of these bifurcations are related to the action of the nonlinearities acting far from Δ. When T is a noninvertible map, as generally occurs in problems of chaos synchronization[13], the global dynamical properties can be usefully described by the method of *critical curves* and the reinjection of the locally repelled trajectories can be described in terms of their folding action. This idea has been recently proposed in Bischi and Gardini, 1998, Bischi and Gardini, 2000 for the study of symmetric maps arising in game theory, and in Bischi et al., 1999a, for the study of the effects of small asymmetries due to parameters mismatches, see also Bischi and Lamantia, 2002b, where the concept of *correlated chaos* is introduced. In these papers, the critical curves have been used to obtain the boundary of a compact trapping region, called *absorbing area* following Mira et al., 1996, inside which intermittency and blowout phenomena are confined. In particular, in Bischi and Gardini, 1998, the concept of *minimal invariant absorbing area* is defined in order to give a global characterization of the different dynamical scenarios related to riddling and blowout bifurcations.

Before giving an example, let us recall some properties of critical curves and absorbing areas (see Mira et al., 1996, chap. 4, or Bischi and Gardini, 1998, for more details).

The critical sets of rank k are defined as the images of rank k of LC_{-1} denoted by $LC_{k-1} = T^k(LC_{-1}) = T^{k-1}(LC)$, LC_0 being LC. Segments of critical curves of *rank-k*, $k = 0, 1, ...$, can be used in order to define trapping regions of the phase plane. An *absorbing area* $\mathcal{A}$ is a bounded region of the plane whose boundary is given by critical curve segments (segments of the critical curve LC and its images) such that a neighborhood $U \supset \mathcal{A}$ exists whose points enter $\mathcal{A}$ after a finite number of iterations and then never escape it, i.e. $T(\mathcal{A}) \subseteq \mathcal{A}$.

Following Mira et al., 1996 (see also Puu, 2000) a practical procedure can be outlined in order to obtain the boundary of an absorbing area (although it is difficult to give a general method). Starting from a portion of LC_{-1}, approximately taken in the region occupied by the area of interest, its images of increasing rank are computed until a closed region is obtained. When such a region is mapped into itself, then it is an absorbing area $\mathcal{A}$. The length of the initial segment is to be taken, in general, by a trial and error method, although several suggestions are given in the books referenced above. Once an absorbing area $\mathcal{A}$ is found, in order to see if it is invariant (or strictly mapped into itself) the same procedure must be repeated by taking only the portion $\gamma = \mathcal{A} \cap LC_{-1}$as the starting segment. Then one of the following two cases occurs:

(i) the union of m iterates of γ (for a suitable m) covers the whole boundary of $\mathcal{A}$; in

[13]In fact the one-dimensional restriction g must be a noninvertible map in order to have chaotic motion along the invariant subspace Δ.

which case $\mathcal{A}$ is an invariant absorbing area, and

$$\partial\mathcal{A} \subset \bigcup_{k=1}^{m} T^k(\gamma) \tag{5.3}$$

(ii) no natural m exists such that $\bigcup_{i=1}^{m} T^i(\gamma)$ covers the whole boundary of $\mathcal{A}$, in which case $\mathcal{A}$ is not invariant but strictly mapped into itself. An invariant absorbing area is obtained by $\cap_{n>0}T^n(\mathcal{A})$.

The *minimal invariant absorbing area* is the smallest absorbing area that includes the Milnor attractor on which the synchronized dynamics occur[14]. Its delimitation is important in order to characterize the global properties which influence the qualitative effects of riddling or blowout bifurcations. In fact, a minimal invariant absorbing area that surrounds a Milnor attractor defines a compact region of the phase plane that acts as a trapping bounded vessel inside which the trajectories starting near Δ are confined. This gives an upper bound for the oscillations (bursts) which characterize both the transient dynamics of the trajectories which eventually synchronize, and the persistent oscillations (on-off intermittency) which describe the dynamics just after a blowout bifurcation. Moreover, contacts between the portions of critical curves bounding the minimal absorbing area surrounding a Milnor attractor and the basin boundaries may mark the transition between local and global riddling phenomena, as it will be shown in the example below.

5.2 A competition model for market share

We consider a dynamic *brand competition model* proposed in Bischi et al., 2000a. This model describes a market where a population of consumers can choose between two brands of homogeneous goods, produced by two competing firms. Let x, y represent the marketing efforts of two firms (advertising, $R\&D$, etc.) and B the total sales potential of the market (in terms of customer market expenditures). Then the share of the market (sales revenue) accruing to firm 1 and to firm 2 is Bs_1 and $Bs_2 = B - Bs_1$, respectively, where

$$s_1 = \frac{ax^{\beta_1}}{ax^{\beta_1} + by^{\beta_2}}\ , \quad s_2 = \frac{by^{\beta_2}}{ax^{\beta_1} + by^{\beta_2}}\ . \tag{5.4}$$

The terms $A_1 = ax^{\beta_1}$ and $A_2 = by^{\beta_2}$ represent the recruitment of customers by firm 1 and 2, respectively, given x and y units of effort, and the parameters a and b denote the relative effectiveness of the effort made by the firms[15]. A dynamic model is obtained by assuming that the two competitors change their marketing efforts adaptively, in response

[14]Boundaries of trapping regions can also be obtained by the union of segments of critical curves and portions of unstable sets of saddle cycles, and in this case we have a so called *absorbing areas of mixed type* (see Mira et al., 1996). We don't enter here in such details, as in the example given below only standard absorbing areas (i.e. completely bounded by critical arcs) are present.

[15]Since $\frac{dA_1}{dx}\frac{x}{A_1} = \beta_1$ and $\frac{dA_2}{dy}\frac{y}{A_2} = \beta_2$, the parameters β_1 and β_2 denote the elasticities of the attraction of firm (or brand) i with regard to its effort.

to the profits achieved in the previous period:

$$T: \begin{cases} x(t+1) = x(t) + \lambda_1 x(t) \left(B \frac{x(t)^{\beta_1}}{x(t)^{\beta_1} + k y(t)^{\beta_2}} - x(t) \right) \\ y(t+1) = y(t) + \lambda_2 y(t) \left(B \frac{k y(t)^{\beta_2}}{x(t)^{\beta_1} + k y(t)^{\beta_2}} - y(t) \right) \end{cases} \tag{5.5}$$

where the parameters $\lambda_i > 0, i = 1, 2$, measure the rate of adjustment and $k = b/a$.

The map (5.5) is a noninvertible map of $Z_4 - Z_2 - Z_0$ type. The set of points for which $\det DT(x, y) = 0$ is given by the union of two branches, say $LC_{-1}^{(a)}$ and $LC_{-1}^{(b)}$, and the shape of the two branches of LC, $LC^{(a)} = T(LC_{-1}^{(a)})$ and $LC^{(b)} = T(LC_{-1}^{(b)})$, as well as the corresponding Riemann foliation, is similar to the one shown in Figure 9.

Following Kopel at al., 2000, Bischi and Gardini, 2000, let us consider the symmetric case of identical firms, obtained for $\lambda_1 = \lambda_2 = \lambda$, $\beta_1 = \beta_2 = \beta$ and $k = 1$, to show some applications of the methods described above. The restriction of the symmetric map to the invariant diagonal is given by

$$g(x) = (1 + \frac{1}{2}\lambda B)x - \lambda x^2. \tag{5.6}$$

which is conjugate to the standard logistic map (2.7), $z' = \mu z(1-z)$, with $\mu = 1 + \frac{1}{2}\lambda B$, by the linear transformation $x = z\,(1 + \lambda B/2)\,/\lambda$. For the symmetric map, the Jacobian matrix, computed at a point of the diagonal Δ, is

$$DT(x, x; \lambda, B, \beta,) = \begin{bmatrix} 1 - 2\lambda x + \frac{\lambda B(\beta+2)}{4} & -\frac{\lambda B \beta}{4} \\ -\frac{\lambda B \beta}{4} & 1 - 2\lambda x + \frac{\lambda B(\beta+2)}{4} \end{bmatrix}. \tag{5.7}$$

Hence, the eigenvalues are $\lambda_{||} = 1 + \frac{1}{2}\lambda B - 2\lambda x$, $\lambda_{\perp} = 1 + \frac{1}{2}\lambda B(1+\beta) - 2\lambda x$, and the transverse Lyapunov exponents are readily obtained:

$$\Lambda_{\perp} = \lim_{N \to \infty} \frac{1}{N} \sum_{n=0}^{N} \ln \left| 1 + \frac{1}{2}\lambda B(1+\beta) - 2\lambda x_n \right|.$$

It is important to note that the parameter β only appears in the transverse eigenvalue $\lambda_{\perp}$, i.e. β is a *normal parameter*: It has no influence on the dynamics along the invariant submanifold Δ, and only influences the transverse stability. This allows us to consider fixed values of the parameters λ and B, such that a chaotic attractor $A_{\Delta} \subset \Delta$ of the map (5.6) exists, with an absolutely continuous invariant measure on it. So, we can study the transverse stability of A_{Δ} as the parameter β varies.

Suitable values of the aggregate parameter λB, at which chaotic intervals for the restriction (5.6) exist, are obtained from the well known properties of the logistic map (see e.g. Collet and Eckmann, 1980, Mira, 1987). For example, at the parameter value $\overline{\mu}_2 = 3.5748049387592...$ the period-4 cycle of the logistic map undergoes the homoclinic bifurcation, at which four cyclic chaotic intervals are obtained by the merging of 8 cyclic chaotic intervals. By using $\lambda B = 2(\overline{\mu}_2 - 1)$ we get a four-band chaotic set A_{Δ} along the diagonal Δ.

Figure 14 shows the results of the numerical computations of the natural transverse Lyapunov exponent $\Lambda_{\perp}^{nat}$ as β varies in the interval $(0, 0.2)$. Observe that a "window" of negative values of $\Lambda_{\perp}^{nat}$ is visible for $0.0575 < \beta < 0.1895$. For example, for $\beta = 0.09$ we have $\Lambda_{\perp}^{nat} = -8.36 \times 10^{-2} < 0$, and we expect that synchronization of the marketing efforts of the two firms occurs for a set of initial conditions with positive Lebesgue measure (this implies that trajectories that synchronize, even starting out of the diagonal, can be numerically observed). The issue of synchronization gets more complex in this case, however, because for this values of the parameters two coexisting attractors inside the feasible set can be numerically observed: the 4-cyclic chaotic set $A_{\Delta} \subset \Delta$ and an attracting cycle of period 2 with periodic points located out of Δ. In Figure 15 the coexisting attractors are represented by black points, each with its own basin of attraction: the white points represent the basin $\mathcal{B}(A_{\Delta})$ of the points generating trajectories that synchronize along A_{Δ}, whereas the light grey points represent the basin $\mathcal{B}(C_2)$ whose points generate trajectories converging to the stable cycle C_2. The dark-grey region represents the set of points which are not feasible, i.e., which generate trajectories involving negative values of the state variables.

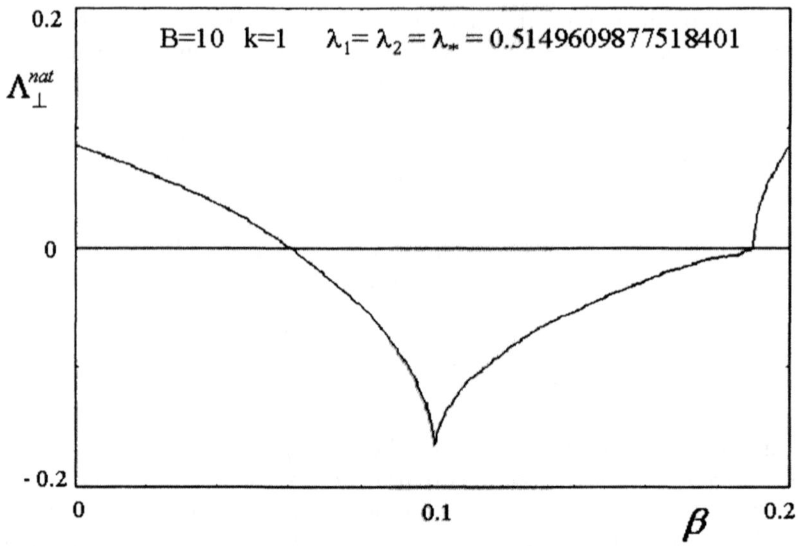

Figure 14.

For the set of parameters used in Figure 15, the four-band chaotic set A_{Δ}, embedded into the invariant diagonal Δ, is not a topological attractor however. In fact, an 8-cycle C_8 embedded inside the diagonal exists, which is transversely repelling. This means that trajectories starting along the local unstable set $W_{\perp}^{u}(C_8)$, issuing from the periodic points of C_8, as well as those starting from narrow tongues along $W_{\perp}^{u}(C_8)$ and from all the infinitely many preimages of the periodic points of C_8 (such preimages are densely distributed along A_Δ due to the fact that A_Δ is a chaotic set with absolutely continuous invariant measure) are repelled away from the diagonal. So, if we consider a sufficiently small neighborhood W of A_Δ, we have that the local unstable set of the transversely unstable cycle intersects ∂W and a set of points with positive Lebesgue measure exists in W whose trajectories exit W in a finite number of iterations. This implies that no neighborhood $V \subset W$ exists such that the definition of Lyapunov stability holds. In this case it is possible to prove that, around the local transverse unstable set of a transversely unstable cycle, open sets of points exist, called "tongues" in Lai et al., 1996 or "wedges" in Alexander et al., 1992, such that the trajectories starting from points of these "tongues" exit W after a finite number of iterations. Similar "tongues" also exist in correspondence of the infinite preimages, along Δ, of the points of C_8. So, A_Δ is not a topological attractor for T, however it is an attractor in Milnor sense because $\Lambda_\perp^{nat} < 0$. In other words, most initial conditions close to A_Δ are attracted to A_Δ, but in any neighborhood of A there exists a dense set that is locally repelled in a direction transverse to it. As argued in the previous section, the locally repelled trajectories may eventually return to A_Δ (i.e. synchronize) after a transient phase in which they make several excursions (bursts) away of Δ, or they may belong to the basin $\mathcal{B}(C_2)$. In the latter case the basin of A_Δ is *riddled* with the basin of C_2. In our case, the locally repelled trajectories are folded back by the action of the global dynamical properties of the map T, and after a transient with some bursts away from Δ occurring, they synchronize in the long-run. The time evolution of the difference of the marketing efforts, $(x_t - y_t)$, during the transient portion of a typical trajectory, starting from the initial allocations $(x_0, y_0) = (6, 6.01)$, is shown in Figure 15b, where the early 300 iterates are represented. After about 40 periods the evolution of the system seems to have reached almost complete synchronization. During the next 40 periods the two competitors behave practically in the same way. At this point the trajectory seems to have definitively settled down on the attractor A_Δ (this would be the case for a topological attractor), and we would tend to conclude that the two-players model can be replaced by a one-player model. However, the trajectory then moves again far away from the diagonal, and the two competitors now act again in a very different fashion. Several bursts of the trajectory, out of Δ, are observed until perfect synchronization of the marketing efforts is eventually obtained. Such an intermittent behavior is a typical characteristic of the convergence to a non-topological Milnor attractor. The pattern of the time series resembles that of a system which is subject to exogenous random shocks, even if the dynamical system that generates such a pattern is completely deterministic. This peculiar dynamical behavior is related to the fact that even if the Milnor attractor attracts "on average" according to the fact that $\Lambda_\perp^{nat} < 0$, the presence of some transversely repelling cycles (even if less influent than the transversely attracting ones) causes sudden bursts when the trajectories happen to get close to them.

However, the locally repelled trajectories cannot reach the other attractor C_2. This is due to the presence of an absorbing area $\mathcal{A}$ around A_Δ, from which the trajectory starting close to A_Δ cannot escape. The boundary $\partial\mathcal{A}$ of such absorbing area, shown in Figure 16a, has been obtained following the procedure outline in the previous section:

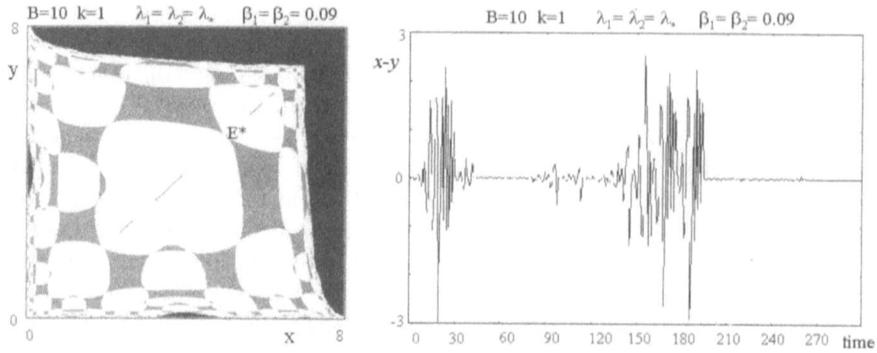

Figure 15.

starting from a portion of LC_{-1}, approximately taken in the region occupied by the area of interest, its images by T of increasing rank are computed until a closed region is obtained. In order to obtain the boundary of the absorbing area $\mathcal{A}$, six images of the generating arc γ are sufficient. However, only the portion of γ belonging to the branch $LC_{-1}^{(b)}$ has been used because the images of the other portion, the one belonging to the upper branch $LC_{-1}^{(a)}$, are always inside the absorbing area, so that they do not form part of the boundary. Hence in Figure 16a we have $\gamma = \mathcal{A} \cap LC_{-1}^{(b)}$ and $\partial\mathcal{A} \subset \bigcup_{k=1}^{6} T^k(\gamma)$.

We remark that $\mathcal{A}$ includes the Milnor chaotic attractor $A_\Delta \subset \Delta$, and all the trajectories starting from a neighborhood of A_Δ, cannot escape $\mathcal{A}$. Loosely speaking $\partial\mathcal{A}$ behaves as a bounded vessel for the intermittency phenomena related to the presence of the transversely repelling cycles embedded inside A_Δ. The local unstable sets of these cycles are folded back (reinjected) by the folding action of the critical curves that form $\partial\mathcal{A}$. The size of the absorbing area containing the Milnor attractor A_Δ gives us firstly an idea of the maximal difference between the marketing efforts of the two firms. Secondly, there is an inverse relationship between the longevity of transients and the values of the natural Lyapunov exponent $\Lambda_\perp^{nat}$. For values of the degree of competition β for which $\Lambda_\perp^{nat}$ is strongly negative the transient phase where bursts occur before the trajectories of marketing efforts settle down along the diagonal is relatively short. Neglecting this relatively short transient period we can conclude that the model of the representative player is a good approximation. On the other hand, if $\Lambda_\perp^{nat}$ is close to zero but negative, then the transient phase is rather long. Frequent and persistent bursts occur before the marketing efforts of the competitors synchronize. It might seem that this justifies, at least in the long run, the assumption, often made in economic models, that homogeneous agents can be considered as synchronized, so that their common behavior can be summarized by the behavior of a representative agent. However, in the situation shown in Figure 16a, the boundary of the absorbing area $\mathcal{A}$ is quite close to the boundary of the basin of the stable cycle C_2. Indeed, a small increase of β causes a contact between the absorbing area and the basin of C_2 which leads to the destruction of the absorbing area, so that some of the trajectories that are repelled from A_Δ can converge to C_2, and the basin of A_Δ becomes riddled (Figure 16b). This example shows a transition from a locally riddled to a globally riddled dynamics caused by a contact between the boundary of a minimal invariant absorbing area and the boundary of its basin of attraction.

After this bifurcation, it is very difficult to forecast if two homogeneous agents will synchronize in the long run, because even starting from an initial condition very close to the diagonal Δ, i.e. such identical agents with quasi-identical starting efforts, the structure of the basins is such that any forecasting about synchronization has no practical meaning. So, the concept of representative agent cannot be applied in such a situation.

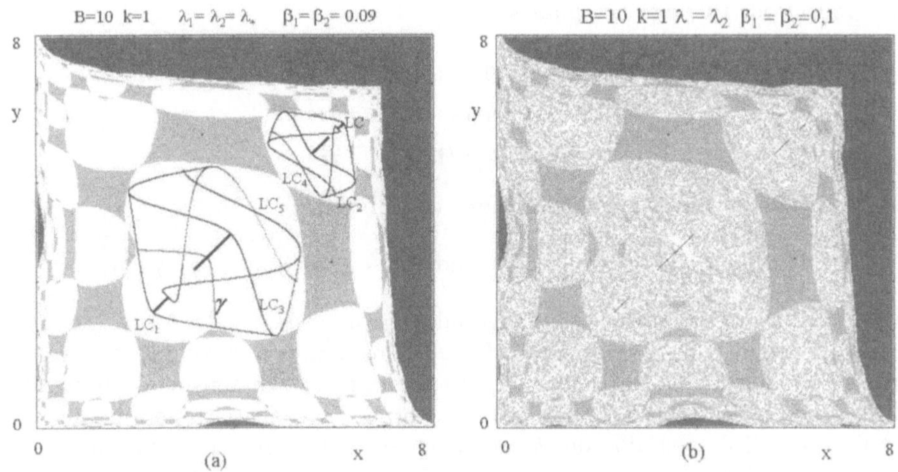

Figure 16.

5.3 Synchronization and partial synchronization in higher dimensional models

Some of the results stated above can be extended with more than two competitors. For example, let us consider a model that describes the interaction between three competitors, and assume that the time evolution of the system is described by the iteration of a map $T : (q_1(t), q_2(t), q_3(t)) \to (q_1(t+1), q_2(t+1), q_3(t+1))$ given by

$$T : \begin{cases} q_1' = T_1(q_1, q_2, q_3) \\ q_2' = T_2(q_1, q_2, q_3) \\ q_3' = T_3(q_1, q_2, q_3) \end{cases}$$

If all competitors are identical, then T is symmetric under the group of permutations

$$D_3 = \{M_{123}, M_{132}, M_{321}, M_{213}, M_{312}, M_{231}\}$$

where

$$M_{ijk}\begin{bmatrix} q_1 \\ q_2 \\ q_3 \end{bmatrix} = \begin{bmatrix} q_i \\ q_j \\ q_k \end{bmatrix}.$$

Obviously $M_{123} = I$ is the identity (trivial symmetry), whereas the three permutations of two coordinates

$$P_1(q_1, q_2, q_3) = (q_1, q_3, q_2)$$
$$P_2(q_1, q_2, q_3) = (q_3, q_2, q_1)$$
$$P_3(q_1, q_2, q_3) = (q_2, q_1, q_3)$$

represent reflections through the planes

$$\Pi_1 = \{(q_1, q_2, q_3) \mid q_2 = q_3\};$$
$$\Pi_2 = \{(q_1, q_2, q_3) \mid q_1 = q_3\};$$
$$\Pi_3 = \{(q_1, q_2, q_3) \mid q_1 = q_2\}$$

and the two cyclic permutations of the three coordinates

$$R_3^1 : (q_1, q_2, q_3) \to (q_3, q_1, q_2) \text{ and } R_3^2 : (q_1, q_2, q_3) \to (q_2, q_3, q_1)$$

represent rotations of $\frac{2}{3}\pi$ around the diagonal $S = \{q_1 = q_2 = q_3\}$.
A dynamical system with a symmetry M has a linear invariant subspace, given by the set of fixed points of M. In particular, Π_i are invariant two-dimensional submanifold for T, and the trajectories embedded inside Π_i, governed by the two-dimensional restriction of T to Π_i are called *partially synchronized* (two of the three players move in a synchronized way). Moreover, the intersection of the three invariant planes Π_i, given by $S = \{(q, q, q) \in \mathbb{R}^3\}$ is an invariant one-dimensional submanifold, and the trajectories embedded inside S, governed by the one-dimensional restriction of T to S, are *fully synchronized trajectories.* More generally, with n identical competitors, we can have *clusters* of $k \leq n$ synchronized competitors coexisting with non-synchronized ones.

Bibliography

R. Abraham, L. Gardini and C. Mira. *Chaos in discrete dynamical systems (a visual introduction in two dimension).* Springer-Verlag, 1997.

H.N. Agiza, G.I. Bischi, and M. Kopel. Multistability in a Dynamic Cournot Game with Three Oligopolists. *Mathematics and Computers in Simulation*, **51**, 63-90, 1999.

A. Agliari, G.I. Bischi, and L. Gardini. Some methods for thr Global Analysis of Dynamic Games represented by Noninvertible Maps. In T. Puu and I. Sushko, editors, *Oligopoly Dynamics: Models and Tools*, Springer Verlag, pp. 31-83, 2002.

J.C. Alexander, J.A. Yorke, Z. You, and I. Kan. Riddled basins. *Int. Jou. of Bif. & Chaos*, **2**, 795-813, 1992.

M. Aoki, *New Approaches to Macroeconomic Modelling.* Cambridge University Press, New York, 1996.

P. Ashwin, J. Buescu, and I. Stewart. From attractor to chaotic saddle: a tale of transverse instability. *Nonlinearity*, **9**, 703-737, 1996.

E. Barucci, G.I. Bischi, and L. Gardini. Endogenous fluctuations in a bounded rationality economy: learning non perfect foresight equilibria. *Journal of Economic Theory*, 87, 243-253, 1999.

K. Binmore. *Fun and Games*. D.C. Heath, 1992.

G.I. Bischi, R. Carini, L. Gardini, and P. Tenti. *Sulle Orme del Caos. Comportamenti complessi in modelli matematici semplici*. Bruno Mondadori Editore, 2004.

G.I. Bischi, H. Dawid, and M. Kopel. Gaining the Competitive Edge Using Internal and External Spillovers: A Dynamic Analysis. *Journal of Economic Dynamics and Control*, vol. 27, 2171-2193, 2003a.

G.I. Bischi, H. Dawid, and M. Kopel. Spillover Effects and the Evolution of Firm Clusters. *Journal of Economic Behavior and Organization*, vol. 50, 47-75, 2003b.

G.I. Bischi, M. Gallegati, and A. Naimzada. Symmetry-Breaking bifurcations and representative firm in dynamic duopoly games. *Annals of Operations Research*, **89**, 253-272, 1999a.

G.I. Bischi and L. Gardini. Role of invariant and minimal absorbing areas in chaos synchronization. *Physical Review E*, **58**, 5710-5719, 1998.

G.I. Bischi and L. Gardini. Global Properties of Symmetric Competition Models with Riddling and Blowout Phenomena. *Discrete Dynamics in Nature and Society*, vol. 5, 149-160, 2000.

G.I. Bischi, L. Gardini, and M. Kopel. Analysis of Global Bifurcations in a Market Share Attraction Model. *Journal of Economic Dynamics and Control*, **24**, 855-879, 2000a.

G.I. Bischi, L. Gardini, and C. Mira. Plane maps with denominator. Part I: some generic properties. *International Journal of Bifurcation and Chaos*, **9(1)**, 119-153, 1999b.

G.I. Bischi, L. Gardini, and C. Mira. Plane Maps with Denominator. Part II: Noninvertible maps with simple focal points. *International Journal of Bifurcation and Chaos*, vol. 13, No. 8, 2253-2277, 2003c.

G.I. Bischi and M. Kopel. Equilibrium Selection in a Nonlinear Duopoly Game with Adaptive Expectations. *Journal of Economic Behavior and Organization*, **46(1)**, 73-100, 2001.

G.I. Bischi and F. Lamantia. Nonlinear Duopoly Games with Positive Cost Externalities due to Spillover Effects. *Chaos, Solitons & Fractals*, vol. 13, 805-822, 2002a.

G.I. Bischi and F. Lamantia. Chaos Synchronization and Intermittency in a Duopoly Game with Spillover Effects. Chapter 8 in T. Puu and I. Sushko, editors, *Oligopoly Dynamics: Models and Tools*, Springer Verlag, 195-217, 2002b.

G.I. Bischi, C. Mammana, and L. Gardini. Multistability and cyclic attractors in duopoly games. *Chaos, Solitons & Fractals*, **11**, 543-564, 2000b.

G.I. Bischi, L. Mroz, and H. Hauser. Studying basin bifurcations in nonlinear triopoly games by using 3D visualization. *Nonlinear Analysis, Theory, Methods & Applications*, **47(8)**, 5325-5341, 2001.

G.I. Bischi and A. Naimzada. Global Analysis of a Duopoly game with Bounded Rationality. *Advances in Dynamic Games and applications*, vol.5, 361-385, Birkhauser, 2000.

W.A. Brock, C. Hommes. A Rational Route to Randomness. *Econometrica*, 65,1059-1095, 1997.

J. Buescu. *Exotic Attractors*, Birkhäuser, Boston, 1997.

C. Chiarella, R. Dieci, and L. Gardini. Asset price dynamics in a financial market with fundamentalists and chartists. *Discrete Dynamics in Nature and Society*, Vol 6, 69-99, 2001.

C. Chiarella, R. Dieci, and L. Gardini. Speculative Behaviour and Complex Asset Price Dynamics: A Global Analysis. *Journal of Economic Behavior and Organization*, 49(1) 173-192, 2002.

P. Collet and J.P. Eckmann. *Iterated maps on the interval as dynamical systems*, Birkhäuser, Boston, 1980.

R.L. Devaney. *An Introduction to Chaotic Dynamical Systems*. The Benjamin / Cummings Publishing Co., Menlo Park, California, 1987.

R. Dieci, G.I. Bischi, and L. Gardini. Multistability and role of noninvertibility in a discrete-time business cycle model. *CEJOR*, vol. 9, 71-96, 2001.

A. Ferretti and N.K. Rahman. A study of coupled logistic maps and its applications in chemical physics. *Chemical Physics*, 119, 275-288, 1988.

H. Fujisaka and T. Yamada. Stability theory of synchronized motion in coupled-oscillator systems. *Progress of Theoretical Physics*, **69 (1)**, 32-47, 1983.

C. Grebogi, E. Ott, and J.A. Yorke. Crises, sudden changes in chaotic attractors and transient chaos. *Physica* **7**D, 81-200, 1983.

J. Guckenheimer and T. Holmes. *Non-linear Oscillations, Dynamical Systems, and Bifurcations of Vector Fields*. Springer, 1983.

R. Guesnerie and M. Woodford. Endogeneous fluctuations. In J. Laffont, editor, *Advances in Economic Theory*, 288-412, Cambridge University Press, 1993.

I. Gumowski and C. Mira. *Dynamique Chaotique,* Cepadues Editions, Toulose, 1980.

M. Hasler and Y. Maistrenko. An introduction to the synchronization of chaotic systems: coupled skew tent maps. *IEEE Trans. Circuits Syst.*, **44 (10),** 856-866, 1997.

A. P. Kirman. Whom or What Does the Representative Individual Represent? *Jou. of Econ. Perspectives,* 6, 117-136, 1992.

M. Kopel. Simple and Complex Adjustment Dynamics in Cournot Duopoly Models. *Chaos, Solitons & Fractals*, **7(12)**, 2031-2048, 1996.

M. Kopel, G.I. Bischi, and L. Gardini. On new phenomena in dynamic promotional competition models with homogeneous and quasi-homo-geneous firms. In D. Delli Gatti, M. Gallegati, and A.P. Kirman, editors, *Interaction and Market Structure. Essays on Heterogeneity in Economics*. Springer-Verlag, pp. 57-87, 2000.

Y.C. Lai, C. Grebogi, and J.A. Yorke. Riddling bifurcation in chaotic dynamical systems. *Physical Review* Letters, 77, 55-58, 1996.

Y.C. Lai and C. Grebogi. Noise-induced riddling in chaotic systems. *Physical Review Letters* **77**, 5047-5050, 1996.

H.W. Lorenz. Multiple attractors, Complex Basin Boundaries, and Transient Motion in Deterministic Economic Systems. In G. Feichtinger, editor, *Dynamic Economic Models and Optimal Control*, 411-430, North-Holland, Amsterdam, 1992.

Y. Maistrenko, T. Kapitaniak, and P. Szuminski. Locally and globally riddled basins in two coupled piecewise-linear maps. *Physical Review E*, **57 (3)**, 6393-6399, 1997.

Y. Maistrenko, V.L. Maistrenko, A. Popovich, and E. Mosekilde. Role of the Absorbing Area in Chaotic Synchronization. *Physical Review Letters*, **80 (8)**, 1638-1641, 1998a.

Y. Maistrenko, V.L. Maistrenko, A. Popovich, and E. Mosekilde. Transverse instability and riddled basins in a system of two coupled logistic maps. *Physical Review E*, **57 (3)**, 2713-2724, 1998b.

J. Milnor. On the concept of attractor. *Commun. Math Phys*, **99**, 177-195, 1985.

C. Mira. *Chaotic Dynamics.* Word Scientific, Singapore, 1987.

C. Mira, J.P. Carcasses, G. Millerioux, and L. Gardini. Plane foliation of two-dimensional noninvertible maps. *International Journal of Bifurcation & Chaos*, vol.6 (8), 1439-1462, 1996.

C. Mira, D. Fournier-Prunaret, L. Gardini, H. Kawakami, and J.C. Cathala. Basin bifurcations of two-dimensional noninvertible maps: fractalization of basins. *International Journal of Bifurcation and Chaos*, **4**, 343-381, 1994.

C. Mira, L. Gardini, A. Barugola, and J.C. Cathala. *Chaotic Dynamics in Two-Dimensional Noninvertible Maps*, World Scientific, Singapore, 1996.

C. Mira and C. Rauzy. Fractal aggregation of basin islands in two-dimensional quadratic noninvertible maps. *International Journal of Bifurcations and Chaos*, **5(4)**, 991-1019, 1995.

Y. Nagai and Y.C. Lai. Periodic-orbit theory of the blowout bifurcation. *Physical Review E*, **56 (4)**, 4031-4041, 1997.

E. Ott and J.C. Sommerer. Blowout bifurcations: the occurrence of riddled basins and on-off intermittency. *Phys. Lett. A*, **188**, 39-47, 1994.

L.M. Pecora and T.L. Carrol. Synchronization in chaotic systems. *Physical Review Letters*, **64 (8)** pp. 821-824, 1990.

T. Puu. *Attractors, Bifurcations and Chaos.* Springer Verlag, Berlin, 2000.

A.S. Soliman. An analysis of the effectiveness of policy based on basins of attraction. *Journal of Macroeconomics*, 21, 165-178, 1999.

S.C. Venkataramani, B.R. Hunt, and E. Ott. Bubbling transition. *Physical Review E*, **54**, 1346-1360, 1996.

J.W. Weibull, *Evolutionary Game Theory.* The MIT Press, 1995.

MIX
Papier aus verantwortungsvollen Quellen
Paper from responsible sources
FSC® C105338

FSC
www.fsc.org

If you have any concerns about our products,
you can contact us on
ProductSafety@springernature.com

In case Publisher is established outside the EU,
the EU authorized representative is:
Springer Nature Customer Service Center GmbH
Europaplatz 3, 69115 Heidelberg, Germany

Printed by Libri Plureos GmbH
in Hamburg, Germany